TRANS CANADA TRAIL

BRITISH COLUMBIA

TRANS CANADA TRAIL

BRITISH COLUMBIA

Bruce Obee

whitecap

Edited by Grace Yaginuma
Proofread by Ann-Marie Metten
Design by Mauve Pagé
Photography by Bruce Obee
Map design by Christine Roy of the Trans Canada Trail Foundation

Printed in Canada by Friesens

Library and Archives Canada Cataloguing in Publication

Obee, Bruce, 1951–
Trans Canada Trail : British Columbia / Bruce Obee.

Includes index.

ISBN 978-1-55285-928-5
1. Trans Canada Trail—Guidebooks. 2. Trails—British Columbia—Guidebooks.
3. British Columbia—Guidebooks. I. Title.

FC3807.O34 2008   917.1104'4   C2007-905570-2

The publisher acknowledges the financial support of the Government of Canada through the
Book Publishing Industry Development Program (BPIDP) and the Province of British Columbia
through the Book Publishing Tax Credit.

For Trans Canada Trail builders
Al Skucas, of Cranbrook,
and Léon Lebrun, of Coquitlam,
men of far-reaching vision
and unremitting devotion

The Trans Canada Trail is the implementation of a uniquely Canadian vision. It is a bold enterprise, as bold as any that has been undertaken in Canadian history—we are creating the first recreational trail that links our oceans, our people, and our land.

The trail covers more than 21,000 kilometres and comprises new and existing trails, waterways, and other links. It is meant to honour past generations and be a gift and inspiration to all those who work toward building the Canadian dream.

Not only are we creating the world's longest recreational trail, we are doing it as only Canadians can. Our trail is being built in more than 800 communities with the support of volunteers, local citizens, local trail-building groups, merchants, municipal leaders, governments, and the media. Each individual plays a role in the creation, promotion, and maintenance of a section of the trail.

Of all the elements that go into this network, Canadian pride is the strongest and most enduring. We hope that this pride is evident in our guidebook and as you travel our Trans Canada Trail.

January 2008
Sanderson Layng
President and CEO *of the Trans Canada Trail*

CONTENTS

FOREWORD

The Trans Canada Trail in British Columbia is a monumental challenge. It's a challenge not only for those who use the trail, but also for builders, who devote their energies making the trail a reality. The trail varies from wheelchair-accessible urban walkways to alpine paths more suited to the hardy outdoor enthusiast—or mountain goat. It ranges from the Pacific shores of Vancouver Island to the Okanagan desert, and east to the Rocky Mountains and its meadows, with numerous climatic transitions along the way. In the province's northeast, the Trans Canada Trail follows the Alaska Highway, traversing evergreen forests and some of the continent's most northerly grain fields.

The Trails Society of British Columbia (also known as Trails BC) was formed in early 1994 to develop a province-wide network of trails that would become an integral part of the Trans Canada Trail. It soon became a registered society and a charity that could issue income tax receipts for donations. As Trails BC evolved, it split into six regional councils across the southern British Columbia TCT route, with a seventh under development in the northeast.

For the trail builder, BC's varied topography tests the best of human and machine. Rainforest trails must often be reopened (and sometimes rediscovered) every year. Urban trails must be developed for and protected from an increasing population density. Railway grades must be redeveloped in treacherous mountain regions. And in eastern British Columbia, the challenge is getting the Trans Canada Trail off the highways and into the quiet backcountry.

Trails BC is facing these tasks head-on. As the society entered its second decade, it helped rebuild the Kettle Valley Railway's Myra Canyon trestles, destroyed by fire in 2003. It was also a key partner in the upgrading of former railway rights-of-way on Vancouver Island and in the BC Interior. These are high profile, multi-million-dollar projects.

There are still thousands of smaller projects that must be undertaken to build and maintain a world-class trail across one of Canada's most unforgiving environments—and your help is needed. To become part of the trail-building team, or to learn more about Trails BC and the Trans Canada Trail, please visit www.trailsbc.ca.

January 2008   Murphy Shewchuk
                                   President of The Trails Society of British Columbia

PREFACE

We agreed from the outset to keep it simple. No buses or backup vans. We'd simply cycle out my back door near Victoria and ride the Trans Canada Trail across British Columbia to the Rockies. A monumental undertaking, in theory; really, it's just a matter of sweat and groceries.

We must have appeared an unlikely pair—Mike LeBlanc, a lanky athlete in his late twenties, and me, a reasonably fit baby boomer, wheeling into town with bicycle trailers in tow. The locals raised their eyebrows when we stopped at every turn to take notes and photographs. Mike, the TCT's trail identification officer, would chat with them about what we were up to while I tapped intently on a hand-held computer.

Our curiosity, we found, was our key to local knowledge. People everywhere were keen to tell all, to show us their towns, their trails, their favourite places. I'd been the beneficiary of this small-town generosity in recent summers when I cycled parts of the TCT in BC and wrote about it for magazines and television. So when I was assigned the task of writing this official guidebook, I assumed I knew a lot about the Trans Canada Trail. I was mistaken.

We soon realized this was more a "route" than a "trail": it was a track through a forest or farmer's field; it was a multi-lane highway, a downtown street, a logging road, an abandoned railway, a dyke; three times it was a ferry; and often it wasn't where we thought it would be.

Some of the challenges were indeed monumental: Paleface Pass in the Cascade Mountains pushed me to the edge of my physical tolerance, and my speed up the western slopes of the Rockies was so pathetic that flies hitchhiked on my face. At the end of the southern TCT route in Elk Pass, 1,758 kilometres from home, the mosquitoes were so thick that we could barely sit still long enough to take a photo of ourselves, flexing our muscles on the Continental Divide.

That was Canada Day, a great day, a great place to be Canadian. All the bugs, the potholes, the horrific climbs were behind us as we whizzed down the eastern slopes of the Rockies into Kananaskis. In 23 days this Trans Canada Trail had gotten us—by bicycle—from my house on the Pacific to the height of the Rocky Mountains.

A challenge? Of course, but really, it's just a matter of sweat and groceries.

January 2008   Bruce Obee

ACKNOWLEDGEMENTS

My thanks—

to John Bellini, former CEO of the Trans Canada Trail Foundation, for inviting me to do this project; to the TCT's Sanderson Layng and James Clark for their insightful suggestions; and a special thanks to Mike LeBlanc for sharing his intimate on-the-ground knowledge of the TCT in BC, for cycling—and re-cycling—the trail with me, and for his ongoing help in assembling a challenging manuscript

to Murphy Shewchuk, Jeannette and George Klein, Léon Lebrun, Jack Harder, Marilyn Hansen, Ernie Hennig, Chris Moslin, Raymond Gaudart, Al Skucas, Don Barnett, and Ava Caldwell of Trails BC

to hikers, equestrians, and cyclists Rod Brown, Kelly Koome, René Bertrand, Linda and John Butterworth, Daryl Farquhar, Craig Henderson, Richie Mann, Ian McNeill, David Carl, and Ann and Roy Kingerlee

to Brian Springinotic of the BC government; Don Foxgord of Tourism BC; Joe Fernandez, Ray Miller, and John Clark of Lake Cowichan; Tom Anderson, Jim Marsh, and Brian Farquhar of the Cowichan Valley Regional District; Tammy Toor of Nanaimo Parks and Recreation; Joan Michel of the Nanaimo Regional District; and Jeff Ward and Don Watmough of Capital Regional District Parks

to Dale Marat of Experience Cycling in Duncan, Brian Fletcher of Chain Reaction in Grand Forks, Bob Dupee of WildWays Adventures in Christina Lake, Steve Stewart of Midway, Ron Sherk of Okanagan GPS, Ken Campbell of the Myra Canyon Trestle Restoration Society, Anne de Jager of Creston Valley Wildlife Management Area, Paul Lautard of Cyclists Rest, Alayna Casselman of Sparwood, Liz Hughes of North Vancouver,

Dr. Stephen Herrero of the University of Calgary, Bob Forbes of Mount Broadwood Heritage Conservation Area, Wayne Pomario of Cycling BC, and Shannon LeBlanc, a welcome smile at the end of a long journey

to Paddy Whidden of Public Works Canada, April Moi and Christine Lucas of Northern Rockies Alaska Highway Tourism Association, Ryan MacIvor and Robin Graham of Tourism Dawson Creek, and Glen Evans of Rolla Agricultural Services

to Tracy Read of Bookmakers Press, Steve Fick of *Canadian Geographic*, Anita Willis of *British Columbia Magazine*, Ron Harrington and Dave Billman of the Knowledge Network, and Bryan McGill and John Thomson

and, as always, to my wife, Janet Barwell-Clarke, and our daughters, Lauren and Nicole Obee

INTRODUCTION

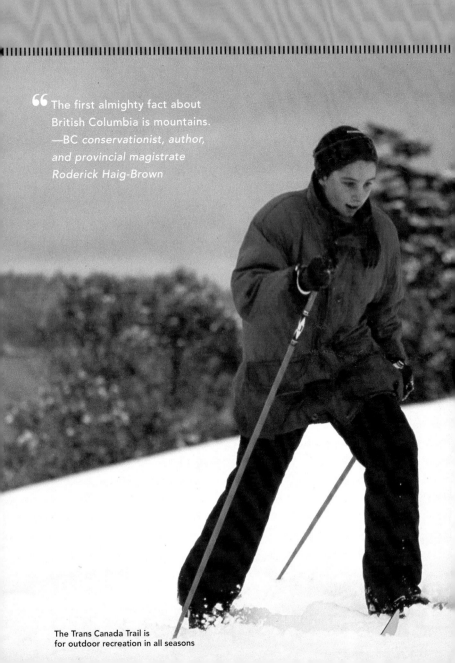

> " The first almighty fact about
> British Columbia is mountains.
> —BC *conservationist, author,*
> *and provincial magistrate*
> *Roderick Haig-Brown*

The Trans Canada Trail is
for outdoor recreation in all seasons

TRAIL TRIVIA

At 947,800 square kilometres, BC is Canada's third-largest province, four times bigger than Great Britain, two-and-a-half times bigger than Japan.

It's natural to expect the odd hill on a trail across British Columbia. This is, after all, the Canadian Cordillera, one of the major mountain systems of the world. The Trans Canada Trail in southern BC runs more than 1,750 kilometres through seven mountain ranges, from "Kilometre 0" on Vancouver Island to Elk Pass on the BC–Alberta border. Elk Pass is one of two points where the TCT crosses the Rocky Mountains; the other is Summit Lake in northern BC, where the TCT route takes the Alaska Highway (see Part Two, starting from page 345).

All 1,758 kilometres of the TCT's continuous route across southern BC, as well as all of the 1,051 kilometres across northern BC, can be cycled and hiked. Much of it can be travelled by wheelchair, on horseback, and on snowshoes and cross-country skis. There are another 46 kilometres of hiking-only sections of the Trans Canada Trail on Vancouver Island and in the Lower Mainland's North Shore mountains.

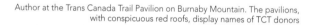

Author at the Trans Canada Trail Pavilion on Burnaby Mountain. The pavilions, with conspicuous red roofs, display names of TCT donors

TRANS CANADA TRAIL DISCOVERY PANELS

Just west of Port Moody a number of Trans Canada Trail "Discovery Panels" over-look the ocean. These interpretive signs are among 2,000 along the TCT across  the country. The bilingual panels, measuring 41 by 61 centimetres, depict geographic and historic features, and indigenous flora and fauna. Funded by the Stephen R. Bronfman Foundation, the TCT Discovery Program covers 170 subjects, providing insights into the areas where the panels appear. In western Canada subjects include lodgepole pine, western hemlock, sphagnum moss, caribou, garter snakes, coastal forests, fire succession, and more.

"This is a great project, which runs parallel to our goals of stimulating people's interest in protecting our environment and our culture," notes Stephen Bronfman. "These are the ties that bind us to our Canadian heritage."

Despite the cordilleran topography, much of the TCT across southern BC is surprisingly flat. Well over one-third of the trail—about 670 kilometres—is comprised of abandoned railway corridors. Dykes make up about 45 kilometres. The grades aren't so easygoing on 520 kilometres of paved roads and highways and 300 kilometres of gravel roads. Only about 220 kilometres of the TCT in southern BC are actual trail.

Like a river with myriad tributaries, the TCT in BC, as in all of Canada, taps into local trail networks as it flows through communities across the province. It was established in 1992 with the aim of building a 21,000-kilometre national recreational trail spanning "every province and territory, linking Canada's three oceans, its people, and its land." While the TCT is comparatively new, many of its components are well-worn trails and cor-ridors travelled by generations of local hikers, cyclists, and equestrians. The same locals bring their brains, brawn, and vision to the TCT in their regions. Though the Trans Canada Trail now is substantially completed, it will always be a work in progress, a trail that will change and improve along with the communities and countryside it spans.

The TCT's roundabout course across the province—it's half as far by highway—is mainly a back-door tour of small-town BC, with masses of forest, farm, and wilderness in between. Rural BC begins just beyond the hum and glitter of Metro Vancouver, the last big town on the TCT as you go east from the Pacific Coast to the far side of the Rockies.

PLANNING YOUR TRIP

The "beginning" (at Km 0) isn't the only place to start a journey on the Trans Canada Trail. The following chapters list more than 100 TCT access points, but there are many more. Each is a gateway to a different stretch of trail, a launching point for day trips or multi-day excursions. And a growing number of travellers, notably cyclists, are making three- or four-week TCT treks across the entire province.

Camping, backpacking, and cycle-touring season starts around Easter on the Coast, late May in the Interior, and continues through summer into early autumn. A cross-province cycling trip on the TCT in southern BC can be done in three weeks, but five or six allows time to linger in the towns, to cool off in the lakes and rivers, or to bike and hike some local trails.

Even seasoned hikers and cyclists in good physical shape find sections of the TCT challenging. Dykes, railway beds, and urban trails, however, can be hiked or cycled by anyone in reasonable health, regardless of age or experience.

A MULTI-USE TRAIL FOR ALL SEASONS

While the majority of TCT users are summer cyclists, this is a multi-use trail shared by hikers, equestrians, snowshoers, cross-country skiers, and, in some places, snowmobilers.

Paved and hard-packed gravel sections of the TCT, mainly in or near communities, are suitable for wheelchairs. For information on accessibility for travellers in wheelchairs, contact the British Columbia Paraplegic Association (780 SW Marine Drive, Vancouver, BC V6P 5Y7; 1-877-324-3611; www.bcpara.org).

Walking/Hiking

All of the Trans Canada Trail in BC is accessible by foot. So, too, are the hiking trails that are connected to the TCT in BC. (The Alaska Highway comprises most of the trail in northern BC, and a few hikers walk the route along the highway's shoulder.)

Cycling/Mountain Biking

Communities along the TCT are prime destinations for mountain bikers and touring cyclists. Trail networks around many TCT towns are extensive, well maintained, and traverse a wide range of terrain. Websites for individual communities may carry information, directions, and maps for local trails. For general information, contact the organization Cycling BC (332–1367 West Broadway, Vancouver, BC V6H 4A9; 604-737-3034; www.cyclingbc.net). Cycling BC also has a Trans Canada Trail website (www.bctrail.ca).

Horseback Riding

Stretches of the TCT that may be attractive to equestrians are noted in following chapters. For more information, check the websites of the Back Country Horsemen of BC (www.bchorsemen.org) and the Horse Council of BC (www.horsecouncilbcsite.com).

Cross-country Skiing/Snowshoeing

In Interior BC, most sections of the TCT that can be cycled in summer can be skied or snowshoed in winter. Trails in provincial and local parks along the TCT route are also used by cross-country skiers and snowshoers. Check websites for individual parks and communities.

Snowmobiling

Parts of the TCT in Interior BC are used by snowmobilers. For links to individual snowmobile clubs across BC, check the BC Snowmobile Federation's website (www.bcsf.org).

Much of the Trans Canada Trail is suitable for horses

All-terrain Vehicles (ATVs)

Although motorized use of the TCT is discouraged or prohibited, some sections of the TCT in BC, notably the Princeton area, are maintained and used by ATVers. The TCT in BC, however, is neither designed nor built for motorized use. ATVs and motorcycles using the TCT can ruin the trail for other users. Motorized vehicles on the TCT have already caused extensive damage, often on newly built sections of trail. ATVers and dirt bikers are asked to look for more appropriate trails by contacting the Quad Riders Association of BC (www.atvbc.ca).

FINDING THE TRANS CANADA TRAIL

Much of the TCT across southern BC is clearly marked and easy to find. But signage on several stretches is minimal, often non-existent in the backwoods, which are plagued by ongoing vandalism. More signs are being erected, and travellers should keep an eye on tree trunks, posts, rocks, or other trailside objects for red and green TCT stickers, or yellow square- or diamond-shaped markers that say "TCT" or show pictures of a hiker or bicycle.

Volunteers from Trails BC erect a Trans Canada Trail marker

In northern BC it's virtually impossible to get lost on the Trans Canada Trail route: it takes the Alaska Highway (BC Highway 97) from Watson Lake, YK, to Dawson Creek, BC, then secondary roads to the BC–Alberta boundary. The northern TCT route is covered in Chapters 22 to 24, comprising Part Two of this book.

The TCT **Access Points** section in each chapter lists several places where you can get on the trail, and includes directions and parking information.

Land

In northern BC the Trans Canada Trail route is mainly the Alaska Highway. In the south, the TCT crosses and follows a number of highways. Greyhound Canada (1-800-661-8747; www .greyhound.ca) and its affiliates have freight and passenger depots at communities along the TCT, and are specifically noted in following chapters. It's cheap and easy to ship a bicycle by bus; bike boxes ($10 at last check) are available at Greyhound depots in larger communities.

Sea and Inland Waterways

Victoria, Km 0 on the Trans Canada Trail, can be reached by ferry from mainland BC and Washington state. The trail continues up Vancouver Island to Nanaimo, where it crosses the Strait of Georgia via BC Ferries and comes ashore in West Vancouver. On the mainland, the TCT takes a

STELLER'S JAY: BC'S AVIAN EMBLEM

The raucous cackle of the Steller's jay (*Cyanocitta stelleri*) is a familiar call to British Columbians, who in 1987 adopted this cousin of the crow as their provincial bird. The only crested jay in the West, the Steller's is a robin-sized iridescent blue freebooter that shamelessly pilfers unguarded picnic tables and campsites. An inhabitant of coniferous forests from the Pacific to the Continental Divide, the Steller's jay is encountered year-round by travellers on the Trans Canada Trail.

In the dead of winter the Steller's jay may survive almost entirely on acorns and pine seeds. It carries acorns in its throat pouch and stores them for later use. It remembers the locations of hundreds of caches, and is thought to be a major factor in the dispersal of oak tree seeds.

ferry across the Fraser River between Albion and Fort Langley, and across Kootenay Lake between Balfour and Kootenay Bay.

Air

Several airlines provide scheduled flights to Vancouver, Victoria, Nanaimo, and other communities along the Trans Canada Trail route in both southern and northern BC. Air Canada (1-888-247-2262; www.aircanada.com) is the main carrier; others are noted in following chapters.

NAVIGATING A WORK IN PROGRESS

While most of the TCT in BC holds a permanent place on the map, some sections are still being fine-tuned: new routes and trails, detours, and other changes may alter directions and kilometre points appearing in this guidebook. Where changes were anticipated at the time of writing, the book suggests websites to check for updates. Peruse the book and check the websites before leaving home. (The website addresses were correct at the time of printing, but keep in mind that they may change.)

A significant route change is expected on the outskirts of Victoria, near the westernmost point of the Trans Canada Trail; other changes are anticipated at points across the province, particularly in the Kootenays and Rocky Mountains. To avoid the need to alter every subsequent chapter

MORE INFORMATION

Travel information for BC and the Trans Canada Trail is available from a variety of sources. More sources may be listed in each chapter under **Communities, Parks, and Places to Stay.**

Trans Canada Trail Foundation This non-profit charity raises funds to build the Trans Canada Trail across the nation. Some money is raised through the sale of TCT–related items, including the series of official guidebooks. Check the TCT website for new books and for details and updates about the trail. 43 Westminster North, Montreal, QC H4X 1Y8; 1-800-465-3636; www.tctrail.ca.

Trails BC The Trails Society of BC is a non-profit charity run by volunteer trail builders developing the TCT and other "shared use and sustainable trail networks." The Trails BC website has a wealth of information about the TCT, including maps and coverage of route changes, alternate routes, special events, news, and more. www.trailsbc.ca

Tourism British Columbia This Crown corporation offers free travel information and a reservation service. Its consumer website is www.hellobc.com, and its "travel counsellors" can be reached at 1-800-435-5622. (Tourism BC also has a website at www.tourismbc.com.) PO Box 9830, Stn Prov Govt, Victoria, BC V8W 9W5

Tourism Regions BC is divided into six tourism regions, each administered by a separate association that provides information and other services for travellers. The Trans Canada Trail routes run through five. Contact information for each region is covered in following chapters.

Visitor Centres Local, regional, and provincial travel information is available from community visitor centres. Usually operated by local chambers of commerce or municipalities, most are staffed by residents who share their local knowledge. Look under the section **Communities, Parks, and Places to Stay** in each chapter.

---

when a change occurs at one point along the TCT's southern route, each chapter begins at Km 0. However, for the northern TCT route, kilometre points begin at Km 0 and continue through all chapters to Km 1,051 at the end of the route. (This is in keeping with the official TCT guidebooks covering other provinces and territories.)

Kilometre Points

Kilometre points in route descriptions are rounded to the nearest 100 metres. Pedometers or cyclocomputers are useful in tracking distances, but their precision can be affected by the unit's calibration, the terrain, and surface conditions. Consider kilometre points on the described TCT routes as approximate and use them in combination with landmarks and other information.

Maps

Kilometre points and other features in the text are tied to those on the accompanying maps, which easily guide TCT travellers along the trail. For a wider overview and more detail consult topographic maps, which include indications of contours and elevations, communities, and roads that may be required for unanticipated detours. Each chapter carries names and numbers of National Topographic System maps at scales of 1:250,000 and 1:50,000. Look for maps at book or map stores, or check the Natural Resources Canada website (http://maps.nrcan.gc.ca). The *British Columbia Road Map & Parks Guide*, produced by Davenport Maps and Tourism BC, is another useful reference that's available from visitor centres and stores throughout the province.

Global Positioning System

Hand-held GPS units add interest to a trek on the TCT and can be helpful when there's a need to know one's exact location. Trail directions in following chapters include longitude and latitude at a few points where trail users could get confused.

LODGING AND CAMPING

There's a range of accommodations along the TCT in BC, from upscale lodges and quiet B&BS to rustic cabins and campsites. The section **Communities, Parks, and Places to Stay** in each chapter lists individual places to stay for smaller centres where there are three or fewer options. Also listed are websites with links to local hotels, motels, resorts, B&BS, and campgrounds.

One of the most up-to-date sources for places to stay, including commercial campgrounds and provincial parks, is the *British Columbia Approved Accommodation Guide*, published annually. This publication offers detail on accommodation in the larger communities, and is available free from visitor centres or can be ordered from Tourism BC (PO Box 9830 Stn Prov Govt, Victoria, BC V8W 9W5; 1-800-435-5622; www.hellobc.com). Tourism BC also has a reservation service.

Details on campgrounds in provincial parks along the TCT route are also provided in each chapter. Campsites in most parks are available on a first-come first-served basis. Reservations are available at some parks, as noted: call Discover Camping (run by BC Parks) at 1-800-689-9025 (or 604-689-9025 in Metro Vancouver) or go to the website www.discovercamping.ca. For information on individual parks, visit BC Parks at www.env.gov.bc.ca/bcparks/ and click on "Find a Park" for an alphabetical listing.

Stanley Park Seawall is part of the Trans Canada Trail in Vancouver

Summer is tourist season in southern BC. Vancouver Island, the southwest coast, and the Okanagan are particularly busy. It is wise to book ahead for accommodation or campsites.

There are also several BC forest service campgrounds along the TCT, basic but pleasant campgrounds that do not offer many amenities but are convenient bases for exploring the TCT.

WEATHER

Winters are mild and often damp on BC's south coast, while spring, summer, and early autumn are usually warm and dry. Winters are colder in the Interior, where the TCT is used by cross-country skiers, snowshoers, and snowmobilers. Interior summers are hot and dry, with temperatures significantly higher than on the Coast: July and August temperatures near the ocean in Victoria may see highs of 22°C, while the thermometer in the village of Midway, halfway across the province, might hit 28°C, or even the mid-30s. In northern BC, summer temperatures are comparable to those on the Coast.

While TCT travellers may swelter in the valleys, the air is generally cooler at higher elevations, where weather is also more changeable. Temperatures in the mountains, where sudden squalls are common, may drop as much as 15°C overnight.

Rain, sometimes heavy, happens any place in any season: good wet-weather gear is essential for TCT travellers.

In northern BC, cycling and camping season is from about mid-June to early September. Even in midsummer it may be cool enough for early rising campers to see their breath, especially at higher elevations. Fort Nelson gets occasional dumps of snow in August. Summer days, however, are more often sunny, with temperatures in the low 20s, falling to 8°C or 10°C at night. In the Peace River area, call 250-784-2244 for recorded forecasts.

For weather forecasts covering the entire province go to the Environment Canada website (www.weatheroffice.gc.ca).

EQUIPMENT AND SUPPLIES

The Trans Canada Trail gets year-round use, but summer is the high season when day trippers share the trail with hikers and cyclists on multi-day journeys. Regardless of season, trail users, especially in the mountains, should prepare for changing weather: reprieve from sweltering sunshine may come as a sudden downpour.

The following lists suggest items for hikers and cyclists to carry on day trips or overnighters.

Essentials

> **Water** A thirsty person is already becoming dehydrated. Carry a minimum of one litre of water per person for day trips and drink frequently. Use a water-purification method for longer outings (see **Cautions** on page 15).
> **Food** Besides enough for meals, pack trail mix, dried fruits, granola bars, and other high-energy snacks.
> **Clothing** Dress in layers with fleece or wool on the outside and moisture-wicking polyester closest to the skin. Quick-drying nylon shorts or pants are light and windproof. Breathable socks made of polyester, nylon, or acrylic are more likely than cotton to keep sweaty feet dry. Light fleece gloves and a headband or toque help take the chill off mountain mornings.
> **Rain gear** A rain hat and waterproof, breathable jacket and pants are essential gear for long journeys and should be carried by day trippers in all but the most promising weather.

> **Skin/Eye protection** Wear sunglasses that protect against ultraviolet A and B rays. Wear a hat. Use sunscreen with a sun protection factor of 15 or higher, and insect repellent with up to 30 percent DEET.
> **First aid kit** Bandages, gauze and adhesive tape, mole skin (for blisters); aspirin or pain reliever, antihistamines, antiseptic; tweezers, scissors, space blanket.
> **Whistle** To attract attention or alert wildlife.
> **Pocket knife** An indispensable multi-purpose tool.
> **Garbage bag** Hold on to trash until you find appropriate disposal facilities.
> **Flashlight** To avoid getting stranded in darkness in the event of an unanticipated delay.
> **Optional**

• toilet paper	• extra socks
• bathing suit and towel	• field guides
• topographic maps	• pen and writing paper
• binoculars	• cell phone
• VHF radio	• hand-held GPS
• camera with extra battery and memory card	

Hikers

> **Footwear** Walking shoes are adequate for nearly all of the Trans Canada Trail. Hiking boots with ankle support are recommended for the Extension Ridge and Haslam Creek trails near Nanaimo, the North Shore mountains on the Lower Mainland, the Chilliwack Valley and Paleface Pass, and Elk Pass over the Rockies. Extra socks and foot powder such as Dr. Scholl's, Desenex, or Gold Bond (from pharmacies) help keep sweaty feet dry and comfortable.
> **Backpack** Whether for day or overnight use, a backpack with an interior frame, and padded shoulder and waist straps, is most comfortable.
> **Pedometer** Measuring distances helps hikers pinpoint locations and adds interest to a journey.
> **Bear aware** Most of the TCT runs through bear country. Carry pepper spray and bear bangers or an air horn in a place where they can be grabbed in a hurry. (See page 18.)

Cyclists

> **Bike** Except for 46 kilometres of hiking-only sections, all of the Trans Canada Trail in BC can be cycled on a standard hybrid or mountain bike, preferably with fenders. Enough food and gear for multi-day trips can be carried in two rear panniers, and a dry bag for tent and sleeping bag. Trailers can also be towed, although the switchbacks of Paleface Pass present a challenge. Single-wheeled trailers are best; dual-wheeled trailers are wide for the narrow stretches of a single-track trail.

Basic repair skills are needed by Trans Canada Trail cyclists

> **Helmet** Wearing a bike helmet is the law in BC.
> **Cyclocomputer** To measure distances and speed. Fancy models indicate elevation and temperature.
> **Footwear** Cycling shoes or other hard-soled shoes for riding, walking shoes for exploring.
> **Water** Cyclists may require more water than hikers. Carry at least two litres per person, and top up bottles at every opportunity.
> **Tools/Parts** Spare inner tube, patches, tire irons, pump; spare chain links, chain breaker; Allen keys, crescent wrench, needle-nose pliers, Phillips and slot screwdrivers; spare brake and gear cables, rag, lubricant; bike lock.
> **Bear aware** Most of the TCT runs through bear country. Carry pepper spray and bear bangers or an air horn in a handy pocket or anywhere they can be grabbed in a hurry. (See page 18.)

For Camping Overnight

> **Tent** With a fly and a light ground sheet.
> **Sleeping bag** Summer campers in northern BC and at higher elevations in the south occasionally wake up to frosty mornings. Use an insulated foam or inflatable mattress and a sleeping bag rated for at least 0°C.
> **Stove** With fuel and dishes.
> **Light** Candle with matches; flashlight or headlamp.
> **Water** Use a purification method (see **Cautions** on page 15).
> **Food** Should be carried and stored in airtight bags. Pack 30 metres of light line to hang a dry bag containing food, toiletries, garbage, and other fragrant items that might attract bears and other night-prowling animals.

> **Soap** Use biodegradable soap well away from lakes, ponds, streams, or other water sources.

TRAIL ETIQUETTE

> **Stay on the trail.** Veering off the TCT to ride or hike over a meadow or animal track damages habitat and disturbs wildlife.

> **Leave no trace.** The TCT's natural and rural beauty is enhanced by being litter free.

> **Mask nature's call.** Where restrooms or outhouses aren't available, human wastes should be buried under 20 centimetres of soil, at least 50 metres from lakes, ponds, streams, or other water sources.

> **Leash dogs.** A dog running free on the TCT may frighten wildlife, horses, and other trail users, or prompt attacks by bears, cougars, or wolves. "Keep pets leashed and under control," advises a BC Parks website. "Better still, don't bring them at all."

> **Share the trail.** A friendly ding on a bike bell warns walkers, dogs, cyclists, or horses of a rider passing from behind. Travel slowly near horses and give them ample room to pass.

> **Respect nature.** Flowers, plants, and mushrooms alongside the trail should remain untouched, for the appreciation of all users of the trail.

> **Respect landowners.** In parts of southern BC, the TCT is a right-of-way, a public trail through private land. Stay on the trail.

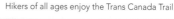

Hikers of all ages enjoy the Trans Canada Trail

› **Cook on a stove.** Open fires in unserviced areas are potentially hazardous and a worry to nearby residents.

CAUTIONS

Accessing Emergency Services

All of the communities along the TCT in southern BC have 911 emergency-call service for police, fire, and ambulance. On the northern TCT/Alaska Highway route, only the larger towns have 911 service.

Advice On the northern TCT route, use emergency telephone numbers listed under **Communities, Parks, and Places to Stay** in each chapter.

Being Out There

Concern Rural areas often have few other travellers as well as poor cell phone reception. There are large tracts of wilderness between communities on the TCT. In northern BC, the TCT route along the Alaska Highway is wilder than in the south and communities are much smaller, but the steady stream of road traffic may ensure emergency help is available.

Advice Be self-sufficient; inform a reliable person of travel plans. Plan to make or receive cell phone calls only at or near communities.

Hunting Season

Concern Don't be mistaken for fair game. Parts of the Trans Canada Trail run through active hunting areas. Hunting seasons may vary region to region and year to year, but generally, spring bear hunt season is from April through June, and autumn hunting for birds and ungulates is from September to November.

Advice Wear bright clothing and make noise.

Drinking Water

Concern Quality of drinking water, especially from streams can vary. Some BC waterways are contaminated by giardiasis (beaver fever), hepatitis A, and other infectious diseases.

Advice Don't drink water taken directly from a lake, stream, or other surface source, even if it looks clean. Use a portable purifier that filters out viruses, bacteria, and protozoa, and buy bottled water when possible. Water can also be boiled for one minute, or treated with iodine or chlorine dioxide. Purified water should be used for drinking, cooking, brushing teeth, rinsing contact lenses, and cleaning fruit and vegetables.

Campfires

Concern Campfires can cause wildfires, and are gradually becoming a pleasure of the past. Outdoor fires are often banned in summer when the woods across BC are tinder dry.

Advice Cook on a camp stove. Don't leave a campfire unattended and ensure it is completely extinguished when leaving the campsite. To report a forest fire call 1-800-663-5555.

Hypothermia

Concern Loss of body heat can cause incoherence, shivering, and reduced coordination.

Advice Wear wind-resistant, waterproof, and breathable clothing that allows moisture to escape from the body while keeping rain and drizzle out. A hypothermic person should be sheltered, given hot drinks, and wrapped in warm, dry clothing or sleeping bags, preferably between two warm people.

Heat Stress

Concern Hiking or cycling on hot, humid days can deplete the body's supply of water and salt, reducing its ability to stay cool. Symptoms include headaches, cramps, nausea, and intense thirst.

Advice Avoid dehydration by drinking lots of liquids. Water and minerals lost by sweating can be replaced by electrolyte drinks such as Gatorade. Wear lightweight, light-coloured clothing; take a break and cool off if a headache develops.

Sun Damage

Concern Sunburn and eye damage.

Advice Wear sunglasses and cover skin with clothing. Wear a wide-brimmed hat or a helmet with a sun visor. On exposed skin, apply sunscreen with an SPF of 15 or higher.

Shellfish Contamination

Concern Harvesting (a saltwater fishing licence is required) and eating shellfish from beaches contaminated by fecal coliforms, or by natural paralytic shellfish poisoning (red tide). Symptoms include tingling of tongue and lips, numbness of toes and fingers, and nausea.

TICKS AND LYME DISEASE

About the size of a sesame seed, a tick is a blood-sucking bug that lives in grass and woodlands across much of British Columbia. Its tiny bite can cause several ailments, including Lyme disease. Two species, the Rocky Mountain wood tick (*Dermacentor andersoni*) and the western black-legged tick (*Ixodes pacificus*) might burrow under the skin of a Trans Canada Trail traveller.

Ticks can often be repelled by tucking T-shirts into pants and pants into socks, and by using insect repellent with up to 30 percent DEET. Clothing and skin surfaces should be checked after travelling in tick territory. An "engorged" tick—its head under the surface of the skin and its blue-grey body sticking out—should be removed immediately and saved for testing at a lab. With tweezers, gently grip the tick near the skin and lift it straight off, ensuring no part of the bug is left behind.

Clean and disinfect the wound, then watch for symptoms of Lyme disease—fever, headache, muscle pain, or paralysis—which may develop within a few hours or over several days.

Advice Check fishing regulations and look for contamination-closure signs posted at beaches by the Department of Fisheries and Oceans. If symptoms occur, induce vomiting and get medical help.

Ticks, Mosquitoes, and Blackflies

Concern Irritating, possibly infectious bug bites. Mosquitoes and ticks are most bothersome across much of BC in spring and early summer. Northern BC is known for its blackflies and trophy-sized mosquitoes. Spring and early summer are worst.

Advice Use insect repellent with up to 30 percent DEET. Avoid campsites near standing water.

Bears

Concern Attacks by black bears or grizzlies. Cyclists or hikers can expect to see black bears, possibly grizzlies, usually from a safe distance. A bear feeding right next to the road, however, might get snarly with strangers riding or walking through its territory.

Advice Take precautions to avoid dangerous encounters on the trail and in campsites. Back off and wait for the bear to finish its meal. (See **Black Bears and Grizzlies** on the next page.)

Bison

Concern Wood bison are a less frequent but (literally) bigger hazard than bears. They might be seen along specific stretches of the TCT's northern

BLACK BEARS AND GRIZZLIES: KNOW THE SIGNS

Bears live nearly everywhere in British Columbia, and are often seen along the Trans Canada Trail. From a safe distance, a sighting of a black bear (*Ursus americanus*) or a grizzly (*Ursus arctos horribilis*) can be fascinating for hikers, equestrians, and cyclists on the TCT. But a sudden close encounter can be frightening, possibly harmful.

Although attacks on humans are rare, precautions and common sense can make them rarer. The right thing to do depends partly on whether the bear is a grizzly or black bear, and if the bear is being defensive or predatory.

ON THE TRAIL

Do:

› Travel in a group.
› Look ahead on trails; scan ridges and hillsides. Keep an eye on the sky for crows or ravens circling over a carcass that might belong to a feeding bear. If a bear is spotted, make a wide detour or back off and wait until the bear moves on.
› Watch for tracks, scat, and trees bearing fur and claw marks.
› Avoid carcasses and seasonal feeding areas such as berry patches or salmon streams, except to observe bears from a safe distance.
› While travelling in bear country, try to stay reasonably noisy. Tinkling bells might only arouse a bear's curiosity. Loud voices, as well as bear bangers or air horns, may be enough to frighten a bear encountered on the trail. Carry pepper spray.

› If a surprised grizzly reacts defensively, play dead: lie on the ground with hands clasped behind the head, face in the knees. However, if a surprised black bear reacts defensively, do not play dead—quickly make a retreat.
› Carry first aid and communication equipment.

Don't:

› Prompt a chase by running from a bear. Back away slowly while speaking quietly. If the bear is a grizzly, try to climb a tree.
› Play dead if a hungry bear is predatory (stalking, approaching a tent at night). Intimidate the bear with noise, sticks, rocks, or other weapons.
› Threaten a surprised bear by making eye contact.

BLACK BEARS AND GRIZZLIES: KNOW THE SIGNS (CONT'D)

IN THE CAMPSITE

Do:

› Sleep in a tent, not under the stars.
› In grizzly country, camp near a possible escape tree.
› Hang food, garbage, toothpaste, soap, cosmetics, insect repellent, and other fragrant items in an airtight bag beyond reach of bears, about five metres above the ground, either on a limb or on a line strung between two trees.
› Cook and store food well downwind of the tent.
› Clean up immediately after meals.

Don't:

› Camp near a bear trail or seasonal feeding ground.
› Camp near fresh tracks or scat.
› Dump dirty dishwater near a campsite. Strain it, pack out the solids, and dump the water in a pit toilet or far downwind of the campsite.

route, but not in the south. Like bears, bison feed on the wide grassy swaths along the roadside. But unlike bears, they travel in herds that are known to wander into the middle of the highway.

Advice A bison bull standing two metres at the shoulder can be intimidating at close range, particularly to cyclists. Back off and wait for the bison to move. It may be safe to pass if all the herd is on one side of the highway, but if the animals are split by the road, and a protective bull stands facing you, it might be wise to back off. They rarely graze in one place for more than an hour or two.

Rattlesnakes

Concern Snake bites are potentially serious, even fatal. (Read more about rattlesnakes on page 194.)

Advice Stay on the trail.

Cougars and Wolves

Concern Cougar densities are highest in the southern third of British Columbia—but sightings from the Trans Canada Trail are rare. Like all wildcats, *Puma concolor* is secretive. A cougar usually shuns contact with

people but occasionally stalks them as prey. Wolves (*Canis lupus*) are not generally aggressive toward humans and are seldom seen in the wild.

Advice Anyone who meets a cougar on the trail should stand upright and face the animal. Back away slowly while talking confidently. Leave the cougar an escape route. If it attacks, fight back, using fists, sticks, stones, or other weapons. Similar methods can be used to deter wolves.

USING THIS BOOK

Where the Trans Canada Trail begins is debatable. While Newfoundlanders may argue for St. John's, British Columbians may claim that Victoria is the official starting point. This claim is backed by a series of TCT guidebooks that are oriented from west to east. When the trail and guidebooks are completed, TCT travellers will be able to open this book beside the Pacific Ocean at Km 0 in Victoria, follow it to Elk Pass in the Rockies, then pick up the next guidebook and continue east across the country to the Atlantic. People starting in Newfoundland would have to read the books backwards.

Each of the 21 chapters covering the TCT's southern route across BC (Part One) describes a stretch of trail that could reasonably be travelled by bicycle in a day. Variations in the lengths of these stretches—from 54.5 kilometres to 117.8—are based largely on availability of campsites and accommodation. Each chapter ends where there's a place to stay overnight, though that often means pitching a tent. The variety of sights and activities, and the difficulty of terrain in certain areas, also has a bearing on the distance covered in each chapter. In a typical day, travellers may be on the trail for eight hours, moving at seven to 15 kilometres an hour, including breaks. In BC's sparsely populated north, however, where tiny communities are linked by long, lonely stretches of highway, the entire 1,051 kilometres are covered in three chapters (in Part Two). Plan your trip carefully, figuring out beforehand where you might stay overnight, and how much of each chapter you think you can cover in a day.

PART ONE: SOUTHERN BC
VICTORIA *to* ELK PASS

> Green space is one of the most important parts of a sustainable plan that everyone can buy into. Wherever you can get green areas they become your future.
> —*Lorne Whyte, former chief executive officer of Tourism Victoria, on the expansion of parkland in Greater Victoria*

BC Parliament Buildings overlook Victoria Harbour

1

TRAIL TRIVIA

Kilometre 0 on the Trans Canada Trail in BC overlooks Juan de Fuca Strait, the province's most southerly location.

TOTAL DISTANCE

62.4 km

HIGHLIGHTS

› Victoria, the capital of British Columbia
› Hatley Park/Royal Roads University
› Goldstream Provincial Park

CONDITIONS

› **Victoria (Km 0) to Sooke Lake Road (Km 45.9)** Paved roads and paved and hard-packed gravel trails; includes a moderately arduous climb up the Trans-Canada Highway's Malahat Drive. → 45.9 km
› **Sooke Lake Road (Km 45.9) to Renfrew Road (Km 58.5)** Good gravel road for 1.4 kilometres, then 11.2 kilometres of gravel railway bed on the Cowichan Valley Trail. → 12.6 km
› **Renfrew Road (Km 58.5) to Koksilah River Provincial Park (Km 62.4)** Good gravel road. → 3.9 km

CAUTIONS

› Not many grocery stores for more than 80 kilometres between Colwood (Km 17.6) and Lake Cowichan (Km 41.7 in the next chapter).
› Black bears, especially beyond Shawnigan Lake.

TOPOGRAPHIC MAPS

1:250,000   Victoria 92B
1:50,000   Sooke 92B/5, Victoria 92B/6, Sidney 92B/11, Shawnigan Lake 92B/12

OVERVIEW

Above the shores of Juan de Fuca Strait near downtown Victoria, Mile 0 on the Trans-Canada Highway is unofficially Km 0 on the Trans Canada Trail. It is customary for people setting off on a cross-continental trek to dip their toes in the Pacific Ocean here and wonder, perhaps, if travellers with equally lofty ambitions are soaking their feet in the Atlantic at St. John's, NL.

Surrounded by ocean on three sides and protected gre
fourth, Victoria has no room to sprawl. It is more likely t(
out, ensuring the farms, forests, and parklands to be enjoyed υ,
lers on the outskirts of town remain intact. This enviable balance betw
city and country is enhanced by a temperate climate, which allows hikers,
cyclists, or equestrians to use the Trans Canada Trail year-round.

Aside from the Lower Mainland, the TCT through Greater Victoria is
the most urbanized part of the trail in BC. Highways, city streets, pathways in neighbourhoods, and trails along railroads ("rail trails") comprise a
TCT route that runs from the centre of British Columbia's capital into the
nearby realm of cougars, bears, and timber wolves.

LOCAL ADVENTURES

Websites for Tourism Victoria (www.tourismvictoria.com) and the Greater
Victoria Cycling Coalition (www.gvcc.bc.ca) detail several cycling and hiking trips on southern Vancouver Island.

Day Trip

› From the TCT's Km 0 at Dallas Road and Douglas Street, hike the ocean-
side walkway to West Bay Marina and board a foot ferry to cruise Victoria
Harbour. → 6.4 km
› From the Johnson Street Bridge in Victoria, cycle the Galloping Goose
Regional Trail to Sooke (→ 55 km), or the Lochside Trail to Sidney (the
first few kilometres on the Galloping Goose; see page 40) (→ 33 km).
Return to Victoria by city bus—one bus carries two bikes. Hikers and
cyclists can get to several Greater Victoria parks on public transit.
› From Km 0, cycle to Royal Roads University/Hatley Park National His-
toric Site (Km 18.9) and tour the elaborate gardens and castle built for BC's
wealthiest family. ⇆ 37.8 km

2 or 3 Days

› Take the Mill Bay Ferry across Saanich Inlet and cycle to Kinsol
Trestle. Return to Victoria the same way (⇆ 87.6 km) or via the TCT
(↺ ±100 km). (See page 37.)
› Take the TCT and Lochside Trail up Saanich Peninsula to Swartz Bay
(→ 33 km), and catch a BC Ferry to Gulf Islands National Park.

TCT ACCESS POINTS

Victoria (Km 0) The intersection of Dallas Road and Douglas Street is Mile 0 on the Trans-Canada Highway, Km 0 on the Trans Canada Trail. **P** *street parking*

Atkins Road (Km 14.7) Take Highways 1 and 1A toward Colwood. Atkins Road is about 100 metres beyond the turnoff from Highway 1 onto 1A. **P** 🚻 *outhouses*

Luxton (Km 22.7) Near Glen Lake Road off Highway 14 (Sooke Road), about five kilometres west of Colwood. **P** *Parking near Luxton fair grounds and Galloping Goose Trail.* 🐎 *Horse trailers can be parked here; horse riders can ride about four kilometres on the TCT/Galloping Goose Trail east toward Royal Roads University, or continue south and then west on the Goose for about 37 kilometres to Leechtown.*

Cowichan Valley Trailhead on Sooke Lake Road (Km 45.9) Follow the TCT route from Highway 1 and Shawnigan Lake Road (Km 40.2) to reach the Cowichan Valley Trailhead. **P** ⑦ 🐎 *Horse trailers can be parked here and the TCT can be travelled by horses (if they're not spooked by trestles) for more than 14 kilometres to Kinsol Trestle. At press time there was debate about whether the derelict Kinsol Trestle would be rebuilt or demolished and replaced; fundraising was under way. With a usable trestle, equestrians will be able to continue another 35 kilometres on the TCT to Lake Cowichan.*

Renfrew Road (Km 58.5) West off Highway 1 at Shawnigan Lake Road (Km 40.2), then north along either side of the lake to Renfrew Road. **P** ⑦ 🚻 *outhouse* ▲

Koksilah River Provincial Park (Km 62.4) Continue on Renfrew Road past the TCT junction (Km 58.5). **P** 🚻 *outhouse* 🚰 *river access*

SOUTHERN VANCOUVER ISLAND

CITY, OCEAN, AND BACKWOODS

From Km 0, the TCT hugs the shoreline through Victoria's city centre then follows an abandoned railway bed—the Galloping Goose Regional Trail—to the city's western outskirts. The TCT leaves "The Goose" and takes paved roads and connecting trails to the Trans-Canada Highway, which runs "up Island" through Goldstream Provincial Park. An off-road TCT route is being planned through the Sooke Hills, joining the Galloping Goose to Shawnigan Lake, where the TCT takes the Cowichan Valley Trail toward Lake Cowichan. It would eliminate the need to hike or bike on the busy highway. (Check for updates at www.trailsbc.ca/v_island_region/ or www.crd.bc.ca/parks/.)

Currently, Goldstream Park is the start of the TCT's climb up the Malahat Drive, part of the Trans-Canada Highway. There are long, fairly steep hills, paved shoulders, and great views over Saanich Inlet and Peninsula, and beyond to the Gulf Islands and American San Juans.

The TCT moves off the highway, and cyclists can coast nearly five kilometres down toward Shawnigan Lake before making a short, steep climb to the 11.2-kilometre Cowichan Valley Trail, a rail trail above the west side of the lake. The rail trail ends near the derelict Kinsol Trestle, one of the highest wooden trestle bridges on earth. A logging road completes the route to Koksilah River Provincial Park, where tents can be pitched and campers can sit by the river and contemplate the challenge that awaits them on the next leg of the TCT—the dreaded Kinsol Trestle detour. (The trestle is expected to be replaced or rebuilt, allowing the TCT to continue on the railbed rather than on this rough detour.)

Ogden Point Breakwater

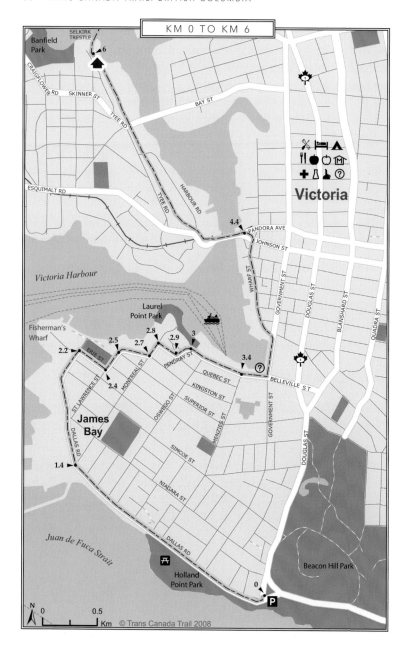

KM 0 TO KM 6

1

THE TRANS CANADA TRAIL

Place names with asterisks are included in the **Communities, Parks, and Places to Stay** section (page 42).

Km 0   *Victoria** The TCT runs west on Dallas Road and follows the shoreline into downtown Victoria.

Km 1.4   *Ogden Point Breakwater* A 750-metre walkable breakwater built in 1917 using 18-tonne granite blocks.

Km 2.2   *Dallas Road + Erie Street* The TCT goes right on Erie; Fisherman's Wharf is to the left.

Km 2.4   *Erie Street + St. Lawrence Street* Go left on St. Lawrence.

Km 2.5   *St. Lawrence Street + Superior Street* At a three-way stop, cyclists cross Superior and veer right on Kingston Street. Walkers, or cyclists pushing their bikes, can go left down to a path that follows the shore for nearly one kilometre to the terminal for ferries from Washington state.

Km 2.7   *Kingston Street + Montreal Street* Veer left on Montreal.

Km 2.8   *Montreal Street + Quebec Street* Veer right on Quebec.

Km 2.9   *Quebec Street + Pendray Street* Veer left on Pendray.

Km 3   *Pendray Street + Belleville Street* Veer right on Belleville. The seaside walkway returns to the road for nearly 100 metres around the ferry docks built for Clipper Navigation and Black Ball Transport.

Km 3.4   *Belleville Street + Menzies Street* Just before this junction at the former Canadian Pacific Railway Steamship Terminal, walkers can take a stairway down to the harbour causeway. Bicycles and wheelchairs can be wheeled from the junction on ramps that switch back down to the causeway. Cycling is not allowed, but bicycles can be pushed on the causeway for one kilometre to Johnson Street Bridge. Cyclists who'd rather ride should stay on the waterfront roads, turning left off Belleville onto Government Street past the Empress Hotel, then, at Victoria Visitor Centre, left off Government onto Wharf Street. At Johnson Street go left across the blue bridge.

Km 4.4   *Johnson Street Bridge* On the west

Artist on the causeway in Victoria Harbour

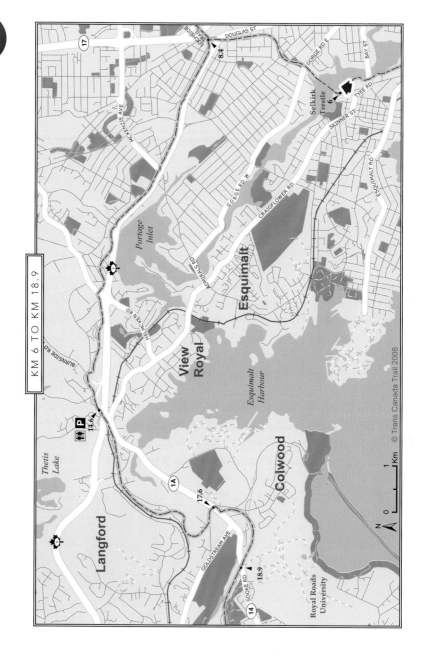

KM 6 TO KM 18.9

Selkirk Trestle

DOUGLAS ST

GORGE RD E

BAY ST

TYEE RD

SKINNER ST

ESQUIMALT RD

GORGE RD W

CRAIGFLOWER RD

ADMIRALS RD

MCKENZIE AVE

LOCHSIDE ROUTE

8.4

6

Portage Inlet

Esquimalt

View Royal

Esquimalt Harbour

HEACKKEN RD

BURNSIDE RD

Thetis Lake

14.6

Langford

1A

17.6

GOLDSTREAM AVE

Colwood

SOOKE RD

18.9

14

Royal Roads University

© Trans Canada Trail 2008

N   0   1   Km

side of the bridge the TCT goes right (north) onto the paved Galloping Goose Regional Trail, a commuter and recreational trail that connects to Victoria's western communities. (The harbourside causeway continues about two kilometres to West Bay, a mooring area for Victoria Harbour Ferries.)

Km 6   *TCT Pavilion, Selkirk Trestle* At the pavilion, turn right and go over the trestle.

Km 8.4   *Galloping Goose Trail, Lochside Trail* Turn left on "The Goose" toward Colwood. (The Lochside Trail heads right and continues for 29 kilometres through the town of Sidney to the BC Ferries terminal at Swartz Bay.)

Km 14.6   *Galloping Goose + Trans-Canada Highway* Continue straight on the Goose.

Km 17.6   *Colwood* Cross the Old Island Highway (Highway 1A) at the traffic light to continue on the Goose.

Km 18.9   *Royal Roads University, Highway 14 (Sooke Road)* Cross the highway to continue on the Goose.

Km 21   *Veterans Memorial Parkway + Kelly Road* The TCT continues kitty corner across this intersection.

Km 22.7   *Luxton, Highway 14 + Glen Lake Road* Turn right off the Goose down Glen Lake Road. Changes to the TCT route in this area were expected as part of the off-road link between the Galloping Goose and Shawnigan Lake: check for updates at www.trailsbc.ca/v_island_region/ or www.crd.bc.ca/parks/. 🐎 Horse trailers can be parked near here at the Luxton fairgrounds.

Km 23.9   *Glenlake Elementary School, Glen Lake Trail* [GPS] north 48.26.559, west 123.31.605. Past the school the TCT takes a 200-metre trail on the left, down a hill and over some railway tracks beside Langford Lake. Turn right on Leigh Road and follow it to Goldstream Avenue (Km 25.1), then turn left.

Km 26.6   *Goldstream Avenue + Trans-Canada Highway* Go left (north) onto the highway.

Km 27.4   *Goldstream Provincial Park* campground turnoff, Trans-Canada Highway + Sooke Lake Road* (Turn left (west) off the highway onto Sooke Lake Road to the provincial park campground.)

Km 29.9   *Entrance to Goldstream Provincial Park** (The park's day-use area is a right turn off the highway.) Continue north up the TCT/Malahat Drive/Trans-Canada Highway.

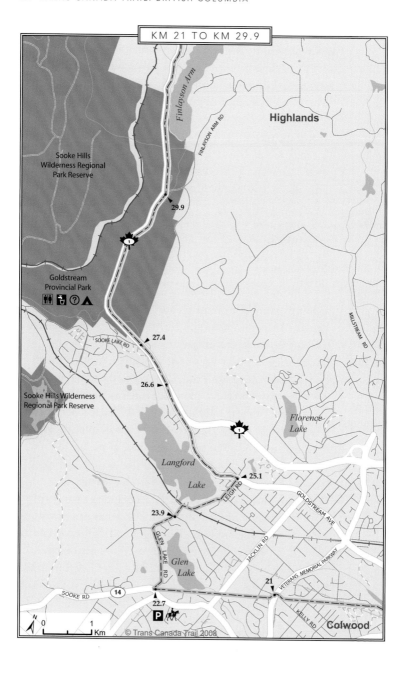

KM 21 TO KM 29.9

Finlayson Arm

Highlands

Sooke Hills
Wilderness Regional
Park Reserve

29.9

FINLAYSON ARM RD

MILLSTREAM RD

Goldstream
Provincial Park

27.4

SOOKE LAKE RD

Sooke Hills Wilderness
Regional Park Reserve

26.6

Florence
Lake

Langford

Lake

25.1

LEIGH RD

GOLDSTREAM AVE

23.9

GLEN LAKE RD

JACKLIN RD

VETERANS MEMORIAL PARKWAY

Glen
Lake

21

SOOKE RD

14

22.7

P

KELLY RD

Colwood

N
0   1
Km   © Trans Canada Trail 2008

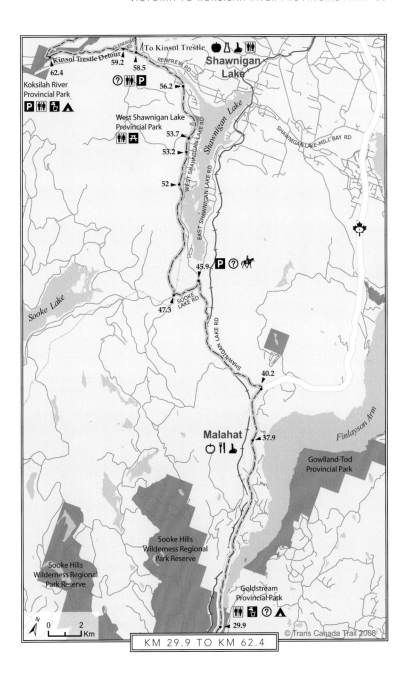

KM 29.9 TO KM 62.4

© Trans Canada Trail 2008

Km 37.9 *Malahat** Continue north on the highway past the community of Malahat.

Km 40.2 *Trans-Canada Highway + Shawnigan Lake Road* Turn left off the highway onto Shawnigan Lake Road.

Spawning salmon in Goldstream River

Km 45.9 *Shawnigan Lake Road + Sooke Lake Road* Turn left onto Sooke Lake Road, a 1.4-kilometre stretch of gravel road with a steep climb to the head of the Cowichan Valley Trail, a hard-packed gravel rail trail.

🏇 Parking for horse trailers is available at the trailhead.

Km 47.3 *Cowichan Valley Trail* Head north on the rail trail.

Km 52 TCT + *West Shawnigan Lake Road* (Turn right if you wish to access West Shawnigan Lake Road.)

Km 53.2 TCT + *West Shawnigan Lake Road* (Again, you can turn right if you wish to access West Shawnigan Lake Road.)

Km 53.7 *McGee Creek Trestle, West Shawnigan Lake Provincial Park* and village of Shawnigan Lake** (To reach the park, turn right off the TCT near the trestle onto West Shawnigan Lake Road, then left. The village of Shawnigan Lake is on the northeast side of the lake.)

Km 56.2 TCT + *Olund Road* **GPS** north 48.38.027, west 123.39.822. The TCT crosses Olund Road. (Kews, Moncur, and West Shawnigan Lake roads are on the right.)

Km 58.5 TCT + *Renfrew Road* The designated TCT route crosses Renfrew Road and carries on for two kilometres to the unusable Kinsol Trestle. Visit the trestle, then take the detour around it by going back to Renfrew Road and heading west on Renfrew. There are plans to either tear down the trestle and replace it, or to rebuild it.

Km 59.2 *Turnoff to Clearwater RV and Tenting, Gleneagles Road* (To reach a 22-site commercial campground, go 500 metres up Gleneagles Road.)

Km 62.4 *Koksilah River Provincial Park** From the park entrance the TCT continues on the bridge across the Koksilah River to the Kinsol Trestle detour.

1

VICTORIA: CANADA'S CYCLING CAPITAL AND A PROMISING START

Travellers who want a picture of themselves setting off on their Trans Canada Trail expedition at Km 0, at the intersection of Dallas Road and Douglas Street in Victoria, might have to line up behind busloads of foreign tourists. This photo-op site is also the Trans-Canada Highway's Mile 0, a landmark where countless adventures begin.

It's a promising departure point for scenery seekers. The snowy peaks of the Olympic Mountains, on the Washington side of Juan de Fuca Strait, are a backdrop for kitesurfers skipping over the whitecaps and paragliders who leap off Victoria's beachfront cliffs. Wildflowers bloom up the sides of Beacon Hill, and at the top of the hill ocean watchers with binoculars glass the sea.

Canada, eh? This is only Km 0. Three kilometres along the TCT, past the Ogden Point Breakwater and Fisherman's Wharf, the downtown streets are awash with tourists fresh

VANCOUVER ISLAND NO SALTY HOLM

About 750,000 people live on Vancouver Island, yet it is not uncommon for Islanders to be asked: "Are there stores? Can we hike it in a day?"

At 31,284 square kilometres, Vancouver Island is North America's largest island in the Pacific, more than five times the size of Prince Edward Island and three times as large as Cape Breton Island. It is Canada's 11th-largest island, stretching 450 kilometres from Victoria to Cape Scott, ranging from 65 to 100 kilometres wide. With peaks to 2,200 metres, the Vancouver Island Mountains are higher than the Russian Urals or Appalachians of the eastern United States, and at 443 metres, Della Falls, in Strathcona Provincial Park, is Canada's highest waterfall. The Island has 3,440 kilometres of coastline and more than 200 kilometres of Trans Canada Trail.

And yes, there are stores, but no, you can't hike Vancouver Island in a day.

Cycling Saanich Peninsula near Victoria

off the mainland ferries. Double-decker buses, horse-drawn carriages, and pedal-powered Kabuki Kabs clog the roads in front of the provincial Parliament Buildings and stately old Empress Hotel. People on the seafront causeway stop to hear buskers or shop the street vendors' wares. Some climb into high-speed whale-watching boats; others board the chubby little double-ended ferries that scuttle about Victoria Harbour.

Every year, well over three million tourists—about ten times Greater Victoria's population—come to BC's capital city. Early blooming gardens and flower-lined streets, an ocean setting and Old World charm—all this remains Victoria's traditional draws, but recent surveys show that visitors are attracted by the same things that keep the locals stuck here like barnacles on a rock: green hills, blue ocean, and skies untainted by urban haze.

Victoria is Canada's 14th-largest metropolis and is about the size of Halifax, one-sixth as big as Metro Vancouver. The entire Capital Region has more than 200 kilometres of bikeways, and plans to more than double that are in the works. At least 7,000 Victorians use their bicycles as daily transportation and about six percent of the workers—the highest ratio in Canada—commute by bicycle. Admittedly, 2,200 hours of annual sunshine and winters with little or no frost give Victoria cyclists an edge over those in snowier climes.

COUGARS NEARBY BUT ELUSIVE

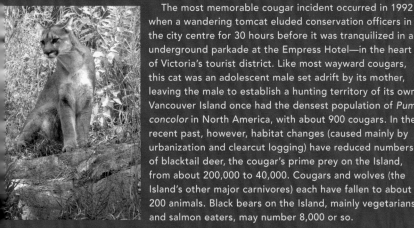

In Greater Victoria, a city of more than 300,000 people, there are hundreds of reports of cougar sightings. As many as two dozen cougars might live within a 20-kilometre radius of the capital city. They've been shot on downtown streets and caught peeking through living-room windows at night.

The most memorable cougar incident occurred in 1992 when a wandering tomcat eluded conservation officers in the city centre for 30 hours before it was tranquilized in an underground parkade at the Empress Hotel—in the heart of Victoria's tourist district. Like most wayward cougars, this cat was an adolescent male set adrift by its mother, leaving the male to establish a hunting territory of its own. Vancouver Island once had the densest population of *Puma concolor* in North America, with about 900 cougars. In the recent past, however, habitat changes (caused mainly by urbanization and clearcut logging) have reduced numbers of blacktail deer, the cougar's prime prey on the Island, from about 200,000 to 40,000. Cougars and wolves (the Island's other major carnivores) each have fallen to about 200 animals. Black bears on the Island, mainly vegetarians and salmon eaters, may number 8,000 or so.

LOCAL ADVENTURE

ACROSS SAANICH INLET TO THE KINSOL TRESTLE
↻ ±100 KM OR ⇆ 87.6 KM

"The Island's most *beautiful* short-cut" is how BC Ferries describes its Brentwood–Mill Bay run across Saanich Inlet. The 25-minute crossing bypasses the uphill Malahat Drive section of the Trans Canada Trail. The terminal nearest Victoria is at Brentwood Bay, on Saanich Peninsula off Highway 17A (West Saanich Road).

Derelict Kinsol Trestle

Here's a scenic round-trip cycling route from Victoria to Kinsol Trestle via the Brentwood–Mill Bay ferry. See maps on page 38 and 39.

Km 0   *Johnson Street Bridge (Victoria)* Head north on the Galloping Goose Trail.

Km 3.8   *Galloping Goose + Lochside Trail* Turn right onto the Lochside Trail.

Km 9.5   *Lochside Trail + Royal Oak Drive* Turn left onto Royal Oak, and continue on an overpass over Highway 17 to Highway 17A.

Km 11.7   *Highway 17A (West Saanich Road)* Turn right (northwest).

Km 13.5   *Alternate route: Interurban rail trail* (For a flatter route turn left at Interurban Road and follow the rail trail north to Wallace Drive. Take Wallace to Hagan Road and go left downhill to Marchant Road, then right on Brentwood Drive to the BC Ferry terminal on Verdier Avenue).

Km 22.2   *Verdier Avenue* Turn left (west).

Km 23.3   *Brentwood–Mill Bay ferry* Cross Saanich Inlet on the ferry. Cycle north along the Mill Bay shore on Mill Bay Road.

Km 29.1   *Highway 1* Turn right (north) at the traffic light.

Km 29.7   *Highway 1 + Shawnigan Lake–Mill Bay Road* Turn left (west) off the highway at the traffic light.

Km 35.3   *Shawnigan Lake village, Shawnigan Lake–Mill Bay Road + East Shawnigan Lake Road* Turn right and continue around the lakeshore.

Km 36.4   *East Shawnigan Lake Road + Renfrew Road* Turn left on Renfrew Road.

Km 40.8   *Renfrew Road + West Shawnigan Lake Road* Stay on Renfrew Road, which veers to the right.

Km 41.8   *Renfrew Road + TCT* **GPS** north 48.39.322, west 123.41.485. Turn right onto the TCT (marked purple on the map on page 39).

Km 43.8   *Kinsol Trestle* South side of the Koksilah River.

Return to Victoria via the TCT (➜ 60.5 km)—the maps from page 28 to 33 show the route between Victoria and the Kinsol Trestle. Or you can do a return trip, boarding the Brentwood–Mill Bay ferry once again.

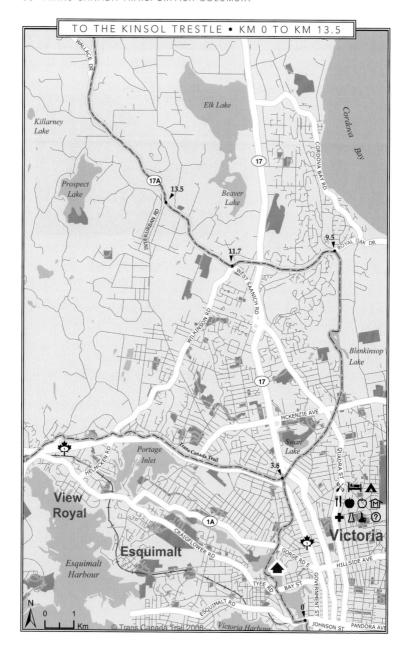

TO THE KINSOL TRESTLE • KM 0 TO KM 13.5

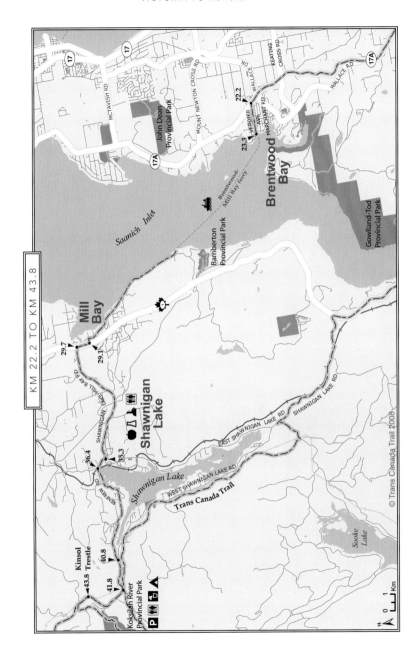

KM 22.2 TO KM 43.8

© Trans Canada Trail 2008

EASY RIDING ON THE GALLOPING GOOSE AND LOCHSIDE TRAILS

The Galloping Goose Regional Trail is the main line in Greater Victoria's growing network of multi-use trails. (Among them is a new 17.5-kilometre hike-and-bike trail, announced as this book went to press, to be built along Victoria's Esquimalt & Nanaimo Railway corridor.) Named for a train that once ran from the city's western outskirts, "The Goose" is now a rail trail stretching 55 kilometres from downtown Victoria, starting from the Johnson Street Bridge (Km 4.4), going toward the village of Sooke, and ending at Leechtown, site of a once-thriving mine.

Galloping Goose Trail

Most of the Goose is for recreation, but the nine kilometres closest to the city centre are mainly paved for commuters who walk or cycle. With several access points, the Goose is a favourite among hikers, cyclists, and equestrians. It takes in the manicured gardens and castle at Royal Roads University, and the beaches, forests, lakes, and farmlands of Metchosin, before passing Sooke Basin and heading up the Sooke River Valley to Leechtown.

Nearly four kilometres from the start of the trail, the Goose intersects the Lochside Trail, a combination of paths, bike lanes, and country roads running 29 kilometres to the BC Ferries terminal at Swartz Bay. Lochside follows an old railway bed along the edge of Swan Lake Christmas Hill Nature Sanctuary, and crosses a 280-metre wooden trestle built over Blenkinsop Lake in 2000, completing an unbroken route between town and country.

For more information, go to www.crd.bc.ca/parks/brochure.htm.

VANCOUVER ISLAND REGION

BC tourism region encompassing Vancouver Island, the neighbouring Gulf Islands, and part of the mainland coast.

› **Population** 750,000

Coho ferry and Victoria Harbour Ferries

> **Visitor Info** *Tourism Vancouver Island* Suite 203, 335 Wesley Street, Nanaimo, BC V9R 2T5; 250-754-3500; www.islands.bc.ca.
> **TCT Info** *Trails BC (Vancouver Island region)* Look up "Vancouver Island" under "BC Regions" on the Trails BC website at www.trailsbc.ca.
> **Transportation** For general information, go to www.islands.bc.ca.

Land The Trans Canada Trail and Trans-Canada Highway share a starting point in Victoria, then take separate courses "up Island." They reunite periodically, until they reach the Departure Bay ferry terminal in Nanaimo, where both routes cross the Strait of Georgia into West Vancouver.

Bus Greyhound Canada (1-800-661-8747; www.greyhound.ca) has bus depots at Victoria, Duncan, Chemainus, Ladysmith, and Nanaimo.

Rail VIA Rail (1-888-842-7245; www.viarail.ca/trains/en_trai_roch_vico .html) runs a passenger service on the Esquimalt & Nanaimo line between Victoria and Courtenay. The railway changed hands recently, and changes to service are expected; bicycles on trains may now be permitted.

Sea BC Ferries (250-386-3431; www.bcferries.com) runs car-and-passenger ships from Tsawwassen and Horseshoe Bay, on the Lower Mainland, to southeastern Vancouver Island at Swartz Bay, outside Victoria, and Duke Point and Departure Bay in Nanaimo. Sailing time is one hour and 35 minutes. *Black Ball Transport* (250-386-2202; www.cohoferry.com) runs daily ferries between downtown Victoria and Port Angeles, WA. *Clipper Navigation* (250-382-8100; www.victoriaclipper.com) operates high-speed ferries daily between Victoria and Seattle. Washington State Ferries

(206-464-6400; www.wsdot.wa.gov/ferries/) runs car-and-passenger ships between Anacortes, WA, and Sidney, BC, which is 27 kilometres from downtown Victoria via the Lochside Trail cycling route.

Air Airlines, charter flights, and commuter aircraft serve Victoria and Nanaimo.

› **Emergency** Call 911.

COMMUNITIES, PARKS, AND PLACES TO STAY

Information on each provincial park in BC can be found on the BC Parks website at www.env.gov.bc.ca/bcparks/.

♣ Greater Victoria (Km 0)

Provincial capital on the southern tip of Vancouver Island. The starting point of both the Trans-Canada Highway and the Trans Canada Trail.

› **Population** 332,000

› **Visitor Info** *Victoria Visitor Centre* 812 Wharf Street, Victoria, BC V8W 1T3; 1-800-663-3883; www.tourismvictoria.com. Check for routes, schedules, and buses with bike racks at www.bctransit.com/regions/vic/. For information about regional parks, go to www.crd.bc.ca/parks/.

› **Attractions** Oceanside walkways, whale watching, BC Parliament Buildings, Ogden Point Breakwater, Beacon Hill Park, Royal BC Museum, Art Gallery of Greater Victoria, Maritime Museum of BC, Royal London Wax Museum, Undersea Gardens, Chinatown.

› **Cycling/Outfitting** *Rider's Cycles* 1092 Cloverdale Avenue; 250-381-1125; www.riderscycles.com. *Russ Hay's The Bicycle Shop* 650 Hillside Avenue; 250-384-4722; www.russhays.com. *Performance Bicycles* 3949-D Quadra Street; 250-727-6655. *Selkirk Station* 80 Regatta Landing (on the TCT/ Galloping Goose Trail); 1-866-383-1466; 250-383-1466; www.switch bridgetours.com.

Victoria International Airport has an *Airport Bicycle Assembly Station*, a sheltered building just outside the terminal, equipped with a pump and basic tools to assemble or disassemble bikes carried off or onto planes in boxes. Storage areas for bicycle boxes and lockers to store bikes are also available. Boxes are often available for free.

› **Greyhound Bus** (1-800-661-8747; www.greyhound.ca) The bus stops at the *Vancouver Island Coach Lines* depot at 700 Douglas Street.

1

⚓ Goldstream Provincial Park (Km 27.4 and Km 29.9)

On Highway 1, 18 kilometres north of Victoria. ⊙ ▲ ♦ 🚻 | *riverside wheel-chair access*

› **Size** 388 hectares
› **Visitor Info** *Freeman King Nature Centre* in park.
› **Attractions** Hiking, nature house. One of the busiest days at Goldstream Provincial Park is November 11, when thousands of salmon are spawning in the river. TCT travellers can stop here to walk beneath 600-year-old Douglas fir and western red cedars, and to watch as many as 200 bald eagles scavenging on fish carcasses.
› **Camping** 163 campsites. *Reservations* 1-800-689-9025 (or 604-689-9025 in Metro Vancouver). www.discovercamping.ca

🌲 Malahat (Km 37.9)

A cluster of buildings along a short stretch of the Trans Canada Trail/Highway 1. ⟳ *general store* ⚓ 🍴 | *post office, telephone*

🌲 Shawnigan Lake (Km 53.7)

From the TCT near McGee Creek Trestle, access West Shawnigan Lake Road and follow it to the village on the northeast side of the lake. ● ⌂ ⚓ 🚻 | *telephone*

› **Attractions** Swimming.

⚓ West Shawnigan Lake Provincial Park (Km 53.7)

Day-use park, on West Shawnigan Lake Road just off the TCT. ⊞ 🚻 *outhouses* 🚰

› **Size** 9 hectares
› **Attractions** Swimming, windsurfing, fishing, canoeing.

⚓ Koksilah River Provincial Park (Km 62.4)

On Renfrew Road about seven kilometres west of the village of Shawnigan Lake. ▲ 🚻 *outhouses* 🚰 *drinking water from river*

› **Size** 210 hectares
› **Attractions** Hiking, chilly swimming.
› **Camping** Walk-in campsites.

"You always hear them coming before you see them, going over the rapids upstream. There are hoots and hollers, a lot of laughing. Then they come out here at the flat section and they're back to suntanning.
—Dave Hignell, co-owner of Sahtlam Lodge, on the inner-tubers on the Cowichan River

Kinsol Trestle detour runs through active logging land

2

TRAIL TRIVIA

With four dozen inlets and some 6,500 islands, BC's total coastline is more than 27,000 kilometres long.

TOTAL DISTANCE

84.5 km

HIGHLIGHTS

› Cowichan River Provincial Park
› Town of Lake Cowichan

CONDITIONS

› **Koksilah River Provincial Park (Km 0) to Kinsol Trestle (Km 6.4)** Detour around derelict trestle on a rough trail that is challenging for cyclists but mercifully short. → 6.4 km
› **Kinsol Trestle (Km 6.4) to Lake Cowichan (Km 41.7)** Hard-packed, double-track railway bed, with a few potholes and puddles. → 35.3 km
› **Lake Cowichan (Km 41.7) to Crofton (Km 84.5)** Paved hilly roads. → 42.8 km

CAUTIONS

› Black bears. Take precautions near corners and rushing water.

TOPOGRAPHIC MAPS

1:250,000   Victoria 92B, Cape Flattery 92C
1:50,000   Shawnigan Lake 92B/12, Duncan 92B/13, Cowichan Lake 92C/16

OVERVIEW

At last check, the future of Kinsol Trestle, a deteriorating assemblage of weatherworn timbers standing 38 metres above the Koksilah River Canyon, was undecided—should it be restored, or demolished and replaced? Fundraising for either solution was under way, and TCT travellers were looking forward to avoiding the rough 6.4-kilometre detour around the 187-metre-long trestle. (Check the status of the trestle and detour at www.trailsbc.ca/v_island_region/ or www.cvrd.bc.ca/parks/.)

The Koksilah and the larger Cowichan River come from different sources but share the same estuary at Cowichan Bay. At 939 square kilometres, the Cowichan watershed is the fourth-largest on Vancouver Island. The TCT flows through the heart of it, following abandoned railway corridors and paved back roads along both sides of the Cowichan River.

The Cowichan Valley is one step removed from the hustle "down Island" in the capital city, and is an idyllic collection of farms and wineries, second-growth forests, small towns, and aboriginal communities. The valley has been identified as a prime area for tourism development under a provincial "rail trails strategy" announced in 2003. (For more on this see page 217.)

The town of Lake Cowichan sits on the lakeshore, split down the middle by the meandering waters of the Cowichan River. The community is the westernmost point on the Trans Canada Trail. There are several places where TCT travellers can stop for a swim in the warm waters of the river and lake. From the town of Lake Cowichan the route heads downstream to cross Highway 1 north of Duncan, then carries on down to the southeast shores of Vancouver Island. There's warm-water swimming in the ocean at Crofton, on Osborne Bay. Hikers on the new seafront walkway can watch fishboats chugging into the harbour next to the terminal for BC Ferries going to Saltspring Island.

Negotiating Burnt Bridge gate on the Kinsol Trestle detour

LOCAL ADVENTURES
Day Trip
› From the town of Lake Cowichan (Km 41.7) hike or cycle a 21 km loop on the TCT down one side of the Cowichan River to Skutz Falls and back up the other side.
› Board a BC Ferry at Crofton (Km 84.5) for a 20-minute sailing to Vesuvius on Saltspring Island. Cycle to villages, mountaintops, lakes, and beaches.

2 or 3 Days
› Stay at Sahtlam Lodge (Km 56.4) (1-877-748-7738; www.sahtlamlodge.com) and explore the TCT and the famous 19 km Cowichan River Footpath; use the lodge as a base for inner-tubing on the river.
› Camp at Cowichan River Provincial Park (Km 32.5, Km 50.4, and Km 56.4) and cycle or hike nearby trails. Other activities include swimming and fishing.

TCT ACCESS POINTS

Koksilah River Provincial Park (Km 0) Take Renfrew Road from the north end of Shawnigan Lake. 🅿 🚻 *outhouse* 🚽 *river access* ▲

Kinsol Trestle, north side (Km 6.4) About four kilometres north of the junction at Highway 1, Cobble Hill Road, and Cowichan Bay Road, turn west off Highway 1 onto Koksilah Road. Go about 2.5 kilometres to Riverside Road and turn south. 🅿 ⦿ *Stay on Riverside about ten kilometres to a parking lot and information kiosk above the trestle.* 🐎 *Horse trailers can be parked here and riders can travel 35 kilometres northwest on the* TCT *to Lake Cowichan.*

Glenora (Km 20.1) From Highway 1 north of the Koksilah River bridge, turn west on Miller Road and go about 2.7 kilometres to Glenora Road. Follow Glenora, then Vaux and Robertson roads west for about seven kilometres to the TCT. 🐎 *parking for horse trailers*

Skutz Falls/Cowichan River Provincial Park (Km 32.5 and Km 50.4) From Highway 1 north of Duncan travel west on Highway 18 for 19 kilometres to Skutz Falls Road (Km 50.4). Turn left (south) and go three kilometres to the park and TCT (Km 32.5). 🐎 *parking for horse trailers*

Lake Cowichan (Km 41.7) Take Highway 18 west from the city of Duncan for 30 kilometres to Lake Cowichan. 🐎 *parking for horse trailers*

THE COWICHAN VALLEY

PASTORAL FARMS, RIVERS, AND SEA

Next to the campsites at Koksilah River Provincial Park, Burnt Bridge is a gated crossing over the river and the start of the Kinsol Trestle detour. Bikes and gear must be passed through the gate. On the north side of the Koksilah River, the marked detour is two kilometres of logging roads and a four-kilometre rainforest trail that's better suited for hikers and horses than touring cyclists: it is steep, winding, uneven, and scenic.

Beyond the detour the TCT is well developed and mainly flat and forested as it follows an old Canadian National Railway right-of-way for 35 kilometres to Lake Cowichan. It crosses a number of recently rebuilt trestles, notably at Holt Creek, and Marie Canyon.

From the town of Lake Cowichan, the TCT follows the original two-lane Cowichan Lake Road between Highway 18 on the left (north) and Cowichan River on the right (south). It is expected that an Esquimalt & Nanaimo Railway spur that runs down the valley will become the official TCT route. In the meantime, the rolling terrain along the old highway is smooth and easy, with light traffic.

After crossing Highway 1 the hills get higher but the scenery gets even better, with views of the mountains on Saltspring Island and of turkey vultures circling over open fields. Crofton's oceanfront walkway overlooks Stuart Channel and the Gulf Islands.

THE TRANS CANADA TRAIL

Place names with asterisks are included in the **Communities, Parks, and Places to Stay** section (see page 53).

Km 0   *Koksilah River Provincial Park*, Burnt Bridge* Negotiate the gate, and cross the bridge across the Koksilah River to the start of a marked logging road up to the right. Continue on this logging road.

Km 1.9   *Kinsol Trestle detour trail* **GPS** north 48.39.208, west 123.44.264. Turn right off the logging road down a steep path.

Km 4.3   *Riverside campsite* (Room for a small number or tents.)

Km 5.3   *Junction* **GPS** north 48.40.222, west 123.41.964. Go right and stay on the main road.

Km 5.9   *Junction* **GPS** north 48.40.415, west 123.41.856. If you go right you will reach a parking area and kiosk, which is 500 metres to the Kinsol Trestle crossing. Going left along the TCT/rail trail will lead you to Lake Cowichan.

Holt Creek Trestle

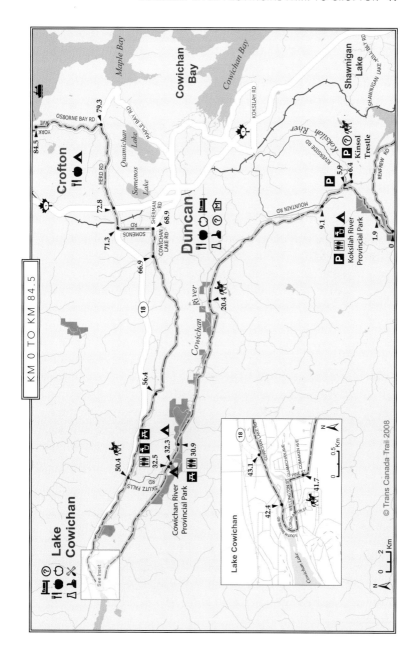

© Trans Canada Trail 2008

Km 6.4   *Kinsol Trestle, north side*
      🐎 A short stretch of the TCT here is often used by horses with carriages. Horse trailer parking is available here.

Km 9.1   TCT + *Mountain Road* The TCT crosses Mountain Road and continues along Hawthorne Road.

Km 20.4   *Holt Creek Trestle*

Km 30.9   *Marie Canyon Trestle* (Picnic tables, outhouses, bike racks.)

Km 32.3   *Cowichan River Provincial Park** The TCT crosses a gravel road at the Horseshoe Bend group campsite.

Km 32.5   *Cowichan River Provincial Park** The TCT comes to the Skutz Falls campground. (Outhouses, drinking water, picnic tables.)

Km 41.7   *Lake Cowichan*, *Pine Street + Comiaken Avenue* The rail trail ends at this junction in the town of Lake Cowichan. Turn right (north) onto Pine Street and go three blocks down to Quamichan Avenue. Just beyond Quamichan, go left (west) on a well-marked railbed that leads to a kiosk describing local trails. This is the westernmost point on the Trans Canada Trail. (A building nearby at the junction of Coronation and Wellington streets was expected to become a trail info centre, with showers for TCT travellers. Check its status at www.trailsbc.ca/v_island_region/.)

    From the town of Lake Cowichan the TCT heads east toward Duncan and Crofton. About 50 metres west from the kiosk on Wellington Street, turn right onto South Shore Road, which parallels the south side of the Cowichan River through Lake Cowichan's downtown core.

Km 42.4   *Cowichan River Bridge* Cross the bridge and continue on the main road (Highway 18) through town.

Km 43.1   *Highway 18 + Cowichan Lake Road* After passing Greendale Road, turn right (east) onto Cowichan Lake Road (known locally as "Old Lake Cowichan Road").

Km 50.4   *Cowichan Lake Road + Skutz Falls Road* The TCT continues straight. (A right turn here leads to Cowichan River Provincial Park*, three kilometres down Skutz Falls Road.)

Km 56.4   *Cowichan Lake Road + Stoltze Road* The TCT continues straight. (A right turn here leads to Cowichan River Provincial Park* and Sahtlam Lodge, both about three kilometres down Stoltze Road.)

Km 66.9   *Cowichan Lake Road + Tansor Road* The TCT/Cowichan Lake

Cowichan River Footpath

Road comes to a stop sign, then continues to the right toward Duncan.

Km 68.9 *Cowichan Lake Road + Somenos Road + Sherman Road* Turn left at this intersection onto Somenos Road. (A right turn goes to downtown Duncan*.)

Km 71.3 *Somenos Road + Highway 18* Turn right onto Highway 18.

Km 72.8 *Highway 18 + Highway 1* Go straight (east) on Highway 18 through the traffic light across Highway 1, where Highway 18 becomes Herd Road.

Km 79.3 *Herd Road + Osborne Bay Road* Turn left (north) on Osborne Bay Road, which becomes York Avenue.

Km 84.5 *Crofton*, York Avenue + Chaplin Street* Go left uphill on Chaplin Street to continue on the TCT, right downhill for BC Ferries to Saltspring Island.

ANGLERS' FOOTPATH MAKES COWICHAN RIVER ACCESSIBLE

The Cowichan, with runs of salmon, steelhead, and a unique stock of brown trout, has always been a stream for anglers. A provincial

"Heritage River," it runs for 47 kilometres from Cowichan Lake down to the southeast shores of Vancouver Island at Cowichan Bay. The Cowichan is a particularly accessible river. In the 1960s anglers cleared a riverside trail, joining a series of crude paths trampled through the bush by the heavy soles of gumboots.

The Cowichan River Footpath follows the riverbanks for 19 kilometres, from Glenora almost to the town of Lake Cowichan. It's an attractive trail through forests of big maple and fir with an understorey of salal and chest-high sword ferns.

Halfway up the footpath, TCT travellers can see Sahtlam Lodge sitting above the opposite bank of the river. Built in the 1920s as a private hunting and fishing retreat, Sahtlam makes a comfortable base for TCT travellers taking time to hike on the footpath, or combining a summer walk with an inner-tube float down the river. The lodge has a private cable crossing to the footpath and TCT (1-877-748-7738; www.sahtlamlodge.com).

TRUMPETER SWAN: THE WINTER MIGRANT

When the Halloween pumpkins are ripe in the fields, Vancouver Islanders keep an eye on the sky and an ear to the wind for the return of the trumpeter swans. It's always impressive: first the distant honking, then the far-off appearance of birds that resemble white pelicans but circle like vultures. These are North America's biggest waterfowl, with two-metre wing-spans and bodies that weigh up to 13 kilos.

Nearly one-third of the world's 35,000 trumpeter swans (*Cygnus buccinator*) fly south from summer nesting grounds in Alaska to winter in BC, mainly on the ice-free Coast. They forage in fields and estuaries and rest on open water, sometimes saltwater bays. As many as 500 might gather at one site; flocks of several dozen are common. They'll occupy an area through winter and begin their northbound migration in early spring. Swans can be spotted by travellers on the Trans Canada Trail in the lower Cowichan Valley, or off the TCT at farms outside Victoria on the Lochside Trail. Over-hunting had reduced them to near-extinction in the 1930s, and hunting swans was banned. With urbanization and industry that choked natural marshes and estuaries, the swans were slow to recover until the late 1960s and early '70s when they discovered the lush, high-protein grasses on dairy farms. Each swan was devouring four or five kilos of cattle food a day, and farmers were risking their livelihoods until they started planting certain fields specifically for the swans.

Now there's an uneasy truce between farmers and swans, and a tinge of satisfaction for Islanders who watch overhead and listen when there's frost on the pumpkins.

Pink fawn lily near Lake Cowichan

VANCOUVER ISLAND REGION

BC tourism region encompassing Vancouver Island, neighbouring Gulf Islands, and part of the mainland coast. For detailed information, go to page 40 in Chapter 1.

COMMUNITIES, PARKS, AND PLACES TO STAY

Information on each provincial park in BC can be found on the BC Parks website at www.env.gov.bc.ca/bcparks/. For regional parks, check out www.cvrd.bc.ca/parks/.

🌲Koksilah River Provincial Park (Km 0)

See page 43 in the previous chapter.

🌲 Cowichan River Provincial Park (Km 32.3, Km 32.5, Km 50.4, and Km 56.4)

From Highway 1 north of Duncan, travel west on Highway 18 for 19 kilometres to Skutz Falls Road (Km 50.4). Turn left (south) and go three kilometres to reach the park (Km 32.5). 🏕 ▲ 🚻 *outhouses* 🚮

› **Size** 873 hectares
› **Attractions** Warm summer snorkelling, inner-tubing, canoeing, fishing, hiking, biking, horseback riding.
› **Camping** 80 campsites in two campgrounds, *Skutz Falls* (Km 32.5 and Km 50.4) and *Stoltz Pool* (Km 56.4). *Reservations* 1-800-689-9025 (or 604-689-9025 in Metro Vancouver). www.discovercamping.ca

🍁 Lake Cowichan (Km 41.7)

The warm waters of Cowichan Lake pour into Cowichan River and flow under a bridge in the centre of town. This is a launching point for anglers and river rafters, a gateway to logging roads leading to Vancouver Island's

BALD EAGLE: A MARITIME RAPTOR

Autumn and winter salmon runs on the coast of BC provide a chance to see congregations of bald eagles (*Haliaeetus leucocephalus*) scavenging on the riverbanks with ravens and noisy gulls. For TCT travellers, the Goldstream and Cowichan rivers are good bets. The eagles feast on salmon until late winter or early spring, then turn to herring that school up to spawn in shallow bays. When the herring disperse the eagles subsist mainly on ducks and seabirds.

Nutrient-rich seas and ice-free winters make coastal BC a prime feeding ground for birds that migrate down from the frozen Interior. Eagle numbers have doubled in BC since the late 1980s. Between 40,000 and 60,000 may winter on the Coast and 15,000 may breed here, staking out nesting territories that they aggressively defend.

TCT travellers across BC can expect to see bald eagles, especially on the Coast but also near rivers, lakes, marshes, and other bodies of water across the province.

southwest coast, and a rest stop for hikers and cyclists on the Trans Canada Trail. ⊘ ● ⌂ ✕ ⏚ ⅋ ⌷ | *many other services for an area population of 7,500*

› **Population** 3,000
› **Visitor Info** *Lake Cowichan tourist/visitor booth* 125C South Shore Road, Box 824, Lake Cowichan, BC VOR 2GO; 250-749-3244; www.cowichan lakecc.ca.
› **Attractions** Summer swimming, fishing, hiking, displays on forestry history.

♣ Duncan (off Km 68.9)

At the junction of Cowichan Lake Road, Somenos Road, and Sherman Road, turn right (off the TCT) onto Cowichan Lake Road for about four kilometres south to the town centre of Duncan. The city is the commercial hub of the Cowichan Valley. *Many amenities and services for a surrounding population of 72,000.*

› **Population** 4,700

> **Visitor Info** *Duncan Visitor Centre* 381A Trans-Canada Highway, Duncan, BC V9L 3R5; 1-888-303-3337; www.city.duncan.bc.ca. *Cowichan Valley Regional Parks* 250-746-2500; www.cvrd.bc.ca/parks/.
> **Attractions** Cowichan Native Village, BC Forest Museum, Somenos Marsh Wildlife Refuge.
> **Cycling/Outfitting** *Experience Cycling* 482 Trans-Canada Highway; 250-746-4041; www.experiencecycling.ca. *Iguana Cycles* 698 Coronation Avenue; 250-748-6803.
> **Greyhound Bus** (1-800-661-8747; www.greyhound.ca) Depot located at *Village Green Mall* at #8–180 Central Way.

Crofton (Km 84.5)

A pulp-mill town with picturesque beaches and warm summer swimming that may be overlooked by hasty travellers. ⓘ ● ⑾ ⛏ ▲ | *terminal for Saltspring Island ferry*

> **Population** 2,500
> **Visitor Info** The *Crofton Visitor Centre* is on the seafront in Crofton's original one-room schoolhouse, circa 1905. The visitor centre is located at 1507 Joan Avenue, Box 128, Crofton, BC V0R 1R0; 250-246-2456; www.croftonbc.com.
> **Attractions** Pulp mill tours.
> **Accommodation/Camping** *Osborne Bay Resort* 250-246-4787; www.osbornebayresort.com

Hiking the TCT near Cowichan River

> "To most people Nanaimo was always just a bottleneck on the highway. Then they bypassed us completely with that new superhighway. But they're missing one of the best parts of Vancouver Island.
> —*Elderly man on Nanaimo's Queen Elizabeth Promenade, looking beyond the boats in the harbour to the Gulf Islands and the Coast Mountains on the mainland*

Statue in Chemainus

TRAIL TRIVIA
Periodic influxes of subtropical currents, known as El Niños, bring sunfish, sea turtles, tuna, and other South Pacific species to coastal BC.

TOTAL DISTANCE
66.4 km

HIGHLIGHTS
› Chemainus murals
› Haslam Creek Suspension Bridge
› The Extension Ridge (Abyss) Trail
› Newcastle Island Provincial Park

CONDITIONS
› For cyclists, paved roads and pathways, some hills but mostly easy back roads; for hikers, separate trails toward Nanaimo, which are described on pages 67 and 68.

CAUTIONS
› Heavy traffic where the Trans Canada Trail uses Highway 1.
› Bears in the backwoods.

TOPOGRAPHIC MAPS
1:250,000   Victoria 92B, Port Alberni 92F, Vancouver 92G
1:50,000   Duncan 91B/13, Nanaimo 92G/4

OVERVIEW
Crofton, Chemainus, and Ladysmith are old communities strung along the southeast shores of Vancouver Island. They are inhabited by Islanders content with a more moderate pace than that in the cities of Victoria or Nanaimo. Travellers who explore these little towns by foot or bicycle get a better sense of the heritage and lifestyle than those who simply drive through.

Beyond Ladysmith some of the TCT south of Nanaimo is for hikers and equestrians only. A wooded trail leads to the Haslam Creek Suspension Bridge and to the Nanaimo River, where a bridge is not yet built. On the north side of the river the TCT hiking route continues on the Extension Ridge (Abyss) Trail toward Nanaimo. Maps on pages 64 and 66 show these hiking routes; directions including access to trailheads are on pages 67 and 68.

For cyclists, a detour bypasses these hiking trails using roads that explore the streams, forests, and clusters of population on Nanaimo's southern outskirts.

Trails under development will eventually eliminate the need for TCT travellers to use short stretches of the Trans-Canada Highway. Within the city of Nanaimo is a well-developed off-road trail system; its backbone is the paved 20-kilometre Parkway Trail, which comprises much of the TCT through town.

LOCAL ADVENTURES

Day Trip

› Tour the Chemainus murals and art galleries (Km 9.4), then take a BC Ferry from Chemainus to Thetis Island.
› Hike over the Haslam Creek Suspension Bridge to Nanaimo River and back. (See page 67.) ⇆ 14 km
› Hike the Extension Ridge (Abyss) Trail. (See page 68.) → 13 km
› Cycle or hike the TCT from the Nanaimo TCT Pavilion (Km 56.9) to the city's waterfront (Km 63.8) and board a foot-passenger ferry to Newcastle Island Provincial Park. → 5.5 km

2 or 3 Days

› Backpack or take a bicycle and camping gear to camp at Newcastle Island Provincial Park (Km 63.8).

TCT ACCESS POINTS

Crofton (Km 0), Chemainus (Km 9.4), Ladysmith (Km 19.1) Accessible from the Trans-Canada Highway north of Victoria, each of these communities makes a good starting point for excursions in either direction on the TCT.

Transfer Beach Park (Ladysmith, Km 21.9) East off Highway 1 in Ladysmith, 87 kilometres north of Victoria. Attractions include a historic locomotive.
🅿 🚻 🚮

Rondalyn Resort From the Trans-Canada Highway, turn west just south of Cassidy Airport, about ten kilometres north of Ladysmith, onto Timberlands Road. Follow it for 2.3 kilometres to Rondalyn Resort. Park here and go left toward a gated industrial area 300 metres down the road to begin a hike to the Haslam Creek Suspension Bridge and beyond to the Nanaimo River.

Cassidy rest stop (Km 38.2) East off Highway 1, about 12 kilometres north of Ladysmith and 14 kilometres south of Nanaimo. 🚻 🛗 🍴 *pub and café*

Colliery Dam Park (Km 55.2) From Highway 1 in south Nanaimo turn west on South Street and continue on Seventh Street to Harewood Mines Road and the TCT. Access to the TCT cycling route and the Extension Ridge (Abyss) Trail. Activities include swimming. 🅿 🚻 🛗 🛱

TCT Pavilion (Km 56.9) From Highway 1 (Terminal Avenue) in Nanaimo go west on Bastion and Fitzwilliam streets to Third Street. The TCT is behind Serauxmen Stadium. 🅿

Buttertubs Marsh (Km 57.7) Take Nanaimo Parkway (Highway 19) to Jingle Pot Road and turn east to the sanctuary entrance. Hiking. 🚻 *outhouse* 🅿

Bowen Park (Km 61.5) From Highway 1 (Terminal Avenue) in Nanaimo go west on Comox and Bowen roads. Extensive network of forested hiking trails, including Millstone Trail. 🚻 🅿

Nanaimo Harbour (Km 63.8) East off Highway 1 (Terminal Avenue) in Nanaimo onto Comox Road, then left to parking behind the arena, next to the downtown walkway/bikeway (Queen Elizabeth Promenade).

Departure Bay BC Ferries (Km 66.4) Take the Trans-Canada Highway to the north side of Nanaimo, where the highway and TCT leave Vancouver Island, crossing the Strait of Georgia on a BC Ferry.

BACK ROADS TO TOWN AND COUNTRY

WOODED TRAILS AND BUSY STREETS

The TCT route north of Crofton begins as paved back roads through groves of maple and fir along the seashore. It stops in the mill-turned-mural town of Chemainus then continues up the coast. The TCT crosses the Trans-Canada Highway into Ladysmith, a miniature rendition of San Francisco

Buttertubs Marsh

with restored heritage buildings on steep hills overlooking Ladysmith Harbour.

North of Ladysmith the TCT crosses Nanaimo River. However, there is currently no bridge over the river so a detour is described. On the north side of Nanaimo River the TCT is the Extension Ridge (Abyss) Trail but it is only for hikers; cyclists must bypass this hiking trail and continue toward Nanaimo. Hiking-only sections are described below. The hiking and cycling routes converge near Colliery Dam Park at the edge of the city of Nanaimo. A number of TCT route changes are anticipated between Ladysmith and Nanaimo: check for updates at the Regional District of Nanaimo website at www.rdn.bc.ca (look for "Parks & Trails" under "Recreation & Parks"), or go to www.trailsbc.ca/v_island_region/.

From Colliery Dam, the final stretch of the TCT on Vancouver Island is less than ten kilometres but it's possible to get lost, particularly if TCT signs have gone missing. It is usually well marked: keep an eye out for trail signs. The TCT route here is a thoughtfully chosen tour of Nanaimo, taking in parks and wildlife reserves, urban streams, and the downtown seafront.

THE TRANS CANADA TRAIL

Place names with asterisks are included in the **Communities, Parks, and Places to Stay** section (page 71).

Km 0   *Crofton*, York Avenue + Chaplin Street* Go left (west) up the hill on Highway 1A as it takes Chaplin Street and then Crofton Road.

Km 3.8   *Chemainus Road + Westholme Road* Go right (north) on Chemainus Road to continue on the TCT to Chemainus. (Going left will bring you to Duncan.)

Km 9.4   *Chemainus** Continue straight, staying on Chemainus Road.

Km 19.1   *Ladysmith*, TCT + Highway 1* South of Ladysmith, cross Highway 1 and head uphill on North Davis Road.

Km 19.5   *Davis Road + Dogwood Drive* Turn right.

Km 21.5   *Dogwood Drive + Methuen Street* Go right downhill on Methuen to a tunnel that takes the TCT under Highway 1 to

KM 0 TO KM 9.4

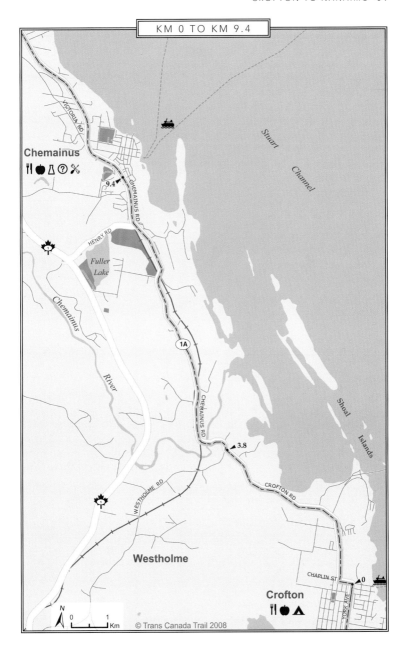

Chemainus

Stuart Channel

VICTORIA RD

9.4

CHEMAINUS RD

HENRY RD

Fuller
Lake

Chemainus

River

1A

CHEMAINUS RD

3.8

Shoal Islands

WESTHOLME RD

CROFTON RD

Westholme

CHAPLIN ST

0

Crofton

YORK AVE

N

0   1
└──────┘Km

© Trans Canada Trail 2008

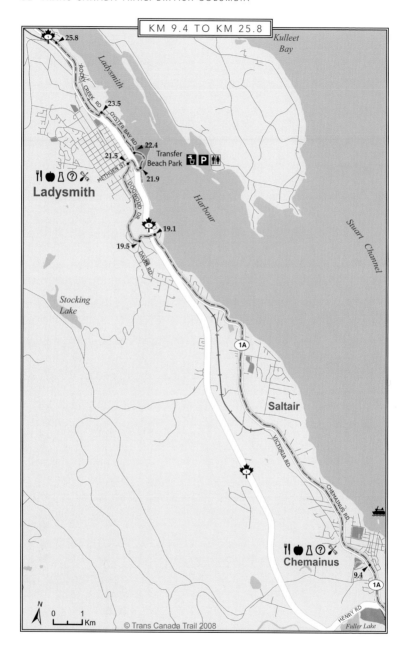

KM 9.4 TO KM 25.8

Kulleet Bay

Ladysmith

Rocky Creek Rd

Oyster Bay Rd

25.8

23.5

22.4

21.5

Methuen St

Dogwood Dr

21.9

Transfer Beach Park

Harbour

Stuart Channel

19.1

19.5

Davie Rd

Stocking Lake

1A

Saltair

Victoria Rd

Chemainus Rd

Chemainus

9.4

1A

Henry Rd

Fuller Lake

N
0   1
└─────┘ Km

© Trans Canada Trail 2008

3

3

Transfer Beach Park. (To see Ladysmith's revitalized downtown heritage, continue straight.)

Km 21.9   *Transfer Beach Park* Turn left (north).

Km 22.4   *Oyster Bay Road* Turn right onto Oyster Bay Road, then veer right at a fork 200 metres up the road.

Km 23.5   *Junction* Turn right downhill, then left.

Km 25.8   *Highway 1* Turn right (north) onto the highway.

Km 26.8   *Highway 1 + Oyster Sto-lo Road* Continue on Highway 1, passing a scenic glimpse of the sea, at the head of Ladysmith Harbour.

Km 29.9   *Highway 1 + Cedar Road* Turn left off Highway 1 at the traffic light onto Cedar, then left again on Thomas Road. Continue for 600 metres to the intersection of Thomas and Takala roads.

Km 30.5   *Thomas Road + Takala Road* Go right up Takala Road to Cameron Road, where you turn right.

Km 33.9   *Cameron Road + Timberlands Road* Go right, then left onto Hallberg Road at the Timberland Pub.

Km 36.6   *Hallberg Road + Vowels Road* Go right for 400 metres to Highway 1. Turn left (north) onto the highway and cross Haslam Creek highway bridge on a narrow wooden walkway.

Km 38.2   *Cassidy rest stop* (Restrooms, drinking water, pub, café.) Continue north on Highway 1 over the Nanaimo River Bridge.

Km 39.1   *Turnoff: Nanaimo River Road* Go right off Highway 1 onto Nanaimo River Road to head west toward White Rapids Road.

Km 39.7   *Nanaimo River Road + South Wellington Road, Nanaimo River Road + E&N Railway tracks* Cross South Wellington Road, and then cross the tracks, and continue up Nanaimo River Road.

Km 43.8   *White Rapids Road* Turn right. (Continue straight if you'd like to take the hikers-only TCT route, the Extension Ridge (Abyss) Trail. It ends at Colliery Dam Park, Km 55.2. See page 68.)

Km 46.6   *Extension Road* Continue straight.

Km 49.6   *Parkway Trail at McKeown Way* Turn left off of Extension Road at a large sign with a map.

Km 54   *Harewood Mines Road* The Extension Ridge (Abyss) Trail ends here near Harewood Mines and Nanaimo River roads;

KM 25.8 TO KM 46.6

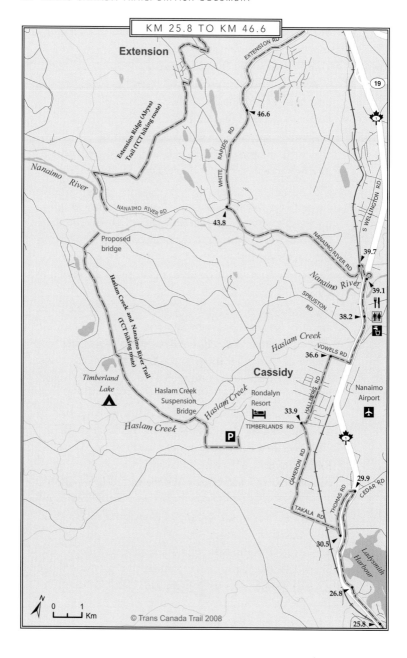

Extension

Extension Ridge (Abyss) Trail (TCT hiking route)

Nanaimo River

NANAIMO RIVER RD

Proposed bridge

Haslam Creek and Nanaimo River Trail (TCT hiking route)

Timberland Lake

Haslam Creek Suspension Bridge

Haslam Creek

Cassidy

Rondalyn Resort

TIMBERLANDS RD

Haslam Creek

Nanaimo River

SPRUSTON RD

Nanaimo Airport

CAMERON RD

THOMAS RD

TAKALA RD

CEDAR RD

Ladysmith Harbour

46.6

43.8

39.7

39.1

38.2

36.6

33.9

29.9

30.5

26.8

25.8

0   1   Km

© Trans Canada Trail 2008

the TCT crosses Harewood Road and continues up the Parkway Trail to Colliery Dam Park (Km 55.2).

Km 55.2   *Colliery Dam Park* The TCT passes Lower Lake in the park, crosses Chase River, then leaves the park on Wakesiah Road. Take the trail along Wakesiah, around Malaspina College campus, to Fourth Street. Turn left.

Km 56.4   *TCT/Parkway Trail* Go right along a paved path.

Km 56.9   *TCT Pavilion* On Third Street behind Serauxmen Stadium. Continue west on the TCT/Parkway Trail as it parallels Third Street; at a fork 500 metres from the pavilion turn right downhill for 300 metres to Third Street and Jingle Pot Road. Cross to the entrance to Buttertubs Marsh.

Km 57.7   *Buttertubs Marsh* A wildlife reserve encircled by 2.4 kilometres of hiking trails, including a stretch of the TCT that follows the marsh to a kiosk at the opposite end. Cyclists ride alongside the marsh on Jingle Pot Road.

Km 58.1   *Jingle Pot Road + Bird Sanctuary Drive* Turn left onto Bird Sanctuary Drive and go 700 metres to the end; take a gravel trail to the left for 100 metres to a kiosk beside the marsh at the end of Buttertubs Drive. From here the TCT continues straight on Buttertubs Drive.

Km 59.5   *Buttertubs Drive + Bowen Road* Cross Bowen Road at the TCT marker and turn left along Bowen Road; go 100 metres and turn right onto the marked Millstone Trail into Bowen Park.

Km 61.5   *Fork* Go right to Millstone Parkway, then left on the parkway to Wall Street, where you turn left.

Km 62.9   *Millstone Trail* Go right off Wall Street onto the paved Millstone Trail, which goes over railway tracks and down a set of stairs. Then turn right and go 200 metres to a footbridge over Millstone River. Cross the bridge and go onto the Harbourside Pathway.

Km 63.3   *Prideaux Street + Mill Street* Go left down Mill Street for 300 metres to the Greyhound bus depot; turn left on a paved path.

Lions Bridge, Nanaimo

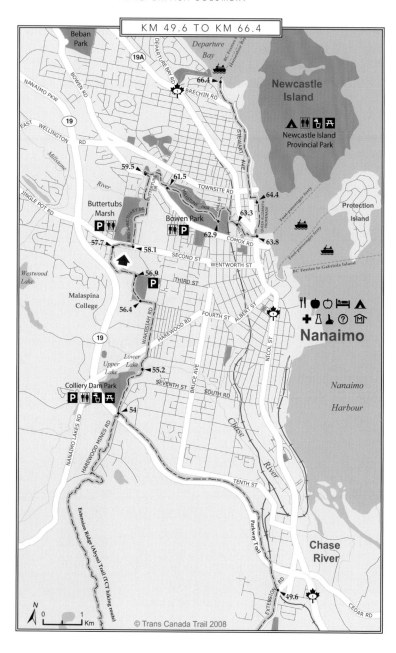

KM 49.6 TO KM 66.4

Beban Park

Departure Bay

19A

BC Ferries to Horseshoe Bay

66.4

BRECHIN RD

Newcastle Island

Newcastle Island Provincial Park

NANAIMO PKW

BOWEN RD

EAST WELLINGTON RD

19

Millstone River

JINGLE POT RD

59.5

61.5

TOWNSITE RD

64.4

Foot-passenger ferry

Protection Island

Buttertubs Marsh

Bowen Park

63.3

Foot-passenger ferry

57.7

58.1

62.9

COMOX RD

63.8

Westwood Lake

SECOND ST

WENTWORTH ST

BC Ferries to Gabriola Island

56.9

THIRD ST

Malaspina College

56.4

FOURTH ST

NICOL ST

ALBERT ST

Nanaimo

19

Upper Lake

Lower Lake

55.2

BRUCE AVE

HAREWOOD RD

WAKESIAH RD

SEVENTH ST

SOUTH RD

Nanaimo Harbour

Colliery Dam Park

54

Chase River

NANAIMO LAKES RD

HAREWOOD MINES RD

TENTH ST

Parkway Trail

Extension Ridge (Abyss) Trail (TCT hiking route)

Chase River

EXTENSION RD

49.6

CEDAR RD

N

0   1
Km

© Trans Canada Trail 2008

Km 63.8   *Nanaimo*, Lions Bridge* This bridge goes over Millstone River on Nanaimo's downtown waterfront. Turn left (north) across the bridge to continue on the TCT/Queen Elizabeth Promenade. (A right (south) turn leads along the shore to ferries to Protection, Gabriola, and Newcastle islands, the last being the location of a provincial park*.)

Km 64.4   *End of Queen Elizabeth Promenade* Turn right onto the road and go 200 metres uphill to Stewart Avenue. Turn right (north).

Km 66.4   *Departure Bay, BC Ferries terminal* The TCT leaves Vancouver Island and crosses the Strait of Georgia to Horseshoe Bay, on BC's Lower Mainland.

TCT FOR HIKERS

HASLAM CREEK AND THE NANAIMO RIVER ⇆ 14 KM

Haslam Creek Suspension Bridge, which opened in 2003, is one of two links in a TCT route that follows old roads and new trails north to Nanaimo's city limits; the second link will be a bridge across the Nanaimo River, but that's yet to come.

    The trail is marked on the main map on page 64. To hike and bike part of the trail, turn left from the Trans-Canada Highway just south of Nanaimo Airport at Cassidy onto Timberlands Road (Km 33.9). Follow it for 2.3 kilometres to Rondalyn Resort and turn left toward a gated industrial area 300 metres down the road. Park at the gate, or at Rondalyn Resort, and follow a marked route, watching for trail markers in trees and other conspicuous locations; bear in mind that TCT markers sometimes disappear in the backwoods. The first four or five kilometres can be cycled.

    About 1.4 kilometres from the gate, Haslam Creek Suspension Bridge dangles 18 metres above a gorge. Beyond the bridge the trail becomes a logging road through clearcuts. Three kilometres from Haslam Creek is a campground at Timberland Lake. About 300 metres farther along is a TCT–marked hiking trail. From there, an hour's hike ends abruptly on the south bank of the Nanaimo River. Until a bridge is built, the way out is the way in. Check for updates at the Regional District of Nanaimo website at www.rdn.bc.ca (click on "Recreation & Parks Services") or the Trails BC website at www.trailsbc.ca ("Vancouver Island").

Haslam Creek Suspension Bridge

TCT FOR HIKERS

THE EXTENSION RIDGE (ABYSS) TRAIL → 13 KM

Officially it's the Extension Ridge, but locals call it the Abyss Trail because of the gaping hole where the earth cracked open. It looks like a glacial crevasse, deep and dark yet narrow enough to jump across. It's one of several earthquake fissures on the Abyss Trail.

The trail is marked on the maps on pages 64 and 66. Until the bridge over the Nanaimo River is built, you must hike along the Nanaimo River to access the southern trailhead. Turn off Highway 1 just north of Cassidy on the Nanaimo River Road turnoff (Km 39.1 on page 63). Stay on Nanaimo River Road, passing White Rapids Road (Km 43.8, where cyclists turn right). Look for a pipeline road marked by TCT signs just under nine kilometres along Nanaimo River Road from Highway 1.

The north bank of Nanaimo River, and some pleasant beaches, are a short walk downhill; the TCT/Abyss Trail goes uphill to the north.

After following a pipeline road and forested trails, this TCT hike moves through the defunct coal-mining town of Extension, originally an extension of the mines at nearby Wellington. Hikers who walk the TCT here today follow in the footsteps of miners who worked at Extension until the 1930s. Some miners' cabins remain amid a few new homes, and the mountains of slag have become racecourses for dirt bikers. Near the entrances to Extension, directions on the backs of TCT signs detail a route through town.

North of Extension the trail climbs a ridge where you can sit at eye level with soaring ravens and peer across a deep valley to Mount Benson. There are distant views of the sea to the east and glimpses of the Nanaimo waterfront. Groves of arbutus, Garry oak, and Douglas fir—an ecosystem unique to the West Coast—border much of the trail (see page 73). This part of the trail is the most "abyssmal," with ominous black rifts that could swallow an unwary hiker.

It's a full day's hike from Nanaimo River to the end of the Extension Ridge Trail near Colliery Dam Park (Km 55.2 on page 65), where the TCT again becomes both a hiking and a cycling route. There's parking near the north end of the trail by Harewood Mines and Nanaimo Lakes roads. This is a "fluid trail": it runs through logging land and is occasionally moved to accommodate timber harvesting. Check for changes at the Regional District of Nanaimo website at www.rdn.bc.ca (look for "Parks & Trails" under "Recreation & Parks") or go to www.trailsbc.ca/v_island_region/.

CHEMAINUS—MILL TO MURALS

Chemainiacs could see the writing on the wall. A one-industry town, an outdated sawmill, construction doldrums of the early 1980s. But natural resources had paid their way in the past, and most everyone agreed they could set the scene for the future: that ocean at the front door and the mountains at the back would make a perfect venue for the "World's Largest Outdoor Art Gallery."

Chemainus mural painted by Paul Ygartua

So they spruced up the streets and buildings and put out a call for artists to paint the town. The mill shut down in the spring of 1982, and by the end of that summer five murals depicting local history adorned downtown walls. Seven more went up the next year, four the next. Tour buses began rerouting off the highway into

BARKING AND FISHY FETOR IDENTIFY SEA LIONS

When the herring return to spawn off the south coast of BC, sea lions are caught in a feeding frenzy that builds through February and March. Their fishy fragrance permeates the air as they haul out by the hundreds, barking incessantly and jostling for space on islets, reefs, and log booms. It's a chaotic scene, with eagles and swarms of gulls squabbling at the surface, waterbirds torpedoing through schools of fish below, and spectators with binoculars and spotting scopes lining nearby shores.

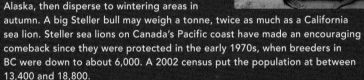

Sea lions are winter residents in southern BC. The barkers are Californias (*Zalophus californianus*) that swim north from their summer breeding rookeries in the United States. About 3,000 forage BC waters through winter. Steller, or northern sea lions (*Eumetopias jubatus*), roar like African lions. They breed on rookeries along BC's central and north coasts and in southeast Alaska, then disperse to wintering areas in autumn. A big Steller bull may weigh a tonne, twice as much as a California sea lion. Steller sea lions on Canada's Pacific coast have made an encouraging comeback since they were protected in the early 1970s, when breeders in BC were down to about 6,000. A 2002 census put the population at between 13,400 and 18,800.

Trans Canada Trail travellers can see, hear, and sometimes smell sea lions not far from the trail. Nanaimo Harbour and the channels through surrounding islands are good sea-lion-spotting areas for BC Ferries passengers.

Chemainus; painters, sculptors, jewellers, and other artisans set up shop; galleries, antique stores, and a performing arts theatre appeared. Now there are three dozen murals—400,000 people a year come to view them. And not far from the revitalized town centre is a new sawmill.

One of the newest attractions to arrive in Chemainus is the Trans Canada Trail—it runs right through the middle of town.

3

VANCOUVER ISLAND REGION

BC tourism region encompassing Vancouver Island, neighbouring Gulf Islands, and part of the mainland coast. For detailed information, see page 40 in Chapter 1.

ORCAMANIA FUELS THRIVING INDUSTRY

Sightings of 50 or 60 killer whales (*Orcinus orca*) from ferries in the Strait of Georgia are fairly frequent, especially in summer. Sometimes a "superpod" totalling about 90 animals is seen; shoals of a dozen or so are more common, but nonetheless spectacular. Viewers may catch them breaching or tail-lobbing or simply resting in a group at the surface.

Whale watching is a multi-million-dollar industry in British Columbia. J, K, and L pods—the southern residents—are the industry's mainstay (in 2001, they were declared endangered in Canada). After recovering from aquarium captures of the 1960s and '70s, numbers have recently plummeted again by 20 percent to about 90 whales. Pollution, dwindling salmon stocks, and marine traffic—including whale watchers—are cited as possible causes.

The northern residents are comprised of more than 200 orcas in 16 pods. Their numbers have fallen less dramatically: they are designated as threatened.

"Resident" orcas are fish-eaters with reasonably predictable migrations, making them the most reliable for whale watchers. From May to October they funnel into inside waters as they follow spawning salmon to their natal streams. Less predictable are "transients," nomadic orcas that feed on the warm-blooded flesh of seals, sea lions, and other marine mammals. They roam widely, hunting in small packs, often changing travel partners. About 250 have been photo-identified in BC waters.

A third population, "offshore" killer whales, makes occasional forays into waters near the shore and causes great excitement when they show up 50 or 60 at a time. About 250 have been photo-identified, but little is known of their diet or habits.

These three orca races have distinctly different dialects, eating habits, and hunting methods. Though they are the same species they are genetically unrelated.

COMMUNITIES, PARKS, AND PLACES TO STAY

Information on each provincial park in BC can be found on the BC Parks website at www.env.gov.bc.ca/bcparks/.

♣ Crofton (Km 0)

See page 55 in the previous chapter.

♣ Chemainus (Km 9.4)

Two kilometres east off Highway 1, 77 kilometres north of Victoria. Fine art and forestry sustain this seaside village. It is a takeoff point for BC Ferries to Thetis Island. (See page 69.) ⑦ ● Δ ✗

› **Population** 3,900
› **Visitor Info** *Chemainus Visitor Centre* 9796 Willow Street, Box 575, Chemainus, BC V0R 1K0; 250-246-3944; www.chemainus.bc.ca.
› **Attractions** The World's Largest Outdoor Art Gallery—three dozen murals depicting local lore and history. Heritage buildings, antiques, artisanal crafts.
› **Greyhound Bus** (1-800-661-8747; www.greyhound.ca) Depot located at *Esso-McBride's Service* at 9616 Chemainus Road.

♣ Ladysmith (Km 19.1)

On Highway 1, 87 kilometres north of Victoria. Once a shipping point for Island coal, now a collection of heritage homes and buildings on hills that face the morning sun. ⑦ ● ✗ Δ ¶

› **Population** 6,700
› **Visitor Info** *Ladysmith tourist/visitor booth* 132C Roberts Street, Box 598, Ladysmith, BC V9G 1A4; 250-245-2112; www.ladysmithcofc.com.
› **Attractions** Refurbished downtown core, Transfer Beach Park.
› **Greyhound Bus** (1-800-661-8747; www.greyhound.ca) Depot located at *Coronation Laundromat* at #8–370 Trans-Canada Highway.

♣ Nanaimo (Km 63.8)

With 80,000 residents, Nanaimo is Vancouver Island's second-largest community. Dubbed the "Harbour City," since 1967 Nanaimo has hosted the Great International World Champion Bathtub Race, a bizarre event in which motorized bathtubs race out into the inhospitable seas in the Strait of Georgia. The ocean and nearby islands make an attractive setting for downtown Nanaimo. The Trans Canada Trail is part of that seaside

Chemainus shops

picture. *Full range of services and amenities, including scheduled flights and ferries to the mainland*

› **Population** 80,000
› **Visitor Info** *Nanaimo Visitor Centre* 2290 Bowen Road, Nanaimo, BC V9T 3K7; 1-800-663-7337; www.tourismnanaimo.com.
› **Attractions** Waterfront walkway, Bowen Park, Buttertubs Marsh, Newcastle Island Provincial Park.
› **Greyhound Bus** (1-800-661-8747; www.greyhound.ca) Depot located at 1 North Terminal Avenue.

🌲 Newcastle Island Provincial Park (off Km 63.8)
In Nanaimo Harbour, on a picturesque island steeped in natural and human history. 🚻 *outhouses* 🏕 ▲ 🚮
› **Size** 336 hectares
› **Attractions** Sandstone beaches and caves; interior lakes and beaver ponds; white raccoons, seals, and orcas; remnants of a sandstone quarry; a shipyard; a fish saltery.
› **Ferry** A foot ferry that carries bicycles (some island roads are rideable) leaves Nanaimo at Maffeo Sutton Park near the Lions Bridge (Km 63.8) on the TCT.
› **Camping** 18 walk-in campsites.

Amid the groves of Garry oak and fir on the leeward side of Vancouver Island, arbutus trees (*Arbutus menziesii*) stand out like twisted, rusty poles, sculpted into abstract forms and sanded as smooth as human skin. Some grow to 30 metres high, with trunks as thick as oil drums and heavy, crooked branches that

sprout off in all directions. Most interesting is the bark, a thin copper-coloured veil that flakes off like old paint to reveal a fresh chartreuse undercoat. Canada's only broad-leafed evergreen, arbutus trees are cloaked year-round in waxy leaves. They produce fragrant clusters of creamy, urn-shaped flowers and red-orange berries that attract winter birds. Known as Pacific madrones in the United States, arbutus trees have a limited range down the West Coast to northern California and up the east side of Vancouver Island and along the opposite mainland shores.

Even more limited in range are Garry oaks (*Quercus garryana*), Canada's only native oak trees on the West Coast. They, too, grow as far south as California, but in Canada are found only on southeast Vancouver Island and neighbouring Gulf Islands, and in two isolated groves on the Lower Mainland.

Both species inhabit dry, rocky, shallow-soiled slopes and meadows and have evolved to withstand drought. They often grow alongside Douglas firs (*Pseudotsuga menziesii*). These are among Canada's tallest trees, reaching 80 metres high and two metres in diameter; some live 600 years.

As intriguing as the trees are the wildflowers that grow in Garry oak meadows. Shooting stars, blue camas, sea blush, chocolate lilies and more—over one-fifth of BC's rarest plants grow here, rare because urbanization is intruding into their limited range. Landowners are being encouraged to protect and restore arbutus, Garry oak, and Douglas fir habitat and their associated wildflowers and plants. TCT travellers see these species along much of the Vancouver Island route. The Extension Ridge (Abyss) Trail, south of Nanaimo, is particularly good.

4 HORSESHOE BAY TO PORT MOODY

66 There is not another large city in the world so close to primeval nature as Vancouver. Vancouver is the edge of the frontier.
—*Canadian columnist Alan Fotheringham*

SeaBus crosses Burrard Inlet to downtown Vancouver

TRAIL TRIVIA

The Trans Canada Trail through Vancouver includes the Stanley Park Seawall, which covers nine kilometres and took 63 years to build.

TOTAL DISTANCE

74.9 km

HIGHLIGHTS

› Capilano River Regional Park
› Lonsdale Quay Market
› World's longest continuous walkway on an urban waterfront

CONDITIONS

› **Horseshoe Bay (Km 0) to SeaBus terminal/Lonsdale Quay (Km 27.3)** Paved roads, hard-packed trails, hilly. → 27.3 km
› **SeaBus terminal/Lonsdale Quay (Km 27.3) to Science World (Km 46.7)** Paved oceanfront trail. → 19.4 km
› **Science World (Km 46.7) to Port Moody (Km 74.9)** City streets, some gravel trail with steep ups and downs, well marked by TCT signs. → 28.2 km

CAUTIONS

› Bears in the woods of the North Shore mountains and around Port Moody.
› Vancouver is a busy city; stay alert.

TOPOGRAPHIC MAPS

1:250,000   Vancouver 92G
1:50,000   North Vancouver 92G/6, Port Coquitlam 92G/7

OVERVIEW

It would seem an impossible task to map out a safe and scenic stretch of the Trans Canada Trail through the multiple jurisdictions of Metro Vancouver. But trail builders here in Trails BC's southwest region have created a TCT route that takes local streets and pathways around much of the traffic. It's a clearly marked, well-chosen journey that showcases the city from the yacht clubs of West Vancouver to the blue-collar neighbourhoods of Burnaby. Industrial sites, parks, shopping malls, and wilderness lie along these 75 kilometres of TCT.

From sea level at Horseshoe Bay the TCT takes separate routes for hikers and cyclists up through the North Shore mountains to Capilano River Park. The routes merge at the park, where the TCT heads back down to the ocean, and a SeaBus runs across Burrard Inlet to downtown Vancouver. From the cruise-ship terminal at Canada Place, the TCT is a paved trail, divided for walkers and joggers on one side (who can travel both directions) and cyclists and skaters on the other (who can travel only one way, counter-clockwise around the seawall). It goes through the busiest urban centre in British Columbia. From the SeaBus terminal near Canada Place, the TCT takes in some of Vancouver's most distinctive landmarks—Stanley Park, Brockton Point, Lions Gate Bridge, Siwash Rock, and more.

Beyond the downtown core there's a steep climb to a TCT Pavilion near the top of Burnaby Mountain. The trail returns to sea level and follows a waterfront path for nearly five kilometres to Rocky Point Park in Port Moody.

The TCT throughout the Lower Mainland and southwest BC is so clearly indicated that it's almost impossible to lose it: keep an eye out for the conspicuous TCT markers.

LOCAL ADVENTURES

Day Trip

› Take a marathon walk on TCT trails from Horseshoe Bay (Km 0) to Capilano Salmon Hatchery (Km 20.5). → 26 km (on hiking-only trails)

› Hike or cycle from the Vancouver SeaBus terminal/CPR station (Km 27.5) to Science World (Km 46.7)—and beyond. → 19.2 km to Science World

2 or 3 Days

› Stay at a downtown hotel or hostel and explore highlights along the TCT and other in-town routes.

TCT ACCESS POINTS

The Trans Canada Trail through the Lower Mainland is accessible from almost anywhere along its route. Use the TCT maps with a street map of Metro Vancouver. Here are some key staging areas and facilities.

Horseshoe Bay (Km 0) 🅿 *parking in local lots* 🚻 *public washrooms at the BC Ferries terminal* For hikers heading into the North Shore mountains (a route described on page 90) there is parking across from Gleneagles

Community Centre on Marine Drive, 1.6 kilometres from the ferry terminal; turn right off Highway 1 onto Eagleridge Drive, then right again onto Marine Drive. 🅿 🚻 *Parking and outhouses can be found on Cypress Bowl Road, 17.2 kilometres from Horseshoe Bay by hiking trail.*

Stevens Drive/Deep Dene Road (Km 17.8) Take Taylor Way north from the Trans-Canada (Upper Levels) Highway; go right on Stevens Drive and continue just beyond Deep Dene Road to Glenmore Park. 🅿 🚻

Capilano River Regional Park (Km 20) From the Trans-Canada Highway head north on Capilano Road to the park. 🅿 🚻

Capilano Park Road/Salmon Hatchery (Km 20.5) Take Capilano Road north from the Trans-Canada Highway, turn left on Capilano Park Road to the hatchery. Attractions include interpretive displays. 🅿 🚻

William Griffin Park (Km 23.4) From the Trans-Canada Highway take Westview Drive north to Queens Road West; go left (west) on Queens to William Griffin Community Centre. 🅿 *parking at the centre (next to the park)* 🚻 🚲

SeaBus terminal/Lonsdale Quay (Km 27.3) Take Lonsdale Avenue south from the Trans-Canada Highway. TCT travellers taking the SeaBus across Burrard Inlet to downtown Vancouver might find more parking spaces here on the north side of Burrard Inlet, near Lonsdale Quay. 🅿 🚻

Downtown Vancouver (Km 27.5 to 46.7) From the SeaBus terminal on Burrard Inlet to Science World there are many places to access the TCT: e.g., Coal Harbour (Km 28.1), Stanley Park (Km 30.2 to 39.2), English Bay (Km 39.5), Sunset Beach (Km 40.3), Vanier Park (Km 42.5), Granville Island (Km 43.7), and Science World (Km 46.7). 🅿 🚻 *parking at all listed locations, as well as an abundance of restrooms and other facilities*

Beyond downtown (Km 46.7 to Km 74.9) Other locations to access the TCT are New Brighton Park (Km 55.2), Confederation Park (Km 57.8), Kensington Park (Km 60.8), Burnaby Mountain (Km 65.2), and Rocky Point Park (Km 74.7). 🅿 🚻 *all these locations have restrooms and parking areas (besides side-street parking)*

FROM NORTH SHORE WOODS
TO AN URBAN CENTRE

FROM SEA LEVEL TO MOUNTAINTOP

There are separate routes for hikers and cyclists from the BC Ferries terminal at Horseshoe Bay. A series of walking trails totalling 26 kilometres make up the hiking route. It climbs into the hills of Cypress Provincial Park and through the North Shore rainforests to Capilano River Regional Park. (Hiking directions from Horseshoe Bay to the Capilano Salmon Hatchery are provided on page 90.)

Cyclists take a tour through the upscale neighbourhoods of West Vancouver then ride through the forests and over the Cleveland Dam in Capilano River Park, where cyclists and hikers meet again. In fewer than ten kilometres, the TCT runs from the semi-wilderness of the North Shore and across Burrard Inlet into the heart of Canada's third-largest city. The route avoids heavy traffic on the Lions Gate or Second Narrows bridges, opting to take the SeaBus for a ten-minute cruise between North Vancouver and the city of Vancouver's downtown core.

Downtown, the TCT is clogged with cyclists, walkers, rollerbladers, baby strollers, and wheelchairs as it loops around Stanley Park on the famous Seawall. Heritage landmarks, outdoor art, beaches, vendors, and playgrounds are among the highlights. Combining new paved trails with the historic Stanley Park Seawall, with a length of 22 kilometres, the TCT here

West Vancouver yatchts

is part of the longest unbroken urban waterfront walkway in the world. At False Creek the trail travels through the site of Expo 86, an industrial area now transformed into a high-density residential and retail centre that will eventually house a population of 110,000.

From Science World at the head of False Creek, the TCT is clearly marked as it takes numerous turns on city streets, many of them designated bikeways. Beyond the Second Narrows Bridge the TCT climbs up one side of Burnaby Mountain and down the other to meet the seashore again—for the last time—near Port Moody.

THE TRANS CANADA TRAIL

Place names with asterisks are included in the **Communities, Parks, and Places to Stay** section (page 94).

Km 0   *Horseshoe Bay, West Vancouver** From the BC Ferries terminal follow the TCT signs up the Upper Levels Highway (Highway 1/99) to Exit #4. (A hiking-only route from Horseshoe Bay to Km 20.5 is described on page 90.)

Km 3.7   *Exit #4* Go right off the highway; continue straight on the exit ramp to a bridge over Highway 1/99 and follow the cycle-commuter signs for nearly 11 kilometres to Taylor Way. The marked TCT route takes Woodgreen Drive, Woodcrest Road, Almondel Road, Ripple Road, Westridge Avenue, and Southridge Avenue to Mathers Avenue.

Km 7.2   *Mathers Avenue, McKechnie Park* Go left down Mathers to a 60-metre trail joining two cul-de-sacs. Take Mathers to 29th Street and turn right to Marine Drive. Go left after one block on Marine to 28th Street (Km 9.8), then left up 28th to Haywood. Turn right onto Haywood, then left at 24th Street.

Km 10.9   *24th Street + Jefferson Avenue* Turn right onto Jefferson, following the cycle-commuter signs past Pauline Johnson School, then along Inglewood Avenue to a left turn up 14th Street, then a right turn on Kings Avenue. Take Kings to Burley Drive, which veers south and intersects with Inglewood Avenue.

Km 14.5   *Inglewood Avenue + Taylor Way* The TCT leaves the cycle-commuter route here. Turn left (north) on Taylor Way and follow the TCT markers to Stevens Drive. Turn right on Stevens alongside the Capilano Golf Club.

Km 17.8   *Stevens Drive + Deep Dene Road* Go right on Deep Dene

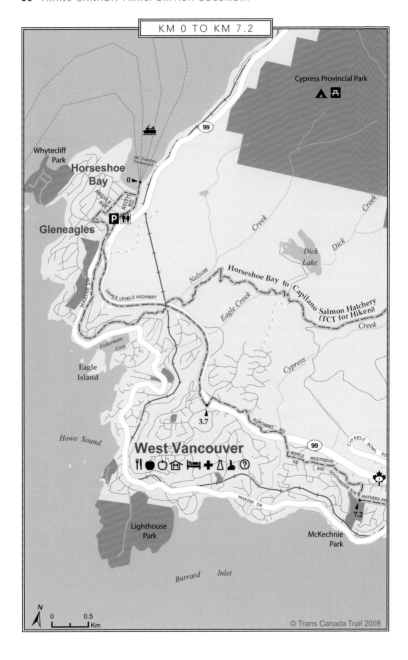

KM 0 TO KM 7.2

Cypress Provincial Park

Whytecliff Park

Horseshoe Bay

BC Ferries Terminal

Gleneagles

ARGYLE AVE

KEITH RD

0

99

Creek

Dick Lake

Dick Creek

Nelson Creek

Horseshoe Bay to Capilano Salmon Hatchery (TCT for Hikers)

UPPER LEVELS HIGHWAY

Eagle Creek

Creek

Fishermans Cove

Eagle Island

Cypress

3.7

ALMONDEL RD

West Vancouver

RIPPLE RD

WESTRIDGE AVE

SOUTHRIDGE AVE

99

CYPRESS BOWL RD

MATHERS AVE

Howe Sound

MARINE DR

7.2

Lighthouse Park

McKechnie Park

Burrard Inlet

N

0   0.5
Km

© Trans Canada Trail 2008

Road, passing a TCT bike-route sign, then left up Glenmore Drive, passing TCT signs that indicate a walking route. Watch on the right for a gravel cycle trail (Km 18.3, before Morven Drive) into Capilano River Park.

Km 20   *Cleveland Dam, Capilano River Regional Park** Cross the dam to the park entrance. From the park entrance take the cycle-commuter road near the information kiosk. (The park is in the District of North Vancouver*.)

Km 20.5   *Capilano Park Road* Go left to continue on the TCT. (If you want to visit the salmon hatchery, go right. An interpretive centre is open every day.)

Km 21.4   *Capilano Park Road + Capilano Road* Turn right. Take Capilano Road south to Edgemont Boulevard (watch for signs to Capilano Suspension Bridge). Turn left on Edgemont, go through Edgemont village, then turn left (east) on Queens Road West to William Griffin Park and Recreation Centre.

Km 23.4   *William Griffin Park* A TCT marker points to the right off Queens Road West. The paved, forested trail follows the west side of Mosquito Creek through the park, crossing under Highway 1 into Mosquito Creek Park.

Km 25.2   *West 16th Street* Cross West 16th and go right down eight stairs to a trail along the east side of Mosquito Creek to Marine Drive. Cross Marine and continue on the trail to Bewicke Avenue. Go left (north) on Bewicke to West Third Street, turn right, then right again on Forbes Avenue. At the end of Forbes, cross West Esplanade, continue over some railway tracks and turn left along the ocean through Waterfront Park to the SeaBus terminal on the north side of Burrard Inlet. Waterfront Park is the site of a TCT aboriginal theme pavilion with welcoming grandmother and grandfather figures carved by Darren Yelton of the Squamish Nation.

Km 27.3   *SeaBus terminal/Lonsdale Quay* Take the SeaBus across Burrard Inlet to the south side of the inlet and the City of Vancouver*.

Km 27.5   *SeaBus terminal/CPR station* Turn right out of the terminal (originally a Canadian Pacific Railway station) and follow the road along the waterfront past Canada Place to the start of a paved seaside trail. It continues onto the Seawall, around Stanley Park.

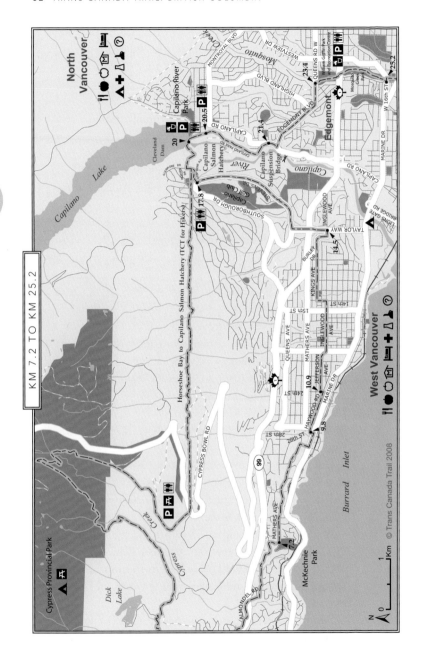

KM 7.2 TO KM 25.2

Horseshoe Bay to Capilano Salmon Hatchery (TCT for Hikers)

© Trans Canada Trail 2008

Km 30.6   *Vancouver Rowing Club* A heritage building, circa 1911.

Km 31.2   *Royal Vancouver Yacht Club* Located here since 1905.

Km 31.6   HMCS Discovery *Naval Reserve Division* Located on Deadman Island. Was once a burial ground; since 1943 it has been used by the Canadian navy.

Km 31.8   *Brockton Point totems* A prominent collection of totems carved by BC natives.

Km 32.1   *Nine O'clock Gun* Fired every night since 1894, except during World War II.

Km 32.4   *Brockton Point light* A beacon for mariners that has blinked here since 1890.

Brockton Point totems
in Stanley Park

Km 32.9   *Brockton Oval* A cricket pitch, rugby field, and clubhouse.

Km 33.2   *Girl in Wet Suit* A bronze sculpture by Elek Imredy, unveiled in 1972, representing Vancouver's dependence on the sea.

Km 33.5   *Water Park* A wet summer play area for kids. (Restrooms, change rooms.)

Km 35   *Lions Gate Bridge* The TCT passes under the bridge, which spans 450 metres across First Narrows.

Km 35.1   *Prospect Point light* Established in 1888.

Km 36.5   *Siwash Rock* A striking tree-topped pinnacle on Burrard Inlet.

Km 36.8   *Third Beach* A sandy beach popular for swimming and sunbathing.

Km 38.4   *Second Beach* Site of a noisy, kid-filled saltwater swimming pool. (Restrooms, change rooms, outdoor shower, concession.)

Km 39.2   *Stanley Park Lawn Bowling Club* At the southwest edge of Stanley Park near tennis courts, putting greens, and other recreational amenities.

Km 40.9   *English Bay* The sand beach has been the venue for the annual New Year's Day Polar Bear Swim since 1920. (Concession stand, restrooms, picnic tables.)

Km 41.1   TCT *markers, Burrard Bridge* Just before the terminal for foot ferries that run in False Creek, the TCT goes up to the streets.

(The seaside trail continues along the north shore of False Creek, past the Plaza of Nations, to rejoin the TCT at Km 47.) To continue on the TCT, which goes up and over Burrard Street Bridge, follow the markers up to Beach Avenue. Cross Beach and go up Thurlow Street on a marked bike route. At the traffic light on Pacific Street turn right and cross Burrard Street Bridge on a sidewalk. Follow the TCT markers to the left off the bridge and into a bike lane at a sign saying, "Welcome to Kitsilano." Go left on Burrard Street, left again on West 1st Avenue, and follow signs toward Granville Island and a junction with a three-way stop.

Km 43.2   *False Creek, Fishermen's Wharf* Turn right at a TCT marker onto an oceanfront trail.

Km 43.5   *Granville Island* Cross under the Granville Bridge to Granville Island Public Market and follow the trail to a sign saying, "Island Park Walk/Birch Walk/Granville Island." A short jog across a footbridge to the left is a TCT Pavilion near the False Creek Community Centre (restrooms, drinking water). The TCT continues east along the seashore.

Km 46.7   *Science World* A former Expo 86 pavilion, the silver geodesic dome is now a conspicuous landmark at the head of False Creek. Just beyond Science World the TCT heads north then

Fishermen's Wharf, False Creek

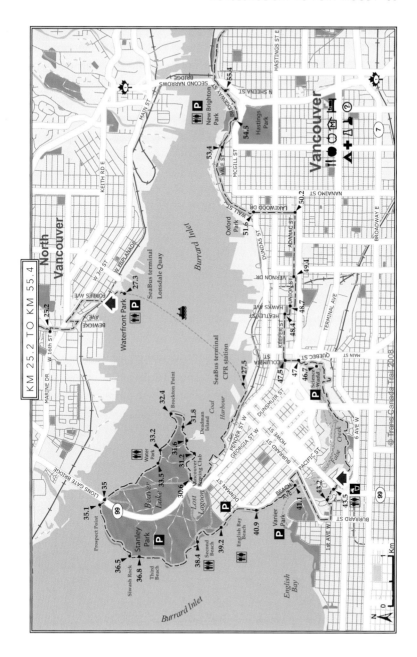

© Trans Canada Trail 2008

east out of town. (The seaside trail continues west (left) along the north shore of False Creek for 3.2 kilometres to rejoin the TCT at Km 41.1, where the TCT goes up to the streets and over Burrard Street Bridge.) From Science World the TCT takes hiking and bike trails around the head of False Creek for nearly 300 metres and then takes to the streets.

Km 47   *Adanac route/Quebec Street* Where the seaside trail continues to the left (west) along False Creek's north shore, the TCT signs point right—to Quebec Street and the Adanac (Canada spelled backwards) bike route. Cross Quebec and follow it north across Union Street to Keefer and Columbia streets.

Km 47.5   *Keefer Street + Columbia Street* Go right (east) on Keefer through Chinatown.

Km 48.4   *Keefer Street + Heatley Avenue* The TCT heads right on Heatley, then left on East Georgia Street.

Km 48.7   *East Georgia Street + Hawks Avenue* East Georgia dead-ends and the TCT goes right on Hawks Avenue, then left on Union Street.

Km 49.4   *Union Street + Vernon Street* The TCT makes a 40-metre jog to the left on Vernon then goes right (east) on Adanac Street.

Km 50.2   *Adanac Street + Lakewood Drive* The TCT goes left on Lakewood Drive which, at this point, is a lane through Templeton High School grounds. Lakewood crosses Dundas Street to Oxford Park.

Km 51.6   *Oxford Park* A short trail to the left through Oxford Park takes the TCT down to Wall Street, part of a route called the Portside Trail. Go right on Wall and follow it along the south shore of Burrard Inlet.

Km 53.4   *Wall Street + Yale Street* After passing Yale Street a first time, continue straight on Wall Street to where it meets Yale Street again at Km 53.4. Go southeast, past vehicle-blocking posts at the end of Wall Street where it meets McGill Street. A TCT road-and-trail route can be taken downhill to the left, but the main TCT route is uphill to a crosswalk that crosses an overpass leading toward the ocean and New Brighton Park. Take the overpass and continue to a stairway that gets hikers down to a seaside trail. Cyclists go 80 metres beyond the stairs and turn right onto a connecting trail. Continue east along the seashore.

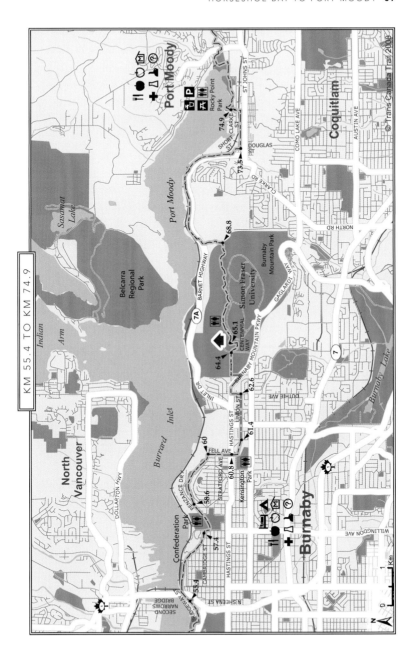

Km 54.5   *Swimming pool/railway underpass* Follow the trail past the
swimming pool, and stay to the right on the sidewalk under
the railway tracks. Just beyond the underpass the TCT goes left
across the road to a paved bike trail that joins another paved
trail. Continue east to Bridgeway Street.

Km 55.4   *Bridgeway Street + North Skeena Street* Where the road makes
a sharp bend to the right up North Skeena Street, the TCT
instead continues straight past a gate that blocks vehicles from
using a paved and hard-packed gravel trail. This is the start of
a pleasant, woodsy trail that gives a unique perspective to the
bustle and industry of Burrard Inlet as the trail crosses under
the Ironworkers Memorial (Second Narrows) Bridge and
over a railway bridge into a forest. (The trail here enters the
municipality of Burnaby*.)

Km 57.4   *Eton Street/Chevron refinery* The TCT runs kitty-corner
across Eton and continues east. Follow the trail and at North
Willingdon Avenue and Cambridge Street cross North Willingdon and continue on the gravel shoulder about 300 metres
up to Penzance Drive. Turn left (northeast) onto a gravel trail
along Penzance.

Km 58.6   *Road crossing* The TCT crosses Penzance and goes up
a hard-packed gravel trail through the woods.

Km 60   *Cambridge Street + Stratford Avenue* Head left downhill
about 200 metres to Fell Avenue. Hikers cross Fell and take
a TCT–marked trail through the forest; cyclists continue
up Fell Avenue.

Km 60.8   *Fell Avenue + Hastings Street* Cross Hastings at the crosswalk
and take the paved trail to the left through Kensington Park,
where the TCT veers right onto the Frances/Union bike route.

Km 61.4   *Union Street + Hammerskjold Drive* The TCT crosses Hammerskjold and continues on Union Street.

Km 62.6   *Union Street + Duthie Avenue* Turn left onto Duthie and
go nearly 300 metres to Hasting Street. The TCT leaves the
Frances/Union bike route here and heads right for about
600 metres up Hastings onto Burnaby Mountain Parkway,
where a crosswalk leads to a gravel trail uphill beside a power
line. It's part-trail, part-road for about 300 metres to a junction that was the corner of Hastings Street and Burnwood

Avenue before the advent of Burnaby Mountain Parkway. Turn right up a steep gravel trail.

Km 64.4   *Centennial Way* A sheltered rest stop sits where the TCT crosses Centennial Way and continues up Burnaby Mountain.

Km 65.1   *Burnaby Mountain Park/TCT Pavilion* At more than 270 metres Burnaby Mountain has commanding views to the north up Indian Arm, and to the southwest over downtown Vancouver. The park features, among other things, a cluster of decorative poles carved by Japanese sculptors. Beyond the TCT Pavilion, the TCT goes up Joe's Trail for 400 metres, then moves down the other side of the mountain.

Km 68.8   *BC Hydro right-of-way* A good but steep gravel path runs for 600 metres down to Barnet Highway (Highway 7A). Cross the highway at the traffic light and head downhill to the ocean. The trail becomes a seaside pathway with TCT Discovery Panels explaining some of the industries and sights along the shore.

Km 73.5   *Douglas Street + Clarke Street* Where the trail makes a brief return to streets, take Short and Douglas streets to Clarke Street and turn left (east), then left again on Moody Street to Rocky Point Park.

Km 74.9   *Rocky Point Park* One of half a dozen contiguous day-use parks on the downtown shoreline of the City of Port Moody*. The TCT continues east along the shoreline as it moves away from the ocean.

SEASIDE TRAIL BYPASSES CITY TRAFFIC

Metro Vancouver is the human nucleus of British Columbia. A metropolis of more than two million and growing, it is home to half the people in BC. With the Pacific Ocean on one side and coastal mountains on the other, the city is a vibrant swath of civilization in the midst of a wilderness.

Travellers on this leg of the TCT quickly get a sense of this wild-versus-urban aura. In Metro Vancouver they have the option of getting right into the hub of it all, or watching the bustle and motion from the North Shore mountains or the top of Burnaby Mountain. This is Canada's gateway to the Pacific, the nation's busiest seaport, and from these lofty viewpoints TCT travellers see a ceaseless flow of jetliners, float planes, helicopters, freighters, tugs, cruise ships, and road traffic. Beyond the downtown harbour and out past Vancouver International Airport, BC Ferries

FROM HORSESHOE BAY TO THE CAPILANO
SALMON HATCHERY → 26 KM

A TCT hiking-only route is comprised of a series of connected trails, from Horseshoe Bay up into Cypress Provincial Park then through the rainforests of West Vancouver to Capilano River Regional Park, site of a federal fish hatchery. (There are also offshoot trails that lead to viewpoints.) It can be hiked by marathoners in a long day, or split into two hikes—one 17.2 kilometres, the other 8.8 kilometres.

This is semi-wilderness: be prepared for changing weather (especially rain), carry lots of drinking water, and allow adequate daylight to complete the journey. From mid-autumn to late winter, snowshoes or cross-country skis may be more useful here than hiking boots.

This trail is marked on the maps on pages 80 and 82. From the BC Ferries terminal at Horseshoe Bay, watch for TCT markers while walking up Keith Road to Argyle Avenue, where a short trail goes to a stairway up to a sidewalk leading to Marine Drive. Cross Marine and head south past the gateway to Gleneagles Golf Club and Community Centre. Marine Drive and Eagleridge Place is the trailhead for a path that follows an old railway bed, offering good views of Fisherman's Cove and Eagle Island. (There is parking at this trailhead.)

The TCT goes over a BC Railway tunnel and an old highway bridge before coming to a water tower. Restrooms are located here. Take the road running north to a second tower and then follow a new path to stairs that climb to a gravel road. A short uphill walk on the road leads to a trail on the left; it goes through the forest to Eagle Lake Access Road. Take this road to the start of West Cypress Creek Trail, which runs upstream with the creek into Cypress Provincial Park*.

At Cypress Creek Bridge the TCT moves south on East Cypress Creek Trail. Stay to the right at a fork just over one kilometre along the path, keeping on a trail running alongside some power lines. Go through a British Pacific Properties gate and turn left to Cypress Bowl Road, where there's a picnic and parking area with toilets and great views of downtown Vancouver, English Bay, and across the Strait of Georgia to Vancouver Island.

A 17.2-kilometre hike could end here, or continue east 8.8 kilometres along the Skyline Trail and a section of the celebrated Baden-Powell Trail toward Capilano River Regional Park. Waterfalls cascade through canyons in the rainforest, where early-day hand-loggers have left springboard cuts in giant stumps. Part of the trail is a Forestry Heritage Walk. Where the TCT reaches Cleveland Dam, stay on the west side of the river and take the Capilano Pacific, Giant Fir, and Second Canyon Viewpoint trails to the Capilano Salmon Hatchery. More than a million coho, chinook, and steelhead smolts, many raised by school kids, are released from the hatchery most years; about 15,000 return as spawning adults.

From the hatchery take the Coho Loop and Chinook Trail. Cross Capilano Park Road to a trail heading north to Eldon Road. Take Eldon to Capilano Road; the TCT hiking and cycling routes merge here.

chug across the Strait of Georgia and through the Gulf Islands to Vancouver Island.

Ruralists unaccustomed to big-city chaos may be intimidated by the prospect of coming down from the hills to cycle or walk through the middle of downtown Vancouver. Yet for the first 13 kilometres the only traffic on the TCT through the city centre is hikers, cyclists, horses, rollerbladers, strollers, and wheelchairs—non-motorized modes of travel. For traffic-shy TCT travellers, this paved, multi-use path around the downtown seashore is a car-free way to tour the heart of Canada's third-largest metropolis.

VANCOUVER, COAST & MOUNTAINS REGION

Tourism region encompassing the Lower Mainland and southern Coast Mountains, from Vancouver to the east beyond Hope, nearly to Princeton. Within this tourism region, Metro Vancouver (formerly the Greater Vancouver Regional District) encompasses more than 2,800 square kilometres on the mainland coast in southwest BC. Comprised of 21 municipalities and

OMNIPRESENT HARBOUR SEALS READILY SEEN

Harbour seals (*Phoca vitulina*) are by far the most ubiquitous of the two dozen marine-mammal species that inhabit the BC coast. TCT travellers can count on seeing them skulking along with their noses just above the surface, their shiny grey heads glistening like glass fishing floats. If there are fish to chase, seals may travel as far up the Fraser River as Pitt Lake, more than 50 kilometres  upstream from the ocean.

Harbour seals haul out on reefs, sand bars, docks, or log booms to bask in the afternoon sun, ready to bounce awkwardly along on their bellies and dive into the ocean at any sign of approaching danger. They can dive deeper than 180 metres and stay submerged for 20 minutes or more.

Weighing 60 or 80 kilograms and measuring up to two metres from nose to hind flippers, they often startle canoeists or kayakers when they pop up from the depths a paddle's length away. Harbour seals are quiet creatures, emitting low-pitched grunts. They do not bark: the so-called barking seals of circus fame are actually California sea lions.

Like other marine mammals, harbour seals were routinely shot by fishermen and fisheries officers until they were protected in the early 1970s. They have made an encouraging comeback on the BC coast from about 10,000 animals to well over 100,000.

one electoral area, it is home to half of the province's total population.

> **Population** 2.1 million

> **Visitor Info** *Vancouver Coast & Mountains Tourism Region* 600–200 West Broadway, Vancouver, BC V5Y 3W2; 604-739-9011; www.coastandmountains.bc.ca. For more information on activities in the Lower Mainland, contact Metro Vancouver, at 4330 Kingsway, Burnaby, BC V5H 4G8; 604-432-6200. The Metro Vancouver website (www.gvrd.bc.ca) has links to Vancouver's 21 municipalities.

> **TCT Info** *Trails BC (southwest region)* Look up "Southwest" under "BC Regions" on the Trails BC website at www.trailsbc.ca. This is a thoroughly detailed section of the Trails BC website edited by Léon Lebrun, the tireless Trails

Siwash Rock on the Stanley Park Seawall

BC director who is largely responsible for the success of the Trans Canada Trail in southwest BC. It covers the TCT from Horseshoe Bay to Brookmere, including turn-by-turn directions, distances, highlights, services, access and staging areas, accommodation and camping, public transportation and shuttles, updates, special events, and links to more information.

WALKER'S ALTERNATIVE

FROM HORSESHOE BAY ALONG THE NORTHWEST SHORES OF BURRARD INLET → 21 KM

Walkers not interested in trekking through the North Shore mountains can take a hike of about 20 kilometres that combines parts of the TCT cycle route with roads and trails above and along the northwest shores of Burrard Inlet. From Horseshoe Bay take the TCT hiking route (as described on page 90) over the BC Railway tunnel and under the Upper Levels Highway. Veer off the TCT route and continue on a service road that goes back under the Upper Levels Highway out to Westport Road. Take Westport to Woodgreen Drive and continue on the TCT cycle route (as described on page 79) as far as Mathers and 31st Street.

Go south on 31st and walk east past the waterfront homes on Procter Park Lane and Bellevue Avenue. Dundarave Park, at the foot of 25th Street, is the start of the Centennial Seawalk, which follows the shore east to Ambleside Park and the mouth of the Capilano River. From here, the Capilano–Pacific Trail runs upstream to the Giant Fir Trail, where TCT signs can be followed over a bridge to Capilano Salmon Hatchery, at Km 20.5 on the Trans Canada Trail.

> **Transportation** Go to www .coastandmountains.bc.ca. For details on city buses, *Sea-Buses*, and the *SkyTrain* commuter rail, contact *Translink* (604-953-3333; www.trans link.bc.ca).

Land Several highways go to Metro Vancouver from the Interior, Washington, and Vancouver Island (via BC Ferries).

Bus A number of bus companies operate from Vancouver; *Greyhound Canada* (1-800-661-8747; www.greyhound .ca) has depots in the Lower Mainland at Vancouver and Vancouver Airport, North Vancouver, Coquitlam, Maple Ridge, Langley, Abbotsford, Chilliwack, and Hope. Depot addresses appear with details for specific communities.

CONNECTING TSAWWASSEN WITH THE TCT

Although the Trans Canada Trail takes a BC Ferry from Vancouver Island to Horseshoe Bay, northwest of Vancouver, a larger number of travellers take a BC Ferry to Tsawwassen, 38 kilometres south of Vancouver. Trails BC volunteers are planning a detailed route from Tsawwassen that links up with the Trans Canada Trail. Its completion is expected to be in conjunction with construction of Golden Ears Bridge over the Fraser River, tentatively scheduled for 2009. The bridge will replace the Albion ferry (Km 44.8 in Chapter 5), and will require significant rerouting of the Trans Canada Trail. Check for updates at www.trailsbc .ca (look up "Southwest" under "BC Regions").

Rail VIA *Rail* (1-888-842-7245; www.viarail.ca) passenger trains run from Pacific Central Station at 1150 Station Street near Science World (TCT Km 46.7). For *Westcoast Express* commuter trains from Mission, check www .translink.bc.ca.

Sea BC *Ferries* (www.bcferries.com) runs car-and-passenger ships between Horseshoe Bay in West Vancouver and Departure Bay and Duke Point in Nanaimo, and between Tsawwassen, 38 kilometres south of Vancouver, and Swartz Bay, 32 kilometres north of Victoria. Sailing time is one hour, 35 minutes. *Aquabus Ferries* (604-689-5858; www.aquabus.bc.ca) carries foot passengers and bicycles from its base at the foot of Hornby Street (near Km 13.8) to Granville Island and other False Creek destinations. *False Creek Ferries* (604-684-7781; www.granvilleislandferries.bc.ca) runs double-ended foot-passenger boats to destinations around False Creek. For information on *SeaBuses* across Burrard Inlet, check www.translink.bc.ca.

Air Vancouver International (www.yvr.ca) is one of Canada's busiest airports with more than 15 million passengers a year. *Abbotsford Airport* (604-855-1135; www.abbotsfordairport.ca) has international flights as well. There are harbour-to-harbour float-plane charters and scheduled flights between downtown Vancouver and other West Coast communities.

> **Emergency** Call 911.

COMMUNITIES, PARKS, AND PLACES TO STAY

Information on each provincial park in BC can be found on the BC Parks website at www.env.gov.bc.ca/bcparks/.

West Vancouver (Km 0)

First community after the TCT arrives on mainland BC at Horseshoe Bay ferry terminal. Metro Vancouver's ritziest municipality.

> **Population** 43,000

> **Visitor Info** *West Vancouver Chamber of Commerce* 1310 Marine Drive, West Vancouver, BC V7T 1B5; 1-888-471-9996; www.westvanchamber.com. A visitor booth operates in summer at Ambleside Beach. *Sewell's Marina* in Horseshoe Bay (604-921-3474; www.sewellsmarina.com) also offers tourist information.

> **Attractions** 34 kilometres of foreshore, oceanfront parks, marinas, sandy beaches, hiking and cycling trails; gateway to Cypress Provincial Park and the Whistler resort municipality.

Ironworkers Memorial Second Narrows Crossing

🌲 Cypress Provincial Park (on hikers-only route
from Horseshoe Bay (Km 0), page 90)

Bounded by Howe Sound on the west, West Vancouver to the south, and
the North Shore mountains on the north and east, "Cypress sits like a ship's
crow's nest high above Vancouver," according to BC Parks. 🚠 🔺

› **Size** 3,012 hectares
› **Attractions** Incredible views of Vancouver, the Strait of Georgia, and Gulf
Islands. Hiking, skiing, and mountain biking trails.
› **Camping** Backcountry camping. See the BC Parks website for a map
and details.

🌳 North Vancouver (Km 20)

The District and the City of North Vancouver are two municipalities on
Metro Vancouver's North Shore, east of West Vancouver.

› **Population** 134,000
› **Visitor Info** The *North Vancouver Chamber of Commerce* provides tour-
ist information for both municipalities. 102–124 West First Street, North
Vancouver, BC V7M 3N9; 604-983-5555; www.nvchamber.bc.ca. A summer
visitor booth operates near the Lions Gate Bridge at Capilano Road and
Marine Drive.
› **Attractions** Capilano River Regional Park, Capilano Suspension Bridge,
Capilano Salmon Hatchery, Grouse Mountain and Skyride, Lonsdale
Quay Market.
› **Greyhound Bus** (1-800-661-8747; www.greyhound.ca) Depot located at
Burrard Wood Mfg. Ltd. at 382 Esplanade.
› **Camping** Between Capilano River and the Lions Gate Bridge, the Cap-
ilano RV Park is one of the few campgrounds near downtown Vancouver.
295 Tomahawk Avenue; 604-987-4722; www.capilanorvpark.com.

🌲 Capilano River Regional Park (Km 20)

In the North Shore mountains above Vancouver, one of the city's most
popular semi-wilderness parks. Accessible from Highway 1: take the Capilano Road/Grouse Mountain Exit #14 and go north to Capilano Salmon
Hatchery, or continue to the Cleveland Dam parking lot. Also accessible
by city bus. ⓘ 🚻 ♿

› **Size** 163 hectares
› **Visitor Info** www.gvrd.bc.ca/parks/CapilanoRiver.htm

› **Attractions** 26 kilometres of hiking trails. Picnicking, fishing, Capilano Salmon Hatchery. Views include Cleveland Dam and Capilano Lake.

♣ City of Vancouver (Km 27.4)

One of the 21 municipalities that make up Metro Vancouver (formerly Greater Vancouver Regional District), and an international business and cultural centre accessible by highways from all directions. (See page 89 for more on the multi-use path around the downtown seashore.)

› **Population** 578,000
› **Visitor Info** *Vancouver Visitor Centre* Plaza Level, 200 Burrard Street, Vancouver, BC V6C 3L6; 604-683-2000; www.tourismvancouver.com.
› **Attractions** University of British Columbia Museum of Anthropology, Vancouver Museum (Canada's largest civic museum), Pacific Space Centre, Vancouver Aquarium, Science World, Stanley Park/Seawall, Granville Island, Chinatown, Gastown, Canada Place; beaches, oceanside walkways/bikeways.
› **Greyhound Bus** (1-800-661-8747; www.greyhound.ca) Main station at 1150 Station Street; Vancouver Airport station at *Tourism Vancouver Info Centre @ The Airport*, at 3211 Grant McConachie Way.

♣ Burnaby (Km 55.7)

Metro Vancouver's third-largest (by population) municipality, east of Vancouver.

› **Population** 206,000
› **Visitor Info** *City Hall* 4949 Canada Way, Burnaby, BC V5K 1A1; 604-294-7944; www.city.burnaby.bc.ca.
› **Attractions** Burnaby Mountain Park, Simon Fraser University, Burnaby Lake Regional Park, Burnaby Fraser Foreshore Park, Metrotown Centre.

♣ Port Moody (Km 74.9)

Small city at the end of a saltwater inlet, between North Vancouver and Burnaby.

› **Population** 26,000
› **Visitor Info** *City of Port Moody* 100 Newport Drive, Box 36, Port Moody, BC V3H 3E1; 604-469-4500; www.cityofportmoody.com.
› **Attractions** Parks and shoreline trails, Port Moody Station Museum, Belcarra Regional Park.
› **Transportation** The Port Moody station for Westcoast Express commuter trains to Vancouver is at 65 Williams Street.

❝ British Columbia shall . . . comprise all such Territories . . . bounded to the South by the Frontier of the United States of America, to the East by the main Chain of the Rocky Mountains, to the North by Simpson's River, and the Finlay Branch of the Peace River, and to the West by the Pacific Ocean, and shall include Queen Charlotte's Island, and all other Islands adjacent to the said Territories . . .
—*Proclamation of British Columbia, issued at Fort Langley on November 19, 1858*

In the Fraser Valley beyond Fort Langley

TRAIL TRIVIA

At 21, the late Terry Fox, a one-legged runner from Port Coquitlam, began his cross-Canada Marathon of Hope on April 12, 1980. His heroic effort to raise money for cancer research ended tragically when the disease claimed his life on June 28, 1981.

TOTAL DISTANCE

75.5 km

TOPOGRAPHIC MAPS

1:250,000	Vancouver 92G
1:50,000	Mission 92G/1, New Westminster 92G/2, Port Coquitlam 92G/7

HIGHLIGHTS

› The Traboulay PoCo Trail
› Dyke hiking and cycling
› The National Historic Site of Fort Langley

CONDITIONS

› **Port Moody (Km 0) to De Boville Slough (Km 15.4)** Paved roads and well-surfaced single- and double-track trails. → 15.4 km
› **De Boville Slough (Km 15.4) to 128 Avenue (Km 32.3)** Hard-packed, double-track gravel dyke trails. Enjoyable hiking and cycling. → 16.9 km
› **128 Avenue (Km 32.3) to Glenmore Road trailhead (Km 72.3)** A combination paved roads and short trails (hard-packed gravel or paved). → 40 km
› **Glenmore Road trailhead (Km 72.3) to Matsqui Trail Regional Park (Km 75.5)** Hard-packed gravel dyke trail. → 3.2 km

CAUTIONS

› Busy traffic in town centres.
› Flooding, if camping at Matsqui Trail Park.

OVERVIEW

With 21 municipalities and a population of more than two million, Metro Vancouver sprawls far up the Fraser Valley before the urbanization gives way to farms and rural communities. Well over half a million people live between Port Moody and the city of Chilliwack, more than 100 kilometres up the valley from downtown Vancouver.

The TCT covers a surprising array of environments here. From the ocean at Port Moody it weaves through parks and city streets, follows forested trails past creeks and urban lakes, takes a ferry across BC's biggest river, explores a heritage town, and gives glimpses of the working Fraser from the dyke in Matsqui Trail Regional Park.

From Coquitlam, the TCT hugs the banks of tributaries to the lower Fraser—the Coquitlam River, De Boville Slough, and Pitt and Alouette rivers—eventually meeting the Fraser upstream at Maple Ridge, where it crosses the river and continues up the valley along the south bank. This is BC's most productive agricultural region, and farms soon dominate the landscape: fruits and vegetables (including cranberries), mushrooms, grains, and more grow on a thousand square kilometres between Vancouver and Hope.

LOCAL ADVENTURES

Day Trip
› From De Boville Slough (Km 15.4), make a return cycle trip to the end of the dyke at 128 Avenue (Km 32.3). ⇆ 33.8 km
› Take the Haney Heritage Walk (Km 36.8).
› Spend a day at Fort Langley (Km 46.2).

2 or 3 Days
› Camp at Matsqui Trail Regional Park (Km 75.5) and hike or cycle the TCT east or west.

TCT ACCESS POINTS

Port Moody/Rocky Point Park (Km 0) On the shoreline near downtown Port Moody at Moody and Esplanade streets. 🅿 🚻 🚮 🏕 🍴 *concession*

Coquitlam/Douglas College and Pinetree Community Centre (Km 6.3) On Pinetree Way across from Town Centre Park. 🅿 🚻 🚮

Coquitlam/Town Centre Park (Km 6.9) On Pinetree Way across from Pinetree Community Centre and Douglas College. 🅿 *parking at tennis courts and stadium near* TCT *Pavilion* 🚻 🚮

Hyde Creek Community Centre (Km 13.5) In Port Coquitlam at 1379 Laurier Avenue. 🅿 🚻 🚮

De Boville Slough (Km 15.4) Small parking area near the start of the dyke trail at Cedar Drive and Lower Victoria Drive.

TCT Pavilion/Harris Road (Km 25.2) Beside Alouette River at the end of Harris Road, accessible off Dewdney Trunk Road. 🅿 🚻 🪧

128 Avenue (Km 32.3) From Dewdney Trunk Road go north on Laity Street, west on 128 Avenue, then north on 210 Street. 🅿 *parking near Neaves Road and 210 Street*

Haney Heritage House/Walk (Km 36.8) Go to Haney on Highway 7 (Lougheed Highway) and turn south on 224th Street to Haney Heritage House. 🅿

Belle Morse Park/Albion Sports Complex (Km 42.2) From Highway 7 (Lougheed Highway) head northeast on 105 Avenue. 🅿 *parking at Albion Sports Complex* 🚻 🪧

Albion Ferry (Km 44.8) Off Highway 7 (Lougheed Highway) at Maple Ridge. There are plans to replace this ten-minute ferry crossing with a bridge downstream. It will require rerouting of the Trans Canada Trail. Check for updates at www.trailsbc.ca (look up "Southwest" under "BC Regions"). 🅿 *limited parking at the ferry terminals and on nearby streets* 🚻 🪧 *drinking water at the terminal on the north side of the Fraser River, but not the south side | telephone*

Fort Langley (Km 46.2) North of Highway 1 between Langley and Maple Ridge. 🅿 🚻 *facilities and street parking in the village of Fort Langley, as well as parking lots at Fort Langley Marina Park on Bedford Channel, and at Fort Langley National Historic Site*

Olund Park (Km 69) From the Trans-Canada Highway east of Aldergrove go north on Mount Lehman Road, then east on Harris Road to Olund Road and Olund Park. 🅿

Glenmore Road trailhead (Km 72.3) From the Trans-Canada Highway east of Aldergrove go north on Mount Lehman Road, east on Downes Road, then north on Glenmore Road to the Matsqui Trail along the Fraser River. 🅿 🚻

Matsqui Trail Regional Park (Km 75.5) Below the Abbotsford–Mission Bridge. From the Trans-Canada Highway west of Aldergrove take Mount Lehman Road north to Harris Road, turn right (east) to Riverside Street and turn left (north) to Page Road and Matsqui Trail Park. **P** 🚻 *outhouses* 🚰 ⛱ ▲ *four camping sites*

DYKE TRAILS TO FARMLANDS

TOWN AND COUNTRY

The TCT through these Fraser Valley population centres has been cleverly planned, utilizing parks and urban trails that avoid busy streets and provide backyard views of local neighbourhoods. Dykes that prevent the Fraser and its tributaries from spilling onto the farms and highways take TCT travellers away from the traffic and into the country. Fields of crops and cattle are spread across the valley, a wide expanse of gold and green hemmed in by the Coast Mountains to the north and the Cascades to the south.

For hikers, cyclists, and equestrians where permitted, these dykes are about as easy as TCT travel gets—flat, double-tracked gravel trails meandering up a broad, fertile flood plain. The water views are constant and frequently idyllic; herons and waterfowl feed in the marshes and backwaters, turtles bask on sun logs, and turkey vultures circle overhead. Sandhill cranes occasionally forage in the fields, and hawks commonly perch on fence posts.

Evidence of human history along the TCT's route through the Fraser Valley is equally intriguing. The trail follows part of the Haney Heritage Walk at Maple Ridge before crossing the Fraser River on the Albion Ferry to Fort Langley, a pioneer town and National Historic Site. The TCT returns to the 21st century and continues on dykes along the Fraser River and on roads through farms to Matsqui.

THE TRANS CANADA TRAIL

Place names with asterisks are included in the **Communities, Parks, and Places to Stay** section (page 112).

Km 0   *Port Moody*, Rocky Point Park* The TCT skirts the shoreline as it heads east then forks about 1.5 kilometres along the trail. Take the right fork, cross some railway tracks, and follow the TCT as it approaches an arena from behind and then moves around to the front. Cross the road to Pioneer Memorial Park

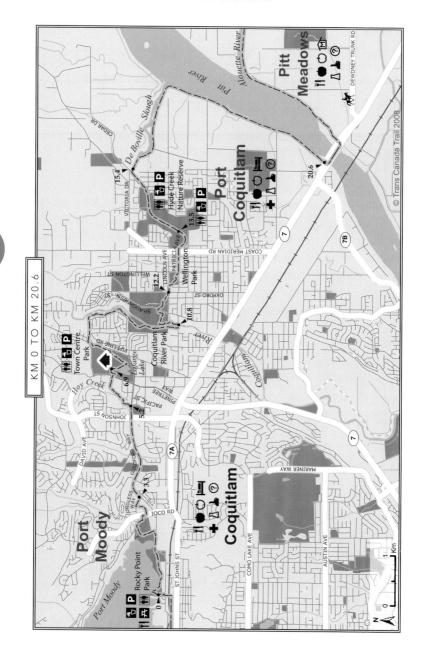

KM 0 TO KM 20.6

(across from City Hall). Take the path through the park, veering right at a TCT marker next to a gazebo. Where the path meets a sidewalk, cross Ioco Road and go through Newport Market Square to Ungless Way. Turn right (east) on Ungless.

Km 3.3 *Ungless Way + Guildford Way* Turn left, but stay on the sidewalk along the left (north) side of Guildford.

Km 5.2 *Guildford Way + Pacific Street* Before Pacific, turn left off the sidewalk onto a gravel trail alongside Hoy Creek. At the first bridge stay on the right (east) side of the creek.

Km 6 *Douglas College turnoff* Turn right to the road behind the college and Pinetree Community Centre; follow the TCT markers straight ahead and cross Pinetree Way to Town Centre Park.

Km 6.9 *Coquitlam*, TCT Pavilion* You will see the pavilion next to Lafarge Lake, near public restrooms. Beyond the lake the TCT takes a bike path to the left. It leaves Town Centre Park and crosses Pipeline Road to a trail leading to Coquitlam River. Turn right (south) at the river and follow the west bank downstream.

Km 10.8 *Coquitlam River Bridge, Port Coquitlam** Cross the river and then take the trail down to the right; it loops under the bridge and follows the east side of the river upstream (north). The TCT then goes on the North Traboulay PoCo Trail, which veers to the east, crosses Shaughnessy Street, and continues through a forest.

Km 12.2 *Oxford Street + Lincoln Avenue* Take Lincoln east to Wellington Park and turn right onto a path through the park. At Wellington Street and Patricia Avenue, continue east on Patricia, crossing Coast Meridian Road to a trail through Hyde Creek Nature Reserve.

Km 13.5 *Hyde Creek Community Centre* (Restrooms, drinking water, parking.) Continue on the creekside trail, crossing a bridge and veering left (north) along the west side of the creek to Cedar and Lower Victoria drives. Turn right (east) toward De Boville Slough.

Km 15.4 *De Boville Slough* Ride or hike the dyke along the south side of the slough toward Pitt River.

Km 20.6 *Pitt River Bridge* While the PoCo Trail continues south to the Fraser River, the TCT goes east (left) on Highway 7 over the Pitt River Bridge and then immediately left on the dyke along

5

KM 20.6 TO KM 44.8

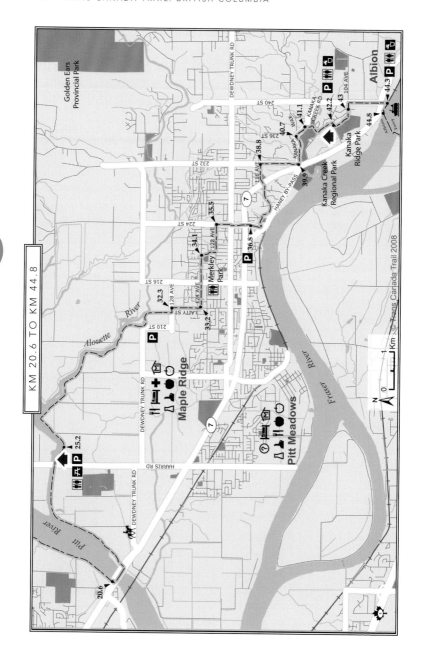

Golden Ears Provincial Park

DEWDNEY TRUNK RD

240 ST

232 ST

224 ST

216 ST

210 ST

KANAKA CREEK RD

104 AVE

43

44.3 **Albion**

42.2

41.1

40.7

236 ST

38.8

116 AVE

HANEY BYPASS

39.9

35.5

36.8

34.1

122 AVE

Merkley Park

128 AVE

LAITY ST

33.2

32.3

River

Alouette

Kanaka Creek Regional Park

Kanaka Ridge Park

44.8

Kanaka WAY

DEWDNEY TRUNK RD

Maple Ridge

7

25.2

DEWDNEY TRUNK RD

Pitt River

HARRIS RD

Pitt Meadows

7

Fraser River

20.6

N

0   1
Km © Trans Canada Trail 2008

the river's east bank. A TCT sign here explains how these trails connect local communities.

🐴 Equestrians continue on the TCT beyond the Pitt River Bridge as far as Harris Road, where a designated horse route begins. Turn left (north) on Harris to cross the South Alouette River, then turn right (east) on a trail just before Fenton Road. Follow the trail to Neaves Road, turn right (south) onto Neaves, then left (southeast) onto another trail. The trail joins 216 Street and takes 216 to another trail which goes to the left (east), roughly paralleling 128 Avenue to 248 Street. Go right (south) on 248, crossing Dewdney Trunk Road and taking a short trail through Kanaka Creek Regional Park to Industrial Avenue. Take Industrial south to 104 Avenue, then turn right (west) to the Albion Ferry (Km 44.8). Horses must be trailered on board the ferry.

Km 25.2   TCT *Pavilion* (Restrooms, picnic tables, parking.) Hikers and cyclists continue on the dyke (to Pitt Meadows*), which passes a marina, then turns right (east) along the Alouette River. Watch for turtles on sun logs.

Km 32.3   *128 Avenue* The dyke trail ends and the TCT goes left (east) on 128 Avenue for 50 metres to Laity Street. Turn right on Laity.

Alouette River

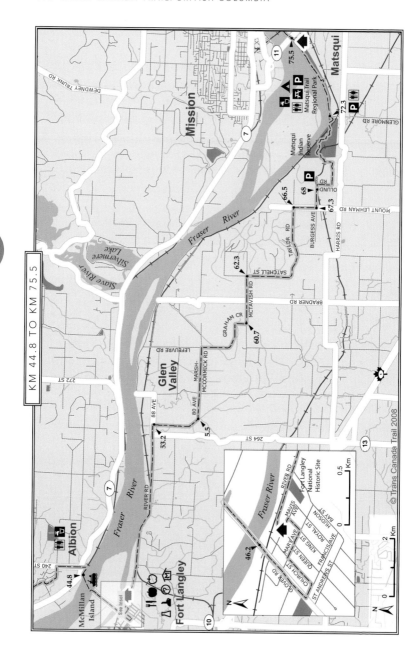

KM 44.8 TO KM 75.5

Km 33.2   *Laity Street + 124 Avenue* Go left (east) on 124 Avenue along a shady street enclosed by big ivy-covered fir trees.

Km 34.1   *Merkley Park* Go right on the trail through the park. At the public restrooms stay left across a gravel area, go past Maple Ridge Secondary School to 122 Avenue, and turn left.

Km 35.5   *224 Street* Turn right (south) to downtown Maple Ridge* and across Highway 7 (Lougheed Highway).

Km 36.8   *Haney Heritage House/Heritage Walk* After crossing Highway 7, go left onto the Heritage Walk. Passing Brickman Park and Maple Ridge Museum, the TCT takes 116 Avenue across Burnet Street, and Highway 7 to 232 Street (Km 38.8). Turn right (south) on 232.

Km 39.9   *Haney Bypass + Lougheed Highway + Kanaka Way* Go left (east) on Kanaka Way. Cross Kanaka to a paved path along the opposite side.

Km 40.7   *Kanaka Way + 236 Street (Gilker Hill Road)* Turn right onto Kanaka Creek Road and into Kanaka Creek Regional Park. Follow the trail along the creek.

Km 41.1   *Rainbow Bridge* Cross the bridge and veer right on a trail to Tamarack Lane. Turn left on Tamarack to 105 Avenue and across to the fairgrounds in Kanaka Ridge Park. Continue past the fairgrounds to Belle Morse Park.

Km 42.2   *Belle Morse Park, TCT Pavilion* Take the trail behind the pavilion and through the parking area behind the Albion Sports Complex. Continue on a gravel trail over a bridge, along the edge of a baseball park, and through a gate. Bear left after the gate.

Km 43   *104 Avenue + Slatford Street* Go straight (east) up 104 and then right (south) on 240 Street and across Highway 7. Near the Fraser River, cross some railway tracks and turn right on River Road (Km 44.3) toward the Albion Ferry.

Km 44.8   *Albion Ferry* A ten-minute cruise for passengers, vehicles, horse trailers, and bikes across the Fraser to historic Fort Langley. This ferry is scheduled to be replaced by a bridge downstream, which will require rerouting of the Trans Canada Trail: check for updates at www.trailsbc.ca.

Km 46.2   *Fort Langley** On the southwest side of a bridge over Bedford Channel, the TCT takes a roundabout tour of the highlights in Fort Langley. Stay on Glover Road to Francis Avenue,

5

Albion Ferry on Fraser River

turn left, then left again on Church Street. Go right at Mary Avenue, and left on King Street to Mavis Avenue. The Fort Langley National Historic Site and a TCT Pavilion are at the junction of Mavis and River Road. The TCT continues east on River Road along the Fraser.

Take Mavis and River roads for 68 kilometres to Keith Wilson Bridge; don't cross the bridge, but continue along a dyke on the southwest side of the Vedder River to Yarrow. An equestrian route beyond Yarrow has not been determined.

Km 53.2   *Nathan Creek Dyke* Go right (south) on the dyke.

Km 55   *80 Avenue/Marsh-McCormick Road* Squeeze through a gate and go left off the dyke onto 80 Avenue, which becomes Marsh-McCormick Road. (Watch for sandhill cranes in the fields.) Turn right at Lefeuvre Road and ascend a particularly challenging hill. Stay on Lefeuvre as it becomes Graham Crescent.

Km 60.7   *Graham Crescent + McTavish Road* Go left (east) on McTavish, then right on Satchell Street (Km 62.3), which becomes Taylor Road.

Km 66.5   *Taylor Road + Mount Lehman Road* Turn right on Mount Lehman and then left on Burgess Avenue (Km 67.3). Where

Burgess forks (Km 68) veer right, cross the railway tracks, and continue up the road to Olund Road and turn right (south). Olund becomes a trail. Turn left on a TCT–marked trail that enters the Matsqui Indian reserve and goes over a set of railway tracks, then under another, and then comes to a T-junction beside a brick building on a slough (Km 71.9). The TCT goes up to the right and continues east along the Fraser River.

Km 72.3   *Glenmore Road trailhead* (Restrooms, parking.) Continue east on the dyke into Matsqui Trail Regional Park.

Km 75.5   *Matsqui Trail Regional Park*, TCT Pavilion* The park is located beside the Fraser with the Abbotsford–Mission Bridge looming overhead. A possible overnight stop with four riverside campsites, with outhouses, picnic tables, and drinking water. (If camping, beware of flooding.) The TCT continues east on the dyke along the Fraser River. (Highway 11 crosses over the bridge and runs south into downtown Abbotsford*.)

HANEY HERITAGE

Haney House (Km 26.8), one the highlights on the Fraser River Heritage Walk in Maple Ridge, was occupied by three generations of Haneys before

Haney House in Maple Ridge

1979, when it was willed by the family to the District of Maple Ridge. Built 101 years earlier as the home of Anne and Thomas Haney, it now is restored and furnished with artifacts left by the family. The wood-frame house near the Fraser River sits in an idyllic garden, where afternoon tea is served.

Thomas Haney, the son of an Irish immigrant, bought land here in 1876 and founded the Port Haney Brick Company. Chinese and aboriginal labourers were employed to excavate local deposits of blue clay. Haney Brick and Tile, as it was later known, operated until 1977.

Another heritage house is the Maple Ridge Museum (22520 116th Avenue), which overlooks the Fraser River. It was built in 1907 and was occupied by the company's manager. This is the starting point for the Fraser River Heritage Walk, which takes a paved path to Haney House and Port Haney Wharf. Historic buildings along the walk—St. Andrew's Heritage Church, the Masonic Hall, the 1911 Bank of Montreal, and a 1930 Japanese kindergarten—are identified by interpretive signs that bring this history to life. The TCT runs right through Anne and Thomas Haney's front yard.

FORT LANGLEY, BIRTHPLACE OF BC

After two false starts, Fort Langley (Km 46.2) finally found a permanent home on the south bank of the Fraser River. The original fort was built in 1827 as part of the Hudson's Bay Company's network of fur-trading posts

Fort Langley railway station

The turtle, with its scaly legs and bizarre body of armour, dropped out of the evolution race 200 million years ago. Dinosaurs came and went, but the lowly turtle endured, unchanged, since the Triassic period.

The painted turtle is the most widespread of 48 North American species.

The western subspecies (*Chrysemys picta belli*), found across southern BC, is the largest, growing up to 25 centimetres long, females being bigger than males.

Trans Canada Trail travellers encounter turtles at several points across the province. Painted turtles occasionally share their habitats with a similar turtle, the red-eared slider (*Chrysemys scripta elegans*), which originate from pet turtles set free in the wild. One of the most visible sites is on Alouette River (Km 31.3), where turtles sunbathe on logs beside the dyke trail.

Temperature regulates much of a turtle's life: it tells the turtle when to retire to the bottom of a pond to dig a hole and hibernate; it signals the time to emerge in spring; and it determines how much a turtle will eat and grow in a season.

When the sunny days of spring arouse the breeding urge, a male swims in front of its intended partner. It floats with palms facing outward on extended forelegs, and gently strokes the female's head. After a 15-minute courtship, the female sinks to the bottom to be mounted by her mate. Eggs are buried in pastures, beaches, or roadsides about 150 metres from the water.

across the West. Furs, salmon, cranberries, and other goods were traded with local First Nations, and Fort Langley became a supply depot and forwarding point for goods destined for the Interior. They were delivered by steamship to the fort, where they were repacked and sent inland.

Salmon from the Fraser River were salted and packed at Fort Langley for all of the HBC's forts west of the Rocky Mountains. Eventually salmon cured at Fort Langley were exported to the Sandwich Islands and Australia. Farming on 800 hectares at Langley Prairie, 11 kilometres from the fort, provided potatoes, peas, grain, pork, and beef for HBC forts and steamships.

The deteriorating fort was vacated in 1839 and a new fort was built four kilometres upstream, closer to the farming operations. Ten months later the new fort burned down, so in 1840 yet another fort was built, which is at the present-day location of the Fort Langley National Historic Site.

The Fraser River gold rush of 1858 brought thousands of hopeful prospectors through Fort Langley to stock up on supplies as they headed upriver to the gold fields. On November 19 that same year, BC's first government was proclaimed at Fort Langley when the British Parliament established the mainland colony of British Columbia.

In 1886 its role as an HBC post officially ended, but a village around the fort survived. The Canadian Pacific Railway station, the Coronation Block, and several other historic buildings date from the early 1900s. At the National Historic Site on the edge of the village, one original structure and several reconstructed buildings are furnished with artifacts from Fort Langley's heyday. Costumed interpreters and special events bring the past to life.

VANCOUVER, COAST & MOUNTAINS REGION

Tourism region encompassing the Lower Mainland and southern Coast Mountains from Vancouver to the east beyond Hope, nearly to Princeton. For detailed information, see page 91 in Chapter 4.

COMMUNITIES, PARKS, AND PLACES TO STAY

🐾 Port Moody (Km 0)

See page 96 in the previous chapter.

🐾 Coquitlam (Km 6.9)

On the Fraser and Coquitlam rivers.

› **Population** 121,000
› **Visitor Info** *Coquitlam tourist/visitor booth* 1209 Pinetree Way, Coquitlam, BC V3B 7Y3; 604-464-2716; www.tricitieschamber.com.
› **Attractions** Maillardville (the Lower Mainland's oldest francophone community).
› **Transportation** The Coquitlam Central Station for the *Westcoast Express* commuter train to Vancouver is at 2920 Barnet Highway.
› **Greyhound Bus** (1-800-661-8747; www.greyhound.ca) Depot located at 100 Woolridge Street.

🐾 Port Coquitlam (Km 10.8)

On the banks of the Coquitlam, Pitt, and Fraser rivers.

› **Population** 56,000

> **Visitor Info** *Coquitlam tourist/visitor booth* 1209 Pinetree Way, Coquitlam, BC V3B 7Y3; 604-464-2716; www.tricitieschamber.com.
> **Attractions** PoCo Trail.
> **Transportation** The station for the *Westcoast Express* commuter train to Vancouver is at 2125 Kingsway Avenue.

♣ Pitt Meadows (Km 25.2)

On the Fraser and Pitt rivers between Port Coquitlam and Maple Ridge.
> **Population** 16,000
> **Visitor Info** *Pitt Meadows Visitor Centre* 12492 Harris Road, Pitt Meadows, BC V3Y 2J4; 604-460-8300; www.mapleridge-pittmeadows.com.
> **Attractions** Pitt Meadows Historical Museum.
> **Transportation** The station for *Westcoast Express* commuter train to Vancouver is at 12258 Harris Road.

♣ Maple Ridge (Km 36.3)

> On the north bank of the Fraser River; Albion Ferry to Fort Langley.
> **Population** 69,000
> **Visitor Info** *Pitt Meadows Visitor Centre* 12492 Harris Road, Pitt Meadows, BC V3Y 2J4; 604-460-8300; www.mapleridge-pittmeadows.com.
> **Attractions** Haney Heritage House/Walk (see page 109).
> **Transportation** The Maple Meadows Station for *Westcoast Express* commuter train to Vancouver is at 20010 Dunn Avenue. For information on the *Albion Ferry*, check www.translink.bc.ca.
> **Greyhound Bus** (1-800-661-8747; www.greyhound.ca) Depot located at *E & Kent* at #4–20214 Lougheed Highway.

♣ Fort Langley (Km 46.2)

A heritage town and National Historic Site on the south bank of the Fraser River (see page 110). ⑦ ● ⊿ ✕ | *most needs and services*
> **Population** 2,700
> **Visitor Info** The *Langley Visitor Centre* is in a historic CN station at 9234 Glover Road in Fort Langley. Unit 1, 5761 Glover Road, Langley, BC V3A 8M8; 604-888-1477; www.fortlangley.com.
> **Attractions** National Historic Site, restored heritage buildings, museum, agricultural museum.
> **Greyhound Bus** (1-800-661-8747; www.greyhound.ca) Depot located at DRK *Agencies Inc.* at 20471 Logan Avenue, Langley.

🌲 Matsqui Trail Regional Park (Km 75.5)

A park beside the Fraser where the Abbotsford–Mission Bridge crosses the river. ⓘ ⛺ 🏞 🚻 *outhouses* 🚮 | TCT *pavilion*

› **Size** 122 hectares
› **Visitor Info** Look up "Matsqui Trail" on the Metro Vancouver website at www.gvrd.bc.ca/parks/.
› **Camping** 4 drive-in campsites next to the TCT. (Read signs warning of possible flooding.)

🍁 Abbotsford (South of Km 75.5)

Known as the "City in the Country." South of the Trans Canada Trail near Clayburn Village.

› **Population** 117,000
› **Visitor Info** *Abbotsford Visitor Centre* 2478 McCallum Road, Abbotsford, BC V2S 3P9; 1-888-332-2229; www.tourismabbotsford.ca.
› **Attractions** Matsqui-Sumas-Abbotsford Museum/Trethewey House.
› **Greyhound Bus** (1-800-661-8747; www.greyhound.ca) Depot located at 2033 Abbotsford Way.

5

Pitt River

6 MATSQUI TO CHILLIWACK LAKE

66 All at once, in hardly more than a mile, the river emerges from the mountains and the jungle to find itself ample elbowroom in a lush and open valley.
—*Bruce Hutchison*, The Fraser

Mount Baker is a snowy backdrop to Fraser Valley farmland

TRAIL TRIVIA

The Trans Canada Trail runs through BC's first company town, the village of Clayburn, where in 1905 Charles Maclure founded a brick factory.

TOTAL DISTANCE

106.4 km

HIGHLIGHTS

> Dyke and riverside trails
> The Great Blue Heron Nature Reserve
> The Rotary Vedder Trail
> Chilliwack Valley trails

CONDITIONS

> **Matsqui Trail Regional Park (Km 0) to Clayburn Creek (Km 18.6)** Easy dyke trails and paved roads through farmland. → 18.6 km
> **Clayburn Creek Trail (Km 18.6) to Blauson Boulevard (Km 20.9)** A climb on a hard-packed, double-track trail. → 2.3 km
> **Blauson Boulevard (Km 20.9) to Sumas River Dyke (Km 25.9)** Paved roads, including a 12 percent downhill grade, and a steep 400-metre gravel track that goes downhill to the dyke. → 5 km
> **Sumas River Dyke (Km 25.9) to Vedder River (Vedder Crossing) Bridge (Km 49.4)** Mainly dykes and a double-track hard-packed gravel trail, except short stints on paved road near the Barrowtown pumping station (Km 34.1) and Keith Wilson Bridge (Km 38.8). → 23.5 km
> **Vedder River (Vedder Crossing) Bridge (Km 49.4) to Vance Road (Km 55.5)** Mostly busy paved roads with paved shoulders, and some short trails. → 6.1 km
> **Vance Road (Km 55.5) to Tamihi Liumchen forest service road (Km 65.2)** Extremely steep, rough and rocky forestry road, with confusing forks; for touring cyclists, one of the roughest sections of the TCT in BC. → 9.7 km
> **Tamihi Liumchen forest service road (Km 65.2) to Chilliwack Lake Provincial Park campground entrance (Km 106.4)** A trail for hikers, cyclists, and horses, with some rough, steep terrain. → 41.2 km

CAUTIONS

> No supplies beyond Cultus Lake, where the trail enters wilderness. Because Cultus Lake has no major grocery stores, consider stocking up in Chilliwack before continuing on the TCT beyond the Vedder River Bridge.

> Beyond Cultus Lake the TCT takes various forest service roads. Forestry roads frequently change and maps are not always up to date. Adding confusion are unnamed roads that veer off main roads into the backwoods, and vandals who rip down TCT signs. In the route description, GPS coordinates are provided where TCT travellers could get lost.
> Bears, especially beyond Cultus Lake.
> Flooding, if camping at Matsqui Trail Regional Park.

TOPOGRAPHIC MAPS

1:250,000   Vancouver 92G, Hope 92H

1:50,000   Mission 92G/1, Skagit River 92H/3, Chilliwack 92H/4

OVERVIEW

For half the distance to Chilliwack Lake the TCT is mainly dykes, trails, and country roads as it funnels up the Fraser Valley between the Coast Mountains and the Skagit Range of the Cascades toward Chilliwack and Hope. The trail passes through the historic village of Clayburn and follows the banks of two more Fraser tributaries—the Sumas and Vedder rivers—as it skirts the southeast side of Sumas Mountain.

At Vedder Crossing (Km 49.4), where the TCT takes a bridge over the Vedder River, touring cyclists must make a choice: either continue on the TCT up the Chilliwack River Valley and do an arduous trek over Paleface Pass to Hope, or take a detour on paved roads.

The Fraser Valley farmlands soon vanish into the background as the TCT is enveloped by mountains over 2,000 metres high. Rivers through the Chilliwack Valley run faster and louder, forests are denser, and the imposing granite peaks of the Cascade Mountains bear the scars of intense alpine glaciation. The TCT here encounters some of its roughest terrain in BC.

These mountains are the northernmost fringe of a range that runs from northern California through Oregon and Washington into southwest BC. Mount Baker, the fifth-highest peak at 3,285 metres, is a volcanic cone, much like its infamous neighbour Mount St. Helens. Baker grumbled briefly in 1975; St. Helens erupted in 1980, killing 62 people, spewing a column of smoke and ash 19 kilometres high. It erupted less forcefully in 2004 and remains somewhat restless: TCT cyclists in the Chilliwack Valley should listen for distant explosions and periodically sniff the air for volcanic ash. If an eruption occurs, pedal faster . . .

LOCAL ADVENTURES

Day Trip

› Cycle from Matsqui Trail Regional Park (Km 0) to Clayburn village (Km 16.6). ⇆ 33.2 km

› Hike or cycle the TCT from Keith Wilson Bridge (Km 38.8) to the Great Blue Heron Nature Reserve (Km 42.3) to explore the trails and interpretive displays. (See page 133.) → 3.5 km

2 or 3 Days

› Set up camp at Thurston Meadows campground (Km 76.8) and take day trips by bicycle or foot on the TCT in either direction from the campground.

TCT ACCESS POINTS

Clayburn village (Km 16.7) From the Abbotsford–Mission Highway, go east on Clayburn Road. **P** *street parking*

Sumas River Dyke (Km 25.9) From the Trans-Canada Highway at Whatcom Road, head northeast on North Parallel Road to where it becomes Eldridge Road. Continue on Eldridge until North Parallel Road rejoins Eldridge and crosses the Sumas River. **P** *limited parking*

McDonald Park (Km 30.3) From Highway 1 east of Clayburn, turn left (west) on No. 3 Road. **P** 🚻 🚰 🛖

Barrowtown pumping station (Km 34.2) From Highway 1 east of Clayburn, turn left (west) on No. 3 Road, then right (northeast) onto North Parallel Road to Barrowtown. **P** *limited parking*

Keith Wilson Bridge (Km 38.8) From the Trans-Canada Highway east of Clayburn, take No. 3 Road east to Boundary Road, turn left (north) to Keith Wilson Road, and cross the bridge. **P**

Great Blue Heron Nature Reserve (Km 42.3) From the Trans-Canada Highway east of Clayburn, take No. 3 Road east to Boundary Road, turn left (north) to Keith Wilson Road, and cross the bridge. Continue on Keith Wilson Road to Sumas Prairie Road, and turn left to Sinclair Road and the nature reserve. To get on the TCT from the reserve, turn right onto a trail near the entrance to the reserve and follow it to the Rotary Vedder Trail. This trail is accessible to wheelchairs. 🅿 🚻 🚽 ⛱

Rotary Vedder Trail accesses (Km 46.1, Km 47.3, Km 49.4) The TCT/Rotary Vedder Trail can be reached from Keith Wilson Road (see above) by turning south at Lickman Road and continuing toward the TCT Pavilion in Chilliwack near the Vedder River (Km 46.1). The TCT can also be reached by turning south off Lickman down Peach Road (Km 47.3) or Vedder Road (Km 49.4). 🅿 🚻 *outhouses*

Cultus Lake (Km 53.2) From the Trans-Canada Highway at Chilliwack go south on Vedder Road, cross the Vedder River onto Vedder Mountain Road, then turn left onto Cultus Lake Road.

Tamihi Creek BC forest service campground (Km 67.4) From the Trans-Canada Highway at Chilliwack go south on Vedder Road, and just before the Vedder River Bridge turn left (east) onto Chilliwack Lake Road. Continue beyond Slesse Road, over the Chilliwack River, then right onto Tamihi Liumchen forest service road. ▲

Chilliwack River rafting

Thurston Meadows Trail/forest service campground (Km 76.8) There are TCT markers on both sides of Chilliwack Lake Road. ▲

Chilliwack Lake Park campground (Km 106.4) On Chilliwack Lake Road at the north end of the lake. 🅿 🚻 *outhouses* 🛁 ▲

BEYOND THE URBANIZED SOUTH COAST

WILDERNESS CHALLENGES

The flat and easy dykes and riverside trails from Matsqui come to an abrupt end at a bridge over the Vedder River at Vedder Crossing (Km 49.4), south of Chilliwack. This is the last chance for cyclists to opt out of the climb over Paleface Pass (described in Chapter 7), one of the hardest tolerance tests for touring cyclists on the TCT in BC. (A detour is described on page 130.)

Those who take up the challenge travel mainly on paved roads through Cultus Lake before embarking on a ten-kilometre stretch of rough logging road to Little Tamihi Creek. From there to Chilliwack Lake Provincial Park the TCT is 41 kilometres of trail, much of it newly built by Trails BC volunteers. It's a grand tour of creeks, rivers, ponds, and fish channels through stands of second-growth timber. Small groves of original forest along with a few clearcuts give TCT travellers a before-and-after look at logging in BC. Many of the streams and fish channels teem with spawning salmon in autumn.

Bicycles can be ridden and pushed on the trail except for short stretches where detours are described. Steep and rocky terrain may dissuade some cyclists who might prefer the 29 kilometres of pavement on Chilliwack Lake Road. The TCT route through the forests meets the road periodically, giving cyclists the chance to "test ride" the trails. Equestrians can ride most of the TCT from Cultus Lake (Km 53.2) to Chilliwack Lake Provincial Park (Km 106.4) and beyond; some detouring around certain creeks and bridges is required.

The trail through Chilliwack Valley is usually well marked: keep an eye on trees or other trailside objects for red-and-green TCT stickers, or diamond-shaped yellow markers.

THE TRANS CANADA TRAIL

Place names with asterisks are included in the **Communities, Parks, and Places to Stay** section (page 133).

Km 0   *Matsqui Trail Regional Park*, TCT Pavilion* From the pavilion below the Abbotsford–Mission Bridge, go east on the dyke along the Fraser River, passing a railway bridge.

Km 7.2   *Page Road park entrance* Turn right onto Page Road for 500 metres, then left on Little Road (Km 7.7) and over the railway tracks. Turn right (west) on Gallagher Road (Km 8.5) then left again on Beharrell Road (Km 9.9). At Beharrell and Fore roads (Km 10.7), go right on Fore for 200 metres then left (south) on Beharrell at a junction where Fore meets Beharrell Road again.

Km 12.6   *Beharrell Road + Hallert Road* Turn right (west) on Hallert, then turn left (south) onto Bell Road (Km 14.2), and left (east) at Clayburn Road (Km 15.8).

Km 16.7   *Village of Clayburn** Historic community with an old-fashioned candy store and restaurant. Continue east on Clayburn Road to Straiton Road (Km 17.3) where you go left.

Km 18.6   *Clayburn Creek Trail* Go right off Straiton Road, cross a bridge, and climb up a double-track gravel trail that runs high above the creek. At a fork (Km 20.3) stay right on the main trail to Blauson Boulevard. Take a short jog to the right and go left on McKee Road.

Km 21.4   *McKee Road + Sumas Mountain Road* Turn right down a hill with a 12-percent grade.

Km 24.1   *Sumas Mountain Road + Atkinson Road* At the bottom of the hill

Clayburn Village Store and Tea Shop

near a Sumas First Nation sign, make a hairpin turn to the left onto Atkinson and follow it to the end (Km 25.4), marked "Thunder Rock" beneath big maple trees. Continue straight down a steep gravel trail and across Eldridge Road. Turn left (north) onto the dyke along the east side of Sumas River.

Km 25.9   *Sumas River Dyke* Continue northeast on the dyke between Sumas River and the Trans-Canada Highway.

Trans-Canada Highway bridge crosses the Vedder Canal

Km 30.3   *McDonald Park/Dark Sky Reserve* City of Abbotsford park
with limited lighting to promote astronomy.

Km 33   *End of dyke* Go left (northeast) on North Parallel Road to
Barrowtown pumping station (Km 34.2) and follow the TCT
signs to the Vedder Canal Dyke.

Km 36.2   *Trans-Canada Highway Bridge* Heading southeast on the dyke,
go under the Highway 1 bridge. (If the dyke trail is flooded,
backtrack to Barrowtown pumping station and cross North
Parallel Road to Inter-Provincial Highway, which becomes a
trail under the Trans-Canada Highway. Continue on Inter-
Provincial Highway about 150 metres to No. 2 Road, then
turn east to the Keith Wilson Bridge.)

Km 38.8   *Keith Wilson Bridge* (To get back onto the dyke, turn left
to go over the bridge, then cross Keith Wilson Road and
continue southeast on the dyke.) At a gravel-storage site just
past Keith Wilson Bridge, the TCT goes down to a trail below
the dyke and continues to the Rotary Vedder Trail along
the Vedder River.

🐎 Don't cross the bridge, but continue along a dyke on the
southwest side of the Vedder River to Yarrow. An equestrian

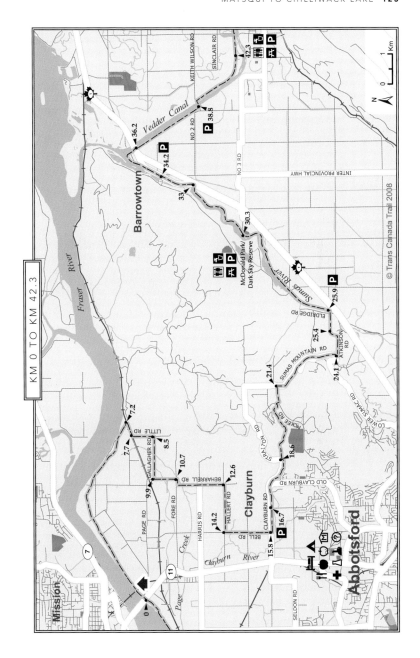

KM 0 TO KM 42.3

© Trans Canada Trail 2008

route beyond Yarrow has not been determined.

Km 42.3   *Rotary Vedder River Trail, Great Blue Heron Nature Reserve* The TCT continues east on the Rotary Vedder River Trail. There are restrooms, picnic tables, parking areas, and benches at viewpoints along this pleasant trail. (For a side trip to the reserve, turn left where the TCT crosses two successive bridges—see page 133. The nature reserve and interpretation centre are located near the junction of Sinclair and Sumas Prairie roads, about 400 metres off the TCT.)

Km 46.1   TCT *Pavilion* (Restrooms, picnic tables.) Watch for ospreys.

Km 49.4   *Vedder Crossing Bridge* Go right (south) across the bridge over Vedder River. (At this point you can turn left (north) onto Vedder Road for a 65-kilometre detour through Chilliwack* to Hope—see page 130 for detour directions.) The TCT leaves the riverside and takes to busy roads. Once across the bridge, continue up Vedder Mountain Road for 600 metres, and turn left (south) uphill on Cultus Lake Road. At a sign for Cultus Lake Provincial Park* (Km 52.5), cross the road and take a 900-metre trail (behind the sign) through a forest of cedar and fir. (Bicycle riders can ignore the sometimes mucky trail and stay on the pavement, turning left on Columbia Valley Road to Sunnyside Boulevard and the community of Cultus Lake.)

Km 53.2   *Cultus Lake** Head south on Sunnyside Boulevard and turn left on Mountain View Road (Km 53.9), which comes to a chain-link fence. Go left onto a one-kilometre trail leading to Columbia Valley Road. Cross the road near Cultus Lake Pub and follow a TCT–marked trail up to a cul-de-sac on Elizabeth Drive. Continue east on Elizabeth.

Km 55.5   *Elizabeth Drive + Vance Road* Turn right onto Vance, which becomes Chilliwack Liumchen West forest service road, a scenic but gruelling ten kilometres, one of the roughest stretches on the TCT in BC.

Km 58.1   *Federal government land* 🅖🅟🅢 north 49.04.466, west 121.56.428 ⛰ 66 metres. Gated property; stay left.

Km 59.4   *Chilliwack Little Tamihi forest service road* 🅖🅟🅢 north 49.04.466, west 121.55.357 ⛰ 197 metres. Veer left.

Km 60.1   *Bridge* 🅖🅟🅢 north 49.04.291, west 121.55.123 ⛰ 146 metres. Cross the bridge.

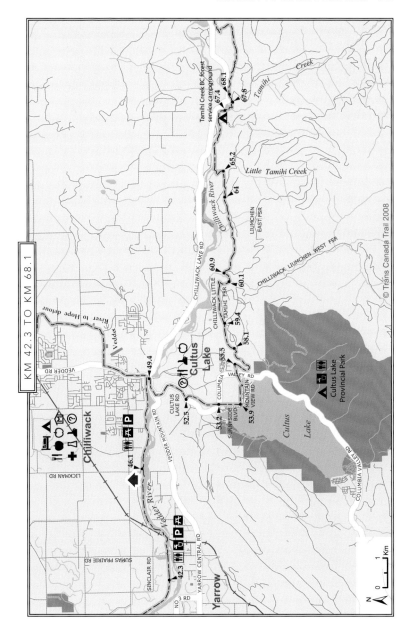

© Trans Canada Trail 2008

6

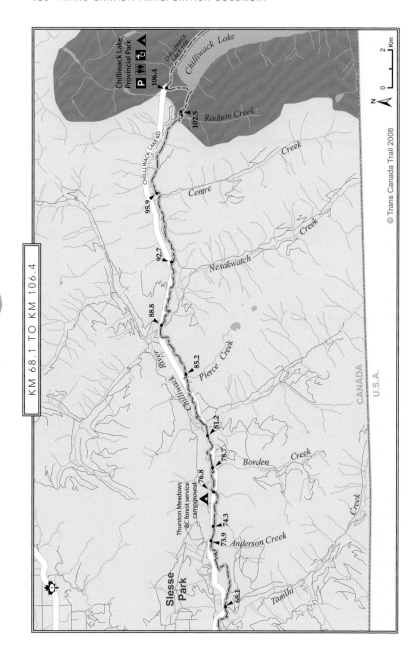

KM 68.1 TO KM 106.4

6

Chilliwack Lake
Provincial Park

Chilliwack Lake

CHILLIWACK LAKE FSR

106.4

102.5 Radium Creek

CHILLIWACK LAKE RD

Creek

Centre

95.9

92.7

Nesakwatch

88.8

Creek

85.2 Pierce Creek

Chilliwack River

81.2

78.7

Borden Creek

76.8

Thurston Meadows
BC forest service
campground

74.3

Creek

73.9 Anderson Creek

Slesse
Park

68.1

Tamihi

CANADA
U.S.A.

© Trans Canada Trail 2008

0   2 Km

N

Km 60.9   *Fork* GPS north 49.04.308, west 121.54.947 ⛰ 182 metres.
           Ignore a trail to the left with a boulder at the entrance. At the
           fork in the main road, go left.

Km 64   *Fork* GPS north 49.04.53, west 121.52.631 ⛰ 190 metres.
           Great mountain and valley views. A TCT marker should
           point to the left.

Km 65.2   *End of rough stretch.* The trail comes to the bottom of a hill
           and meets Little Tamihi Creek. Take the Fishermen's Trail
           to the right along the Chilliwack River.

Km 67.4   *Tamihi Creek BC forest service campground* Continue through
           the campground on the TCT to a gate at Liumchen Creek
           forest service road. Turn left and go about 100 metres
           on the road to Chilliwack–Tamihi Creek forest service road
           (Km 67.6).

Km 67.8   *Liumchen Creek forest service road + Chilliwack–Tamihi Creek
           forest service road* Go right (south) up Chilliwack–Tamihi
           Creek Road for 400 metres to a TCT marker on the left side
           of the road. The trail is rideable but rough for bikes for the
           next six kilometres, with an elevation gain of 120 metres.
           (Cyclists who prefer pavement and easier terrain can continue
           on Liumchen Creek Road past Chilliwack–Tamihi Road for
           about 200 metres to Chilliwack Lake Road where they turn
           right (east).)

Km 68.1   *Tolmie Trail* Travellers who stay on the TCT go left off
           Chilliwack–Tamihi Road at the TCT marker and follow
           the trail through forests of fir, cottonwood, and maple.

Km 73.9   *Anderson Creek, Chilliwack Lake Road* The TCT meets
           Chilliwack Lake Road at Anderson Creek Pond. Go right
           (east) on the road and cross the bridge over Anderson Creek,
           then take a trail along the edge of a pond. At the eastern end
           of the pond return to the road for about 300 metres.

Km 74.3   *Thurston Trail* The TCT goes right (south) off the road and
           continues east through the forest, passing some fish channels.

Km 76.8   *Thurston Meadows BC forest service campground* The TCT
           crosses Chilliwack Lake Road and continues east through the
           campground, passing fish channels and following parts of an
           old logging railway grade. The trail leaves the forest and takes
           the road for about 200 metres.

Km 78.7   *Borden Creek* The TCT crosses Borden Creek on the road then returns to the forest. Beyond the forested area cyclists should take the road while hikers take the trail. The TCT returns to the road to cross Slesse Creek.

Km 81.2   *Chilliwack River Salmonid Enhancement Facility* The TCT continues on Chilliwack Lake Road for about 100 metres, then goes left (north) off the road into the forest on the Larsen Bench Trail. It makes a steep climb with a hairpin turn near the top of Larsen Hill. (Cyclists might prefer the paved road, but the grade is 13 percent, the steepest grade on the TCT in BC.) The trail continues from the top of the hill through the forest for about three kilometres before meeting Chilliwack Lake Road. Go east on the road for about 200 metres, then cross over to a trail through some federal government (Department of National Defence) property to Pierce Creek.

Km 85.2   *Pierce Creek* Cross the creek and continue on the TCT through the woods, following an old logging road and trail to a gravel pit. The TCT skirts around the pit and continues out to Chilliwack Lake Road.

Km 88.8   *Chilliwack River Bridge* The TCT continues about 100 metres on Chilliwack Lake Road over the Chilliwack River and turns right (south) onto the Nesakwatch Trail. The trail crosses a log bridge and enters a fishy area known as the Angelwing Pond Complex. Cyclists and horse riders stay on the road for about 400 metres to a road on the right; take the road to a trail which goes to the left (east).

Km 92.7   *Former Riverside BC forest service campground, Chilliwack River crossing* The trail returns to Chilliwack Lake Road for about 150 metres then passes through a former campground to the Centennial Fish Channels and another crossing of the Chilliwack River. Cyclists may prefer to remain on the road here as there are rocky sections and a particularly steep climb ahead on the Centre Creek Trail.

Km 95.9   *Centre Creek Trail* The trail continues east beyond the fish channels through a timber-harvest area where the trees here today could be gone tomorrow. Look in the forest for huge hollow cedar stumps that were used as shelters by shake-block cutters.

Km 102.5 *Radium Creek Trail* After a steep 500-metre climb (a serious push for cyclists) the TCT travels from a bluff through the forest, passing a short detour to a suspension bridge, then crossing Radium Creek before switchbacking down to a footbridge across the outlet of Chilliwack Lake. The trail wanders through Chilliwack Lake Provincial Park to the park entrance on Chilliwack Lake Road.

Trails BC director
Léon Lebrun

Km 106.4 *Chilliwack Lake Provincial Park* entrance*
The TCT continues through the park on Chilliwack Lake forest service road, a rutted route that follows the eastern lakeshore.

TCT DYKES CREATE FRASER VALLEY FARMLAND

The "muddy Fraser," as it's widely known, is the source of some of North America's richest soil. The minerals and silt carried down through Interior British Columbia fan into a broad alluvial plain downstream from Hope, where the Fraser Valley encompasses 25,000 square kilometres. For untold millennia spring freshets flooded the valley, delivering an annual load of fertile soil. As the valley became populated, dykes and ditches were built to hold back or redirect the floodwaters and reclaim agricultural land.

If the Trans Canada Trail had been here before the 1920s, it would have looked over a vast lake east of Sumas River, instead of the 130 square kilometres of dairy farms and crops such as hops and berries seen here today. Sumas Lake was drained to create Sumas Prairie, and the riverside dyke that helps hold the water at bay is the TCT route. In all, there are 600 kilometres of dykes on the lower Fraser system between the mouth of the river and Chilliwack, 100 kilometres upstream.

More than 100,000 hectares are farmed between Vancouver and Hope. Most of Metro Vancouver's 6,000 farms are here, producing well over half of BC's agricultural revenue. The Fraser Valley is one of the most intensely farmed regions in the province. Vegetables, fruit, hay, grain, livestock, poultry, mushrooms, and much more are grown or raised here close to major markets.

VANCOUVER, COAST & MOUNTAINS REGION

Tourism region encompassing the Lower Mainland and southern Coast Mountains from Vancouver to the east beyond Hope, nearly to Princeton. For detailed information, see page 91 in Chapter 4.

DETOUR

VEDDER RIVER TO HOPE → 65.1 KM

Many cyclists would rather pass on Paleface Pass, a steep and gruelling slog beyond the north end of Chilliwack Lake (described in Chapter 7). Those who do, however, cut out more than 100 kilometres of Trans Canada Trail through the upper Chilliwack Valley and over the mountains to Hope. This alternate 65-kilometre road route to Hope, through the city of Chilliwack and along the north side of the Fraser River, is not as adventurous, but is scenic and considerably easier.

Km 0   *Vedder River Bridge* From the bridge head left (north) on Vedder Road.

Km 1.6   *Vedder Road + Promontory Road* Go right (east) on Promontory Road.

Km 2.7   *Promontory Road + Chilliwack River Road* Go left on Chilliwack River Road.

Km 8.3   *Chilliwack River Road + Prairie Central Road* Go left to the Highway 1 underpass and through the traffic light at Young Road and Luckakuck Way. Travel through Chilliwack on Young Road.

Km 12.5   *Young Road + Hope River Road* Turn right (east) at Hope River Road and follow the river's north bank through agricultural land with fields, orchards, berry farms, and marshes.

Km 15.2   *Hope River Kinsmen Park*

Km 16.6   *Hope River Road + Kitchen Road + Camp River Road* Turn right (east) along Camp River Road, which crosses McGrath Road to become Ferry Road.

Km 25.1   *McGrath Road + Ferry Road* Continue straight.

Km 26.3   *"No Exit" sign* Turn left down Rosedale Ferry Road (a "Road Closed" sign in a tree) and follow it along the Fraser River, under the Agassiz Bridge and up to Highway 9.

Km 26.9   *Highway 9* Go over the bridge, heading north across the river.

Km 33.1   *Highway 9/Highway 7* Keep right onto Highway 7.

Km 45.7   *Rest stop.*

Km 61.2   *Highway 7 + Highway 1* The road joins Highway 1, which crosses the Fraser River and meets the Trans Canada Trail at the Hope Visitor Centre.

Km 65.1   *Hope Visitor Centre* The TCT route from Hope is described in Chapter 8.

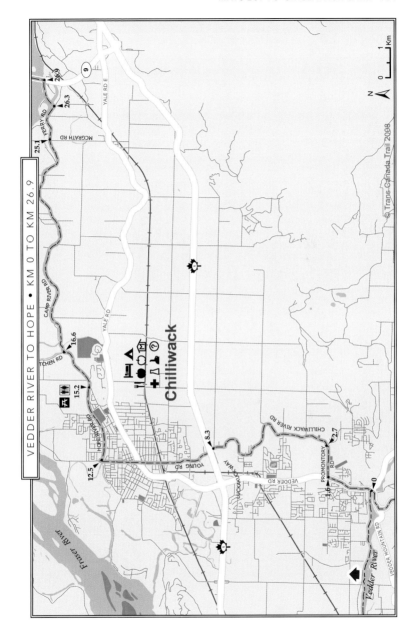

VEDDER RIVER TO HOPE • KM 0 TO KM 26.9

Chilliwack

Fraser River

Vedder River

Km

N

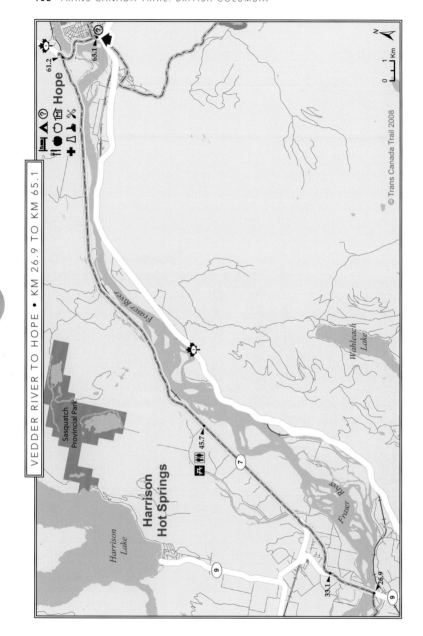

COMMUNITIES, PARKS, AND PLACES TO STAY

Information on each provincial park in BC can be found on the BC Parks website at www.env.gov.bc.ca/bcparks/.

Matsqui Trail Regional Park (Km 0)

See page 114 in the previous chapter.

Clayburn (Km 16.7)

A heritage village on the west side of Sumas Mountain.

> **Visitor Info** Click on "Heritage Sites" at www.fraservalleyguide.com.
> **Attractions** Clayburn Village Store and Tea Shop, heritage church, school, old brick plant site. Gifts, art. Fresh farm produce.

GREAT BLUE: BC'S BIGGEST HERON

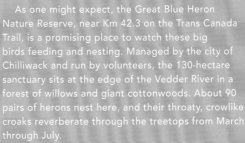

As tall as a five-year-old child, the great blue heron (*Ardea herodias*) is the largest of BC's five heron species and the most widespread in North America. It lives year-round in southwest BC, feeding in intertidal zones, wet meadows, irrigation ponds, and sloughs. Small fish, frogs and salamanders, lizards and snakes, even mice and grasshoppers round out a heron's diet.

As one might expect, the Great Blue Heron Nature Reserve, near Km 42.3 on the Trans Canada Trail, is a promising place to watch these big birds feeding and nesting. Managed by the city of Chilliwack and run by volunteers, the 130-hectare sanctuary sits at the edge of the Vedder River in a forest of willows and giant cottonwoods. About 90 pairs of herons nest here, and their throaty, crowlike croaks reverberate through the treetops from March through July.

The luckiest observers catch the herons performing their elaborate courtship rituals. With feathers fluffed and neck outstretched to half its body length, an amorous male flamboyantly shakes a twig in its long bill. Both sexes raise their feathered crests and noisily clap their bills before copulating.

The birds nesting at the reserve are coastal great blues (*Ardea herodias fannini*), designated in 1997 as "vulnerable," two strikes from "endangered." Pollution, loss of nesting sites to urbanization, and predation by growing numbers of eagles are cited as probable causes of recent declines.

The great blue is one of about 80 bird species recorded at the reserve. Visitors may also see carp, spawning salmon, river otters, frogs, and turtles. For information, call the reserve's Rotary Interpretive Centre at 604-823-6603 or look up "Great Blue Heron Nature Reserve" at www.chilliwack.com.

Cascade Mountains and Chilliwack Valley

🌲 Chilliwack (Km 49.4)

Agricultural centre on Highway 1 between Cultus Lake and the Fraser River.

› **Population** 70,000
› **Visitor Info** *Chilliwack Visitor Centre* 44150 Luckakuck Way, Chilliwack, BC V2R 4A7; 1-800-567-9535; www.tourismchilliwack.com.
› **Attractions** Farm tours, Atchelitz Threshermen's Antique Powerland.
› **Greyhound Bus** (1-800-661-8747; www.greyhound.ca) Depot located at *Kerrox Agencies* at 45745 Luckakuck Way.

RED CAP DISTINGUISHES SANDHILL CRANE

Great blue heron watchers in the Fraser Valley sometimes unexpectedly focus on a sandhill crane. Similar in size and shape to a heron, the sandhill is distinguished by its red cap and feathery bustle. Its high, incessant call is quite dissimilar to the heron's croak, and in flight its neck is outstretched while the heron's is held close to the body.

Most of the sandhill cranes seen in British Columbia are migrating between wintering grounds in the southern United States and Mexico and nesting areas in Alaska. A few breed in the Fraser lowlands near Pitt Meadows and Fort Langley. TCT travellers occasionally spot them in farmers' fields. Other areas along the TCT in southern BC where sandhill cranes have been reported are Nanaimo and Summerland. On the northern TCT route they could be spotted near Liard River Hot Springs, Fort Nelson, and Fort St. John.

Cultus Lake Provincial Park (Km 52.5)
Popular with campers from the Lower Mainland who like to fish, hike, water ski, and windsurf. ▲ 🚻 🚰 | *hot showers in campgrounds*
› **Size** 2,561 hectares
› **Camping** 314 campsites in four campgrounds. *Reservations* 1-800-689-9025 (or 604-689-9025 in Metro Vancouver). www.discovercamping.ca

Cultus Lake (Km 53.2)
A Coney Island kind of holiday spot for Lower Mainlanders. ⏱ *convenience stores* ⑦ 🏪 🍴 | *note that food stores may not be well stocked—TCT travellers headed for the wilderness beyond Chilliwack Lake may want to detour at Vedder River Bridge for shopping in Chilliwack*
› **Visitor Info** www.cultuslake.bc.ca
› **Attractions** Waterslides, bumper boats, jet ski rentals, minigolf, petting zoo.

Chilliwack Lake Provincial Park (Km 106.4)
A lakeside park with old-growth forests, alpine and subalpine ridges, and 40 kilometres of hiking trails. ▲ 🚻 *outhouses* 🚰
› **Size** 9,258 hectares
› **Camping** 146 drive-in campsites, walk-in wilderness camping.

7 CHILLIWACK LAKE TO HOPE

> 66 You're taking your bikes over Paleface Pass?!
> —Chilliwack bear hunter who'd unsuccessfully attempted
> to climb Paleface Pass in his four-wheel-drive truck

Skagit Range of the Cascade Mountains

TRAIL TRIVIA
An estimated 140,000 black bears and 17,000 grizzlies live in BC. Much of the TCT runs through bear country.

TOTAL DISTANCE
58.8 km

HIGHLIGHTS
› Paleface Pass, one of the most challenging sections on the TCT in BC
› Outstanding mountain views

CONDITIONS
› **Chilliwack Lake Provincial Park campground (Km 0) to Paleface Creek (Km 7.9)** Road worsens as it follows the east side of Chilliwack Lake. Rocks, potholes, busy weekend recreation traffic. → 7.9 km
› **Paleface Creek (Km 7.9) to Upper Silverhope Valley (Km 16)** 5.1 kilometres of rough, steep, deactivated logging road followed by three kilometres of unforgiving switchbacks. An extremely rough stretch for cyclists, yet a scenic, albeit steep, hike. → 8.1 km
› **Upper Silverhope (Km 16) to TCT marker/gate (Km 26.9)** Unused logging road with wide "deactivation" trenches dug to block vehicle traffic. The trenches have been modified by volunteers to make them passable for cyclists. → 10.9 km
› **TCT marker (Km 26.9) to Hope (Km 58.8)** Four kilometres of single-track trail, 24 kilometres of well-maintained, well-used logging roads, and four kilometres of paved road. → 31.9 km

CAUTIONS
› Weekend-recreation traffic and weekday logging trucks on both sides of Paleface Pass.
› Summer snow in Paleface Pass. (The Pass is physically challenging with or without snow.)
› Bears and remote wilderness, especially between Chilliwack Lake and Hope.

TOPOGRAPHIC MAPS
1:250,000	Hope 92H
1:50,000	Skagit River 92H/3, Hope 92H/6

OVERVIEW

The Skagit Range of the Cascade Mountains is a hundred kilometres inland, yet the influence of the Pacific Ocean is still evident along the Trans Canada Trail. Hemlock, cedar, grand fir, and other giant conifers of the temperate rainforest thrive on the seaward slopes. Some stands of old growth remain, but much of the forest here has been logged at least once. The journey on the TCT from Chilliwack Lake to Hope offers some insight into BC's logging industry: using active and deactivated logging roads, the TCT travels through everything from old-growth forests to recent clearcuts.

The valleys in these mountains are deep, steep, and narrow, and the peaks and ridges above the treeline are sharp and barren. Summits over 2,000 metres on both sides of the TCT may be covered in snow year-round. This mountain scenery is overwhelming.

Equestrians can ride from Chilliwack Lake Provincial Park (Km 0) to Flood Hope Road (Km 55.4), just over three kilometres from downtown Hope. This remote section of the TCT includes the infamous Paleface Pass, an overland link between Chilliwack River Valley on the south and the Fraser River and Hope to the north. It's a moderate challenge for equestrians and for hikers in good shape; for cyclists it is undeniably one of the most difficult stretches of the TCT in BC. Trails BC director Léon Lebrun says that Paleface Pass will be a "real grunt for cyclists but doable if you are in great condition and are prepared to push your bike."

LOCAL ADVENTURES

Day Trip

› Hike from Chilliwack Lake (Km 7.9) to the top of Paleface Pass (Km 15.2) and back. ⇆ 14.6 km

2 or 3 Days

› Set up camp at Chilliwack Lake Provincial Park (Km 0), and explore the TCT hiking trails to the west along Chilliwack Lake Road.

TCT ACCESS POINTS

Chilliwack Lake Provincial Park campground (Km 0) From the Trans-Canada Highway at Chilliwack, go south on Vedder Road. Just before the bridge at Vedder Crossing turn left (east) onto Chilliwack Lake Road and follow it to the north end of the lake. **P** 🚻 *outhouses* 🚰 ⛰

Hope Visitor Centre/TCT Pavilion (Km 58.8) The TCT runs from the visitor centre (919 Water Avenue) through downtown. **P** *plenty of street parking in downtown Hope*

PALEFACE PASS

GATEWAY TO MOUNTAIN VISTAS

The gravel road beyond Chilliwack Lake Provincial Park Campground worsens as it runs down the east shore of the lake to Paleface Creek. It's hard to take in the scenery while dodging rocks and potholes, but there are viewpoints where you can stop for pictures of Mount Meroniuk, Paleface Mountain, and others in the Skagit Range.

From Paleface Creek—which is at an elevation of 650 metres—the trail goes up, up, and up. Here the TCT is a deactivated logging road with metre-wide, 20-centimetre-deep trenches plowed across the route. Trailblazers have cut shallow tracks perpendicularly across the trenches to help cyclists wheel through. The first 5.1 kilometres may take three hours: this is a warm-up for the next 2.2 kilometres over the 1,410-metre summit of Paleface Pass. This is a trail better suited for hikers and equestrians than cyclists. Extremely steep terrain, boulders, exposed tree roots, tight switchbacks, and snow that may linger into July conspire against cyclists carrying loaded panniers, or worse, towing trailers.

"You must be a very fit and hardy cyclist to go beyond Chilliwack Lake," warns the Trails BC website. "This is a very tough grind but very rewarding." The reward: stunning mountain vistas.

The TCT's descent to Hope takes logging roads down Silverhope Creek Valley northward toward its confluence with the Fraser River near Hope. The terrain is steep, often rough, with scenic waterfalls and stretches of whitewater alongside the TCT.

THE TRANS CANADA TRAIL

Place names with asterisks are included in the **Communities, Parks, and Places to Stay** section (page 144).

Km 0   *Chilliwack Lake Provincial Park* campground* From the campground, go on the gravel road along the eastern lakeshore.

Km 7.9   *Paleface Creek* Base of Paleface Pass. Tents can be pitched on the grass; there are no facilities. On the north side of Paleface Creek, the TCT goes up the rocky road beside the campsite.

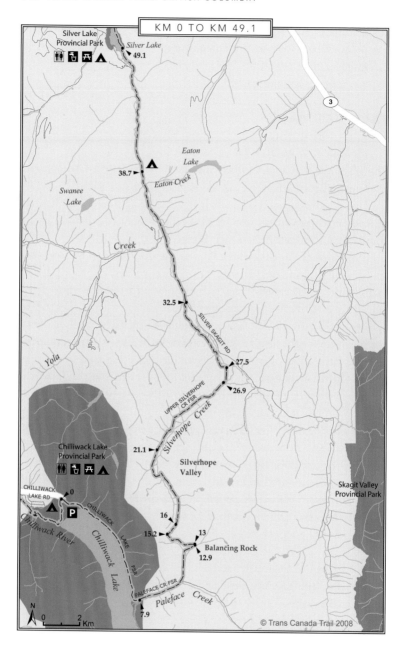

KM 0 TO KM 49.1

Silver Lake
Provincial Park

Silver Lake
49.1

3

Eaton
Lake

38.7

Eaton Creek

Swanee
Lake

Creek

32.5

SILVER SKAGIT RD

27.5

Yola

26.9

UPPER SILVERHOPE
CR FSR

Silverhope Creek

Chilliwack Lake
Provincial Park

21.1

Silverhope
Valley

Skagit Valley
Provincial Park

CHILLIWACK
LAKE RD

0

P

CHILLIWACK

LAKE

FSR

16

15.2

13

Balancing Rock

12.9

Chilliwack River

Chilliwack Lake

PALEFACE CR FSR

Paleface Creek

7.9

N

0   2
Km

© Trans Canada Trail 2008

7

Km 12.9   *Fork*  north 49.04.373, west 121.21.314
          1,214 metres. A TCT marker on a tree
          stump to the left points to a hairpin turn
          up to "Balancing Rock."

Km 13   *Balancing Rock* TCT/Paleface Pass signs
          are attached to a stump supporting a large
          boulder. Continue past the boulder on
          the marked trail.

Km 15.2   *End of Paleface Pass Trail* north
          49.04.685, west 121.22.599 1,410
          metres. Continue on a marked gravel road
          to upper Silverhope Valley.

Cascade Mountains
and Chilliwack Lake

Km 16   TCT *marker/fork* north 49.04.963,
          west 121.22.199 1,390 metres. Another
          deactivated logging road takes the TCT on
          its downhill journey toward Hope. A soft
          surface and deactivation trenches every
          50 or 60 metres (dug to block vehicle traf-
          fic, some filled with runoff water) make
          the first 12 kilometres a frustrating slog.

Km 21.1   TCT *marker/fork* north 49.07.102,
          west 122.23.009 1,105 metres.
          Continue straight.

Km 26.9   TCT *marker/gate* north 49.08.917,
          west 121.19.790. End of trenched road;
          continue straight.

Km 27.5   TCT *marker/trail* north 49.09.428,
          west 121.19.790 616 metres. The Silver
          Skagit forest service road to Hope is
          500 metres ahead, but the TCT takes

Balancing Rock
at Paleface Pass

          the path to the left (northwest) through
          the bush. The path parallels Silver Skagit Road for four
          kilometres. At the end of the path, a left turn leads to the Old
          Centennial Trail, an alternate walking route to Chilliwack
          Lake. The TCT, however, goes right, down a one-kilometre dirt
          road that joins Silver Skagit Road.

Km 32.5   *Silver Skagit Road + Centennial Trail turnoff* Continue north
          on Silver Skagit toward Hope.

Km 38.7   *Eaton Creek* BC *forest service campground* (Turn right on a

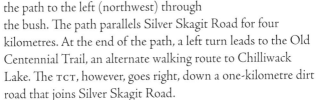

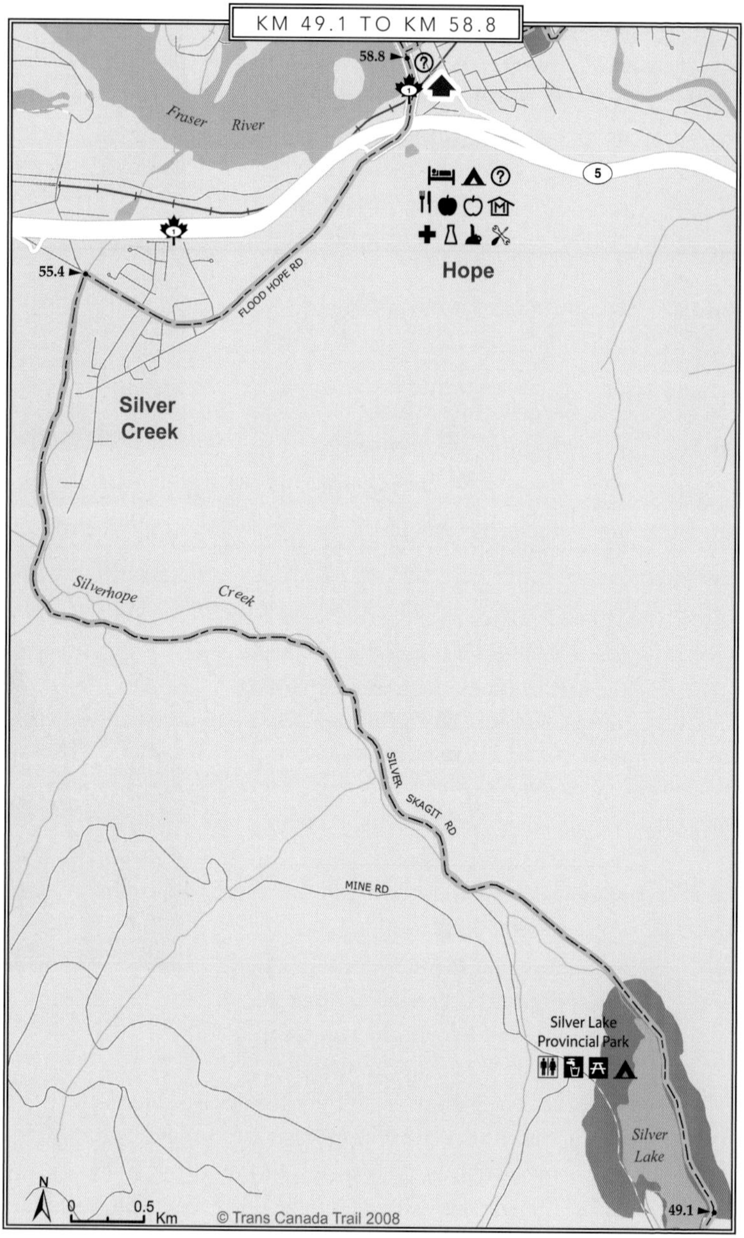

KM 49.1 TO KM 58.8

58.8 ►

5

Fraser River

55.4 ►

Hope

FLOOD HOPE RD

Silver
Creek

Silverhope   Creek

SILVER SKAGIT RD

MINE RD

Silver Lake
Provincial Park

Silver
Lake

49.1 ►

N

0   0.5
└──┴──┘ Km

© Trans Canada Trail 2008

7

Cascade Mountains, approaching Hope

gravel road that goes about one kilometre to a campsite with room for two tents.) To continue on the TCT, go north toward Hope.

Km 49.1   *Silver Lake Provincial Park** (Turn left from Silver Skagit into this campground.) To continue on the TCT, go north toward Hope.

Km 55.4   *Flood Hope Road* A TCT sign points right toward Hope.

Km 58.8   *Hope* Visitor Centre/*TCT *Pavilion* Beyond Hope, the TCT takes city streets to reach the Kettle Valley Railway trail.

FRASER RIVER SYSTEM PROVIDES TCT ROUTES

With its notorious rapids and whirlpools safely upstream, the Fraser River slips down between the Cascade and Coast mountains past Hope and mellows into a more leisurely pace. From here it drops fewer than 50 metres as it wanders 150 kilometres through an expansive estuary to the ocean at Vancouver. At Hope the river has already come more than 1,200 kilometres from its source in the spruce swamps of Fraser Pass, on the western slopes of the Continental Divide.

With a catchment basin of over 230,000 square kilometres—about a quarter of BC—the Fraser is the fifth-largest river system in Canada. Each year it delivers 121 billion cubic metres of fresh water to the Pacific Ocean.

The water transports 12 million cubic metres of sand and sediment and adds it to the delta, a process that has been happening about 8,000 years.

Fraser River

The Fraser River is the world's largest salmon-producing system, sometimes with annual returns of 12 million fish. All five Pacific salmon species spawn in the Fraser watershed.

Much of the TCT route from Vancouver to Hope follows the Fraser River and some of its tributaries. Beyond Hope the TCT continues alongside yet another Fraser tributary, the Coquihalla River.

VANCOUVER, COAST & MOUNTAINS REGION

Tourism region encompassing the Lower Mainland and southern Coast Mountains from Vancouver to the east beyond Hope, nearly to Princeton. For detailed information, see page 91 in Chapter 4.

COMMUNITIES, PARKS, AND PLACES TO STAY

Information on each provincial park in BC can be found on the BC Parks website at www.env.gov.bc.ca/bcparks/.

♣♣ Chilliwack Lake Provincial Park (Km 0)

See page 135 in the previous chapter.

♣♣ Silver Lake Provincial Park (Km 49.1)

Undeveloped park in a mountain and lakeshore setting. A "rustic camping experience," according to BC Parks. ▲ ⛽ ♦ *outhouses* ⬛

› **Size** 77 hectares
› **Camping** 25 campsites

🏕 Hope (Km 58.8)

On the edge of the Fraser River at the junction of Highways 1, 3, 5, and 7, squeezed between the Cascade and Coast mountains. Hope has been known as the "Chainsaw Carving Capital" since 1991 when a big rot-infested tree in the city's Memorial Park was slated to fall under the woodman's axe.

Hope artist Pete Ryan transformed the four-metre-high stump into an eagle clutching a salmon. The locals admired his work; now the streets and parks of Hope are adorned by 20 of Ryan's carvings, many depicting native wildlife. ⑦ 🍎 ⛺ ✂ 🍴

› **Population** 6,800
› **Visitor Info** *Hope Visitor Centre* 919 Water Avenue, PO Box 370, Hope, BC V0X 1L0; 1-866-467-3842; www.destinationhopeandbeyond.com; www.hopebc.ca. Thorough websites tell all there is about Hope, including its history, businesses, arts and culture, recreational activities, and events. You will also find maps, and weather and accommodation information.

One of Pete Ryan's wood carvings in Hope

› **Attractions** Chainsaw carvings, Blue Moose Deli & Coffee Bar, Hope Station House community arts centre, Japanese Friendship Gardens in Memorial Park (downtown), Hope Museum.
› **Cycling/Outfitting** *Cheyenne Sporting Goods* 267 Wallace Street; 604-869-5062.
› **Greyhound Bus** (1-800-661-8747; www.greyhound.ca) Depot located at *Hope Drycleaners* at #1–800 Third Avenue.

7

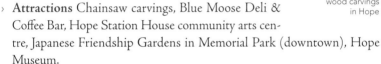

BLACKTAIL DEER: THE MOST VISIBLE "BIG GAME"

Of all the so-called "big game" animals in British Columbia, blacktail deer (*Odocoileus hemionus*) is the species most commonly seen along the Trans Canada Trail. From the rainforests of the coast to the sagebrush of the southern Interior, individual deer, does with fawns, and small bands of bucks are frequently spotted foraging the fields or resting in the shade. On the coast, the subspecies Columbian blacktail is most common, while farther inland the mule deer is the largest and most widespread blacktail subspecies in BC.

Unlike animals that escape human encroachment by retreating farther into the wilderness, deer are adaptable. They regularly feast on urban flower and vegetable gardens, and are often seen on riverbanks, lakeshores, and beaches in and around towns.

8 HOPE TO COQUIHALLA LAKES

> But I haven't got any teeth. —Hope bushman Cecil MacDonald, when asked to smile for a snapshot. He lives in the woods, travels by bicycle, and is an encyclopedia on the TCT and other local trails. Catch him if you can.

Bushman Cecil MacDonald

TRAIL TRIVIA

Four people were killed in 1965 when the Hope Slide buried a three-kilometre stretch of the Hope–Princeton Highway.

TOTAL DISTANCE

61.2 km

HIGHLIGHTS

› The Coquihalla Canyon and the Quintette tunnels
› The falls of Fallslake Creek (Bridal Veil)

CONDITIONS

› **Hope (Km 0) to Coquihalla Canyon (Km 8.9)** Paved roads. Good single-track trail and double-track railway bed. → 8.9 km
› **Coquihalla Canyon (Km 8.9) to Portia (Km 35.3)** Sections of paved road, including Highway 5 (Coquihalla Highway), and some rough and steep dirt road and trail. → 26.4 km
› **Portia (Km 35.3) to Coquihalla Lakes (Km 61.2)** Mainly well-surfaced double-track railbed and industrial road with a few irritating patches of loose gravel. → 25.9 km

CAUTIONS

› Possible trail closures at Portia (Km 35.3). Get updates from the Hope Visitor Centre or Coquihalla Lakes Lodge before setting out.
› Bears.

TOPOGRAPHIC MAPS

1:250,000   Hope 92H
1:50,000   Hope 92H/6, Spuzzum 92H/11

OVERVIEW

With Highways 1, 3, 5, and 7 all converging at Hope, the only time it's quiet at the visitor centre is when it's closed. The TCT Pavilion outside the visitor centre is conspicuous testimony of the community's support for the trail. TCT stickers are pasted in storefront windows throughout the downtown core and the route is well marked.

Hope is the start of a long rail trail journey. Except for a few stretches of road or trail, from here the TCT utilizes abandoned train corridors for more than 600 kilometres to Castlegar. These are ready-made off-road routes, hacked and dynamited through the backcountry a century ago, then surrendered to the wilderness with the coming of highways, trucks, and private cars.

Andrew McCulloch, the chief engineer who oversaw construction of the Kettle Valley Railway from Midway to Hope, was known to recite Shakespeare to workers around evening campfires. He named train stations after the Bard's characters—Juliet, Romeo, Portia, Jessica, Lear, and Iago. Best known is Othello (just outside Hope), site of the Quintette tunnels in the Coquihalla Canyon. This railway became known as "McCulloch's Wonder," and anyone who travels these rail trails today wonders how anyone could overcome such formidable odds. (For more on the KVR, see page 155.)

LOCAL ADVENTURES

Day Trip

› Hike or bike the TCT from Hope to the Quintette tunnels (Km 8.9). ⇆ 17.8 km

› Cycle a TCT–Othello Road loop to the Quintette tunnels. (See page 157.) ↺ 18.5 km

2 or 3 Days

› Rent a cabin or campsite at Coquihalla Lakes Lodge (Km 61.2), and take day trips on foot or by bicycle on the TCT between Portia Station (Km 35.3) and Brodie Station (Chapter 9, Km 24). Highway 5 can be incorporated into cycling loops.

TCT ACCESS POINTS

Hope Visitor Centre (Km 0) At 919 Water Avenue (Trans-Canada Highway). A junction of major highways to and from the Lower Mainland. **P** *ample street parking* 🚻 🚮

Coquihalla Canyon Provincial Park (Km 9.4) From Sixth Avenue in Hope take Kawkawa Lake Road to Othello Road, which leads to Tunnels Road and the park. **P** *parking at the beginning of a 500-metre trail to Quintette tunnels* 🚻 *outhouses*

Portia Station (Km 35.3) Take Highway 5 to Portia Exit #202. **P** *limited roadside parking at the gate across the TCT/Terasen Pipelines road*

Coquihalla toll plaza (off Km 60.3) On Highway 5 (Coquihalla Highway), 55 kilometres northeast of Hope. Hikers and cyclists can pass through the toll booths without paying. They take a short, steep road down from the highway (right/east) to the TCT near the northeast end of the Terasen Pipelines road. From the parking area near the south side of the toll plaza there is a break in the highway dividers to allow vehicles to return south on the highway without going through the toll booths. **P** *parking at a rest stop on Highway 5 on the south side of the toll plaza* 🚻 🛉

THE KETTLE VALLEY RAILWAY

BC'S FAMOUS RAIL TRAIL

Parts of the historic Kettle Valley Railway from Hope have been washed out by rivers, bulldozed by industrial road builders, or paved over by highways. But trail builders are committed to preserving what remains of the KVR as part of the TCT across southern BC. Outside Hope, the TCT is on and off the KVR, criss-crossing Highway 5 as it follows the Coquihalla River upstream.

From Portia, at an elevation of 650 metres, the TCT climbs another 450 metres on the Coquihalla Summit Trail to Coquihalla Lakes Lodge. Part pipeline road, part railway bed, this section of the TCT is also part human history, part natural history. Derelict trestles have tumbled into ravines, collapsed tunnels have become impassable, and constructed stone walls still hold the railbed tight against the cliffs. Five kilometres before Coquihalla Lakes, the trail passes the falls of Fallslake Creek (Bridal Veil) as it runs between Needle Peak on the west and Coquihalla Mountain on the east. The scenery's great, the history is visible, and the route is a welcome reprieve from the traffic on Highway 5.

THE TRANS CANADA TRAIL

Place names with asterisks are included in the **Communities, Parks, and Places to Stay** section (page 157).

Km 0   *Hope*, Hudson Bay Street + Water Avenue* From the Hope Visitor Centre, the TCT takes Hudson Bay east for 200 metres to Fraser Avenue. Turn left (north) and go two blocks to Wallace Street, then right (east) for four blocks and again right (south) on Sixth Avenue.

KM 0 TO KM 22.7

8

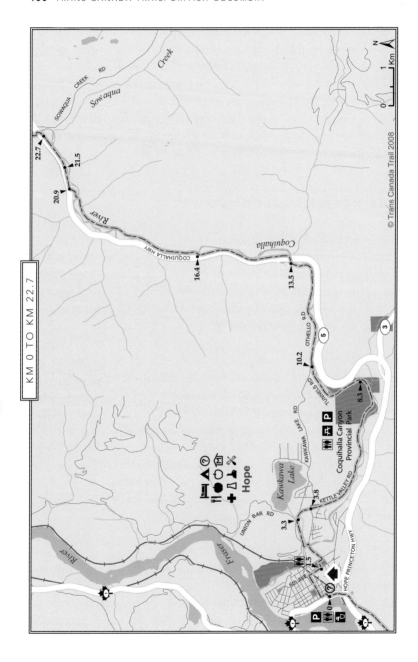

© Trans Canada Trail 2008

Km 1.5   *The Hope and District Recreation Complex* Turn left into the rec centre parking lot and follow the TCT signs through a park that is behind. Where the road meets Seventh Avenue and Kawkawa Lake Road, turn left (east) on Kawkawa Lake Road, and go 600 metres and over a wooden bridge across the Coquihalla River. Turn left on Union Bar Road (Km 2.4), and go around a corner to the right and into a small parking lot at a trailhead. (An outhouse is located here.) Take the trail.

Km 3.3   *Fence* Lift bikes over a chest-high fence. Walkers can squeeze through an opening.

Km 3.8   *Kawkawa Lake Road + Kettle Valley Road* Cross Kawkawa Lake Road and travel 300 metres southeast to a gate at the end of Kettle Valley Road. Continue straight on a rail trail.

Km 8.3   *Coquihalla Canyon* First of four Quintette tunnels in Coquihalla Canyon Provincial Park*.

Km 8.9   *Last Quintette tunnel* Follow the trail through the parking lot and up Tunnels Road to Othello Road (Km 10.2) and continue straight (east) on Othello Road.

Km 13.5   TCT *marker/fork* Turn right, then right again after 200 metres onto a road paralleling Highway 5.

Km 16.4   TCT *marker* Near an aerial cable car, move onto the shoulder of Highway 5 and continue north.

Km 20.9   TCT *marker* A TCT sign points to a dirt road between Coquihalla River and the highway, but a concrete barrier blocks access to the TCT. Either lift bikes over the barrier to get onto the trail, or stay on Highway 5 for about 200 metres to the end of the barrier, where the trail is easily accessed.

Km 21.5   TCT *marker (visible from the highway)/Jessica Trail* GPS north 49.26.456, west 121.17.031 ⛰ 233 metres. If the trail is overgrown, stay on the highway and access the Jessica Trail farther up the road.

Km 22.7   *Jessica Trail* GPS north 49.26.764, west 121.16.303 ⛰ 258 metres. If following the highway, watch for a dirt road off the highway that leads back to the Jessica Trail. Go right onto the trail, which goes under the highway at Sowaqua Creek, then crosses a dirt road to a steep, TCT–marked trail for 350 metres up to the Kettle Valley Railway grade.

Km 25.1   TCT *markers and gates* The TCT is well marked as it takes a wooded trail that passes some private cabins. Stay on the trail.

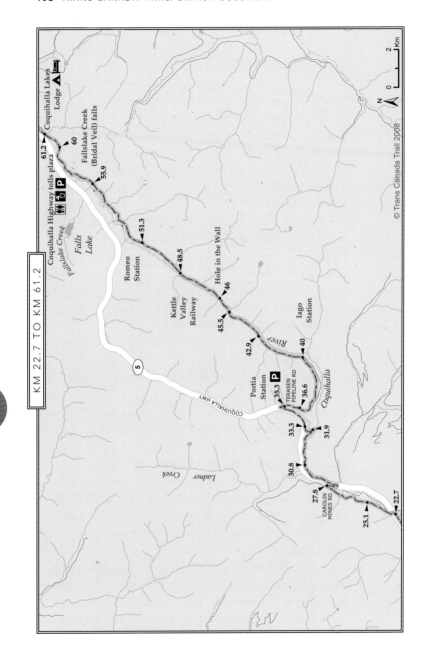

KM 22.7 TO KM 61.2

8

Derelict snow shed beyond Iago Station

Go under the gate and continue straight for 2.5 kilometres to another gate.

Km 27.8   *Carolin Mines Road* Go right, down a frighteningly steep road of loose rock for 500 metres to Highway 5. A TCT marker directs travellers to the right, under the highway, to a service road that runs along the east side of the highway.

Km 30.8   *Ladner Creek Bridge* The trail crosses Ladner Creek on a Bailey bridge. (For a side trip, watch for a road going under the highway; it leads to a trail that goes to an old KVR trestle.)

Km 31.9   *TCT marker/fork* Take the left fork on the main road.

Km 33.3   *TCT marker/fork* The gravel ends; a paved road goes up to the left, but a TCT marker points down a trail on the right, which leads to Portia. If the trail surface is soft, cyclists might prefer to ride the highway shoulder to the Portia Exit #202.

Km 35.3   *Portia Station, Terasen Pipelines road gate* Go past the gate and take the road toward Coquihalla Lakes.

Km 36.6   *Pipeline road joins the KVR* Go straight on the railway through the woods.

Km 40   *KVR + pipeline road* Go left onto the pipeline road.

Km 42.9   *TCT sign/Iago Station* Old concrete foundations.

Km 45.5   *Tunnel* A derelict snow shed stands beside the TCT.

Km 46   *"Hole in the Wall"* A stream flows through a natural tunnel under a bridge that the TCT crosses. (About 20 metres past the bridge, volunteers have restored 2.7 kilometres of the original rail grade as a walking trail, which makes a nice side trip off the TCT. Along with a few switchbacks and rough spots are great views,

Creek crossing beyond Bridal Veil Falls

collapsed snow sheds, and remnants of the Kettle Valley Railway. A shorter hike from the TCT from Km 48.5, at the other end of this walking trail, also leads to good views. Just before crossing a bridge at the confluence of Needle Creek and the Coquihalla River, watch for signs leading from the TCT up an old rock-haul road.)

Km 48.5   *Rock-haul road/walking trail* (A left turn off the TCT takes the side trip up to the rail grade/walking trail.) TCT travellers continue straight on the main trail.

Km 51.3   *TCT sign/Romeo Station* Little evidence of this former KVR station.

Km 55.9   *The falls of Fallslake Creek (Bridal Veil)* KVR remnants.

Km 60   *Gate* Lift bikes over the gate and continue straight. (About 300 metres farther along the TCT, the Coquihalla Highway toll plaza can be reached by making a sharp left turn up a steep access road. Cyclists and hikers don't pay.)

Km 61.2   *Coquihalla Lakes Lodge** The TCT continues north following much of the Kettle Valley Railway trail.

Bridal Veil Falls cascade near KVR remnants

RAILWAY NOW A TOURIST ATTRACTION

The Quintette tunnels, just over eight kilometres outside Hope at Coqui-halla Canyon Provincial Park, are an engineering marvel. They rivalled the famous trestles of the Okanagan's Myra Canyon as a near-impossible chal-lenge to 20th-century railway builders. Sheer walls of granite more than 90 metres high tower over the seething river as it swishes through a narrow horseshoe-shaped gorge. Though only 500 meters long, the treacherous gorge taxed the engineering creativity of Andrew McCulloch to the limit.

McCulloch, chief engineer for the construction of the Kettle Valley Railway, spent weeks in the canyon dangling from a woven basket sus-pended by ropes from the clifftops. Shouting over the incessant roar of the river, he and other engineers cut small ledges into the rock walls to set up surveying equipment. Contrary to the opinions of other railway build-ers, McCulloch determined that four tunnels and two bridges could bring the tracks through the gorge in a straight line. By the summer of 1916 the KVR's Coquihalla line was complete, and trains were steaming through the Quintette tunnels.

Quintette tunnels at Coquihalla Canyon

The 60-kilometre stretch of railway from Hope to the Coquihalla summit reportedly cost an average of $136,000 per mile, about five times the going rate for railway construction at the time. A single mile near the summit cost $300,000, purported to be the most expensive mile of railway track in the world. Included in the Coquihalla line's extraordinary costs were 43 bridges, 13 tunnels, and 16 snowsheds.

"Quintette" is actually a misnomer as there are four, not five, tunnels, but daylight in the third gives the illusion of an additional tunnel. Hikers or cyclists on this leg of the Trans Canada Trail travel through the tunnels and readily see why dramatic scenes from movies such as *Rambo: First Blood* were filmed here.

The railway stopped running here in 1959. The tunnels, now within the 150-hectare Coquihalla Canyon Provincial Park, are protected. An interesting, moderately hilly 18.5-kilometre route to the park combines paved back roads with the TCT. Take the TCT from Hope to the junction of Kawkawa Lake and Kettle Valley roads. Rather than take the TCT down Kettle Valley Road, continue east on Kawkawa Lake Road to Othello Road. Turn right onto Othello and go nearly five kilometres to Tunnels Road. Turn right and travel one kilometre to the park. Return to Hope via the TCT.

VANCOUVER, COAST & MOUNTAINS REGION

Tourism region encompassing the Lower Mainland and southern Coast Mountains from Vancouver to the east beyond Hope, nearly to Princeton. For detailed information, see page 91 in Chapter 4.

COMMUNITIES, PARKS, AND PLACES TO STAY

Information on each provincial park in BC can be found on the BC Parks website at www.env.gov.bc.ca/bcparks/.

🌲 Hope (Km 0)

See page 144 in the previous chapter.

🌲 Coquihalla Canyon Provincial Park (Km 9.4)

A line of tunnels between the granite walls of a deep gorge. ⛺ 🚻 *outhouses*
› **Size** 159 hectares
› **Attractions** The park protects the Quintette tunnels.

🛏 ⛺ Coquihalla Lakes Lodge (Km 61.2)

Cabins and campsites on 3.2 wooded hectares near the lakes with the TCT at the front door. Box 817, Merritt, BC V1K 1B8; 1-877-978-2096; www.coquihallalakeslodge.com.

> "Population: Varies . . . Industry: None . . . Chief Sports: Sleeping and Day Dreaming . . . All clubs and lodges hold their meetings at midnight on the sixth Tuesday of each month.
> —*Sign at the village of Coalmont*

Reminders of the Kettle Valley Railway at Brookmere

TRAIL TRIVIA

TCT travellers should keep an eye out for the sasquatch or bigfoot. There have been more than 360 sasquatch-related reports in BC.

TOTAL DISTANCE

91.5 km

HIGHLIGHTS

› Otter Lake Provincial Park
› Tulameen and Coalmont
› Red cliffs along the Tulameen River

CONDITIONS

› **Coquihalla Lakes (Km 0) to Brodie Station (Km 24)** Mainly flat but rugged, with rough trails around two washouts. Cyclists loaded with gear may prefer Highway 5. → 24 km
› **Brodie Station (Km 24) to missing trestle ten kilometres southeast of Brookmere (Km 39.1)** Depending on recent use and maintenance, the railway bed may consist of loose gravel for nearly seven kilometres to Brookmere, followed by washboard for ten kilometres, then a steep, narrow bypass trail around a missing trestle. → 15.1 km
› **Missing trestle (Km 39.1) to Princeton (Km 91.5)** Generally good double-track railbed, sometimes rocky or sandy. → 52.4 km

CAUTIONS

› The second of two washouts (Km 15.9) perhaps too rough for cyclists. Take Highway 5 instead.
› Parr Tunnel is dark—travel with a flashlight or headlamp.
› Bears.

TOPOGRAPHIC MAPS

1:250,000	Hope 92H
1:50,000	Princeton 92H/7, Tulameen 92H/10, Spuzzum 92H/11, Boston Bar 92H/14, Aspen Grove 92H/15

OVERVIEW

Like the TCT from Hope up the Coquihalla Valley, this route is comprised of industrial roads, railway beds, and trails. It weaves back and forth across Highway 5 as it follows the Coldwater River north to the KVR's Brodie

Station, and then veers east to Brookmere, a divisional point between two Kettle Valley Railway subdivisions. (There are six in total in BC.) The Merritt subdivision heads north, while the Princeton subdivision, which the TCT takes, heads east through the Okanagan region.

Brookmere is also the dividing point between Trails BC's Southwest and Okanagan regions. The community's old water tower and CPR caboose are reminders of this region's railroad history. Most of the TCT from here east to Castlegar, more than 550 kilometres along the trail, is uninterrupted railway corridor that's usually easy to follow. Horses that are not trestle-shy can travel on this corridor.

Here the TCT crosses a climatic divide, between the wet and rocky coastal ranges of the southwest and the more subdued terrain and drier weather of the Interior. While cities like Vancouver, on the rainy, western side, may get more than 100 centimetres of precipitation a year, the Okanagan, in the rain shadow of the coastal mountains, may get only 30. Variations in temperature, too, are just as wide: summer days near the coast may linger in the mid 20s (Celsius) while the southern Interior could swelter in the mid 30s.

The climatic differences are notable in the vegetation as coastal forests of hemlock, cedar, and fir with dense understories give way to pine trees, prickly pear cactus, and open grasslands. Reclusive scorpions and rattlesnakes live in this arid habitat, but coyotes and yellow-bellied marmots are better bets for wildlife watchers.

LOCAL ADVENTURES
Day Trip
› Hike from Brodie Station (Km 24) to Brookmere (Km 29.2) and back. ⇆ 10.4 km
› From Otter Lake Provincial Park (Km 65.2) near Tulameen, hike or cycle to Coalmont (Km 72.5) and back. ⇆ 14.6 km
› From Princeton (Km 91.5), cycle to Coalmont (Km 72.5) or to Tulameen (Km 65.9) and back via the TCT and Coalmont Road. ↻ 38 km to Coalmont, ↻ 51 km to Tulameen

5 or 6 Days
› Cycle a 460 km road-and-rail loop through Douglas Lake Ranch (see page 168).

TCT ACCESS POINTS

Britton Creek rest area (Km 1.4) From the Coquihalla toll plaza on Highway 5, 55 kilometres northeast of Hope, go 2.7 kilometres and take Exit #228. At a junction about 300 metres from the highway, go straight for 200 metres into the rest area. A right (south) turn at this junction goes to Coquihalla Lakes Lodge. 🅿 🚻 🔋 🏕

Brodie Station (Km 24) From the Coquihalla toll plaza go about 27 kilometres and take Exit #250 at Larson Hill. Head south along the east side of the highway down to a bridge near the KVR's Brodie Station. 🅿

Brookmere (Km 29.2) Take Exit #258 off Highway 5 and follow Coldwater Road to Brookmere. 🅿 *trailside parking*

Tulameen (Km 65.9) Take Coalmont Road west from Princeton for 25 kilometres. 🅿 *street parking* 🛏 ⭕ | *small-town services*

Coalmont (Km 72.5) Take Coalmont Road west from Princeton for 18 kilometres. The Coalmont Hotel may provide the town's only services. 🅿 *trailside parking*

Princeton (Km 91.5) Community of 3,000 at the junction of Coalmont Road and Highways 3 and 5A. 🅿 *parking near the TCT at a number of points in town*

THE RAILWAY THROUGH THE OKANAGAN

INTO THE RAIN SHADOW

Trail builders here have been relentless in their quest to secure an off-road route: parts of the abandoned Kettle Valley Railway corridor have been resurrected, industrial roads have been utilized, new bridges and trails have been constructed. In the Princeton area, snowmobilers, dirt bikers, and ATVers help build and maintain trails; expect to meet them on the TCT.

The TCT from Brodie Station to Brookmere and beyond is proof that flat terrain doesn't necessarily guarantee easy travel. Depending on recent use and maintenance, the railway surface might be sandy or rough, with stretches of washboard that can rattle the sunglasses off a cyclist's face.

There's hardly a blemish on the landscape. This is farming and ranching territory. Much of the land on either side of the TCT is private; there are cattle guards, and livestock gates that must be kept closed. Old log barns and cabins, railway remnants and ranches, marmots and loons are part of the scene as the trail follows Otter Creek and the Tulameen and Similkameen rivers. It passes warm swimming lakes and the historic towns of Tulameen and Coalmont. It may get hot on the leeward side of the coastal ranges, but there are plenty of lakes and streams to rinse off the trail dust.

THE TRANS CANADA TRAIL

Place names with asterisks are included in the **Communities, Parks, and Places to Stay** section (page 169).

Km 0   *Coquihalla Lakes Lodge** On the road/TCT at the lodge entrance, head north.

Km 1.4   *Britton Creek Rest Area* The Trans Canada Trail continues straight. A right turn here leads 200 metres to Britton Creek rest area, where there are restrooms, parking, drinking water, picnic tables, and a kiosk with details on local trails (including the TCT).

Km 2.2   *Exit #228* Turn left to Highway 5 where the TCT takes an overpass over the highway to connect to the old Kettle Valley Railway bed. Cross the bridge over the Coldwater River and go under the dual Highway 5 bridges, which also cross the Coldwater. Turn left and go about 70 metres onto the rail trail.

Km 5.7   *Exit #231, Mine Creek Road* Near this highway exit, continue on the TCT between the highway and Coldwater River and cross Mine Creek (Km 6.3). Continue on the trail. Where the Coldwater River runs close to the highway, the trail is narrow; cyclists may have to walk a short distance.

Km 13   *Exit #240* Four hundred metres south of Juliet Station the TCT goes under Highway 5 to the west side. Cyclists can get on the highway here to avoid two washouts farther up the trail. Hikers can get around the washouts, but the second is tough for cyclists.

Km 13.5   *High fence* Access through a self-closing gate.

Km 15.1   *Washout* A marked trail (which requires repair after each winter) bypasses the washout.

Km 15.9   *Washout* A temporary trail, rebuilt after each winter, goes

KM 0 TO KM 59.8

Brookmere

29.2

24
Brodie
Station
23.2

COQUIHALLA HWY

THYNNE MTN FSR

39
39.9
38.7

15.9
15.1

13

Coldwater River
Provincial Park

River

Kettle
Valley
Railway

Coldwater

VALLEY RD

5.7

Thynne
Lake
50.5
51.8

5

2.2

TULAMEEN-OTTER

1.4

0

9

Frembd
Lake
57

59.8

Otter Lake
Provincial Park

N
0   2
Km   © Trans Canada Trail 2008

Otter
Lake

through this washout. It is steep, sandy, and difficult for touring cyclists, who may have to unload bikes and make two trips. Watch for material sliding down from above. At low water it's possible to go down to the river and scramble along the riverbank for about 150 metres, then get back on the rail trail on the downstream side of the washout.

Km 23.2 *Highway 5 crossing* The TCT goes under the highway to the east side and continues to Brodie Station.

Km 24 *Brodie Station* Cross the bridge and follow the rail trail as it heads east toward Brookmere. Beware of soft, loose rock in the centre of the trail.

Km 29.2 *Brookmere** A sleepy community with minimal facilities and one of the last, if not *the* last, wooden water towers on the Kettle Valley Railway. Also beside the trail stands a CPR caboose. Depending on recent maintenance, this part of the TCT could be the start of ten kilometres of washboard where the trail is shared with vehicles.

Km 38.7 *Fork* Veer left on the railway bed.

Km 39 *Landslide, outhouse* Walk around the landslide. Just past the outhouse, take a trail down to the right. It bypasses a missing trestle. Cross the road and a footbridge, then climb back up to the rail grade. Check for marmots lurking in the broken trestle timbers.

Km 39.9 TCT *marker/Otter Valley* Scenic farmland. Look for log barns at Km 44.1 and by Thynne Lake at Km 50.5.

Km 51.8 *Otter Creek Bridge* Continue across the bridge.

Km 57 *Frembd Lake* Watch for loons.

Km 59.8 *Otter Lake* Good swimming and fishing.

Km 65.2 *Trestle and Otter Lake Provincial Park** The park has a shady picnic site and sandy beach. (The park campground across the lake can be reached by road from Tulameen. Head north up the western shore for 5.5 kilometres.)

Otter Lake Trestle near Tulameen

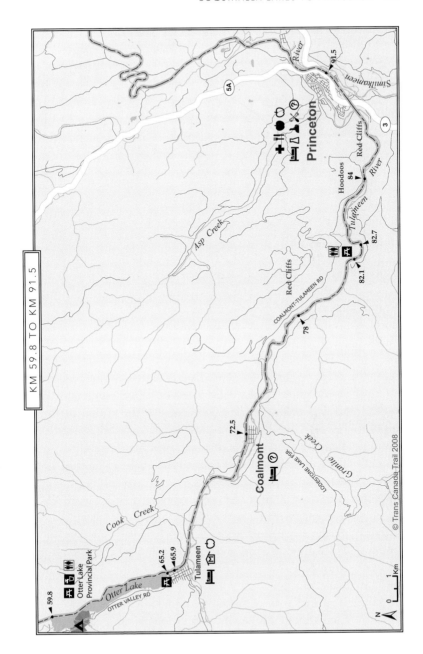

KM 59.8 TO KM 91.5

Princeton

91.5

Similkameen

3

Red-Cliffs

84 Hoodoos

Tulameen River

82.7

82.1

Red Cliffs

COALMONT-TULAMEEN RD

78

Asp Creek

72.5

Coalmont

Granite Creek

LODSTONE LAKE FSR

Cook Creek

65.2

65.9

Tulameen

Otter Lake

OTTER VALLEY RD

59.8

Otter Lake
Provincial Park

© Trans Canada Trail 2008

9

N

0   1
Km

5A

Red cliffs above Tulameen River

Km 65.9	*Tulameen** Idyllic lakeside village. On the way out of town, watch for the famous "Shoe Tree" beside the Tulameen River.
Km 72.5	*Coalmont** See the next page for more on this town.
Km 78	*Red cliffs* "Tulameen" is a native word for "red earth." Rocks along the Tulameen River were a source of ochre.
Km 82.1	*Outhouse/picnic table* Dilapidated but usable facilities just beyond a walkable landslide.
Km 82.7	*Parr Tunnel* Curved, 147-metre tunnel that is too long to see both ends at once. Travel with a flashlight or headlamp. A gazebo 100 metres beyond the tunnel overlooks the river.
Km 84	*Hoodoos* Natural rock spires sculpted by wind and rain.
Km 86.4	*Red cliffs*
Km 87.9	*More red cliffs*
Km 91.5	*Princeton** Town at the confluence of the Tulameen and Similkameen rivers on the southern end of the Thompson Plateau. (The TCT goes through Princeton and continues east on the Kettle Valley Railway trail.)

HISTORIC COALMONT A TRAIL RIDER'S MECCA

TCT travellers who roll into Coalmont (Km 72.5) are given fair warning: "To all doorstep salesmen—especially those selling magazines, encyclopedias, and fire-bells—your safe passage is not guaranteed in this village," announces a sign at the town's entrance. "Women beware! There is a predomenance [*sic*] of bachelors living here."

Really, there's not much human "predomenance" at all. If there's any action, it's over at the pub in the Coalmont Hotel, circa 1911, at last check the only surviving business.

Seems a ghostly demise for a town that was founded upon the "largest body of coal yet discovered in North America," according to the Coalmont *Courier*. Through the early 1900s coal was taken from Blakeburn, high on a mountain above Coalmont. The grades were so steep that an aerial tram was built in 1921 to bring the coal down to the railway. The Blakeburn mine became one of BC's biggest producers, shipping more than 160,000 tonnes a year. But an explosion in 1930 claimed the lives of 45 workers: it was the beginning of the end for Coalmont. A decade later the mine shut down.

Coalmont today calls itself the "Snowmachine Capital of Canada," with the TCT and literally hundreds of kilometres of other trails the main attractions. While motorized use of the Kettle Valley Railway and Trans Canada Trail is discouraged, in this part of BC the trails are maintained and used largely by snowmobilers, ATVers, and motorcyclists.

VANCOUVER, COAST & MOUNTAINS REGION

Tourism region encompassing the Lower Mainland and southern Coast Mountains from Vancouver to the east beyond Hope, nearly to Princeton. For detailed information, see page 91 in Chapter 4.

THOMPSON OKANAGAN REGION

Tourism region at the southern end of the Thompson Plateau, north and east of the Cascade Mountains, west of the Monashees, with the Okanagan Highland between.

› **Visitor Info** *Thompson Okanagan Tourism Association* 2280-D Leckie Road, Kelowna, BC V1X 6G6; 1-800-567-2275/250-860-5999; www.totabc .com/rg/.

› **TCT Info** *Trails BC (Okanagan region)* Look up "Okanagan" under "BC Regions" on the Trails BC website at www.trailsbc.ca.

LOCAL ADVENTURE

DOUGLAS LAKE LOOP
AMONG BC'S MOST SCENIC ROUTES ↻ 460 KM

Canada's largest ranch, encompassing more than 2,000 square kilometres of grasslands in British Columbia's southern Interior, is the highlight of a 460-kilometre loop combining highways, back roads, and the Trans Canada Trail. This is arguably one of the most scenic backcountry bicycle tours in a province renowned for its "super, natural" scenery. Cyclists see ospreys snatching fish from roadside lakes, sometimes dropping them on the road. Deer wander the fields, and the skies are alive with turkey vultures, hawks, and a plethora of other birds.

Douglas Lake Road

Douglas and other small lakes are surrounded by hills of velvet-brown grass rolling up from the shores. A small community, including a school, is located on the ranch. Douglas Lake Cattle Company, incorporated in 1886, is BC's fifth-oldest company. The ranch runs 20,000 head of cattle, and is involved in timber harvesting, sales of ranch equipment, and tourism.

Directions. A good starting point is Merritt, about 40 kilometres north of the TCT at Brookmere (Km 29.2). Take Coldwater Road, a paved back road, south from Merritt to Brookmere, and head east on the TCT/Kettle Valley Railway for 163 kilometres to Summerland, on Okanagan Lake. From there the route follows the western lakeshore north for just over 100 kilometres (on Highway 97 and then on Westside Road). Just beyond the north end of the lake, reconnect to Highway 97 and go west for 48 kilometres to Douglas Lake Road (1.5 kilometres west of Westwold), a well-maintained, lightly travelled gravel road running 80 kilometres to Nicola Lake. A final 28 kilometres southwest on Highway 5A completes the loop to Merritt.

› **Transportation**
Land Greyhound Canada (1-800-661-8747; www.greyhound.ca) stops in the South Okanagan at Princeton, Keremeos, Summerland, Kelowna, Westbank, Penticton, Okanagan Falls, Oliver, and Osoyoos.
Air Westjet Airlines (1-888-937-8538; www.westjet.com) has scheduled flights to Kelowna, 44 kilometres north of Summerland via Highway 97.

Air Canada (1-888-247-2262; www.aircanada.com) serves Kelowna and Penticton.
› **Emergency** Call 911.

COMMUNITIES, PARKS, AND PLACES TO STAY

Information on each provincial park in BC can be found on the BC Parks website at www.env.gov.bc.ca/bcparks/.

⊨ ▲ Coquihalla Lakes Lodge (Km 0)

See page 157 in the previous chapter.

♣ Brookmere (Km 29.2)

Quiet hamlet known for its trailside caboose and water tower. *Few amenities, though new real estate development may soon bring a store, accommodation, and other services*
› **Accommodation** *Marshall Springs Resort & Spa* was under development with expectations of offering accommodation and other amenities in 2008. Check www.marshallsprings.com.

♣♣ Otter Lake Provincial Park (Km 65.2)

A two-part park with a picnic area and beach on the TCT at the south end of the lake and a campground on the northwest side. ⛱ ▲ ♿ *outhouses* 🚽
› **Size** 51 hectares
› **Attractions** BC Parks describes Otter Lake as "ideal for old-fashioned camping." Fishing for lake trout is good, and the campground makes a good base to explore nearby Tulameen and Coalmont. Beavers, red squirrels, mountain goats, cougars, and grizzly bears live in the area.
› **Camping** 45 sites. The park campground is across the lake from the TCT. Head north from Tulameen up the western shore for 5.5 kilometres. *Reservations* 1-800-689-9025 (or 604-689-9025 in Metro Vancouver). www.discovercamping.ca

♣ Tulameen (Km 65.9)

Small town on the edge of the Tulameen River and Otter Lake. ⑦ ♻ *general store—the Tulameen Trading Post* ⊨ *| laundromat and pay showers at Otter Sleep Inn*
› **Population** 250
› **Visitor Info** www.tulameenbc.com

> **Attractions** Museum in a log cabin near the general store.
> **Cycling** *Backroads Bike Shop* Fifth and Nicola; 250-295-3735; www .cyclelogicpress.com/backroads. html. *Tulameen Adventure Tours* Offers shuttle services on the TCT in southern BC; 250-295-6681; www.tulameentours.com.
> **Accommodation** *Otter Sleep Inn* 1-866-467-0202; www.ottersleep inn.netfirms.com. See also www .tulameenbc.com.

Tulameen shoe tree

♣ Coalmont (Km 72.5)

Once a busy coal town, now a snoozy backwater in attractive surroundings. (See page 167.)
visitor info on the TCT and other trails, as well as outdoor activities, may be available at Coalmont Hotel

> **Accommodation** *Coalmont Hotel*, in the heart of downtown Coalmont. 1853 Main St, Coalmont, BC V0X 1G0; 250-295-6066. Pub located in hotel.

♣ Princeton (Km 91.5)

At the junctions of the Tulameen and Similkameen rivers and of Highways 3 and 5A. ⑦ 🛏 ▲ ● 🛆 ✂ | *most services*

> **Population** 3,000
> **Visitor Info** The *Princeton Visitor Centre* is located on the left side of Highway 3 over the blue bridge just east of Bridge Street. 105 Highway 3 East, Box 540, Princeton, BC V0X 1W0; 250-295-3103; www.princetonbc.info.
> **Attractions** Princeton and District Pioneer Museum
> **Cycling** *Backroads Bike Shop* 308 Bridge Street; 250-295-3722; www.cycle logicpress.com/backroads.html.
> **Greyhound Bus** (1-800-661-8747; www.greyhound.ca) Depot located at *Argee Enterprises* at 301 Vermillion Avenue.
> **Accommodation/Camping** *Princeton Castle Resort* (Chapter 10 Km 3.7) is a full-service resort, providing a lodge, cabins, and RV and tent sites. 1-888-228-8881; www.castleresort.com.

10 PRINCETON TO SUMMERLAND

> 66 Beats walkin'.
> —Ten-year-old Luke Mulcahy
> from Kamloops, halfway through
> a 600-kilometre bicycle trip
> with his family

Osprey Lake on the KVR rail trail

TRAIL TRIVIA

The Okanagan, with 200 roadside fruit stands, is one of Canada's three major tree-fruit regions.

TOTAL DISTANCE

105.4 km

HIGHLIGHTS

› Kettle Valley Steam Railway
› Summerland's lakeshore and theme shops

CONDITIONS

› **Princeton (Km 0) to Erris Tunnel (Km 25.5)** Double-track railbed in good condition; easy and scenic. → 25.5 km
› **Erris Tunnel (Km 25.5) to Bankeir (Km 47.1)** Slow-going on soft, bumpy rail trail surface through bush. → 21.6 km
› **Bankeir (Km 47.1) to Discovery Panel on beaver (Km 81.4)** Rail grade improves. Mainly hard-packed surface with some soft stretches. → 34.3 km
› **Discover Panel (Km 81.4) to Faulder (Km 88.3)** Soft and sandy—cycling is difficult. → 6.9 km
› **Faulder (Km 88.3) to Summerland (Km 105.4)** The trail surface is good for just over two kilometres, then becomes soft with potholes and occasional good stretches. → 17.1 km

CAUTIONS

› Rattlesnakes—watch your step and stay on the trail, which snakes tend to avoid.

10

TOPOGRAPHIC MAPS

| 1:250,000 | Penticton 82E, Hope 92H |
| 1:50,000 | Summerland 82E/12, Princeton 92H/7, Hedley 92H/8, Bankeir 92H/9 |

OVERVIEW

Princeton sits at the confluence of the Tulameen and Similkameen rivers, both tributaries of the Columbia River system. These waterways, with the Okanagan River to the east, dissect the southern end of the Thompson

Plateau, a gently rolling upland at elevations of 1,200 to 1,500 metres. This is a transition zone between the jagged Cascade Mountains to the west and the rounded ridges and open slopes of the Okanagan Highland to the east.

Not far outside Princeton the landscape takes on that distinct Okanagan look. Smooth hills baked gold by the sun roll away from the TCT in all directions. Groves of giant ponderosa pines, their cinnamon-coloured bark brightened by sunlight, offer shade for deer that rest in the grass. Alkali ponds are fringed by salty white crusts. Magpies flash their long tails as they hunt for bugs and carrion, violet-green swallows sweep the air for insects, red-tailed hawks call overhead, and killdeer feign broken wings to distract humans and predators away from their nests. Yellow-bellied marmots like to sun themselves on old trestle timbers, and coyotes occasionally dash across the trail.

Four small trailside lakes beckon hot and dusty travellers as the TCT climbs Hayes Creek Valley toward Osprey Lake, then runs downstream with Trout Creek to Summerland on the west side of Okanagan Lake. At the Prairie Valley train station west of Summerland, TCT travellers encounter the Kettle Valley Steam Railway, which runs on a short stretch of active KVR track. (For more on the railway, see page 181.)

Downtown Summerland, with its Old English theme shops, overlooks Okanagan Lake. Among the town's most prominent natural features is Giants Head, an 841-metre mountain in the midst of lush green vineyards and orchards. Summerland's lakeshore is nicely developed with parks and beaches, walkways, and piers. (There are plenty of restrooms and picnic areas.)

LOCAL ADVENTURES
Day Trip
› From Princeton (Km 0) explore the TCT in either direction by foot or bicycle.
› At Summerland (Km 105.4) walk the beaches, browse the Old English shops, and ride the Kettle Valley Steam Railway.

3 or 4 Days
› Cycle a 235 km loop on the TCT from Princeton (Km 0) to Summerland (Km 105.4), returning via Highways 97, 3A, and 3, and Old Hedley Road.

10

TCT ACCESS POINTS

Princeton (Km 0) Community of 3,000. Coalmont Road/Tulameen Avenue and Highways 3 and 5A all go to Princeton. **P** *parking near the* TCT *at a number of points in town*

Faulder (Km 88.3) On Princeton–Summerland Road approximately 12 kilometres west of Summerland. **P** *limited roadside parking where Kettle Place comes off the* TCT *to meet Princeton–Summerland Road*

Prairie Valley Station TCT kiosk (Km 93.7) Located behind the Kettle Valley Steam Railway station. From Highway 97 at Summerland take Prairie Valley Road for about five kilometres to Doherty Avenue. Turn right (north) on Doherty and then left (east) on Bathville Road, and continue about 1.4 kilometres to the kiosk. **P**

Summerland (Km 105.4) On Highway 97, 16 kilometres north of Penticton. **P** *Roadside parking near the* TCT. *Inquire about multi-day parking at the visitor centre on Highway 97.*

MORE RAIL TRAILS AND BACK ROADS

ACCESS TO ADVENTURE

Like bookends on opposite sides of the Thompson Plateau, Princeton and Summerland are somewhat of a matched pair. The rounded brown hills and the sagebrush and ponderosa pines that surround both communities are hallmarks of the Okanagan landscape. Both were former Kettle Valley Railway stations, and both are service centres and takeoff points for hikers, cyclists, anglers, birders, and other outdoor recreationists. Summerland, the larger of the two, is the TCT's gateway to Okanagan Lake, Interior BC's long-established family-holiday spot.

These bookends are joined by both the TCT/KVR run) and Princeton–Summerland Road, backcountry alternatives to Highways 3, 3A, and 97. The western half of the 92-kilometre Princeton–Summerland Road is paved; the eastern end is winding and often washboarded. Quality of this road as well as the trail varies with seasons, use, and maintenance. The road and TCT run side by side for much of this route, occasionally crossing paths. On the outskirts of Summerland the TCT takes paved roads. Equestrians can take the TCT all the way from Princeton.

10

THE TRANS CANADA TRAIL

Place names with asterisks are included in the **Communities, Parks, and Places to Stay** section (page 182).

Km 0   *Princeton*, TCT trailhead* From the wooden arches marking
         Princeton's TCT trailhead, turn right on Highway 3 and go
         400 metres to Bridge Street. Turn left by the Petro-Canada
         station, following signs to Highway 5A to Merritt, Kamloops,
         and the town centre. Take the first right onto Tapton Avenue
         (Hwy 5A) and follow signs to Merritt and Tulameen.

Km 1.1   *Bridge* Cross a bridge over the Tulameen River and about
         50 metres past the bridge turn right onto the TCT/Kettle
         Valley Railway.

Km 3.7   *Access to Princeton Castle Resort** A full-service resort; accom-
         modation and camping.

Km 14.1 *Trailside pond* Good birding.

Km 17.5 *Gazebo* Good birding, shelter from sun or rain. (Outhouse.)

Km 25.5 *Erris Tunnel* More than 90 metres long.

Km 32.8 *Spukunne Creek*

Km 35.5 *Princeton–Summerland Road* (You
         can access this road by going right.)

Km 41.2 *Chain Lake BC forest service
         campground* (A right turn onto
         a short road leads down to lakeside
         camping. Also note that you can
         access Princeton–Summerland
         Road from this point of the trail.)
         The TCT continues
         on the railroad bed.

Erris Tunnel on the KVR rail trail

Km 47.1 *Community of Bankeir, Princeton–
         Summerland Road* The TCT/KVR
         crosses Princeton–Summerland
         Road. From here this road follows
         the north side of Osprey Lake, but
         the TCT takes the south shore.
         (3 Lakes General Store at Bankeir, 300 metres ahead, is reach-
         able by both the road and trail. To get to the campground on
         Osprey Lake, stay on the road.) The TCT stays on the railway.

Km 49   *Link Lake forest service campground* (Access to lakeside
         BC camping.)

KM 0 TO KM 88.3

© Trans Canada Trail 2008

Faulder

88.3

Darke Creek

Darke Lake
Provincial Park

75.3
76.4

81.4

74.1
76.2

PRINCETON-SUMMERLAND RD

68.8

Trout Creek

60.7

59.9

Thirsk
Lake

54.9

54.1
52.6

Osprey
Lake

50.7

Link
Lake

49

47.1

Bankeir

41.2

35.5

Spukunne Creek

PRINCETON-SUMMERLAND RD

32.8

Kettle
Valley
Railway

25.5
Erris
Tunnel

17.5

14.1

Princeton
Castle Resort

3.7

3

5A

Princeton

River

Tulameen River

Similkameen

Princeton

VERMILION AVE. ST. BRIDGE

1.1

0

3

5A

10

Km 50.7 *Osprey Lake* Continue east on the railbed.

Km 52.6 TCT + *Princeton–Summerland Road* The TCT/railway bed and the road meet again. Continue east on the TCT/KVR.

Km 54.1 *Trout Creek detour* The railway bridge is gone, so take the short road to the right, and then go left and cross the creek on Princeton–Summerland Road.

Km 54.9 *Returning to the rail trail* Go left off of Princeton–Summerland Road onto a 200-metre dirt road to the railway grade. About 2.5 kilometres along, the road and railway become the same route for 2.3 kilometres.

Km 59.9 *Thirsk Lake campground* The TCT runs off the road and up to the left on the railbed. (To reach the campground, stay on the road for about 150 metres beyond the marked TCT/KVR turnoff.)

Km 60.7 *Discovery Panel* Information on the great horned owl.

Km 68.8 *Discovery Panel* Information on the trembling aspen.

Km 74.1 *Trestle* A trestle that crosses Trout Creek.

Km 75.3 TCT/KVR + *Princeton–Summerland Road* The TCT crosses Princeton–Summerland Road. Continue on the railbed.

Km 76.2 *Trestle* Another trestle that crosses Trout Creek.

Km 76.4 *Discovery Panel* Information on the black bear.

Km 81.4 *Discovery Panel* Information on the beaver. The TCT crosses a back road here. There are pleasant views of Trout Creek on the south (right) side of the trail. The

KVR rail trail northwest of Faulder

trail becomes rough and soft for seven kilometres as it moves toward Faulder through canyonlike scenery.

Km 88.3 *Faulder* A cluster of homes and farms, with a local campground beside the TCT (the Kettle Valley Campground/ B&B*). Trail quality improves as it runs toward Prairie Valley Station.

Km 90.6   *Trail becomes soft* The surface of the TCT becomes soft
as it runs alongside some railway tracks.

Km 91.1   *Railway crossing* The TCT crosses railway tracks.

Km 91.2   *Railway crossing* The TCT crosses railway tracks again.

Km 92.3   *Discovery Panel* Information on the black-capped chickadee.
The trail surface becomes softer with potholes, making it
difficult for cyclists.

Km 93.2   *Irrigation flume* The TCT passes an irrigation flume
and goes around a gate.

Km 93.6   *Bathville Road, Prairie Valley Station* The TCT reaches Bathville
Road which leads to Prairie Valley Station (where a steam
train runs on a short stretch of KVR track). Turn right onto
the road and continue behind the station to a TCT kiosk that
shows the route to Summerland.

Km 93.7   *TCT kiosk* A sign shows the TCT route from Princeton
to Summerland.

Km 94.2   *Gate* The TCT passes through a gate where an irrigation
flume can be seen behind a chain-link fence.

Km 94.4   *Fork* The TCT continues straight (left fork).

Km 96.3   *Conkle Mountain Gazebo* Great views of farms, vineyards,
and Giants Head mountain.

Km 96.8   *Fork* The TCT goes down to the left.

View from Conkle Mountain Gazebo near Summerland

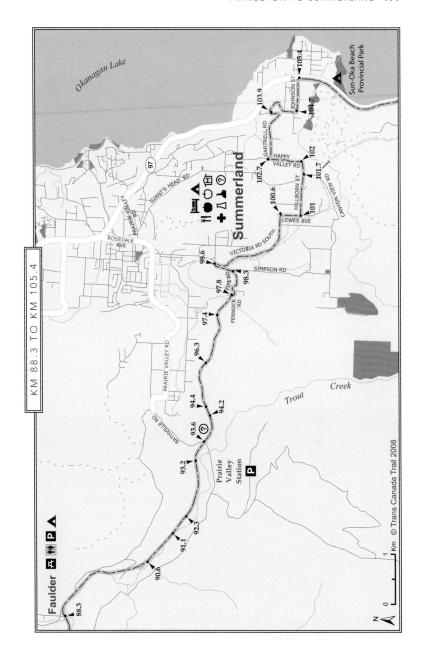

KM 88.3 TO KM 105.4

Okanagan Lake

Sun-Oka Beach
Provincial Park

105.4

JOHNSON ST

103.9

104.7

GARTRELL RD

102.7

HAPPY
VALLEY RD

102

HILLBORN ST

101.7

101

100.6

Summerland

CANYON VIEW RD

LEWES AVE

PRAIRIE VALLEY DR

GIANT'S HEAD RD

ROSEDALE
AVE

VICTORIA RD SOUTH

98.6

SIMPSON RD

98.3

97.8

FIFE RD

FENWICK RD

97.4

PRAIRIE VALLEY RD

96.3

94.4

94.2

BATHVILLE RD

93.6

93.2

Prairie
Valley
Station

Trout

Creek

Faulder

92.3

91.1

90.6

88.3

© Trans Canada Trail 2008

Km

N

0   1

10

Km 97.4   *Gate* The TCT passes
through a gate for a
short, rough, and steep
downhill stretch.

Km 97.7   *Fenwick Road* The trail
ends and the TCT fol-
lows roads through the
outskirts of Summer-
land, beginning with
Fenwick Road, down to
Highway 97.

Trout Creek Trestle near Summerland

Km 97.8   *Fenwick Road + Fyffe
Road* Turn right (east)
onto Fyffe Road.

Km 98.3   *Fyffe Road + Simpson Road* Continue straight through
to Simpson Road at the stop sign.

Km 98.6   *Simpson Road + Victoria Road South* The TCT makes a hairpin
turn to the right, crossing railway tracks and continuing
downhill on Victoria Road South. (To reach downtown
Summerland, go left (north) on Victoria Road South, leaving
the TCT route.)

Km 100.6   *Victoria Road South + Lewes Avenue* Turn right (south)
onto Lewes Avenue.

Km 101   *Lewes Avenue + Hillborn Street* Turn left (east) up
Hillborn Street.

Km 101.7   *Hillborn Street + Canyon View Road* The TCT continues
straight on Hillborn Street. (For a view of the spectacular
Trout Creek trestle, turn right (south) down Canyon
View Road and follow it for 400 metres to the KVR tracks
and trestle.)

Km 102   *Hillborn Street + Happy Valley Road* Take Happy Valley Road
to the left.

Km 102.7   *Happy Valley Road + Gartrell Road* Go downhill to the right
on Gartrell Road.

Km 103.9   *Gartrell Road + Arkell Road* The TCT route continues downhill to the right, onto Fir Avenue.

Km 104.7   *Fir Avenue + Johnson Street* The TCT route veers left (east).

Km 105.4   *Johnson Street + Highway 97* On the outskirts of Summerland*. The TCT then takes Highway 97 south to Penticton.

10

OKANAGAN FRUIT STIMULATES OLFACTORY SENSES

Apricot trees are first to bring the fragrance of spring to the South Okanagan. The blossoms appear in early April and soon are followed by peaches, pears, plums, and cherries. The scent of apple blossoms permeates the air by late April or early May. As wind-blown petals litter the orchards, the fruits begin to ripen on the trees.

By late June, drooping clusters of ruby-red cherries are ready for harvest and are first to appear at local fruit stands. Fresh-picked peaches and apricots come in mid-July through August. Pears, plums, and apples are harvested through August and September; some apples are picked just before the frosts of late October.

Across southern British Columbia about 2,000 orchardists produce fruit on nearly 10,000 hectares in the Okanagan, Similkameen, Creston, and Fraser valleys, growing 35 percent of Canada's apples and most of the country's soft fruits. Summer pickers come to the Okanagan from far-off places such as Ontario or Quebec to help harvest more than 140 million kilograms of fruit. It's estimated that BC's tree-fruit industry generates $700 million a year and employs 7,500 workers.

Not only are these thousands of fruit trees aromatic, they give areas such as the South Okanagan a lush green parklike ambiance that is equally appealing to the eye.

VOLUNTEERS KEEP RAILWAY HISTORY ALIVE

Passengers were gone by the 1960s and freight trains vanished from the Kettle Valley Railway in the 1980s, but the whistle of a steam locomotive still resounds through the Okanagan hills near Summerland. Passengers climb aboard at Prairie Valley Station (Km 93.6) for a short journey to Canyon View Station and back.

Volunteers from the Kettle Valley Railway Society run the train from mid-May to mid-October, transporting tourists, backpackers, and cyclists. As the train clatters through a landscape of sagebrush, orchards, and vineyards, attendants dressed in traditional uniforms tell the story of "McCulloch's Wonder." (For more on the KVR, see page 155 in Chapter 8.)

The KVR survived the Great Depression and World War II, but the opening of the Hope–Princeton Highway in 1949 was the start of its demise. After the mid-1960s it was mainly freight trains that kept the railway alive as travellers took to driving automobiles. But with frequent and expensive washouts in the Coquihalla, rerouting of connecting trains from the Kootenays, and the expansion of competing modes of modern transportation, stretches of the KVR were shut down and tracks were torn up. The last train rain in 1989.

All that survived into the 21st century are the tracks near Summerland used by the KVR Steam Railway.

Climb aboard at Prairie Valley Station to hear the story of McCulloch's Wonder from a genuine trainman on a genuine steam train. (For more information, call 1-877-494-8424 or go to www.kettlevalleyrail.org.)

Kettle Valley steam train

THOMPSON OKANAGAN REGION

Tourism region at the southern end of the Thompson Plateau, north and east of the Cascade Mountains, west of the Monashees, with the Okanagan Highland between. For detailed information, see page 167 in Chapter 9.

COMMUNITIES, PARKS, AND PLACES TO STAY

There are several BC forest service campgrounds along this route, basic but pleasant campgrounds that are convenient bases for exploring the TCT: Chain Lake (Km 41.2), Link Lake (Km 49), Osprey Lake (Km 50.7), Thirsk Lake (Km 59.9), and Trout Creek (Km 75.3).

♣ Princeton (Km 0)

See page 170 in the previous chapter.

🛏 ⛺ Princeton Castle Resort (Km 3.7)

Full-service resort, with lodge, cabins, RV, and tent sites. 250-295-7988; www.castleresort.com.

🛏 ⛺ Kettle Valley Campground/B&B (Faulder, Km 88.3)

Ten tent sites on Trout Creek beside the TCT, catering to hikers and cyclists. Refreshing splash in shallow creek. 250-494-4130; jap@vip.net. 🚻 🚻 *flush toilets | showers*

♣ Summerland (Km 105.4)

Quintessential small-town Okanagan, Summerland sits in the arid hills overlooking BC's ninth-largest lake. It is surrounded by orchards and vineyards and is a major fruit-processing centre. Billing itself as the "Okanagan's Old English Town," its downtown features a number of British theme shops.

› **Population** 11,000
› **Visitor Info** *Summerland Visitor Centre* 15600 Highway 97, Box 130, Summerland, BC V0H 1Z0; 250-494-2686; www.summerlandchamber .bc.ca.
› **Attractions** Giants Head Park, Kettle Valley Steam Railway, wineries and vineyards, Kettle Valley Dried Fruits, Summerland Sweets, Summerland Trout Hatchery, Summerland Museum, Summerland Art Centre & Gallery, Okanagan Lake beaches
› **Greyhound Bus** (1-800-661-8747; www.greyhound.ca) Depot located at *Summerland Necessities* at 13415 Rosedale Avenue.
› **Camping** *Peach Orchard Campground*, on Peach Orchard Road between Highway 97 and Okanagan Lake; municipally operated. 250-494-9649; www.peachorchard.ca.

Giants Head Mountain in Summerland

11 SUMMERLAND TO CHUTE LAKE

> 66 They're most of the business now—about 90 percent—
> because the trail is so busy.
> —*Chute Lake Resort's Doreen Reed,*
> *on the flood of cyclists on the TCT/KVR*

Chute Lake Resort

TRAIL TRIVIA
About 45 kinds of wine are produced in the Okanagan Valley.

TOTAL DISTANCE
54.5 km

HIGHLIGHTS
› Views of Okanagan Lake
› The Penticton waterfront
› Rock ovens in Rock Ovens Park
› Chute Lake

CONDITIONS
› **Summerland (Km 0) to Penticton/TCT Pavilion (Km 12.6)** Highway and paved trail and streets. → 12.6 km
› **Penticton (Km 12.6) to Chute Lake (Km 54.5)** Paved streets and hard-packed double-track railway bed that climbs relentlessly at a two-percent grade. Moderately hard on the legs. → 41.9 km

CAUTIONS
› Rattlesnakes—watch your step and stay on the trail.

TOPOGRAPHIC MAPS
1:250,000   Penticton 82E
1:50,000   Penticton 82E/5, Summerland 82E/12

OVERVIEW
It's not hard to ignore the traffic and take in the view over southern Okanagan Lake as you take the TCT from Summerland down Highway 97 to Penticton. On a hot summer day the Penticton waterfront looks like southern California. Diners at open-air bistros on Lakeshore Drive watch an unending stream of skateboarders, mountain bikers, rollerbladers, and the bikini clad. Beyond the crowded beach, water skiers and parasailers soar over the waves between the dry brown cliffs on either side of the lake. This is a suitable quenching spot for thirsty TCT travellers about to climb to those clifftops.

From the lakeshore in Penticton's Rotary Park the TCT begins its trek across the Okanagan Highland, a geographic transition between the

11

rolling hills of the Thompson Plateau to the west and the sharp peaks of the Monashee Mountains to the east.

For travellers going east, Penticton is the start of the Kettle Valley Railway's Carmi subdivision, one of six KVR subdivisions. (The community of Midway, nearly 220 kilometres up the tracks, is the KVR's "Kilometre 0," going east to west.) The railway covers more than 500 kilometres across southern BC, and is the most popular rail trail in the province, with lodges and campgrounds every 50 or 60 kilometres. The route includes Myra Canyon (a National Historic Site—see page 203 in the next chapter) and a landscape unlike any other found on the TCT—orchards and vineyards greening the benchlands high above Okanagan Lake, turkey vultures soaring off the clifftops, and families of California quail scampering over the rail trail. Much of the trail is lined in pastel-green sagebrush and the air is enriched with its fragrance.

The views get bigger, better, and more unbelievable as the trail climbs above the lakeshore and around the back side of Okanagan Mountain to Chute Lake. A photograph often used in Trans Canada Trail advertisements was taken along this leg—it depicts cyclists emerging from Little Tunnel (Km 29.9), 340 metres above the glittering blue surface of Okanagan Lake.

LOCAL ADVENTURES
Day Trip
› Take a shuttle from Penticton (Km 12.6) to Chute Lake (Km 54.5) and cycle back downhill. → 41.9 km
› Hike the TCT from Penticton (Km 12.6) to McCulloch Trestle (Km 16.4) for a picnic and hike back to Penticton. ⇆ 7.6 km

2 or 3 Days
› Cycle a loop from Midway, incorporating the TCT with highways, back roads, and local trails. (See page 216 in Chapter 13.) ↻ 360 km

TCT ACCCESS POINTS
Summerland (Km 0) On Highway 97, 16 kilometres north of Penticton. **P** *Roadside parking near the TCT. Inquire about multi-day parking at the visitor centre on Highway 97.*

11

Penticton (Km 12.6) On Highway 97 between Okanagan and Skaha lakes. **P** *Parking at Rotary Park on Lakeshore Drive. Inquire about long-term parking at the visitor centre (553 Railway Street).* 🚻 🚮

Smethurst Road (Km 25.4) From Naramata Road on the eastern edge of Naramata, turn east onto Smethurst Road. **P** *parking where Smethurst Road meets the* TCT

THE OKANAGAN LURE

BIG LAKES AND SUNSHINE

Summerland's commanding views over Okanagan Lake are a taste of what's to come for TCT travellers headed for the clifftops on the opposite shore. Though they're not far, reaching them could take a while: people commonly get stalled in Penticton, the South Okanagan's second-largest city. Like Kelowna, its big sister to the north, Penticton sits on the lakeshore, surrounded by golden-brown hills baked by 2,000 hours of annual sunshine.

Okanagan Lake
in Penticton

At 352 square kilometres, Okanagan Lake is the ninth-largest in BC. Only three or four kilometres wide, it funnels down the Okanagan Valley for more than 100 kilometres from Vernon in the north to Penticton in the south. From Penticton, the Okanagan River—renowned inner-tubing territory—flows through to Skaha Lake. (Beside this river is a well-used bike/hike trail.) Penticton's enviable setting between these two sun-drenched lakes has made it one of southern BC's prime vacation spots.

Rail trails are a priority here, and the city of Penticton has done superb work on the Trans Canada Trail. A well-maintained gravel path climbs the Kettle Valley Railway bed up the eastern shore of the lake. Benches and interpretive signs overlook the lake. Keep an eye out for Ogopogo, the legendary lake monster.

Beyond the city limits the TCT is a double-track gravel rail trail that's usually hard but softens occasionally in dry weather. Awesome scenery helps divert attention from aching legs: this is a two-percent incline for 42 kilometres to Chute Lake, an elevation gain of over 800 metres.

11

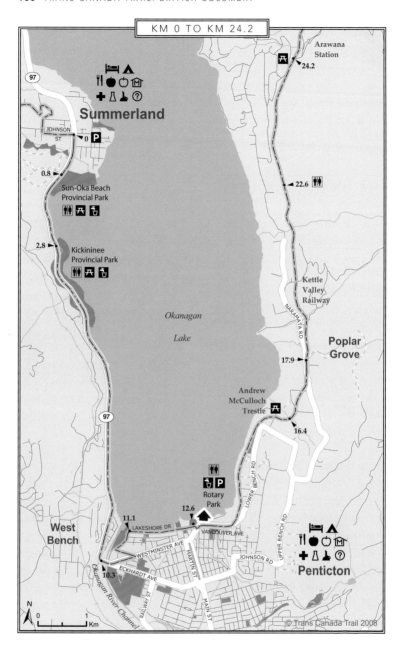

KM 0 TO KM 24.2

Arawana
Station
24.2

97

Summerland

JOHNSON
ST
0
P

0.8

Sun-Oka Beach
Provincial Park

22.6

2.8

Kickininee
Provincial Park

Okanagan

Lake

Kettle
Valley
Railway

NARAMATA RD

Poplar
Grove

17.9

97

Andrew
McCulloch
Trestle

16.4

Rotary
Park

LOWER BENCH RD

12.6

11.1

West
Bench

LAKESHORE DR

VANCOUVER AVE

UPPER BENCH RD

WESTMINSTER AVE

MARTIN ST

JOHNSON RD

Penticton

10.3

ECKHARDT AVE

RAILWAY ST

MAIN ST

Okanagan River Channel

N

0   1
          Km

© Trans Canada Trail 2008

11

Catching a shuttle from Penticton to the top and cycling down is easier and makes a good side trip.

Floating on the Okanagan River channel in Penticton

THE TRANS CANADA TRAIL

Place names with asterisks are included in the **Communities, Parks, and Places to Stay** section (page 193).

Km 0	*Summerland*, Johnson Street + Highway 97* The TCT takes the highway south down a steep hill along the west side of Okanagan Lake. It's busy but the paved shoulder is wide.
Km 0.8	*Sun-Oka Beach Provincial Park** A favourite local swimming spot on Okanagan Lake.
Km 2.8	*Kickininee Provincial Park** Another lakefront swimming and picnic site.
Km 10.3	*Eckhardt Avenue* Just beyond the south end of Okanagan Lake, Highway 97 veers left onto Eckhardt Avenue. Continue over the bridge across the Okanagan River Channel, then turn left onto a paved riverside trail that heads upstream toward the lakeshore. (Trails along both sides of the river channel between Okanagan and Skaha lakes make great hiking and cycling, while the channel is popular for summer inner-tubers.)

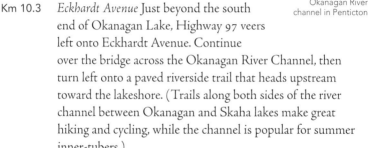

SS Sicamous, Penticton

KM 24.2 TO KM 54.5

Chute Lake

54.5 ►

Chute Lake Resort

54.2

Chute Lake forest service campground

Okanagan Mountain

Provincial Park

CHUTE LAKE RD

53.6

Elinor Lake

34.4

34.2

Naramata Lake

Kettle Valley Railway

ELINOR LAKE FSR

NARAMATA RD

Robinson Creek

38.6

38.9

45.4

29.9

39.9

40.3

44.5

Rock Ovens Regional Park

Okanagan

43.1

27.4

42.2 Adra Tunnel

Lake

Naramata

Naramata Creek

11

ROBINSON AVE

SMETHURST RD

25.4 P

N

0   1

Km

Arawana Station

24.2

© Trans Canada Trail 2008

Km 11.1   *ss Sicamous* At the beached paddlewheeler, turn right onto
            Lakeshore Drive and continue along the south shore of
            Okanagan Lake.

Km 12.6   *Penticton*, TCT Pavilion/Rotary Park* Take Lakeshore Drive
            east from Rotary Park, and go up the hill on Vancouver
            Avenue for 900 metres to a TCT sign on the right side of the
            road. Cross Vancouver Avenue at the crosswalk and go up
            Vancouver Place to the start of the TCT/Kettle Valley Railway
            trail.

Km 16.4   *Andrew McCulloch Trestle* The trestle was built in 2002,
            named in honour of the KVR builder. (Here you will find a
            picnic table.)

Km 17.9   *TCT + Naramata Road* Cross the road and continue up the
            TCT toward Chute Lake. (Take Naramata Road to get to
            Naramata*.)

Km 22.6   *Outhouse*

Km 24.2   *Arawana Station* (Sheltered picnic table.)

Km 25.4   *TCT + Smethurst Road* Cross Smethurst to continue on the
            TCT. (To reach the community of Naramata about four
            kilometres to the west, turn left (west) off the TCT onto
            Smethurst, left (south) on North Naramata Road, then right
            (west) on Robinson Avenue.)

Km 27.4   *Outhouse*

Km 29.9   *Little Tunnel* Just before the tunnel, there are dramatic views
            of Okanagan Lake and the communities of Naramata, Sum-
            merland, and Penticton, as well as Skaha Lake. Perhaps the
            most popular vantage point for photographs on the Kettle
            Valley Railway. Go through the tunnel and continue on the
            rail trail.

Km 34.2   *Outhouse*

Km 34.4   *Glenfir Station* The TCT makes a hairpin turn to the right and
            continues south on the rail trail.

Km 38.6   *Rock ovens* See sidebar on the next page. (A short trail off
            the TCT/KVR leads to rock oven #6 in Rock Ovens Regional
            Park.)

Km 38.9   *Rock ovens #4, 5, and 7*

Km 39.9   *Outhouse* Near the trail is one of many nest boxes put up by
            the Southern Interior Bluebird Society, hanging in a tree next

11

ROCK OVENS USED BY BACKWOODS BAKERS

The aroma of fresh-baked bread no longer emanates from the "Naramata ovens," but from 1911 to 1915 this aroma melded with the scent of pine trees in the Chute Lake area. Hungry Kettle Valley Railway builders were well fed in the field, thanks to the dome-shaped mounds of boulders—outdoor baking ovens—in Rock Oven Park.

A dozen are tucked away in the woods between Naramata and Chute Lake, most a few metres off the Trans Canada Trail. Built of local stone and mortared with mud to make them airtight, they look like mossy rock igloos, about two metres in height and diameter, with a front door wide enough for a human, or a bear, to crawl inside.

to one of several benches installed along the trail by Naramata Parks and KVR Woodwackers.

Km 40.3	*Rock ovens #1, 2, and 3*
Km 42.2	*Adra Tunnel bypass* Turn left where the TCT leaves the railway bed, and go about 100 metres to curve around a corner and rejoin the rail grade. Once back on the railbed, go right a short distance to see the tunnel (closed due to hazards), and then go left to continue on the TCT/KVR.
Km 43.1	*Rock oven #8*
Km 44.5	*Rock oven #9*
Km 45.4	*Rock oven #11* (Outhouse.)
Km 53.6	*Rock oven #12*
Km 54.2	*Chute Lake BC forest service campground* Wooded camping at the south end of the lake.
Km 54.5	*Chute Lake Resort** The TCT/KVR continues north along the lakeshore.

11

THOMPSON OKANAGAN REGION

Tourism region at the southern end of the Thompson Plateau, north and east of the Cascade Mountains, west of the Monashees, with the Okanagan Highland between. For detailed information, see page 167 in Chapter 9.

COMMUNITIES, PARKS, AND PLACES TO STAY

♠ Provincial Day-use Parks: Sun-Oka and Kickininee

Four picnic sites in two provincial parks are spaced along the shore of Okanagan Lake between Summerland and Penticton. Each has restrooms, drinking water, picnic tables, and summer swimming. *Sun-Oka Beach* (an abbreviation for "Sunny Okanagan"), three kilometres south of Summerland, is 30 hectares and well used by locals. *Kickininee Park*, 49 hectares, has three beaches/picnic sites—Pyramid, Soorimpt, and Kickininee—between five and eight kilometres south of Summerland. The Kickininee site is accessible from Highway 97 only to northbound travellers, but there are left-turn lanes to Pyramid and Soorimpt that provide access from the north or south. Watch for park signs along the highway. Look both up on the BC Parks website at www.env.gov.bc.ca/bcparks/.

♠ Summerland (Km 0)

See page 183 in the previous chapter.

BURROWING OWL: A DIMINUTIVE RAPTOR

Owl watchers normally look up at trees, but in the Okanagan there's one species that nests underground. The burrowing owl (*Athene cunicularia*), a spindle-legged, robin-sized raptor, sets up house in the abandoned den of a ground squirrel or badger. During summer nesting season it makes brief appearances in the light of day to hunt. It is occasionally seen standing outside the burrow or on a fence post.

As creatures of grasslands, burrowing owls were never abundant: grasslands comprise less than three percent of British Columbia's land. The species, however, was fairly stable and widespread, ranging from the South Okanagan and Kootenay rivers up through the Thompson Valley. Since the mid-19th century, cattle overgrazing the grasslands wiped out hiding places for prey such as mice. And the eradication of tunnelling mammals left few nesting burrows for the owls. In 1975, burrowing owls were declared endangered in BC and were designated nationally endangered in 1995.

Yet the future for this diminutive raptor is not entirely gloomy. Ranchers have been letting grasses grow longer to provide better habitat for voles and other prey, and they've been working with recovery teams to build and monitor artificial burrows on their land. The future for the species now depends largely on owls bred in captivity and released in the wild.

Trans Canada Trail travellers would be lucky indeed to spot a wild burrowing owl. Keep an eye peeled in the West Bench area in the hills between Summerland and Penticton.

A sign at the entrance to Rock Oven Park warns: "April through October is rattlesnake season. Use caution travelling this route." Though British Columbia's only poisonous viper may be lurking near the Trans Canada Trail, it is not likely to strike unless it gets stepped on. The western rattlesnake (*Crotalus viridis*) is a mild-mannered serpent that would rather slink away from danger than confront it. Nonetheless, summer travellers on the TCT in the Okanagan Valley, and farther east in the Kettle Valley, should stick to the trail.

Measuring 60 to 145 centimetres long, the western rattler spends most of its life within a couple of kilometres of its winter den. It prefers sunny, south-facing hillsides with talus slopes or rock ridges where crevices are deep enough to avoid sub-zero temperatures. Two hundred or more rattlesnakes may hibernate in one den, spending more than half the year underground. In spring they disperse to bask in the sun between meals of voles or deer mice.

These timid reptiles are protected under the *BC Wildlife Act*.

♣ Penticton (Km 12.6)

The South Okanagan's second-largest city, Penticton is known to tourists as a place to bask in the sun and cool off in the lake. It is also a major processing and shipping centre for apples and soft fruits that tourists see growing around them. Over ten square kilometres of orchards growing within Penticton's city limits make it a particularly fragrant town at spring-blossom time.

› **Population** 42,000

› **Visitor Info** *Penticton Visitor Centre* 553 Railway Street, Penticton, BC V2A 8S3; 1-800-663-5052; www.penticton.ca; www.penticton.org/tourism/.

› **Attractions** Kettle Valley Railway, Okanagan River Channel inner-tubing, SS *Sicamous*, Penticton (RN Atkinson) Museum, Art Gallery of the South Okanagan, Wonderful Waterworld, Skaha climbing bluffs, vineyard tours, kokanee spawning at Penticton Creek.

› **Cycling/Outfitting** *The Bike Barn* 300 Westminster Avenue; 250-492-4140; www.bikebarn.ca. *Freedom* 533 Main Street, 250-493-0686; www.freedombikeshop.com.

› **Greyhound Bus** (1-800-661-8747; www.greyhound.ca) Depot located at 307 Ellis Street.

♣ Naramata (off Km 17.9)

A quaint village in the heart of Okanagan winery country, overlooking the orchards and vineyards above the lake. The TCT crosses Naramata Road at Km 17.9.

› **Population** 2,500
› **Visitor Info** www.discovernaramata.com
› **Attractions** Wining and dining, Kettle Valley Railway.

🛏 🅰 Chute Lake Resort (Km 54.5)

A landmark on the TCT/KVR with rustic cabins, a lodge, a pub, and campsites. Pitch a tent on the grass beside the lake and hear the ghostly yip-yipping of coyotes over the crackle of a campfire. Anglers were originally the main clientele here; while still important customers, they're outnumbered now by cyclists on the TCT. At the height of the tourist season as many as 75 meals a night are served in the pub. Chute Lake Resort is a Trans Canada Trail highlight that survived the Okanagan Mountain wildfire of 2003. (See page 203.) Go to www.chutelakeresort.com for detailed directions, as the resort is located in semi-wilderness. 250-493-3535
🍴 | *showers, laundromat, canoe and boat rentals*

› **Attractions** Wildlife, including moose, coyotes, and waterfowl such as loons and geese; fishing and swimming; a barn full of artifacts collected from flea markets and garage sales around Interior BC.

Chute Lake Resort pub and lodge

12 CHUTE LAKE TO BEAVERDELL

66 Aren't you afraid you're gonna die?
—Nine-year-old boy to cyclists on a 300-kilometre trip

Myra Canyon,
Kettle Valley rail trail

TRAIL TRIVIA
Southern BC is the northern fringe of the monarch butterfly's continental range.

TOTAL DISTANCE
105.8 km

HIGHLIGHTS
› Myra Canyon
› Community of Beaverdell

CONDITIONS
› **Chute Lake (Km 0) to Myra Canyon (Km 25.5)** Potholes, washboard, and oversized puddles on wet days make for an obstacle course on this rail trail. → 25.5 km
› **Through Myra Canyon (Km 25.5 to Km 36.5)** Hard, double-track railbed with a few puddles and potholes. → 11 km
› **Myra Canyon (Km 36.5) to McCulloch Lake (Km 50.2)** Railbed with potholes, washboard, and puddles of unknown depth, some the size of small ponds. (A crude bypass trail has been cut around one semi-permanent puddle.) → 13.7 km
› **McCulloch Lake (Km 50.2) to Beaverdell (Km 105.8)** Mainly hard-packed double-track rail grade. Rough patches outside of McCulloch Lake and Beaverdell. → 55.6 km

CAUTIONS
› Rattlesnakes.
› Bears.

TOPOGRAPHIC MAPS
1:250,000   Penticton 82E
1:50,000   Beaverdell 82E/6, Wilkinson Creek 82E/11, Summerland 82E/12, Kelowna 82E/14

OVERVIEW
The TCT/KVR climbs over the Okanagan Highland to the east and then begins a barely perceptible descent at about the middle of Myra Canyon. Wildfire destroyed several trestles here in 2003, breaking the continuity of the TCT in the canyon and forcing travellers to take a detour. However,

12

the trestles were rebuilt and reopened in 2008, allowing hikers and cyclists to continue their journey on the abandoned KVR corridor uninterrupted. (See page 203.)

McCulloch Lake, with its myriad bays and islands, was a gathering place for cyclists, anglers, and other outdoor explorers. It was named for Andrew McCulloch, the chief engineer who oversaw construction of the KVR line from Midway to Hope. A lodge was built in 1998 to resemble a railway station during the heyday of the KVR's passenger service—1915 to the early 1960s. The lodge closed after the 2003 fire in Myra Canyon, and its status was unknown as this book went to press.

Beyond McCulloch Lake is Summit Lake, where a gazebo makes a good blind for birders scouring the wetlands for waterfowl. The trail then wanders past swamps, pine groves, and rock slides to a rustic campground at Arlington Lakes. Campers can step out of their tents into the water and float on their backs for views of summer snow on Big White Mountain, 19 kilometres to the northeast. The TCT/KVR then follows the West Kettle River through the old mining community of Carmi down to the outskirts of Beaverdell.

LOCAL ADVENTURES

Day Trip
› Hike or cycle Myra Canyon (Km 25.5 to Km 36.5). → 11 km
› Take a room or pitch a tent at Beaverdell (Km 105.8) and cycle to Arlington Lakes (Km 74.2) and back. ⇆ 63.2 km

2 or 3 Days
› From Penticton, catch a shuttle to Midway or Beaverdell (Monashee Adventure Tours; 1-888-762-9253; www.monasheeadventuretours.com), and return via the TCT/KVR. → 220 km from Midway, 150 km from Beaverdell

TCT ACCESS POINTS

Myra Canyon, west end (Km 25.5) *From Kelowna, 44 kilometres north of Summerland on Highway 97* (Map on facing page.) Set your odometer at Km 0 on the east side of the Highway 97 bridge across Okanagan Lake. Stay on Highway 97 (Harvey Avenue) until you reach Pandosy Street (Km 0.8), where you turn right (south). Continue to the junction of Pandosy, Lakeshore Drive, Cedar Avenue, and KLO Road (Km 3.2), and turn left (east) on KLO. At the East Kelowna community hall, veer right onto McCulloch

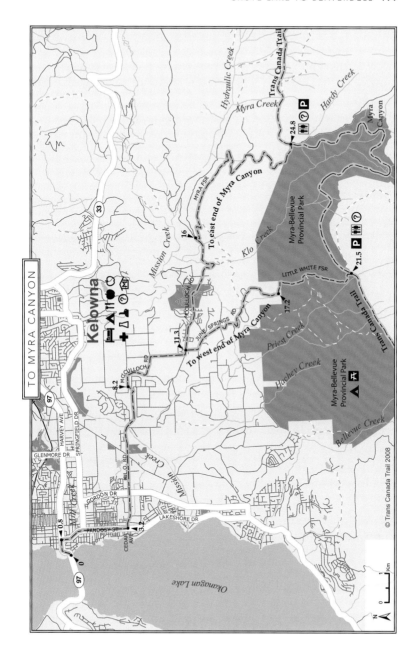

TO MYRA CANYON

Kelowna

Myra-Bellevue Provincial Park

Myra-Bellevue Provincial Park

To east end of Myra Canyon

To west end of Myra Canyon

Trans Canada Trail

Trans Canada Trail

Hydraulic Creek

Myra Creek

Hardy Creek

Myra Canyon

Mission Creek

Klo Creek

Priest Creek

Hachey Creek

Bellevue Creek

Mill Creek

Okanagan Lake

MYRA FSR

McCULLOCH RD

JUNE SPRINGS RD

LITTLE WHITE FSR

McCULLOCH RD

McCULLOCH RD

KLO RD

GORDON DR

SPRINGFIELD DR

GLENMORE DR

HARVEY AVE

PANDOSY ST

CEDAR AVE

LAKESHORE DR

24.8

21.5

17.2

16

11.3

8.2

3.2

0.8

0

33

97

97

© Trans Canada Trail 2008

N

0   1 Km

12

Road (Km 8.2), where a sign points toward the Myra Canyon trestles. Stay on McCulloch, watching road signs carefully as it makes several turns before reaching June Springs Road (Km 11.3), where you turn right. (To reach the east end of Myra Canyon, continue straight on McCulloch.) Turn left at a T-junction, following signs to Myra Canyon.

The pavement ends at the Little White forest service road (Km 17.2), an unmaintained dirt road that goes up to Myra Canyon—the road is a rough, steep, and winding 4.3 kilometres. At a fork (Km 20.3), follow the Myra Canyon signs to the left. The Little White forest service road then intersects the TCT/KVR (Km 21.5), where a parking area is located. Travellers can either take the rail trail east through Myra Canyon toward McCulloch Lake and Beaverdell, or west toward Chute Lake. (For more on Myra Canyon see page 203.) This is also the start of a 15-kilometre trail that was originally opened as a detour after fire destroyed the trestles in 2003. Although the detour is no longer needed, there were plans to keep it open, giving cyclists and hikers an optional circle route that incorporates the canyon. **P** ** outhouses ⑦ *information kiosk*

Myra Canyon, east end (Km 36.5) *From Kelowna, 44 kilometres north of Summerland on Highway 97* (Map on page 199.) From Kelowna, follow the same route as described above to Myra Canyon's west end, until you reach the junction of McCulloch and June Springs roads (Km 11.3). Instead of turning right onto June Springs, continue straight on McCulloch to Myra forest service road (Km 16), the start of a maintained 8.8-kilometre gravel road to Myra Canyon. Turn right at the parking lot and continue to the main parking area (Km 24.8) for the canyon's east end. **P** ** ⑦ *interpretive signs and outhouses by the main parking area*

Beaverdell (Km 105.8) Take Highway 33 north from Rock Creek for 47 kilometres. **P** ○

A PASSENGER'S VIEW

BACKWOODS TO WHISTLE STOPS

Despite a few puddles and potholes, the TCT route here is mostly a mosey through pine forests and farmsteads. It's not uncommon for those who get an early start from Chute Lake to see a cow moose and calf foraging in the shallows. Or to spot a downy loon chick hitching a ride on its mother's

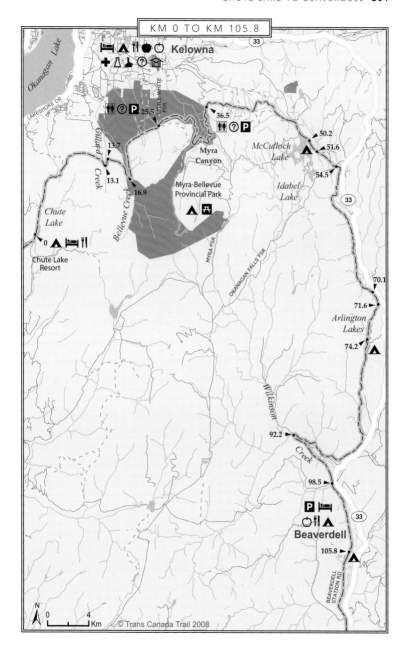

KM 0 TO KM 105.8

Kelowna

Okanagan Lake

LAKESHORE DR

25.5

LITTLE WHITE FSR

36.5

Gillard Creek

13.7

13.1

Myra Canyon

McCulloch Lake

50.2

51.6

54.5

Idabel Lake

16.9

Chute Lake

Bellevue Creek

Myra-Bellevue Provincial Park

0

Chute Lake Resort

MYRA FSR

OKANAGAN FALLS FSR

70.1

71.6

Arlington Lakes

74.2

Wilkinson

92.2

Creek

98.5

Beaverdell

105.8

BEAVERDELL STATION RD

N

0   4
|____| Km   © Trans Canada Trail 2008

12

back. Snowshoe hares are everywhere, flashing their oversized white feet as they thump across the trail, and chipmunks hang around rest stops to beg for handouts from tourists. Deer in the fields are more common than cows, but they're skittish—be quiet and sneaky if you want to take photographs.

Trailside display at Carmi

TCT travellers see the Okanagan backcountry from the perspective of early 20th-century train passengers as the rail trail climbs at a moderate grade through Myra Canyon toward McCulloch Lake, then runs downhill to Beaverdell. Gorges, trestles, warm-water lakes, and backwater communities make up the scenery, much of it unchanged since the railroad days.

A few railway and mining relics decorate the yards in Carmi, where a unique trailside display of dolls and stuffed animals is accompanied by a sign that warns: "Stage riders take note! Spit with the wind, not against it." Past Carmi, the TCT continues along the west side of West Kettle River to the outskirts of Beaverdell. Take the 1.5-kilometre detour off the TCT to get to Beaverdell, to the east and across the river up to Highway 33. You can pitch a tent beside a creek in Zach's Campground or book into the Beaverdell Hotel (circa 1910), and mingle with the locals in the pub or dine across the road at Our Place Café. Or just settle onto a bench outside the general store and be absorbed into the Beaverdellian lifestream.

THE TRANS CANADA TRAIL

Place names with asterisks are included in the **Communities, Parks, and Places to Stay** section (page 205).

Km 0   *Chute Lake Resort** The TCT/KVR runs north along the lakeshore.

Km 13.1   *Gillard Creek* Trestle ruins.

Km 13.7   *Views of Kelowna and Westbank* Glimpses through the trees of Okanagan Lake and the region's largest metropolitan centre.

Km 16.9   *Bellevue Creek Trestle* Survived the Okanagan Mountain wildfire of 2003.

Km 25.5   *Myra Canyon, west end* Trestle #1 ahead, the first of 18. (Outhouses, kiosk, and road access to Kelowna*—see TCT Access Points on page 198.)

Km 26.4   *Outhouses*

12

Km 32.9   *Outhouses*

Km 36.5   *Myra Canyon, east end* The TCT contin-
ues southwest on the railway corridor.
(Outhouses, kiosk, and road access to
Kelowna—see page 200.)

Km 50.2   *McCulloch Lake* (A BC forest service
campground is just ahead. McCulloch
Lake Lodge may or may not be open.)

Km 51.6   *Summit Lake* A trailside gazebo overlooks a marshy lake.

Km 54.5   *Idabel Lake turnoff* (To reach Idabel
Lake Resort*, turn right on a gravel
road that crosses the TCT/KVR, and
continue for four kilometres to a sign
pointing to the resort.)

Gillard Creek Trestle ruins

Km 70.1   *Rock slide* Sizable slide, but the trail
is navigable.

Km 71.6   *Fork* 📟 north 49.37.840, west 119.05.014 ⛰ 1,062 metres.
Veer right.

Km 74.2   *Arlington Lakes* At a three-way fork, keep left toward the lake
and BC forest service campground. From Arlington Lakes the
TCT veers away from West Kettle River to follow Hall Creek,
a West Kettle tributary.

Km 92.2   *Bridge over Wilkinson Creek* Cyclists forded this creek until
the bridge opened in 2002.

Km 98.5   *Carmi* Old mining town. Gold was discovered here in the late
1800s but the community's heyday was over by the 1940s.

Km 105.8   *Beaverdell Station Road and Beaverdell* * The TCT joins Beaverdell Station Road. (The village of Beaverdell is off the TCT:
at the juncture, turn left onto Beaverdell Station Road, and
go 1.5 kilometres east.) From Km 105.8 the TCT heads right
(south) on Beaverdell Station Road, following the West Kettle
and Kettle rivers.

MYRA CANYON: A SECOND RESURRECTION

The trestles were still smouldering in the canyon when governments and
volunteers vowed to replace them. With its 18 previously restored trestles
and two tunnels, Myra Canyon had been declared a National Historic Site
in 2002. This was the undisputed highlight of the Trans Canada Trail in

Myra Canyon trestle
rebuilding, 2007

British Columbia, perhaps in all of Canada. People from around the world—as many as 50,000 a year—were coming with their bikes and backpacks to see why. This site, everyone agreed, was too valuable to lose.

BC's new rail trail tourism industry was germinating in Myra Canyon when wildfires ravaged the area in the summer of 2003. As residents were fleeing their homes near Kelowna, the Okanagan Mountain forest fire swept toward Myra Canyon. By the time firefighters had control, 12 of 16 wooden trestles were destroyed and two steel bridges were damaged.

The monumental task of restoring the Myra Canyon trestles was still a fresh memory for 300 volunteers who'd taken on the same project in the mid-1990s. Their selfless efforts ensured—forever, it was believed—the continuity of both the historic Kettle Valley Railway corridor and the Trans Canada Trail.

Heartbroken but undaunted by the fire of 2003, they were among the first to contribute their trestle-rescuing expertise. While the federal and provincial governments came up with $17 million, businesses stepped in—once again—with offers of equipment and materials. Lotteries and raffles, benefit concerts, telethons, and other fundraisers were launched to help accumulate the millions needed to bring back the trestles.

Though less than a dozen kilometres from end to end, Myra Canyon is a nationally significant link in the Trans Canada Trail. Construction workers, working through winter, steamed ahead with look-alike trestles, and by the end of 2007 the new trestles were ready for a grand re-opening in the spring of 2008. Visitor numbers are expected to double to 100,000 a year.

THOMPSON OKANAGAN REGION

Tourism region at the southern end of the Thompson Plateau, north and east of the Cascade Mountains, west of the Monashees, with the Okanagan Highland between. For detailed information, see page 167 in Chapter 9.

12

STICKY-TOED TREEFROG A PROFICIENT CLIMBER

Campers at Chute Lake, and along much of the Trans Canada Trail across southern British Columbia, may be roused from their sleep by the birdlike chirps of Pacific treefrogs (*Hyla regilla*). Treefrogs are ubiquitous, found in ponds and ditches, moist meadows or fields, forests, and even urban balconies with potted plants. With long legs and adhesive toe pads, these minuscule amphibians hunt spiders and insects as they climb about on trees, shrubs, or blades of tall grass.

A big treefrog is about half the length of a human index finger; some are smaller than a thumbnail. In response to changes in temperature or humidity, they may alter colours from pale grey to olive-brown or emerald-green.

At breeding time in early spring, Pacific treefrogs move to "ephemeral wetlands," which dry shortly after their tadpoles have metamorphosed, thereby avoiding predation by fish or bullfrogs that require deeper, permanent water.

The emergence of Pacific treefrogs from winter hibernation is dependent on weather. While scientists use them as barometers to measure changes in climate, moviemakers use their distinctive songs as soundtracks for tropical scenes.

BOUNDARY COUNTRY

The area between McCulloch Lake (Km 50.2) and Christina Lake to the east (Chapter 14, Km 77.6) is known as Boundary Country. Here the TCT crosses the Midway and Christina ranges of the Monashee Mountains.

› **Visitor Info** A website maintained by the *Boundary Economic Development Commission* (www.boundary.bc.ca) shows community profiles, activities, and a wealth of other information.

› **TCT Info** *Trails BC (Boundary region)* Look up "Boundary" under "BC Regions" on the Trails BC website at www.trailsbc.ca.

› **Transportation** Highway 3 (Crowsnest Highway) is the main thoroughfare through Boundary Country. Greyhound Canada buses (1-800-661-8747; www.greyhound.ca) stop at Kelowna, Rock Creek, Midway, Greenwood, Grand Forks, and Christina Lake.

COMMUNITIES, PARKS, AND PLACES TO STAY

🛏️ ⛺ Chute Lake Resort (Km 0)

See page 195 in the previous chapter.

♣ Kelowna

The Okanagan's largest city. Not on the Trans Canada Trail, but the community closest to Myra Canyon. (For directions to Myra Canyon, refer to TCT Access Points on page 198.)

› **Population** 96,000

› **Visitor Info** *Tourism Kelowna Visitors and Convention Centre* 544 Harvey Avenue, Kelowna, BC V1Y 6C9; 1-800-663-4345; www.tourismkelowna .com.

› **Attractions** Beachfront parks and walking/cycling paths, BC Orchard Industry and Wine Museum, winery tours, Kelowna Art Gallery.

› **Cycling/Outfitting** *Monashee Adventure Tours* runs organized and custom bicycle and snowshoe tours, as well as shuttle services between Princeton and Nelson. 1-888-762-9253; www.monasheeadventuretours.com. *The Cyclepath* 2169 Springfield Road; 250-868-0122; www.cyclepathkelowna .com. *Kelowna Cycle* 103–2949 Pandosy Street; 250-762-2453; www.kelowna cycle.ca. *Gerick Cycle & Sports* 1969 Harvey Avenue; 250-868-3007.

› **Greyhound Bus** (1-800-661-8747; www.greyhound.ca) Depot located at *Kelowna Terminals* at 2366 Leckie Road. Greyhound buses also stop at Kelowna International Airport.

⊨ Idabel Lake Resort (Km 54.5)

Lakeside lodge suites and cottages. Three kilometres beyond Summit Lake, turn right on a gravel road that crosses the TCT/KVR trail. It is four kilometres to the resort, which is near the north end of Idabel Lake. 250-765-9511; www.idabellakeresort.com. *no camping or restaurant*

Beaverdell Hotel, circa 1910

♣ Beaverdell (Km 105.8)

A laid-back community on Highway 33, halfway between Kelowna and Rock Creek. The *Chef Moz Dining Guide* describes Our Place Café as a "great small-town café." There's more dining across the road at Beaverdell Hotel (check the three-meal deal for TCT travellers). ☼ *general store* ⊨ ▲ ⊺❙ | *post office*

› **Population** 300

› **Accommodation/Camping** *Beaverdell Hotel* 250-484-5513. *Zach's Campground and Rooms* 250-484-5532.

13 BEAVERDELL TO MIDWAY

TCT staffer Mike LeBlanc on the KVR rail trail near Midway

13

TRAIL TRIVIA
Although the village of Midway is "midway" across BC, it is believed the name is actually based on the Midway Plaisance at the Chicago World's Fair of 1893, the year the BC townsite was laid out.

TOTAL DISTANCE
71.2 km

HIGHLIGHTS
› Midway, Kettle Valley Railway's Kilometre 0
› Rhone Canyon
› Paul Lautard's Cyclists Rest
› The Kettle River Recreation Area

CONDITIONS
› **Beaverdell (Km 0) to Rhone Canyon (Km 21)** Part road, part railbed. The surface is rough and washboarded where the TCT is shared with vehicles. → 21 km
› **Rhone Canyon (Km 21) to Midway (Km 71.2)** Hard-packed railbed for most of the way. → 50.2 km

CAUTIONS
› Gates on the public right-of-way. When opening or closing gates, be careful with the barbed wire and sharp edges not to puncture tires or tear clothing. Some gates may be locked; carry maps that show alternate road routes.

TOPOGRAPHIC MAPS
› 1:250,000   Penticton 82E
› 1:50,000   Greenwood 82E/2, Osoyoos 82E/3, Beaverdell 82E/6

OVERVIEW
The plateaus, highlands, and mountain ranges continue to unfold as the TCT follows the Kettle and West Kettle rivers for more than 70 kilometres to Midway. These valleys separate the Okanagan Highland to the west from the Monashee Mountains to the east. Unlike the sharp, massive peaks in the northern Monashees, the hills here in the south are more rounded, bearing a closer resemblance to the Okanagan countryside. As

13

the trail moves toward the west-facing slopes, typical Interior trees such as Engelmann spruce and ponderosa pine mix with coastal hemlock and Douglas fir.

The rivers and TCT run side by side for much of this journey. The most dramatic encounter comes at Rhone Canyon where the West Kettle River roars down between sheer rock walls.

At "Cyclists Rest," cyclists are greeted by the legendary Paul Lautard, who created this rest stop for weary TCT travellers. Born here in the early 1920s, he has a memory full of local lore and history. (See page 215.)

Near the ranchlands and farms of Rock Creek, the Kettle River curls around the southern tip of the Midway Range before flowing through the community of Midway. Here it crosses the Canada–U.S. border into Washington, reappearing in Canada at Grand Forks.

LOCAL ADVENTURES

Day Trip

› Cycle from Beaverdell (Km 0) to Rhone Canyon (Km 21) and back. ⇆ 42 km
› Hike or cycle a loop on the TCT and Highway 33 between Kettle River Recreation Area (Km 44.1) and Rock Creek (Km 51.1). ↻ 14 km

2 or 3 Days

› Set up camp at Kettle River Recreation Area (Km 44.1) and take day trips on the TCT.

4 or 5 Days

› Ride the Osoyoos loop combining the TCT with roads and other trails. (See page 216.) ↻ 360 km

TCT ACCESS POINTS

Beaverdell (Km 0) On Highway 33, 47 kilometres north of Rock Creek. From the general store on Highway 33 in downtown Beaverdell, go west for 1.5 kilometres on Beaverdell Station Road, down the hill and across West Kettle River to the TCT.

Westbridge (Km 36.2) On Highway 33, 13 kilometres north of Rock Creek. The TCT crosses the highway here. ↻

13

Kettle River Recreation Area (Km 44.1) On Highway 33, 6.5 kilometres north of Rock Creek (at Highway 3). Turn right (east) and go one kilometre to the park. ⚧ *outhouses* 🚻 ▲ | *telephone*

Rock Creek (Km 51.1) Just southwest of the junction of Highway 3 and Highway 33. To reach the TCT from the junction, take the road over a bridge across the Kettle River. At the junction of Kettle River East Road and Kettle Valley South Road, the TCT heads southeast on Kettle Valley South Road. 🍴 🛏 ☉

Midway (Km 71.2) On Highway 3, 18 kilometres east of Rock Creek.

CROSSING THE KETTLE
AND WEST KETTLE RIVERS

STAYING COOL IN THE SUMMER HEAT

When the Okanagan heat hits the 30s, often before noon, relief may be a few steps off the trail. It would be unwise to jump into the whirlpools of Rhone Canyon, but there are plenty of swimming holes downstream. Some TCT travellers leap in fully clad and continue on in wet, cool clothes until the sun bakes them dry.

Except for a few potholes and stretches of washboard, this is an easy ride or hike through an attractive river valley with deep gorges and open farmlands. From Beaverdell, the TCT alternates between rail trail and road, repeatedly crossing the Kettle and West Kettle rivers. Highway 33 (Kettle Valley Highway) crosses and closely parallels the TCT/KVR at several points, but for much of the route to Midway the highway and railroad are separated by the river, making this leg of the TCT somewhat isolated.

People occasionally encounter locked gates on the railbed, clues that not everyone in these parts is enamoured with the Trans Canada Trail. The public right-of-way traverses large tracts of private farmland and some farmers claim that careless trail users cause livestock injuries or losses. TCT travellers should carry a map that gives an overview of roads in this area, in case of an unexpected detour.

THE TRANS CANADA TRAIL

Place names with asterisks are included in the **Communities, Parks, and Places to Stay** section (page 218).

13

Km 0   *Beaverdell* (1.5 kilometres east of the TCT)* From the general store on Highway 33 in downtown Beaverdell, go west on Beaverdell Station Road, down the hill, and across West Kettle River. The TCT continues on the road as it veers south along the west side of West Kettle River.

Km 2.8 *TCT/KVR sign, fork* Go right onto the trail that runs beside the road. (Vehicles and motorized traffic are not permitted.)

Km 7.8 *Road shared with vehicles* Unpleasant washboard for about 11.5 kilometres.

Km 19.3 *Trail marker* The TCT is closed to vehicles.

Km 20.4 *Bridge over West Kettle River*

Km 21   *Rhone Canyon* The trail hugs the cliffs as it cuts through a narrow gorge. Photogenic views of West Kettle River gushing through the canyon and around a bend toward the mountains.

Km 24   *Blythe–Rhone Road* The TCT takes Blythe–Roane Road, continuing south and crossing a bridge back to the west side of the river.

Km 25.7 *Little Dipper Hideaway Campground and B&B** Pitch a tent beside the river.

Km 28.7 *Cyclists Rest** Marked by a KVR caboose replica on a slope above the road. Be treated to the enthusiastic hospitality of

Mike LeBlanc on the KVR rail trail near Westbridge

13

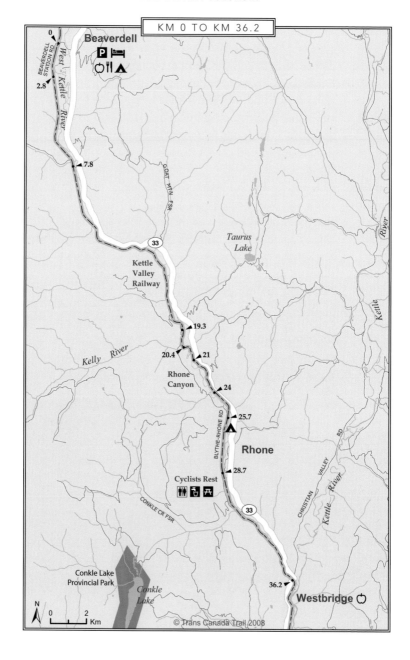

KM 0 TO KM 36.2

Beaverdell

Taurus Lake

Kettle Valley Railway

Rhone Canyon

Rhone

Cyclists Rest

Conkle Lake Provincial Park

Conkle Lake

Westbridge

© Trans Canada Trail 2008

N
0   2
Km

octogenarian Paul Lautard—read more about him on page 215. (Outhouses, fresh water, emergency shelter.)

Km 31.3   *Fork* The TCT veers right onto Jim Dandy Road.

Km 32.6   *Fork* Stay left.

Km 33.4   TCT *marker* The TCT continues on the railway bed, which is closed to vehicles here.

Km 36.2   *Westbridge** The TCT/KVR comes to Highway 33 near a bridge over the West Kettle River. Cross the highway (not the bridge) to pick up the trail on the other side. The West Kettle River merges with the Kettle River, which the TCT follows south along the west side. Watch for ground squirrels, hawks, and deer.

Km 43.3   *Pine island* An island of tall pine trees lies near a bend in the river; good fishing hole.

Island of pine trees in Kettle River

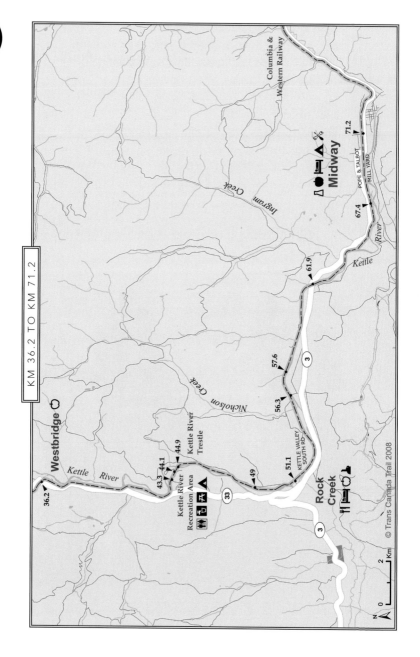

KM 36.2 TO KM 71.2

Columbia & Western Railway

Ingram Creek

71.2

Midway

POPE & TALBOT
MILL YARD

67.4

Kettle River

61.9

Westbridge

Kettle River

Nicholson Creek

57.6

56.3

Kettle River Trestle

44.9

44.1

43.3

Kettle River Recreation Area

51.1

KETTLE VALLEY SOUTH RD.

49

Rock Creek

36.2

33

3

3

© Trans Canada Trail 2008

0   2 Km

N

Km 44.1 *Kettle River Recreation Area** Appealing riverside campground in a forest of ponderosa pine. (Access to Highway 33.)

Km 44.9 *Kettle River Trestle* A black steel truss bridge crossing the Kettle River. Sandy riverbank and good swimming below.

Km 49 *Possibility of blocked trail* (If the trail is blocked, turn left (southeast) onto a paved and scenic back road that runs south along the Kettle River's eastern bank toward Rock Creek.)

Km 51.1 *Kettle River East Road + Kettle Valley South Road, Community of Rock Creek** The TCT continues to the southeast along Kettle Valley South Road. (To reach Rock Creek, turn right (southwest) on a road that crosses a bridge over the Kettle River and meets Highway 33 near its intersection with Highway 3. Rock Creek is near this highway junction. Highway 3 (Crowsnest Highway) meets the TCT periodically as it follows the Kettle River east toward Midway.)

Km 56.3 *Kettle Valley South Road + railbed/TCT marker* Where the road turns south across the river, bear left onto the railway bed.

Km 57.6 *Possibility of blocked trail* (If the trail is blocked, backtrack 1.3 kilometres, cross the river to the south side, and turn left (east) on Highway 3. Take the highway bridge over the river and return to the railway bed below the bridge (Km 61.9).)

Km 61.9 *Highway 3 bridge over Kettle River* The TCT continues under the bridge on the railway bed.

Km 67.4 *Pope & Talbot mill* The TCT continues off-road toward Midway. It leaves the railway bed and takes a trail through the Pope & Talbot mill yard. Highway 3 is an alternative for the final stretch into Midway, but you will miss the sign on the railbed: "Midway, BC. 'Mile 0' of the KVR, Warmly Welcomes Cyclists."

Km 71.2 *Midway Station, Midway** Halfway across British Columbia, the KVR's Midway Station sits in the shade of an old maple tree between the rail trail and Highway 3. (The TCT continues east on the Columbia & Western Railway trail.)

CYCLISTS REST: A TCT LANDMARK

Some of the cyclists wheeling past his house on the Trans Canada Trail looked hot, thirsty, and weary, so Paul Lautard decided to show them some down-home hospitality. In 1998 he erected a wood-framed shelter

13

LOCAL ADVENTURE FOR CYCLISTS

OSOYOOS LOOP FROM KVR'S MILE 0 ↻ 360 KM

The 220 kilometres of Trans Canada Trail on the Kettle Valley Railway in the Carmi subdivision can be combined with highways and back roads to make up a 360-kilometre bicycling loop that encircles the southern end of the Okanagan Highland.

Starting in Midway, head west on Highway 3 for 73 kilometres to Osoyoos. The road rolls through a landscape of sparse forests and farms where deer, ground squirrels, vultures, and hawks are common. (Johnstone Creek Provincial Park, about 25 kilometres west of Midway, has 16 campsites.) The highway goes up 650 metres in elevation over Anarchist Summit, then drops 1,000 metres over 32 kilometres of switchbacks to Osoyoos, taking in endless views over Osoyoos Lake and Washington state. Take Highway 97 north along the west side of Osoyoos Lake, stopping at the Desert Centre to stroll the boardwalks. This so-called Pocket Desert is one of Canada's rarest ecosystems with species such as the Great Basin spadefoot toad (*Scaphiopus intermontanus*), western rattlesnake (*Crotalus viridis*), and night snake (*Hypsiglena torquata*).

At the north end of Osoyoos Lake, turn right (east) off the highway to Haynes' Lease Ecological Reserve, and take an 18-kilometre trail along the Okanagan River. The trail passes the Oxbows, a series of bends in the river with swampy islands and peninsulas of critical wildlife habitat. Continue upstream through the community of Oliver to McAlpine Bridge, where the river and Highway 97 intersect.

Take the highway to Vaseux Lake, where there's good birdwatching and bighorn-sheep viewing, then continue to Okanagan Falls, a picturesque town on Skaha Lake (with a 25-site provincial campground). From there, Eastside Road then Lakeshore Road are off-highway routes through the orchards along the eastern shore of Skaha Lake to Penticton. Get on the TCT/KVR in Penticton, which is Km 12.6 in Chapter 11, and ride nearly 220 kilometres back to Midway (following the directions in Chapters 11, 12, and 13).

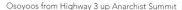

Osoyoos from Highway 3 up Anarchist Summit

and strung up some hammocks, and named it Cyclists Rest. Now it's a landmark (Km 28.7, near Rhone), and Lautard is somewhat of a legend in these parts.

13

A youthful, gregarious octogenarian, Lautard is the son of a Kettle Valley Railway maintenance foreman. He spent half his life as an indus-trial carpenter in Vancouver before coming home to Rhone. From his house above Cyclists Rest, he keeps an eye out for visitors, then whizzes down on his ATV with a jug of ice-cold water and his dog, Stubby. He invites TCT travellers to sign their names on the rafters—"if you can find a spot"—while Stubby per-forms tricks.

His first year, 452 cyclists came by to accept his hospitality. Numbers increased to more than 1,700 some

Paul Lautard and Stubby at Cyclists Rest

years, although there was a decline after the Myra Canyon burned in 2003. "I see cyclists from everywhere—Latvia, Sweden, South Africa, Australia, Germany."

At Cyclists Rest, Lautard has provided outhouses and picnic tables, and in 2002 he built a full-sized replica of a KVR caboose, decked out with a wood stove, first aid supplies, and bunks for cyclists or hikers who get caught in bad weather.

"I know what it's like to be away from home," says Lautard, who stormed the beaches of Normandy in 1944. "If I can help them, I will."

RAIL TRAILS MAKE FOR WORRY-FREE BICYCLE TOURS

Halfway across southern British Columbia, the village of Midway is the birthplace of a bourgeoning industry—rail trail tourism in BC. From Mid-way, officially Mile 0 on the Kettle Valley Railway, KVR trains ran for nearly 500 kilometres west to Hope in the 1900s. Nowadays the KVR is a rail trail, and Midway is the starting point for many TCT travellers, mainly cyclists, going westbound.

The first 220 kilometres to Penticton make up the KVR's Carmi sub-division, which is also part of the Trans Canada Trail. This is BC's most popular multi-day cycle tour, with campsites and accommodation, stores, communities, and whistle stops spaced along the route. This area was

MIDWAY, BC
"MILE 0" of KVR
Warmly Welcomes Cyclists
Info Centre 1 km

Mike LeBlanc prepares
to ride into Midway

singled out for a pilot project under a provincial rail trails strategy, launched in 2003, to determine travel-industry standards for trail maintenance, signage, and facilities, as well as marketing. There are 2,000 kilometres of abandoned railway corridors in BC; half are already developed to some degree and used by hikers, equestrians, cyclists, skiers, and snowshoers, among others.

Rail trails are a worry-free way to travel. Away from traffic, they showcase the province from a "back door" perspective, especially through small towns. Anyone in reasonable shape can handle 40 or 50 kilometres a day on a well-maintained rail trail. While people of all ages ride BC's rail trails, it seems the majority are aging baby boomers who enjoy the outdoors and a moderate all-day aerobic workout but aren't interested in scaling mountains or packing a week's worth of camping gear.

BOUNDARY COUNTRY REGION

The area between McCulloch Lake and Christina Lake is known as Boundary Country. Here the TCT crosses the Midway and Christina ranges of the Monashee Mountains. For detailed information, see page 205 in Chapter 12.

COMMUNITIES, PARKS, AND PLACES TO STAY

Information on each provincial park in BC can be found on the BC Parks website at www.env.gov.bc.ca/bcparks/.

♣ Beaverdell (Km 0)

See page 206 in the previous chapter.

⊨ ▲ Little Dipper Hideaway Campground and B&B (Km 25.7)

Tent and RV sites, rooms, and a cabin beside the West Kettle River. Off Highway 33, ten kilometres north of Westbridge. 250-446-2213; www .littledipperhideaway.com.

13

⚶ Cyclists Rest (Km 28.7)

Free hospitality and history lessons from a spry octogenarian whose father was a local railway man. (See page 215.) At 3505 Blythe–Rhone Road, 7.5 kilometres northwest of Westbridge. 🚻 *outhouses* 🚰 | *first aid, emergency overnight shelter*

♣ Westbridge (Km 36.2)

On Highway 33, 13 kilometres north of Rock Creek.
🍎 *general store* | *post office, access to Highway 33*

♣♣ Kettle River Recreation Area (Km 44.1)

Off Highway 33, five kilometres north of Rock Creek. Summer swimming, tubing, canoeing; winter cross-country skiing and snowshoeing on the TCT. 🏕 ⛺ 🚻 *outhouses* 🚰 | *telephone*

Midway Station, KVR Mile 0

13

> **Size** 179 hectares
> **Attractions** Open forests of ponderosa pine and bunchgrass, also old-growth cottonwoods. The BC Parks website has a good map of the park and its hiking trails.
> **Camping** 87 drive-in sites. *Reservations* 1-800-689-9025 (or 604-689-9025 in Metro Vancouver). www.discovercamping.ca

Rock Creek (Km 51.1)

At the junction of Highway 3 and Highway 33. Once a mining town, now an agricultural community in the Kettle Valley. ⑦ ⊨ ⊘ *convenience stores* ⚓ ⱺ *pub | gift shop, fruit stands, ice cream*

> **Population** 300
> **Visitor Info** Search for "Rock Creek" at www.britishcolumbia.com.
> **Attractions** Horse riding on logging roads and skidding trails.
> **Greyhound Bus** (1-800-661-8747; www.greyhound.ca) Depot located at *Rock Creek Service* at the junction of Highways 3 and 33.
> **Accommodation** *Rock Creek Hotel*, circa 1893.

Midway (Km 71.2)

Halfway across BC, 504 kilometres by highway from Victoria on the Pacific Ocean and from Sparwood in the Rocky Mountains. "Mile 0" (or "Kilometre 0") on the Kettle Valley Railway, in the Carmi subdivision. Once a railway and mining town, now a sawmilling and agricultural community, Midway's most notable landmark is the old railway station, sporting a new coat of paint behind a white picket fence. It rests in the shade of a giant maple between Highway 3 and the Trans Canada Trail. The station's next-door neighbour is the Kettle River Museum, a good source of local information. ⑦ ● ⌂ ✕ ⱺ *pub* ▲ *| bakery, canoe rentals*

> **Population** 700
> **Visitor Info** *Village of Midway* 661 Eighth Avenue, Midway, BC V0H 1M0; 250-449-2222; www.midwaybc.cjb.net.
> **Attractions** Hiking and equestrian trails, Entwined Trees, heritage homes and buildings.
> **Greyhound Bus** (1-800-661-8747; www.greyhound.ca) Depot located at *Midway Spot* at 728 Palmerston Avenue.
> **Camping** *Riverfront Park village campsite* at the edge of the Kettle River; showers, grassy tent sites, cooking shelter for tenters.

14 MIDWAY TO CHRISTINA LAKE

66 Did you guys know they made a movie about this town, too.
It's called *Snow Falling on Cedars*. You can rent it at the
video store.
—*A Greenwood resident calling
from her passing car to TCT cyclists*

Kettle River near Christina Lake

TRAIL TRIVIA

It is said that Christina Lake was named in the 1860s for the daughter of Hudson's Bay Company merchant Angus McDonald. The story is that she once plunged into a stream that ran from the lake to retrieve her father's papers that had fallen from shore.

TOTAL DISTANCE

77.6 km

HIGHLIGHTS

› Greenwood
› Grand Forks
› Kettle River trestle south of Christina Lake
› Christina Lake

CONDITIONS

› **Midway (Km 0) to Eholt Station (Km 29.2)** Mainly single-track and some double-track hard-packed railway bed. → 29.2 km
› **Eholt Station (Km 29.2) to Grand Forks (Km 52.3)** Rocky, particularly the last 16 kilometres. → 23.1 km
› **Grand Forks (Km 52.3) to Christina Lake (Km 77.6)** Mainly hard double-track railbed, but soft and weedy in places. Rocky beyond the trestle over the Kettle River near Christina Lake. → 25.3 km

CAUTIONS

› Greenwood (Km 13.9) is the last chance for supplies for nearly 40 kilometres to Grand Forks (Km 52.3).

TOPOGRAPHIC MAPS

1:250,000 Penticton 82E
1:50,000 Grand Forks 82E/1, Greenwood 82E/2

OVERVIEW

Having followed the Kettle Valley Railway's Coquihalla, Princeton, and Carmi subdivisions to Midway, the Trans Canada Trail continues east on yet another abandoned railway corridor—the Columbia & Western. Like the KVR, the C&W is an off-road saunter that reveals a side of BC history often overlooked by highway travellers—mountains of mining slag at Greenwood, crumbling trestle footings, and trestles newly restored.

From Midway to Christina Lake, Highway 3 and the TCT/C&W run through the same valleys for much of way. But they often are separated by streams, hills, and forests, making the TCT mildly remote here. The remoteness intensifies beyond the defunct Eholt Station, where Highway 3 makes an abrupt turn south while the TCT continues east. The TCT heads south eventually, following a cliff-hugging track high above the Granby River Valley.

The highway and TCT are reunited at Grand Forks. So, too, are the Kettle River and British Columbia: after looping down from Midway through Washington state, the river re-enters BC near Carson, a non-descript Canada Customs post on the southwest outskirts of Grand Forks. As the river heads east to Christina Lake, it once again provides the corridor for the highway and TCT.

LOCAL ADVENTURES

Day Trip

› Cycle from Midway (Km 0) to Greenwood (Km 13.9) and back. ⇆ 27.8 km
› Cycle from Greenwood (Km 13.9) to Eholt Station (Km 29.2) and back. ⇆ 30.6 km
› Cycle from Grand Forks (Km 52.3) to Christina Lake (Km 77.6) and back. ⇆ 50.6 km

2 or 3 Days

› From Grand Forks (Km 52.3), cycle a loop to Midway (Km 0), going one way on the trail and returning on Highway 3, or vice versa. ↺ 108 km
› Or cycle a longer loop on the trail to Rock Creek (Chapter 13, Km 51.1), returning to Grand Forks on Highway 3. ↺ 145 km
› Stay at Grand Forks (Km 52.3) and explore the TCT on both sides of town.

TCT ACCESS POINTS

Midway (Km 0) On Highway 3, 18 kilometres east of Rock Creek.

Greenwood (Km 13.9) On Highway 3, 16 kilometres east of Midway.

Tunnel of Flags (Km 17) On Highway 3, about two kilometres north of Greenwood. **P** *parking in a small roadside pullout*

14

Eholt Station (Km 29.2) About 12.5 kilometres northeast of Greenwood, turn left (northeast) off Highway 3 on Eholt Road.

Grand Forks (Km 52.3) On Highway 3, 40 kilometres southeast of Greenwood. 🅿 *parking lots, on-street parking*

Christina Lake (Km 77.6) On Highway 3, 21 kilometres east of Grand Forks. Turn right (south) off the highway onto Santa Rosa Road, and go 1.4 kilometres to a parking area where the TCT/C&W railway bed crosses the road. From here the TCT heads north on the C&W railway bed to Castlegar. Hikers and horses can continue with touring cyclists on the TCT, or take the Dewdney Trail east to Rossland. 🅿 🐎

BROAD VALLEY VIEWS AND ROUGH SPOTS

TAKE TIME OUT FOR SCENERY

The TCT quickly blends into a landscape of farms and forests as it takes the C&W Railway corridor northeast from Midway. Both the TCT and Highway 3 run next to Boundary Creek before veering east along Eholt Creek to Eholt Station. Aching legs here are reminders that railway grades are not flat: even a subtle climb of less than 1.5 percent is tiring over 30 kilometres.

En route to Eholt Station, Greenwood is the last urban stop before heading deeper into the southern Monashees. If the views across the Granby River Valley don't slow travellers between Eholt and Grand Forks, the railway surface will. The second half is rocky, requiring undivided attention to avoid dumping. The trail improves east of Grand Forks, where it follows the Kettle River, eventually crossing it over a scenic gorge, and again on a spectacular trestle south of Christina Lake.

THE TRANS CANADA TRAIL

Place names with asterisks are included in the **Communities, Parks, and Places to Stay** section (page 232).

Km 0   *Midway Station* Get on the C&W railway bed by the big maple tree next to the restored station in Midway* and head east. It's nearly impossible to get lost.

Km 11.3   *Boundary Creek Provincial Park** (Campsites available at this park. To reach the park, leave the TCT and take a road to the

West Kootenay Power Building in Greenwood

right (east) that leads to Highway 3. Turn right (south) at the highway and go one kilometre to the park.)

Km 13.4   *West Kootenay Power Building* The TCT crosses a bridge behind a brick building, circa 1906, which is expected to be developed as a showcase for local history. You will also see nearby slag piles and a 36-metre brick smokestack. (Outhouse.)

Km 13.9   TCT + *Washington Road, Greenwood** Washington Road intersects the TCT. (To get to Greenwood, turn right at Washington Road. A bridge crosses over Boundary Creek and leads to Highway 3 in Greenwood.) The TCT continues straight, along the west side of the creek. (The mammoth slag piles at Lotzkar Memorial Park are a short way up a dirt road to the left—read more on page 230.)

Km 14.5   TCT + *Louisa Street* (A second access to Highway 3 and Greenwood—turn right.)

Km 16.9   *Boundary Creek* At this photogenic spot, the trail crosses Boundary Creek for the last time.

Km 17   *Tunnel of Flags,* TCT + *Highway 3* The unsightly ruins of a 1913 railway trestle were transformed into a global landmark in

14

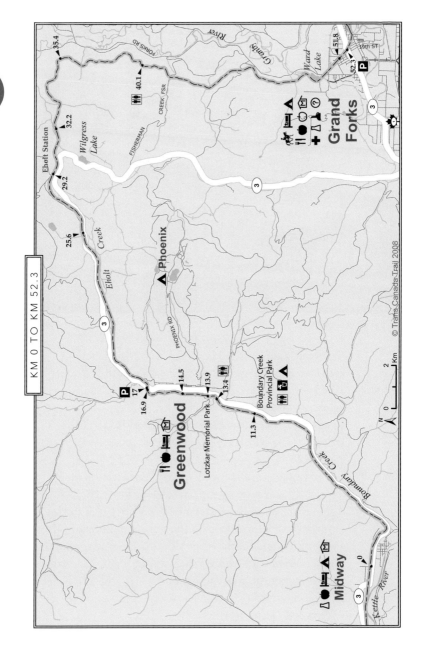

KM 0 TO KM 52.3

© Trans Canada Trail 2008

2000 by Greenwood Mayor Arno Hennig, who painted flags from around the world on the concrete face. The TCT drops down off the rail grade and crosses the highway. On the other side, don't go straight up the hillside: look for TCT markers delineating a longer but easier trail that switchbacks up to the rail grade and begins following Eholt Creek eastward.

Km 25.6   *TCT + Highway 3* The railway bed crosses the highway near the headwaters of Eholt Creek. Continue on the railway.

Km 29.2   *Eholt Station* No sign of hotels or houses that stood near the tracks in the early 1900s. The TCT crosses a road here. A right (south) turn leads to Highway 3; straight across the road, the TCT continues on the railway. The trail is shared with vehicles for three kilometres.

Km 32.2   *End of shared road* The TCT crosses a road and resumes on a double-track railbed.

Km 35.4   *Tunnel* Much of the railway bed on the 17 kilometres from here to Grand Forks is uncomfortably rocky. Don't be distracted by the phenomenal views of the Granby River Valley. The descent reaches grades of more than two percent as the railbed comes down to river level in Grand Forks.

Tunnel of Flags north of Greenwood

Km 40.1   *Tunnel* An outhouse and emergency shelter overlook the Granby River, just beyond the south end of this tunnel.

Km 51.8   *Grand Forks Station* The station is now a pub that serves more hikers, cyclists, and horse riders than train passengers. Continue straight on the trail.

Km 52.3   *Grand Forks*, TCT + Highway 3* A route of about three kilometres takes the TCT through Grand Forks. The TCT crosses the highway on the rail grade, near Motel 99. Use the traffic lights one block west at 19th Street if the highway is busy. (A left turn on the highway here goes to downtown Grand Forks.) Pick up the trail on the other side and head east.

Km 53.1   *Kettle River Trestle* Don't cross the trestle; turn left (east) on Kettle River Drive and follow the TCT markers along the north bank of the river.

Km 53.6   *Kettle River Drive + Eighth Street* The trail leaves the city

14

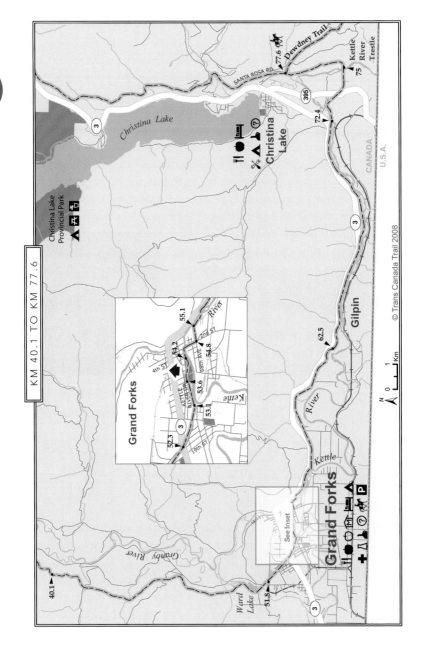

KM 40.1 TO KM 77.6

Christina Lake

Christina Lake Provincial Park

Christina Lake

SANTA ROSA RD

Dewdney Trail

77.6

Kettle River Trestle

75

395

72.4

CANADA

U.S.A.

3

62.5

Gilpin

Kettle River

© Trans Canada Trail 2008

N

0   1
Km

Grand Forks

River

55.1

2nd ST

54.2

4th ST

54.8

68th AVE

53.6

KETTLE RIVER DR

53.1

Kettle

3

52.3

19th ST

Grand Forks

See Inset

Kettle

Granby River

Ward Lake

51.8

40.1

3

streets and goes to the right down a gravel path into City Park. It then heads right onto a paved trail to the river.

Km 54.2   *City Hall* The TCT comes out of City Park at a parking lot behind City Hall and heads right on a lane between Home Hardware and River Park Estates. At Second Street turn right (south) over a bridge across the Kettle River.

Km 54.8   *Second Street + 68th Avenue* Turn left (east) onto 68th.

Km 55.1   *Kettle River Bridge* Don't cross the bridge. Instead, just before the bridge take the trail down to the right. The trail soon crosses a trestle and follows a gas pipeline on a new gravel surface. It travels between Highway 3 and the Kettle River through lightly treed mountains and farms with lots of gates. It's quiet here, mainly birds and crickets.

Km 62.5   *Trail surface changes* The quality of trail surface tends to deteriorate as it moves away from Grand Forks. While new gravel has been laid on some stretches, it is soft and weedy in places. For the most part it's an easy hike or ride.

Km 72.4   *Kettle River Trestle* The TCT crosses the river at a scenic gorge.

Km 75   *Kettle River Trestle* The easternmost trestle over the Kettle River in BC. It covers a high, breathtaking span with great

Kettle River Trestle near Christina Lake, in 2003 before decking and rails were added

14

views up and down the river. In the summer of 2003, decking and safety rails were built on this trestle by members of the 44 Field Engineer Squadron from Trail, BC, along with Britain's 21 Royal Engineer Regiment. Near this trestle the river makes a hairpin turn and flows south into Washington to join the Columbia River.

Km 77.6   *Christina Lake*, TCT + Santa Rosa Road* At the junction of the TCT/C&W Railway and Santa Rosa Road, there are two other options besides continuing on the TCT (which combines railway corridor, roads, and trails for nearly 120 kilometres to the city of Trail—see Chapter 15). You can either: 1) go left on Santa Rosa Road for 1.4 kilometres to Highway 3 and the community of Christina Lake, or 2) hike or ride a horse on a 38-kilometre stretch of the historic Dewdney Trail, a non-cycling route that eventually leads to the cities of Rossland and Trail in the West Kootenay region. (Dewdney Trail directions are provided in Chapter 15 on page 249.)

THE ONCE-MOLTEN SLAG OF HELL'S BELLS

Trans Canada Trail travellers know they're almost at Greenwood when they spot a 36-metre brick smokestack on the southern outskirts of town. The prominent landmark is a remnant from an industrious past when

Hell's bells in Greenwood

Greenwood had 3,000 residents, 20 hotels and restaurants, saloons, and a smelter that operated 'round the clock.

The Boundary region was one of the world's largest copper-producing areas. The smokestack at Anaconda, about one kilometre from Greenwood, was built by BC Copper Company, which ran the smelter from 1901 to 1918. The plant was sold to Leon Lotzkar, who disposed of the machinery and gave the land to Greenwood.

A mountain of slag at what now is Lotzkar Memorial Park, just off the TCT near Km 13.9, looks like a vast glacier of black glass, complete with gaping crevasses. Most notable are the "hell's bells," huge mounds of slag dumped by 25-tonne bell-shaped rail cars.

Near Lotzkar Park, the brick West Kootenay Power Building, built in 1906, is expected to be developed as an interpretive centre displaying the area's industrial past.

THE KETTLE RIVER SYSTEM PROVIDES HISTORIC ROUTES

The Kettle and West Kettle rivers are a constant companion for travellers along much of the Trans Canada Trail. The first close encounter is just south of Carmi, where the TCT runs parallel to the West Kettle River. The river comes and goes from view as the trail follows it down to Westbridge, where it joins the main Kettle River. From there to Midway the TCT continues along the Kettle River Valley until the river flows across the Canada–U.S. border into Washington. It returns to Canada near Grand Forks and again provides a travel corridor for the TCT. At the second trestle south of Christina Lake (Km 75), the Kettle River makes a sharp turn south, back down to Washington, where it flows into the Columbia River.

In 1997 the West Kettle River was proclaimed a British Columbia Heritage River, giving special recognition to its natural, cultural, historic, and recreational importance. Flowing nearly 300 kilometres from its headwaters in the Monashee Mountains to the Columbia River, the Kettle River system drains 9,800 square kilometres, including 1,500 in the U.S. It generates power and provides water for homes and farms; it sustains trout, salmon, and the rare Umatilla dace (*Rhinichthys umatilla*); and it holds few hazards for canoeists. Undoubtedly the Kettle River is best known as a travel corridor for railways, highways, and the Trans Canada Trail.

14

BOUNDARY COUNTRY

The area between McCulloch Lake and Christina Lake is known as Boundary Country. Here the TCT crosses the Midway and Christina ranges of the Monashee Mountains. For detailed information, see page 205 in Chapter 12.

COMMUNITIES, PARKS, AND PLACES TO STAY

Information on each provincial park in BC can be found on the BC Parks website at www.env.gov.bc.ca/bcparks/.

Midway (Km 0)

See page 220 in the previous chapter.

Boundary Creek Provincial Park (Km 11.3)

Four kilometres west of Greenwood on Highway 3. Comfortable base for hike or bike trips to Greenwood or Midway. ▲ 🚻 🗑 | *no telephone*
› **Size** 2 hectares
› **Camping** 18 campsites shaded by cottonwood, Douglas fir, spruce, and pine trees.

Greenwood (Km 13.9)

Named in 2002 by *Harrowsmith Country Life* magazine as one of the top ten places to live in Canada. Greenwood looks like the last century to

CACTUS: A NATIVE MEDICINE

People who walk barefoot in the grasslands or pine forests of British Columbia's southern Interior risk a painful encounter with prickly pear cactus (*Opuntia fragilis*). This prostrate perennial is widespread at lower elevations, where it grows in spiny mats over the arid landscapes.

The spines, one to three centimetres long, are actually leaves attached to fleshy green stems. The cactus produces brilliant yellow flowers and tiny pear-shaped berries. The succulent stems were collected by aboriginals and cooked for use in soups, cakes, and cough syrup.

Downtown Greenwood

people who roll in on the Trans Canada Trail. City Hall, the post office, and other buildings from the early 1900s look like new. In the "Hotel Block" downtown, hanging baskets overflowing with summer flowers embellish the Copper Eagle Cappuccino and Bakery. Next door, the bay windows on the Greenwood Saloon Inn are freshly painted. On the outskirts of town the brick smokestack from a copper smelter rises over a mountain of steely black slag. Greenwood Museum is a good start for history buffs to get oriented. ⓘ ● ⅞ 🏛 | *post office*

› **Population** 800
› **Visitor Info** *Greenwood Museum and Visitor Centre* 214 South Copper Street, Box 399, Greenwood, BC V0H 1J0; 250-445-6355; www.greenwood museum.com. *City of Greenwood* 202 Government Avenue, Greenwood, BC V0H 1J0; 250-445-6644; www.greenwoodcity.com.
› **Attractions** Heritage building walking tour, Lotzkar Memorial Park "hell's bells" (described on page 230).
› **Greyhound Bus** (1-800-661-8747; www.greyhound.ca) Depot located at *Evening Star Motel* on Highway 3.

♣ Grand Forks (Km 52.3)

At the confluence of two major rivers, the Kettle and the Granby, Grand Forks was once home to the largest non-ferrous copper smelter in the British Empire. The smelter closed in 1919, but the abrasive slag is still used for sandblasting. Forestry is the mainstay here nowadays, along with agriculture, tourism, and mining. Grand Forks is rather like a larger version of Greenwood with early 20th-century buildings along shady, tree-lined streets, with rivers that run through the heart of town and mountains on all sides. ⑦ ▲ ● ⌂ ✕ ⑪ | *most needs and services*

› **Population** 4,000

› **Visitor Info** *Grand Forks Visitor Centre* 7362 Fifth Street, Box 1086, Grand Forks, BC V0H 1H0; 1-866-442-2833; 250-442-2833; www.grandforks chamber.com; www.boundary.bc.ca.

› **Attractions** Downtown heritage walking tour, horse riding, rock candy safari mine tour, Grand Forks Art Gallery, Mountain View Doukhobor Museum.

› **Cycling** *Chain Reaction Bike and Board* 7236 Third Street; 250-442-0118; www.chainreactionrideandslide.com.

› **Greyhound Bus** (1-800-661-8747; www.greyhound.ca) Depot located at *K Star Enterprises* at 2–7500 Donaldson Drive.

› **Camping** *Grand Forks City Park,* a municipal campground. 7362 Fifth Street; 250-442-2833; www.boundary.bc.ca.

♣ Christina Lake (Km 77.6)

A vacation community on a lake that warms up to 23°C. The population quadruples in summer. ⑦ ↻ ● ✕ ⑪

› **Population** 1,500

› **Visitor Info** *Christina Lake Chamber of Commerce* Highway 3 & Kimura Road, Christina Lake, BC V0H 1E2; 250-447-6161; www.christinalake .com.

› **Attractions** Kettle River trestle (Km 75), Dewdney Trail (Km 77.6—see page 249 for trail directions), horseback riding, Christina Lake Provincial Park (day use).

› **Cycling** *WildWays Adventure Sports* has a bike sales, rental, and repair shop that also offers tours and shuttle services. On Highway 3; 1-888-945-3929; 250-447-6561; www.wildways.com.

› **Greyhound Bus** (1-800-661-8747; www.greyhound.ca) Depot located at *Lakeside General Store* at 1819 Todesco Road.

15 CHRISTINA LAKE TO TRAIL

66 I consider this a huge opportunity. It's going to take millions of dollars to get all the trestles, the tunnels, and railbeds in shape, but I also believe it's going to contribute millions and millions to the provincial economy.
— *Don Foxgord, Tourism British Columbia's vice-president of business development, on rail trail tourism*

The Columbia River between Castlegar and Trail

TRAIL TRIVIA

The Columbia River system produces one-third of BC Hydro's power, and more than one-third of all the electricity used by the United States.

TOTAL DISTANCE

117.8 km

HIGHLIGHTS

> The Columbia & Western rail trail
> The Teck Cominco smelter

CONDITIONS

> **C&W rail trail/Christina Lake (Km 0) to Keenleyside Dam (Km 78.4)** Generally good cycling surface with six kilometres of rough ballast near the end. → 78.4 km
> **Keenleyside Dam (Km 78.4) to Trail (Km 117.8)** Paved roads for 16.5 km, rough but cyclable trail for 19.2 kilometres, and finally paved roads for 3.7 kilometres. → 39.4 km

CAUTIONS

> No amenities on the rail trail between Christina Lake (Km 0) and Castlegar (Km 86.9). Accessible water is scarce; refill at every opportunity.
> Voracious mosquitoes at the Farron campsite.
> Dark tunnels. Use a flashlight or headlamp though Bulldog and Coykendahl tunnels.
> Bears.

TOPOGRAPHIC MAPS

| 1:250,000 | Penticton 82E, Nelson 82F |
| 1:50,000 | Grand Forks 82E/1, Deer Park 82E/8, Rossland–Trail 82F/4, Castlegar 82F/5 |

OVERVIEW

From Christina Lake, the Trans Canada Trail continues north and then east on the Columbia & Western rail trail to Castlegar. The C&W trail, well travelled by cyclists but also used by hikers and equestrians, is part of a 118-kilometre route to the city of Trail. After climbing high above Christina Lake, the route runs north along the west side of the Rossland Range to a high ridge overlooking the Selkirk Mountains and Lower Arrow Lake, part of a reservoir on the Columbia River. The rail trail moves downstream to end at Hugh Keenleyside Dam. The TCT takes a short jaunt through Castlegar, then crosses the Columbia River and follows it downstream along the west side of the Bonnington Range toward Trail.

Hikers and equestrians (but not cyclists) have the option of leaving the TCT at Christina Lake and travelling back in time to the gold-rush era of the 1860s. The historic Dewdney Trail (see page 249) is a route east to Rossland, a city of 3,800 in the southern Monashee Mountains. Part of a path to gold fields across southern BC, this 37.5-kilometre section of the Dewdney Trail is much like it was in its heyday—scenic, steep, and challenging. (From Rossland, travellers can take a road and railbed route to Trail, where they can rejoin the TCT.)

LOCAL ADVENTURES

Day Trip

› Get a shuttle from Christina Lake to Bonanza Siding (Km 28.9), and cycle the railway bed for 29 km back to Christina Lake or 58 km to Castlegar (Km 86.9). (For shuttles, call WildWays in Christina Lake at 1-888-945-3929.)

› Cycle a Trail–Rossland loop on highways, roads, and rail trails. (See page 246 for directions.) ↻ 26.4 km

2 or 3 Days

› Cycle a loop between Christina Lake (Km 0) and Castlegar (Km 86.9) using the TCT/Columbia & Western rail trail and Highway 3. ↻ 160 km

TCT ACCESS POINTS

Christina Lake (Km 0) On Highway 3, 21 kilometres east of Grand Forks. To get to the TCT, turn southeast off the highway onto Santa Rosa Road, and go 1.4 kilometres to a parking area, where the C&W Railbed crosses the road. From here the rail trail/TCT heads north.

Bonanza Siding (Km 28.9) On the C&W railway bed between Christina Lake and Castlegar. Take Paulson Detour Road, on the northwest side of Highway 3, about 22 kilometres west of Highway 3B. Via the rail trail, Castlegar is 58 kilometres northeast of Bonanza Siding, and Christina Lake is 29 kilometres to the southwest.

Hugh Keenleyside Dam (Km 78.4) Take Columbia Avenue and Arrow Lakes Drive west from Castlegar. **P** *limited parking at the end of the* C&W *Railway bed near the Keenleyside Dam*

Castlegar (Km 86.9) At the junction of Highways 3, 3A, and 22. **P** *Parking lots, on-street parking. Inquire about long-term parking at the visitor centre.*

Trail (Km 117.8) 26 kilometres south of Highway 3 via Highway 22. **P** *parking lots, on-street parking*

THE MONASHEE MOUNTAINS TO THE SELKIRKS

RIVERS AND A RAIL TRAIL

There's little sign of civilization along the rail trail as the TCT leaves the Monashee Mountains and moves east toward the Selkirks. Except for tunnels and trestles, there are few relics from the railroading era. It is not hard, however, to envision a string of rail cars slinking around the cliff faces high over the Columbia Valley. Or trains marooned on the tracks, waiting for maintenance crews to clear the rock slides.

Speedboats on Christina Lake appear as minuscule streams of white foam to those on the rail trail, which climbs about 240 metres above the lake's eastern shore. Grades reach more than two percent on both sides of the highest point, an elevation of 1,212 metres at Farron, a former railway station. The trail climbs 700 metres in the first 35 kilometres to Farron, then descends nearly 800 metres over 43 kilometres to the northwestern outskirts of Castlegar.

Just beyond a tunnel that's nearly one kilometre long, the rail trail opens to huge views of Lower Arrow Lake, which fills the long, narrow Columbia Valley some 400 metres below. The mountains across the lake to the east—Pine Ridge, Ladybird Mountain, and the Norns Range of the Selkirks—seem a bit rough around the edges. Only one range stands between the Selkirks and the Rocky Mountains and already the terrain bears a subtle resemblance to the Rockies—sharper, craggier peaks with year-round snow and dense forests.

To the north, Deer Park Mountain, more than 1,100 metres high, stands prominently above the eastern lakeshore. The views come and go as the rail trail drops down to lake level over the next 25 kilometres, which include about six kilometres of rough riding on railway ballast.

Christina Lake

From the end of the rail trail at Hugh Keenleyside Dam, the TCT takes roads through Castlegar to the city's southern outskirts. The TCT route to Trail is a rough and narrow path down the east side of the Columbia River. Keep a close watch for TCT signs.

THE TRANS CANADA TRAIL

Place names with asterisks are included in the **Communities, Parks, and Places to Stay** section (page 251).

Km 0   *Christina Lake*,* TCT/C&W *Railway + Santa Rosa Road*
The C&W railbed intersects Santa Rosa Road and runs north, high above the eastern shore of Christina Lake. (To get on the TCT from Christina Lake, go south on Highway 3, then make a southeast (left) turn off Highway 3 onto Santa Rosa Road and proceed for 1.4 kilometres to a sharp turn and parking area beside the TCT.)

Km 4   *Fife Station* The C&W Railway crosses a road where a small shed may be the only reminder of Fife Station. Replenish water bottles at a tap near the edge of the road to the left.

Km 25.3   *Paulson Tunnel* 111-metre-long tunnel.

Km 25.8   *Paulson Bridge* A bridge high overhead on Highway 3 that

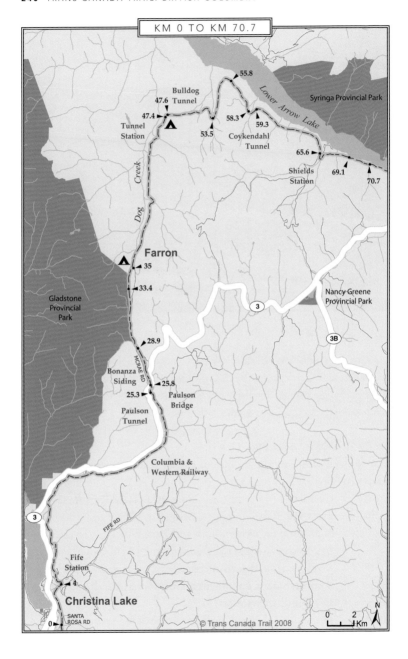

KM 0 TO KM 70.7

55.8

Bulldog
Tunnel
47.6

47.4

Tunnel
Station

53.5

58.3

59.3

Coykendahl
Tunnel

Lower Arrow Lake

Syringa Provincial Park

65.6

Shields
Station

69.1

70.7

Dog Creek

Farron

35

33.4

Gladstone
Provincial
Park

28.9

3

Nancy Greene
Provincial
Park

3B

Bonanza
Siding

25.8

25.3

Paulson
Bridge

MCRAE RD

Paulson
Tunnel

Columbia &
Western Railway

3

FIFE RD

Fife
Station

4

Christina Lake

0

SANTA
ROSA RD

© Trans Canada Trail 2008

0   2
Km

N

Paulson Bridge above the C&W rail trail

crosses the rail trail and McRae Creek. No highway access.
Just beyond the bridge are some flat, grassy areas that make
usable campsites. They are, however, beside beaver ponds
which may attract mosquitoes.

Km 28.9   *McRae Road, Bonanza Siding* In an area known as Bonanza
Siding, the railbed continues straight across a road that leads
down to a farm on the left. On the right is a road that parallels
the railbed: if you turn right, Highway 3 is about 2.6 kilometres to the east.

Km 33.4   *Farron Explosion monument* A short path to the left leads to a
monument commemorating the death of Doukhobor leader
Peter Verigin. He was assassinated in 1924 when his train was
bombed here. Eight other passengers died. (See page 245 for
more on the Doukhobors.)

Km 35   *Farron* There is little here except old concrete ruins that mark
a widening of the trail with grassy spots to camp on either
side. The most secluded site is up a short hill to the right,
where there's an outdoor biffy in the trees. Drinking water
can be filtered from a creek that flows under the railway bed

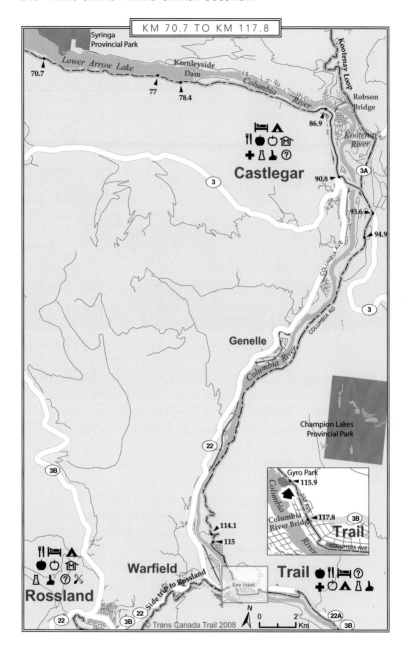

KM 70.7 TO KM 117.8

Syringa
Provincial Park

Lower Arrow Lake

70.7

Keenleyside
Dam

Columbia River

Kootenay Loop

77

78.4

Robson
Bridge

86.9

Kootenay River

Castlegar

3

3A

90.8

93.6

94.9

COLUMBIA AVE

3

Genelle

Columbia River

COLUMBIA RD

Champion Lakes
Provincial Park

22

Gyro Park

115.9

Columbia

3RD AVE

117.8

3B

Columbia
River Bridge

Trail

COLUMBIA AVE

114.1

115

3B

Warfield

Side trip to Rossland

Trail

Rossland

22

22

3B

© Trans Canada Trail 2008

N   0   2
                     Km

22A

3B

15

about 600 metres back down the trail. Mosquitoes here in early summer can be monstrous, abundant, and voracious. At just over 1,200 metres, Farron is the highest point on the C&W Railway between Grand Forks and Castlegar. The tiring two-percent climb becomes a descent of similar gradient down Dog Creek Valley. But there's rough road ahead.

Km 47.4 *Tunnel Station* Concrete ruins of train station. Usable trailside tent sites on both sides of Bulldog Tunnel.

Km 47.6 *Bulldog Tunnel* Although there's light at the end of the tunnel, it's too far away—930 metres—to illuminate the middle. A flashlight is needed. The surface is rocky, and water dripping from the ceiling fills puddles below. Best to walk. After the tunnel, the rail trail turns east toward Lower Arrow Lake.

Km 53.5 *Arrow Lakes Reservoir* Views of BC's third-largest reservoir (more than 500 square kilometres) and beyond to the Selkirk Mountains.

Km 55.8 *Rock slide* A track worn by use can be used to squeeze around a pile of boulders that have tumbled onto the trail.

Km 58.3 *Coykendahl Station* Little evidence of the station.

Km 59.3 *Coykendahl Tunnel* It's only 90 metres long, but Coykendahl Tunnel curves in the middle, blocking the light from the other end. Walk with a flashlight.

Km 65.6 *Shields Station* No evidence of the station.

Km 69.1 *View of the Keenleyside Dam* Hugh Keenleyside Dam at the eastern end of Lower Arrow Lake is visible, with pulp mills and sawmills downstream on the Columbia River.

Km 70.7 *Rough surface* Start of a nerve-racking 6.3-kilometre stretch surfaced with apple-sized railway ballast.

Km 77 *End of ballast* The surface changes from rough ballast to smoother gravel. The rail ties are removed but the steel rails are still in place.

Km 78.4 *End of C&W Railway trail* At the end of the railway continue 900 metres toward Keenleyside Dam, and turn right onto the paved road that parallels the south side of the Columbia River toward Castlegar. A pleasant, shaded route with wide views of the river and mountains.

Km 86.9 *Castlegar*, Robson Bridge* Don't cross the bridge: just before it, take Columbia Avenue to the right (southeast) into Castlegar and continue south toward Trail.

15

Peter Verigin monument near Farron Station

Km 90.8 *Columbia Avenue (Highway 22) + Highway 3* Turn left (east) onto Highway 3 and take the sidewalk on the bridge across the Columbia River. (From here the TCT's combination of trails and old roads may be difficult for cyclists. Those who prefer pavement should not head toward this Highway 3 bridge, but stay on Columbia Avenue (Highway 22). It is 26 kilometres from Castlegar to Trail (Km 117.8).)

Km 93.6 *Highway 3 + Columbia Road* Turn right (south) onto Columbia Road.

Km 94.9 *Columbia Road + Prairie Road* Veer right onto Prairie Road. Continue toward the landfill and beyond the pavement to the marked TCT route along the Columbia River down to Trail. Keep a close watch for TCT signs.

Km 114.1 *Pavement + Sandpit Road* Go left onto Sandpit Road, which runs downhill.

Km 115 *Marianna Crescent* At the bottom of the hill, bear right along Marianna and Hazelwood Drive through a neighbourhood along the Columbia River.

Km 115.9 *Gyro Park* Stay on the riverside road through the park, where you will find a Trans Canada Trail Pavilion. Head toward Highway 3B/the Columbia River Bridge in downtown Trail.

Km 117.8 *Downtown Trail*, TCT + Highway 3B (Columbia River Bridge)* The TCT crosses the highway. (Turning right will lead to the Columbia River Bridge.) From here the trail goes east along the Columbia River and beyond toward the Purcell and

Rocky mountains. An optional itinerary is to go to the town of Rossland* to the west and loop back by taking a 16-kilometre road-and-trail route (see page 246). You can also start farther west at Christina Lake, and take the Dewdney Trail to Rossland (see page 249). Both options are described in detail next.

DOUKHOBOR MURDER A MYSTERY

Tucked away in the bush beside the Columbia & Western Railway trail near Farron Station is an inconspicuous monument commemorating the assassination of Doukhobor leader Peter "the Lordly" Verigin (Km 33.4). He was one of nine passengers killed on October 29, 1924, when a night train bound for Grand Forks was blown up, reportedly by the first time bomb ever made in Canada.

A religious sect of pacifists who had rejected the Russian Orthodox Church, the Doukhobors (or "Spirit Wrestlers") immigrated to Canada in the early 1900s. About 5,000 built settlements in the Grand Forks, Castlegar, and Kootenay areas, where they acquired land and lived by their motto Toil and Peaceful Life. They planted orchards, packed fruits, manufactured bricks, and built sawmills and a jam factory.

Despite their industriousness, the Doukhobors' pacifist views and resistance to authority caused friction with governments and neighbouring communities. Their communal lifestyle started to deteriorate after Verigin's murder, a crime that remains unsolved.

Except for the odd cluster of derelict buildings, little remains today of some 90 Doukhobor communes that once thrived in this region. The Union of Spiritual Communities of Christ, the world's most active Doukhobor organization, is headquartered in Grand Forks and Castlegar, where several thousand Doukhobors now have integrated into mainstream society. It's estimated that well over 30,000 Doukhobors live in British Columbia, most in the Grand Forks, Castlegar, and Kootenay regions.

To get a taste of Doukhobor life in the early 1900s, visit Mountain View Doukhobor Museum, in a restored 1912 Doukhobor communal house west of Grand Forks (3655 Hardy Mountain Road; 250-442-8855), and Doukhobor Discovery Centre, a reconstructed community above the Columbia River in Castlegar (112 Heritage Way in Castlegar; 250-365-5327; http://kdhs.kics.bc.ca). A bread-baking oven, wood-fired *banya* (sauna), naturally dyed homemade fabrics, and tools are among 1,000 artifacts of old Doukhobor life.

LOCAL ADVENTURE

FROM TRAIL TO ROSSLAND AND BACK ↻ 26.4 KM

Touring cyclists can combine a ten-kilometre stretch of highway with 16.4 kilometres of trails and roads for a loop that goes from Trail to Rossland and back. From Trail, start with a steep climb up Highway 22/3B to Rossland, or take a BC Transit bus, which carries up to two bicycles. In Rossland, head west on Columbia Avenue, then veer left (southwest) onto Dunn Crescent to Black Bear Drive and the Rossland Lions Park campground, about one kilometre from downtown Rossland. A kiosk in the campground shows a map and local trail detail.

Downtown Rossland

Km 0   *Rossland Lions Park campground* At the campground gates, head left (northwest) up Black Bear Road for 400 metres and turn left onto Drakes Trail.

Km 2.7   *Drakes Trail and Doukhobor Draw Trail* Travellers headed for the city of Trail stay on Drakes Trail as it continues to the left (south). (The Doukhobor Draw Trail goes right to Highway 22 and the Dewdney Trail's eastern trailhead.)

Km 3.1   *Drakes Road* The trail comes out at a cul-de-sac and takes Drakes Road to the left (east) for about 400 metres, then veers right off the road onto a trail.

Km 4.2   *Railgrade Trail* The trail crosses Gelesz Road to the start of a scenic eight-kilometre rail trail to the village of Warfield.

Km 12.1   *Warfield* From a kiosk at the eastern end of the Railgrade Trail, go straight and cross Highway 22/3B at a crosswalk to Arnold Lauriente Way, a continuation of the rail trail. After about 900 metres the route crosses Highway 22/3B at Webster School, then continues just past Forrest Drive onto a trail through a municipal park.

Km 13.4   *Montcalm Road* The trail comes to Montcalm Road, where you turn right and go downhill. Continue about 400 metres and cross a bridge over Trail Creek to the left. Turn left after the bridge and stay to the left along the roads.

Km 15.8   *Reservoir Road + Binns Street* Take a hairpin turn to the left onto Binns, and go down to Highway 22/3B, where you turn right. Continue to the bridge across the Columbia River to downtown Trail.

Km 16.4   *Columbia River Bridge* The route from Rossland* intercepts the TCT route from Castlegar on the eastern side of the bridge. Cross the bridge and turn right (southeast) on Second Avenue to continue on the TCT toward the Purcell and Rocky mountains.

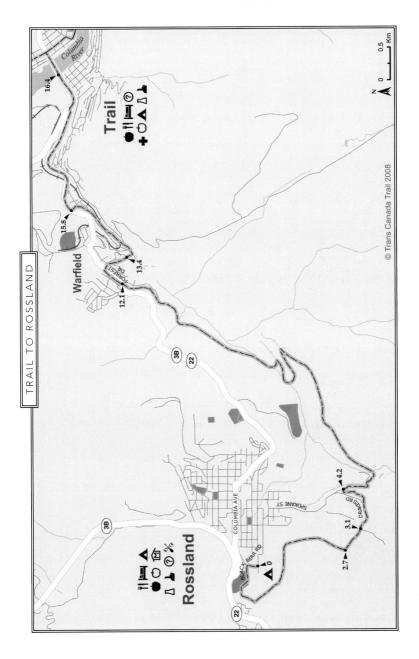

15

TRAIL TO ROSSLAND

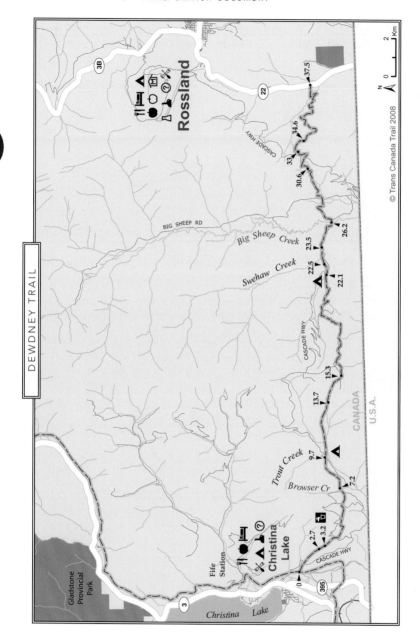

DEWDNEY TRAIL

15

© Trans Canada Trail 2008

LOCAL ADVENTURE

THE DEWDNEY TRAIL FROM
CHRISTINA LAKE TO ROSSLAND → 37.5 KM

The fact that modern-day Canadians can load up a horse or backpack and travel like 19th-century gold miners gives the Dewdney Trail prominence in this part of southern BC. This is living history, a chance to get a sense of the adventure, the hardship, and the landscapes experienced by travellers in pioneering times.

The 37.5-kilometre track from Christina Lake to Rossland is about one-fifteenth of the original Dewdney Trail. Built between 1860 and 1865 to access gold claims, the Dewdney ran 576 kilometres across southern BC, from Hope in the west to

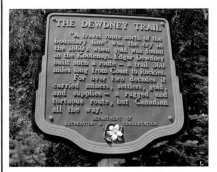

Sign on Highway 22, eight kilometres south of near Rossland

Wild Horse Creek in the Rockies. The Dewdney remained the main route through this area until the advent in the 1920s of the Cascade Highway, which is more dirt track than highway. The road and trail meet at various points.

This is two or three days in the backcountry. Drinking water can be filtered from creeks; water is scarcer at higher elevations. There are well-used campsites about 10 and 22 kilometres from the western trailhead, as well as a few other places where tents can be pitched.

To get to the western trailhead from Christina Lake, go south on Highway 3, then make a southeast turn onto Santa Rosa Road and proceed for 1.4 kilometres. Near a sharp bend, the road is intersected by the TCT/Columbia & Western Railway. There's parking here. Go down onto the railbed on the south side of Santa Rosa Road and find the trail leading steeply up into the forest. It is often obscured by bush.

Richie Mann, of the Trail Horsemen's Society, provided these kilometre points and most of the detail.

Km 0   *Christina Lake, Dewdney (western) trailhead* Take the trail up into the bush.

Km 2.7   *Boulder* A massive rock is believed to have crashed down the hillside to block the trail in the 1950s.

Km 3.2   *Dewdney Spring* A spring named for the trail on which it originates. Good drinking water.

Km 7.2   *Bowser Creek* One of a number of homesteads along the trail.

Km 9.7   *Trout Creek campsite* A concrete fireplace at this small campsite was built in the 1920s by highway workers.

Km 13.7   *Alder Creek* Remains of an old campsite used by a prospector or

15

15

LOCAL ADVENTURE (CONTINUED)

trapper are visible on the south bank of the creek.

Km 15.3 *Highest elevation* At about 1,500 metres, the highest point between the west and east sections of the trail.

Km 22.1 *Santa Rosa BC forest service campground* A 300-metre trail leads to the campground.

Km 22.5 *Wooden bridge* The bridge was here before the West Kootenay Power and Light Company's transmission line, circa 1905.

Km 23.5 *Waterfall* A feature noted on maps that accompanied Edgar Dewdney's reports in 1865.

Km 26.2 *Big Sheep Creek*

Km 30.6 *Stone retaining wall* Original rock work.

Km 33 *Rossland summit* Elevation of about 1,400 metres.

Km 34.6 *New trail* Four hundred metres of trail were built in 1974 to restore continuity broken by logging.

Km 37.5 *Rossland*, Dewdney (eastern) trailhead* At Highway 22, about eight kilometres southwest of downtown Rossland. A provincial "Stop of Interest" sign marks the trailhead.

KOOTENAY ROCKIES REGION

Tourism region that encompasses British Columbia's mountainous southeast corner, including the southern Monashees, Selkirks, Purcells, and Rockies. The TCT winds a course through the valleys and passes up to the Continental Divide.

› **Visitor Info** *Kootenay Rockies Tourism* 1905 Warren Avenue, Box 10, Kimberley, BC V1A 2Y5; 1-800-661-6603; 250-427-4838; www.bcrockies.com.

› **TCT Info** Not far from Christina Lake the TCT crosses into what Trails BC refers to as the West Kootenay region. Look up "West Kootenay" under "BC Regions" on the their website at www.trailsbc.ca.

› **Transportation**

Land Greyhound Canada (1-800-661-8747; www.greyhound.ca) has bus depots and stops in the Kootenay Rockies region at Castlegar, Nelson, Salmo, Trail, Creston, Yahk, Cranbrook, Jaffray, Elko, Fernie, and Sparwood.

Air Castlegar and Cranbrook are served by *Air Canada* (1-888-247-2262; www.aircanada.com) and *Central Mountain Air* (1-888-865-8585; www.flycma.com).

CHRISTINA LAKE TO TRAIL **251**

COMMUNITIES, PARKS, AND PLACES TO STAY

Backcountry Camping

There are no services or official campsites along the railbed from Christina Lake to Castlegar. Widenings of the trail provide limited tent space, notably at Paulson Bridge (Km 25.8), Farron (Km 35), and Tunnel Station (Km 47.4). Farron, the trail's high point, has drinking water, an outdoor toilet, and hordes of mosquitoes.

🌲 Christina Lake (Km 0)

See page 234 in the previous chapter.

🌲 Castlegar (Km 86.9)

At the confluence of the Columbia and Kootenay rivers downstream from Hugh Keenleyside Dam, Castlegar bills itself as the "Best Dam City." It is also at the confluence of Highways 3, 3A, and 22. There are at least seven bridges in and around the town.

› **Population** 7,000
› **Visitor Info** *Castlegar Visitor Centre* 1995 Sixth Avenue, Castlegar, BC VIN 4B7; 250-365-6313; www.castlegar.com.

ARROW LAKES: BC'S THIRD-LARGEST RESERVOIR

Joined by a 30-kilometre stretch of the Columbia River, Upper and Lower Arrow lakes became a single 518-square-kilometre reservoir in the 1960s with construction of the Hugh Keenleyside Dam on the Columbia. Extending from the dam for 232 kilometres upstream to Revelstoke, this is BC's third-largest reservoir.

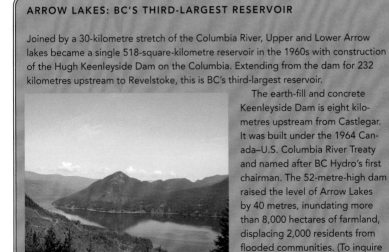

The earth-fill and concrete Keenleyside Dam is eight kilometres upstream from Castlegar. It was built under the 1964 Canada–U.S. Columbia River Treaty and named after BC Hydro's first chairman. The 52-metre-high dam raised the level of Arrow Lakes by 40 metres, inundating more than 8,000 hectares of farmland, displacing 2,000 residents from flooded communities. (To inquire about a tour of the Keenleyside Dam call 250-365-5299.)

Lower Arrow Lake

Castlegar railway station and museum

> **Attractions** Castlegar Railway Station/Museum, Doukhobor Village Museum, Zuckerberg Island Heritage Park, Hugh Keenleyside Dam, Kootenay Gallery of Art, History, and Science.
> **Cycling/Outfitting** *Mallard's Source for Sports* 660 18th Street; 250-365-5588.
> **Greyhound Bus** (1-800-661-8747; www.greyhound.ca) Depot located at 601 23rd Street.

🏕 Trail (Km 117.8)

Trail has been an ore-processing town since 1895 when the first smelter was built to treat gold and copper (see sidebar below). The industry expanded to make Trail the world's largest producer of lead and zinc in the 1920s and '30s. Teck Cominco Limited's smelter is still the biggest on the planet.

> **Population** 7,600
> **Visitor Info** *Trail Visitor Centre* 200–1199 Bay Avenue, Trail, BC VIR 4A4; 1-877-636-9569; www.trailchamber.bc.ca.
> **Attractions** Smelter tours, Little Italy.
> **Cycling/Outfitting** *Gerick Cycle & Sports* 908 Rossland Avenue; 250-364-1661; www.gericks.com.
> **Greyhound Bus** (1-800-661-8747; www.greyhound.ca) Depot located at *Dicken Bus Lines* at 1355 Bay Avenue.
> **Accommodation/Camping** *City of Trail* RV *Park* Highway 3B at east entrance to city; 1-877-636-9569; 250-368-3144; www.trail.ca. *Kiwanis Beaver Creek Campsite & Park* Off Highway 22A, on the TCT route

15

TRAIL SMELTER: ONE OF THE WORLD'S LARGEST

Teck Cominco's smelter beside the Columbia River at Trail (Km 117.8) has been in operation since 1896. Now the complex is one of the world's biggest zinc and lead

smelting and refining operations; in recent years it has produced more than 260,000 tonnes of zinc and over 80,000 tonnes of lead. Other commodities produced at the Trail complex include silver, gold, copper arsenate, sulphuric acid, and fertilizer. With more than 1,500 employees at Trail, Teck Cominco is a major regional employer.

2.1 kilometres beyond the Old Waneta Road/Highway 22A junction (Chapter 16); 250-367-9165.

♣ Rossland (beyond Km 117.8)

An alpine city at an elevation of more than 1,000 metres, with steep roof-tops, a ski hill that spawns Olympians, and the odd bear on the back porch in spring. Though just beyond the TCT route, trail enthusiasts here have made major contributions to the TCT and the development of an extensive trail network in this region. Fame came to Rossland in the 1960s and '90s when local girls Nancy Greene and Kerrin Lee-Gartner brought home Olympic gold. When not skiing Red Mountain in winter, Rosslanders are hiking, biking, and riding horses on surrounding trails. The town bills itself as the "Mountain Biking Capital of Canada" and is known for its variety in terrain and difficulty. The Kootenay Columbia Trail Society runs an excellent website (www.rosslandtrails.ca) with maps and descriptions of trails, including the TCT. ⊘ ▲ ● ⏁ ✗ | *most needs*

> **Population** 3,800
> **Visitor Info** *Rossland Visitor Centre* Highways 3B/22, Box 26, Rossland, BC V0G 1Y0; 1-888-448-7444; www.rossland.com.
> **Attractions** Rossland Historical Museum, Le Roi Gold Mine tour, heritage walking tour, trails.
> **Cycling** *Revolution Cycles and Service* 2044 Columbia Avenue; 250-362-5688; www.revolutioncycles.ca. *Adrenaline Adventures* (at Prestige Mountain Resort) offers mountain bike tours and shuttle services on the Trans Canada Trail and local trails. 1909 Columbia Avenue; 250-362-7421; www.rushbc.com.
> **Camping** *Rossland Lions Park* is a campground in town. 932 Black Bear Drive; 250-362-9410. See also www.rossland.com.

16 TRAIL TO SALMO

> If you boys are interested, we're doin' karaoke down at the Silver Dollar pub at nine.
> —Woman inviting
> Trans Canada Trail cyclists
> to share the Salmo nightlife

Farm on Waneta-Nelway Road,
above the Pend d'Oreille River Valley

TRAIL TRIVIA

The Columbia River has the second-greatest water flow of any river in North America, after the Mississippi.

TOTAL DISTANCE

75.9 km

HIGHLIGHTS

› Views of the Columbia and Pend d'Oreille rivers
› The Seven Mile Dam
› Columbian ground squirrels

CONDITIONS

› Trail (Km 0) to the intersection of Highway 22A and Waneta–Nelway Road (Km 17.6) Paved roads. → 17.6 km
› Waneta–Nelway Road (Km 17.6) to Nelway (Km 50.6) Gravel uphill for almost three kilometres, followed by four kilometres of pavement, then nearly 24 kilometres of gravel. Pavement resumes just over two kilometres before reaching Nelway at Highway 6. → 33 km
› Nelway (Km 50.6) to Salmo (Km 75.9) Paved highway. → 25.3 km

CAUTIONS

› No communities and no amenities for more than 70 kilometres between Trail and Salmo.
› Bears.

TOPOGRAPHIC MAPS

1:250,000	Nelson 82F
1:50,000	Creston 82F/2, Salmo 82F/3, Rossland–Trail 82F/4, Castlegar 82F/5, Nelson 82/F6, Boswell 82F/7, Crawford Bay 82F/10, Kokanee Peak 82F/11

OVERVIEW

Industry in a scenic setting of big rivers and mountains is a theme that continues from the smelter at Trail through the Columbia and Pend d'Oreille river valleys. Dams, transmission lines, and big reservoirs are part of a hydroelectricity system that generates power for local, provincial, and international use.

Southeast of Trail, the Columbia River completes a 739-kilometre run through British Columbia, draining an area of more than 103,000 square kilometres. It crosses the Canada–u.s. border near Waneta and continues southwest for another 1,261 kilometres to the Pacific Ocean, forming much of the boundary between Washington and Oregon states. The Columbia in this area of the TCT divides the Monashee Mountains to the west from the Selkirks on the east. From here, with each step toward the Continental Divide, the ranges get craggier, the terrain gets steeper, and the valleys become more deeply incised.

LOCAL ADVENTURES

Day Trip

› Ride a bicycle for a 60 km return trip on the TCT from Trail to the Seven Mile Dam.

3 or 4 Days

› Cycle the Kootenay Loop, which connects Salmo, Nelson, Castlegar, and Trail. (See page 262.) ↻ 198.8 km

TCT ACCESS POINTS

Trail (Km 0) 26 kilometres south of Castlegar via Highway 22; 9 kilometres east of Rossland via Highway 22/3B. **P** *parking lots and on-street parking*

Nelway (Km 50.6) On Highway 6 at the Canada–u.s. border, 25.3 kilometres south of Salmo. **P** *limited road parking*

Salmo (Km 75.9) Near the junction of Highways 6 and 3, 15 kilometres north of the Salmo–Creston Skyway (a.k.a. Crowsnest Highway/Highway 3), and 41 kilometres south of Nelson.

THE PEND D'OREILLE

OFF THE BEATEN TRACK

The TCT route out of downtown Trail follows paved roads and highways above the Columbia River. Where the Columbia crosses the u.s. boundary near Waneta, the river is joined by its major tributary from the east, the Pend d'Oreille. Here, the TCT takes a scenic, unhurried journey up the Pend d'Oreille Valley. It's a remote, lightly travelled route along industrial roads, where pavement turns to gravel and the roads get hillier. Not far along, travellers can choose between the gravel TCT route or a paved road above the river to Seven Mile Dam. The two roads merge just beyond the dam, and the TCT continues on a gravel road that deteriorates as it moves east.

The pavement resumes just over two kilometres before Nelway, on the Canada–U.S. border, where the TCT takes Highway 6 north for another 25 kilometres to Salmo.

THE TRANS CANADA TRAIL

Place names with asterisks are included in the **Communities, Parks, and Places to Stay** section (page 264).

Km 0   *Trail** On the east side of the Columbia River Bridge (Highway 3B) in Trail, the TCT continues southeast on Second Avenue.

Km 1.8   *Second Avenue + McQuarrie Street* Go right on McQuarrie, then left on Columbia Avenue, which becomes Highway Drive.

Km 5   *Highway Drive + Rosewood Drive + Cottonwood Drive* Go right onto Rosewood, and then at the next junction, keep right onto Carnation Drive. This road goes along the river and then veers left.

Km 6   *Carnation Drive + Highway 3B* Turn right (east) onto the highway.

Km 7.7   *Highway 3B + Old Waneta Road* Turn right onto Old Waneta.

Km 9.4   *Old Waneta Road + Highway 22A* Turn right onto the highway.

Km 11.5   *Kiwanis Beaver Creek Campground* Creekside camping.

Km 14.6   *Highway 22A + Seven Mile Dam Road* (Turn left if you wish to take a paved, alternate route toward Seven Mile Dam; it intersects the TCT three kilometres up the road.) The TCT here continues south on Highway 22A.

Km 17.6   *Highway 22A + Waneta–Nelway Road* Turn left (east) up Waneta–Nelway, a gravel road that crosses some railway tracks and switchbacks up steep hills toward Seven Mile Dam Road.

Km 20.4   *Waneta–Nelway Road + Seven Mile Dam Road* The TCT/ Waneta–Nelway Road crosses Seven Mile Dam Road and continues east above the Pend d'Oreille River for ten kilometres. (Travellers can go the same distance on a lower paved

Pend d'Oreille River Reservoir behind Seven Mile Dam

16

road that takes in views of the river and stops at a picnic site and viewpoint below Seven Mile Dam. About 1.4 kilometres beyond the dam, this road intersects the TCT at the eastern end of Waneta–Nelway Road.)

Km 30.2 *Waneta–Nelway Road (east end) + Pend d'Oreille Road* The TCT continues east on the gravel Pend d'Oreille Road along the north side of the Pend d'Oreille River. (For a spectacular view of the Seven Mile Dam, head west about 1.4 kilometres.)

Km 31.4 *Buckley picnic area and campground** A large, near-treeless campground on the Pend d'Oreille River Reservoir, located off Pend d'Oreille Road, 900 metres down a washboarded road.

Km 39.2 *Riverside campsite* Small tent site across the road from a waterfall.

Km 42.6 *Salmo River* About 400 metres beyond a bridge across Salmo River is a "user maintained" campsite with a small fishing dock on the river. No facilities.

Km 43.5 *Remac* Old mine ruins.

Km 45.2 *Boundary Dam* Seen through the trees, on the Pend d'Oreille River just across the international boundary in Washington state.

16

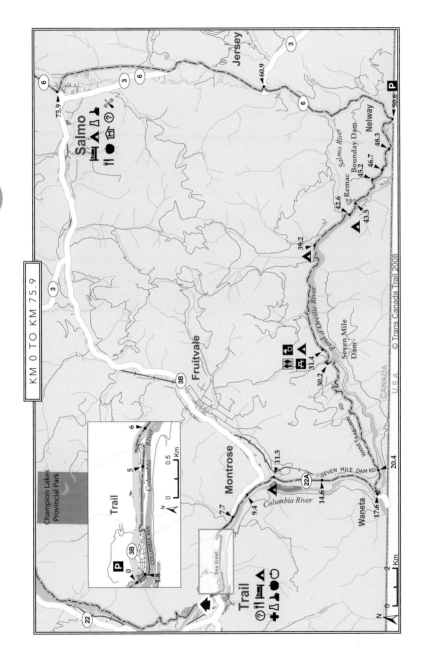

KM 0 TO KM 75.9

Salmo

75.9

Jersey
60.9

Nelway
58.6 P

48.3
46.7
45.2 Boundary Dam
43.5
42.6 Remac Salmo River

39.2

Fruitvale

Pend d'Oreille River

31.4
30.2 Seven Mile Dam

3B

WANETA-SHEEP RD

20.4
SEVEN MILE DAM RD

Montrose

11.5

22A

14.6 Columbia River

Waneta

17.6

9.4

7.7

22

© Trans Canada Trail 2008

CANADA
U.S.A.

Champion Lakes
Provincial Park

Trail

Columbia River

6
5

0.5 Km
N 0

3B COLUMBIA AVE
P 0

See Inset

Trail

0 1 2 Km

N

Km 46.7   *Hydro station* Watch for cows on the road.

Km 48.3   *Gravel road ends, pavement begins*

Km 50.6   *Highway 6, Nelway border crossing* Turn right to go to the United States. The TCT turns left (north) up Highway 6 toward Salmo.

Km 60.9   *Highway 6/3 + Highway 3 (Crowsnest Highway/Salmo–Creston Skyway)* The TCT continues north up Highway 6, which also becomes Highway 3 at this point.

Km 75.9   *Salmo*, Tourist Information and Museum on Highway 6* A pleasant town for TCT travellers to rest and restock. (From here the TCT takes the Great Northern Trail north to Nelson.)

Washington's Boundary Dam

GROUND SQUIRREL: A DILIGENT DIGGER

A patch of grass on the western outskirts of Salmo, at the junction of Highways 6 and 3, is a hangout for Columbian ground squirrels (*Spermophilus columbianus*). These tawny rodents are plentiful throughout the Kootenays and other parts of BC's southern Interior. They perch outside their burrows and chirp indignantly at passing Trans Canada Trail travellers.

These squirrels spend much of the summer escaping the heat of the noonday sun in cool, subterranean lairs. A metre or so below the surface, tunnels three to 20 metres long radiate from a central chamber that is about a metre in diameter and comfortably lined with grasses. The summer burrow may have a dozen or more entrances and escape exits, each marked on the surface by a mound of dirt.

Hibernation dens are offshoots of the summer burrows and are often twice as deep. Near the entrance to the sleeping chamber is a sump to drain water that could flood the den. They plug this entrance with the earth left over from digging the sump and seal off the chamber from the summer burrow system. Ground squirrels may spend seven or eight months hibernating. In spring they dig straight up to the surface into the light of day.

LOCAL ADVENTURE

THE KOOTENAY LOOP ↻ 198.8 KM

A route known as the Kootenay Loop, which connects Salmo, Nelson, Castlegar, and Trail, is a favourite among touring cyclists. Combining parts of the Trans Canada Trail with scenic back roads to Castlegar, this is a trip through a mountain wilderness interspersed with hamlets and acreages settled by back-to-the-landers. A good starting point is Salmo, where the Great Northern Trail to Nelson begins, just across Highway 6 from the Salmo Museum. This rail trail is described in greater detail in Chapter 17.

Km 0   *Salmo* Tourist Information and Museum* Go north on the rail trail. Follow the directions to Km 42.7, Nelson City Hall, as described in Chapter 17 on pages 268 and 271.

Km 42.7   *Nelson City Hall, Vernon Street + Ward Street* The TCT goes north toward Front Street, while this Kootenay Loop takes Highway 3A (Vernon Street) west from Nelson City Hall.

Km 45.2   *Highway 3A + Granite Road* Turn left off the highway onto Granite.

Km 50   *Granite Road + Blewett Road* Turn left onto Blewett and follow it across Kootenay Canal and Kootenay River. Good stop for photos of West Kootenay Power's Lower Bonnington Dam.

Km 63.6   *Blewett Road + Highway 3A/6* Turn left (southwest) onto Highway 3A/6 through to South Slocan, and then right (west) onto Highway 6 at the community of Crescent Valley.

Km 68.8   *Crescent Valley* Go left over the bridge across the Slocan River and head left (south) onto Pass Creek Road, a route that winds up and down through small clusters of population between long stretches of farm and forest. This paved road skirts the backside of Sentinel Mountain toward Castlegar.

Km 90.5   *Pass Creek Road + Broadwater Road, Castlegar* The cycling route turns right onto Broadwater and goes 1.5 kilometres across Robson Bridge and into Castlegar. To close this loop, go south on the TCT route from Castlegar (Chapter 15, Km 86.9) through to Trail (Chapter 15, Km 117.8), and then from Trail through the Pend d'Oreille Valley up to Salmo, as described in the main TCT directions in this chapter.

Km 198.8 *Salmo* After 106.8 kilometres from Castlegar to Salmo, the loop is complete.

Cycling from Salmo to Christina Lake is another great ride. Follow the directions above from Salmo to Castlegar. Instead of going south toward downtown Castlegar and Trail, after the Robson Bridge head west toward Christina Lake on the TCT/Columbia & Western rail trail. A one-way trip is a total of 180 kilometres.

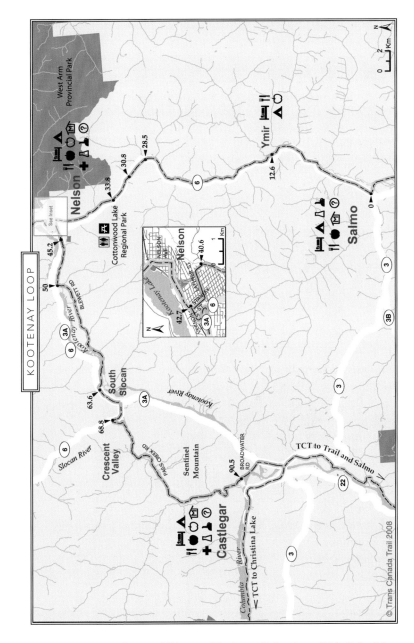

See page 242 for map of Castlegar to Trail, and page 260 for Trail to Salmo.

KOOTENAY ROCKIES REGION

Tourism region that encompasses British Columbia's mountainous southeast corner, including the southern Monashees, Selkirks, Purcells, and Rockies. For detailed information, see page 250 in Chapter 15.

COMMUNITIES, PARKS, AND PLACES TO STAY

♣ Trail (Km 0)

Please see page 253 in the previous chapter.

♠ Buckley Picnic Area and Campground at Pend d'Oreille (Km 31.4)

Recreation area 900 metres off the TCT on the Pend d'Oreille Reservoir, which is used for the generation of electricity. ⑦ 🏕 ▲ 🚻 *outhouses* 🔋

› **Visitor Info** Click on "Pend d'Oreille" at www.bchydro.com/recreation/.
› **Attractions** Sandy beach. (Beware of fluctuating water levels.)
› **Camping** 22 campsites.

♣ Salmo (Km 75.9)

Fifteen kilometres north of the Salmo–Creston Skyway, where Highway 3 heads east over Kootenay Pass. Once a mining and railroad town, Salmo now relies on sawmills and Teck Cominco's smelter at Trail for employment. Its 1930s buildings, its setting between mountains (the Bonnington and Nelson ranges of the Selkirks), and its laid-back aura are typical Kootenays. ⑦ ● ⌂ 🍴 ▲ 🛏 🏛

› **Population** 1,200
› **Visitor Info** *Salmo and District Chamber of Commerce* 100 Fourth Street, Salmo, BC V0G 1Z0; 250-357-2596; www.salmo.net.
› **Attractions** Salmo Museum, School of Stone Masonry, World's Oldest Telephone Booth.
› **Greyhound Bus** (1-800-661-8747; www.greyhound.ca) Depot located at 205 Fourth Street.
› **Camping** *Salmo Village Park campground* Located a couple of blocks east of Highway 6. 250-357-9344

17 SALMO TO GRAY CREEK

> 66 Something old, something new.
> That's the spirit of the Kootenays.
> —*Knowledge Network's*
> *Malcolm Stewart*
> *on Nelson, a town rich*
> *with architectural*
> *and industrial history*

Nelson and the Kootenay River
from the Great Northern Trail

TRAIL TRIVIA

About 140 ospreys breed in the Nelson–Creston area of the Kootenays, making it one of the most concentrated osprey-nesting regions in the world.

TOTAL DISTANCE

88.1 km

HIGHLIGHTS

> Great Northern Trail
> Heritage-rich Nelson
> Kootenay Lake ferry

CONDITIONS

> **Salmo (Km 0) to Nelson (Km 42.7)** Well-surfaced rail trail, subject to occasional flooding. Paved city streets for last 1.1 kilometres. → 42.7 km
> **Nelson (Km 42.7) to Gray Creek (Km 88.1)** Paved Highway 3A, and a Kootenay Lake ferry crossing. → 45.4 km

CAUTIONS

> Grizzly bears on the Great Northern Trail.
> Occasional flooding on the Great Northern Trail, near a junction with Highway 6 (Km 28.5). Use Highway 6, which rejoins the TCT after five kilometres.

TOPOGRAPHIC MAPS

1:250,000   Nelson 82F, Lardeau 82K
1:50,000   Salmo 82F/3, Castlegar 82F/5, Nelson 82F/6, Crawford Bay 82F/10, Kokanee Peak 82F/11, Passmore 82F/12, Slocan 82F/14, Kaslo 82F/15, Rosebery 82F/3

OVERVIEW

Rugged mountain ranges separated by deep, wide valleys with big lakes and fast-flowing rivers characterize the Kootenays. Most of this region in southeastern British Columbia is drained by the Columbia River and its major tributary, the Kootenay River. The largest lakes in the Kootenays—Kinbasket, Upper and Lower Arrow, Kootenay, and Duncan—are reservoirs created by dams on the Columbia system.

The Kootenays are also characterized by a laid-back lifestyle. This area has long been a haven for pacifists, beginning with Doukhobors in the early 1900s, then Quakers in the 1950s, and American draft dodgers in the 1960s and '70s. These pacifists remain a part of the social fabric of the Kootenays, which includes a lingering hippie culture. The city of Nelson has one of the highest concentrations of artists in BC, inspired, no doubt, by the extraordinary scenery around them. And with its abundance of Victorian-era homes and buildings, Nelson is unquestionably the most beautiful city in BC's Interior. A day or two (or longer) could easily be spent exploring the town's historic architecture. (See page 273 for more on Nelson.)

LOCAL ADVENTURES
Day Trip
› Take a return hike or bicycle ride on the Great Northern Trail from Mountain Station, above Nelson, to Troup. ⇆ 16 km
› Ride a bicycle loop between Nelson and Salmo on the Great Northern Trail and back on Highway 6. ↺ 82 km

TCT ACCESS POINTS
Salmo (Km 0) Near the junction of Highways 6 and 3, 15 kilometres north of the Salmo–Creston Skyway (a.k.a. Crowsnest Highway/Highway 3), and 41 kilometres south of Nelson.

Ymir (Km 12.6) A sleepy hamlet on Highway 6, 12 kilometres north of Salmo.

Nelson (Km 42.7) 41 kilometres northeast of Castlegar at the junction of Highways 6 and 3A, on Kootenay Lake's West Arm.

Balfour (Km 75.5) Small community and ferry terminal on the west side of Kootenay Lake, on Highway 3A, 32 kilometres northeast of Nelson.

Kootenay Bay (Km 75.8) and Crawford Bay (Km 79.1) Neighbouring communities on the east side of Kootenay Lake near the ferry terminal, at the north end of Highway 3A that runs up the east side of Kootenay Lake.

Gray Creek (Km 88.1) Hamlet on Highway 3A, 12 kilometres south of the Kootenay Bay ferry terminal, and 67 kilometres north of Creston.

17

AN EASY AND SCENIC ROUTE
THROUGH THE KOOTENAYS

A RAIL TRAIL, A HIGHWAY, AND AN INLAND FERRY

The Trans Canada Trail north from Salmo to Nelson takes the Great Northern Trail, which follows Salmo River and Cottonwood Creek between the Bonnington and Nelson ranges of the Selkirk Mountains. Highway 6, which is visible along much of the way, provides an alternate route if sections of the trail are flooded. From Nelson, the TCT takes a bridge across Kootenay Lake's West Arm and follows the north shore east on Highway 3A to Balfour, where a ferry crosses the lake. (No fares are charged.)

Ospreys nesting on a navigational beacon just outside Balfour seem unfazed by tourists clicking snapshots on the ferry. On the 35-minute crossing to Kootenay Bay, the TCT leaves the eastern foothills of the Selkirk Mountains to arrive at the western edge of the Purcells. The route then follows the eastern shore of Kootenay Lake south to Gray Creek. At this point travellers must choose between the TCT's steep and rugged 80-kilometre trek over Gray Creek Pass to Kimberley—one of the roughest stretches on the TCT in BC—or a scenic 202-kilometre highway detour to Kimberley via Creston and Cranbrook. (See page 288 in the next chapter.)

THE TRANS CANADA TRAIL

Place names with asterisks are included in the **Communities, Parks, and Places to Stay** section (page 274).

Km 0   *Salmo* tourist information and museum on Highway 6* The TCT takes the Great Northern Trail, which begins across Highway 6 from the museum. Go north on the rail trail as it follows the Salmo River upstream.

Km 12.6   *Ymir** Tiny town with hotels, a store, and restaurants.

Km 28.5   *Rail trail + Highway 6* The rail trail crosses the highway. If the trail ahead is flooded, use

Marker at summit of the Great Northern Trail

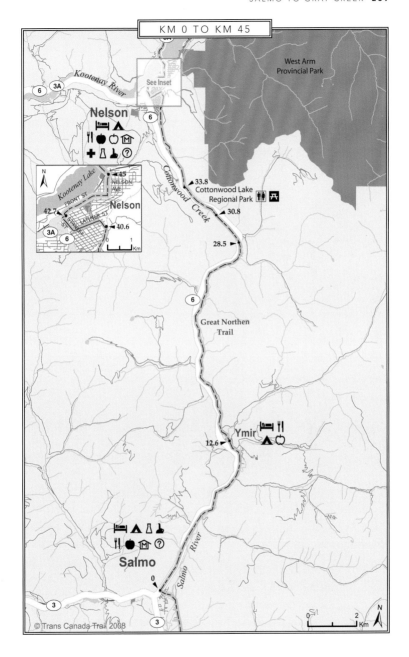

KM 0 TO KM 45

West Arm
Provincial Park

Kootenay River

Nelson

See Inset

Cottonwood Creek

▲ 33.8
Cottonwood Lake
Regional Park

▲ 30.8

28.5 ►

Great Northen
Trail

Ymir

12.6 ►

Salmo

Salmo River

0

3

3

© Trans Canada Trail 2008

17

Inset:

N

Kootenay Lake

45
NELSON
AVE

FRONT ST

42.7

Nelson

STANLEY ST
LATIMER ST

40.6

3A   6

0   1
Km

0   2
Km

N

17

KM 45 TO KM 88.1

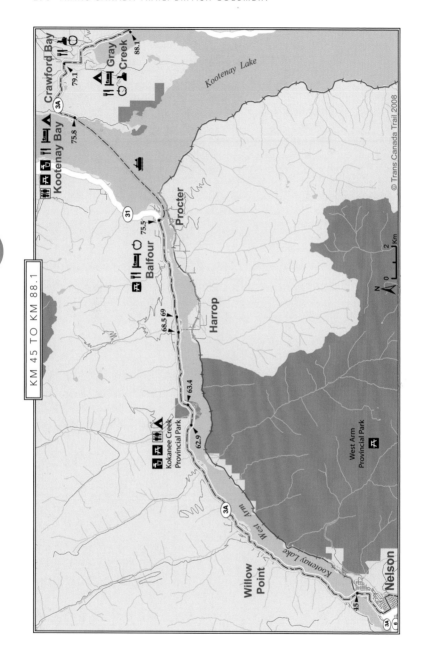

Crawford Bay

Gray Creek

88.1

79.1

Kootenay Lake

75.8

Kootenay Bay

3A

31

Procter

75.5

Balfour

Harrop

68.5, 69

63.4

62.9

Kokanee Creek
Provincial Park

West Arm
Provincial Park

3A

West Arm

Willow
Point

Kootenay Lake

Nelson

45

3A
6

© Trans Canada Trail 2008

2 Km

N

0

Harrop

Highway 6, which rejoins the rail trail about five kilometres ahead.

Km 30.8   *Trail summit* At an elevation of nearly 1,000 metres, the summit of the Great Northern Trail is marked by an animal skull on a post. The trail moves alongside Cottonwood Creek and follows it down toward Nelson.

Km 33.8   *Highway 6/Cottonwood Lake Regional Park* The rail trail crosses Highway 6 near the entrance to an eight-hectare day-use park, where there are footpaths and a swimming beach. (Outhouses, picnic shelter.)

Km 40.6   *Mountain Station* This former railway station is the Nelson end of the Great Northern Trail. From here, the rail trail continues another 7.9 kilometres to Troup where it dead-ends; the TCT, however, heads downhill from the Mountain Station parking lot into downtown Nelson. Take the dirt road down to Observatory and South Cherry streets, and continue down South Cherry to Latimer Street. Turn left onto Latimer, and go seven blocks to Stanley Street, where you turn right. After seven blocks on Stanley you'll reach Vernon Street, where you turn right for one block to Nelson City Hall. (This switchback route is commonly used by locals cycling uphill to Mountain Station.)

Km 42.7   *Nelson* City Hall, Vernon Street + Ward Street* From City Hall, the TCT continues north down Front Street (Highway 3A) toward the bridge over Kootenay Lake's West Arm: Highway 3A continues northeast on Front Street, goes right (east) onto Anderson Street, and then left (north) onto Nelson Avenue. (To reach Nelson City Campground and RV Park on High Street, go right (south) off of Anderson Street onto Nelson Avenue, then right (southwest) onto High Street.)

Km 45   *Nelson Bridge* The TCT/Nelson Avenue veers left toward the bridge. Cross the 700-metre Nelson Bridge, and continue on Highway 3A along the West

Nelson City Hall

Kootenay Lake ferry *Osprey* at Balfour

Arm. There are paved bike lanes on both sides of the highway.

Km 62.9   *Kokanee Creek Provincial Park*, Redfish campground* One of Kootenay Lake's most popular family-camping destinations.

Km 63.4   *Kokanee Creek Provincial Park*, main entrance* Turn right off the highway for another lakeside campground, or for picnicking.

Km 68.5   TCT/*Highway* 3A + *Harrop Ferry Road* (Turn right if you wish to visit the communities of Harrop and Procter via a cable ferry that crosses the West Arm.)

Km 69   *Redfish Creek* Highway 3A crosses the creek. Watch for bright red spawning kokanee in August and September.

Km 75.5   *Balfour*, Kootenay Lake ferry terminal* The TCT/Highway 3A takes a 35-minute cruise aboard the *Osprey* or *Balfour*, free car-and-passenger ferries that cross Kootenay Lake. Near the start of the journey watch for ospreys nesting on a navigational beacon. In the middle of Kootenay Lake, the ferry crosses from Pacific Time to Mountain Time—set your clock to one hour later. (To reach Ainsworth Hot Springs* continue north from Balfour on Highway 31 for 15 kilometres.)

Km 75.8   *Kootenay Bay** Ferry terminal on the east side of Kootenay Lake. Continue up the hill on Highway 3A.

Km 79.1   *Crawford Bay**

Km 88.1   *Gray Creek** Continue east on Highway 3A to reach Gray Creek. (This is the start of an extremely challenging TCT route on a rough gravel road over Gray Creek Pass to Kimberley. Travellers have the option of taking a much longer detour on Highways 3A, 3, and 95A. See page 288 in Chapter 18.)

HERITAGE-RICH NELSON

If it weren't for all the cappuccino bars, modern cars, and high-end mountain bikes, Nelson would look much like a Canadian frontier town in the 19th century. New houses do stand amid trees in the younger parts of town, but most of Nelson is a colourful assemblage of homes and buildings from the late 1800s and early 1900s.

At the turn of the 20th century, Nelson was BC's third-largest city, a busy mining town with architecture just as elegant as in the much bigger cities of Vancouver and Victoria. Architect Francis Rattenbury, who designed the Vancouver Art Galley and Victoria's Parliament Buildings and Empress Hotel, also crested Nelson's Courthouse and City Hall.

A multi-million-dollar restoration of historic buildings in downtown Nelson has revitalized the city since the 1980s. Many vintage homes overlooking Kootenay Lake have also been lovingly restored by their owners. Nelson now has more than 350 buildings with heritage status. Pick up a free map from Nelson's visitor centre (225 Hall Street) for a heritage walking tour of the town.

INLAND FERRIES EXTEND BC'S HIGHWAY SYSTEM

Ferries are water-borne links in British Columbia's intricate network of roads and highways. They connect coastal communities and shuttle

Downtown Nelson heritage buildings

commuters, cattle, and freight across Interior lakes and rivers. Cruising waterways once plied by aboriginals and fur traders, ferries are windows to everyday life in BC.

In the BC Interior, the provincial government operates 17 inland ferries, moving more than three million people and over 1.6 million vehicles a year.

The *Osprey*, launched in 2000 to run across Kootenay Lake between Balfour and Kootenay Bay, is a typical self-propelled car-and-passenger vessel. Cable ferries also run in this region—essentially platforms on pontoons that are pulled across rivers or narrow lakes on cables powered by shoreside winches. The oldest in BC, in operation since 1910, runs across the Kootenay River southeast of Nelson, serving the isolated community of Glade; another has been running since 1924 across Kootenay Lake's West Arm to Harrop, not far from Balfour.

Even more unusual are "reaction ferries" that use the force of river currents to propel them across. They consist of two steel pontoons bridged by a Bailey structure and are used to transport vehicles—usually one or two at a time—as well as equipment, livestock, and passengers. Without engines they are noiseless and cheap, and are operated by a single crew person. At one time the province had no fewer than 75 reaction ferries; now only six remain. These oddball ferries are a living slice of BC's transportation history.

KOOTENAY ROCKIES REGION

Tourism region that encompasses British Columbia's mountainous southeast corner, including the southern Monashees, Selkirks, Purcells, and Rockies. For detailed information, see page 250 in Chapter 15.

COMMUNITIES, PARKS, AND PLACES TO STAY

Information on each provincial park in BC can be found on the BC Parks website at www.env.gov.bc.ca/bcparks/.

♣ Salmo (Km 0)

See page 264 in the previous chapter.

♣ Ymir (Km 12.6)

Village 12 kilometres north of Salmo off Highway 6 (go northeast off highway onto First Avenue). ⟳ ⵜ ▲ ⊨

› **Population** 233
› **Visitor Info** www.ymirbc.com
› **Accommodation/Camping** An unmaintained campground, which offers free camping, is nestled between downtown and the Salmo River. 🅿 🏕 🚻 *outhouses* There are also two heritage hotels: *Hotel Ymir* (250-357-9611) and *Ymir Palace Inn* (1-866-964-7466 or 250-357-2466).

🌲 Nelson (Km 42.7)

A vibrant community in the heart of BC's Kootenay region, with a refurbished town centre and more than 350 heritage homes and buildings. Restored Victorian houses grace the steep streets above Kootenay Lake's West Arm. Downtown, kids on mountain bikes whiz past cappuccino drinkers at outdoor cafés. Tourists nose about the antique stores and snap pictures of century-old buildings with a Selkirk Mountain backdrop. (See page 273.)

› **Population** 9,300
› **Visitor Info** *Nelson Visitor Centre* 225 Hall Street, Nelson, BC V1L 5X4; 1-877-663-5706; www.discovernelson.com. *City of Nelson* 502 Vernon Street, Nelson, BC V1L 5P4; 250-352-5511; www.city.nelson.bc.ca.
› **Attractions** Heritage walking tour, Streetcar No. 23 Restored, Nelson Museum, Chamber of Mines Eastern BC Museum, Lakeside Park.
› **Cycling** *The Sacred Ride* 213 Baker Street; 250-354-3831; www.sacredride.ca. *Gerick Cycle & Sports* 702 Baker Street; 1-877-437-4251; www.gericks.com.
› **Greyhound Bus** (1-800-661-8747; www.greyhound.ca) Depot located at 1112A Lakeside Drive.
› **Camping** Camp at the edge of downtown at *Nelson City Campground and RV Park* 90 High Street; 250-352-7618.

Osprey nest near Balfour ferry terminal

🦆 Kokanee Creek Provincial Park (Km 62.9, Km 63.4)

On Highway 3A, 21 kilometres northeast of Nelson. Idyllic forested campsites near the beaches of Kootenay Lake's West Arm. ▲ 🚻 *flush toilets* 🚾 | *showers, boat launch, children's playground, sani-station*

17

> **Size** 260 hectares
> **Attractions** Warm swimming, hiking trails, boating, fishing, birding, spawning kokanee.
> **Camping** 168 campsites in two campgrounds.

Balfour (Km 75.5)

Lakeside hamlet and ferry terminal on Highway 3A, on the west side of Kootenay Lake. ○ *general store* ⊓ *pub* ⊞ ⊨ | *marinas*

> **Population** 240
> **Attractions** Golf course.

Ainsworth Hot Springs (15 km north of Km 75.5)

On Highway 31 north of the TCT on the west side of Kootenay Lake, 15 kilometres north of Balfour. Resort built around a U-shaped cave that was originally a mine shaft. ○ ⊓ *roadside coffee bar*

> **Population** 90
> **Attractions** Museums.

Kootenay Bay (Km 75.8)

On Highway 3A on the east side of Kootenay Lake, a collection of buildings above the Kootenay Bay ferry terminal. ⊓ ⊞ ⊨ ⛰ ⛹ ⛏

> **Population** 40

Crawford Bay (Km 79.1)

Village on Kootenay Lake's eastern shore near the north end of Highway 3A. ○ ⛴ ⊓

> **Population** 350
> **Attractions** Artisans, beach, marina.

Gray Creek (Km 88.1)

Collection of buildings on Highway 3A, 12.3 kilometres south of the Kootenay Bay ferry terminal. ○ *general store* ⛴ ⊓ ⊨ ⛰ | *laundromat, boat ramp, nearby restaurants*

> **Population** 150
> **Attractions** Artisans.
> **Camping** *Cedar Grove Campground* 15060 Highway 3A, General Delivery, Box 65, Gray Creek, BC V0B 1S0; 250-227-9492.

18 GRAY CREEK TO KIMBERLEY

mberley
ature Park

TRAIL TRIVIA

About 200,000 avalanches occur in BC each year. BC has 1,200 kilometres of provincial roads in 60 avalanche-prone areas.

TOTAL DISTANCE

88.5 km

HIGHLIGHTS

› Kimberley Nature Park

CONDITIONS

› **Gray Creek (Km 0) to Kimberley Nature Park (Km 79.2)** Steep and extraordinarily rough 17.6 kilometres going uphill, steeper (up to 14-percent grade) downhill gravel road for 47.8 kilometres, often potholed and washboarded. Finally, 13.8 kilometres of pavement. → 79.2 km
› **Kimberley Nature Park (Km 79.2) to Kimberley (Km 88.5)** Eight kilometres of often steep and sometimes rough wooded trail, followed by 1.3 kilometres of downtown streets. → 9.3 km

CAUTIONS

› Extremely arduous journey in the wilderness; minimal amenities, no supplies, and patchy cell phone service for most of the route. Cyclists should carry spare front and back brakes and know how to install them. Chain breakers, Allen keys, wrenches, tire irons, patches, pumps, and other equipment required for mechanical self-sufficiency are essential.
› Forestry roads change with use, and maps are not always up to date. GPS coordinates are provided in the directions in this chapter.
› Possible summer snow at high elevations.
› Bears.

TOPOGRAPHIC MAPS

1:250,000   Nelson 82F, Fernie 82/G
1:50,000   St. Mary Lake 82F/9, Crawford Bay 82/F10, Cranbrook
             82G/12

OVERVIEW

From the eastern shore of Kootenay Lake, the Trans Canada Trail climbs over the Purcell Mountains to the alpine town of Kimberley, purported to be the highest city in British Columbia at an elevation of 1,113 metres. The TCT route, which takes Gray Creek Pass forest service road and St. Mary Lake Road, reaches a summit of 2,053 metres, the highest point on the TCT in BC.

This route rivals Paleface Pass (between Chilliwack Lake and Hope) as the roughest, most challenging stretch of TCT in BC. Both are endurance tests that push the limits. Paleface Pass, however, is shorter; Gray Creek Pass is a long, arduous trek requiring physical strength and, if cycling, the know-how to repair bikes. Nearly 80 kilometres of wilderness, this strenuous—some might say onerous—journey may be too long for cyclists to complete in a single day.

But, like Paleface Pass, it is a feast of mountain scenery with frosty peaks, massive rock slides, ice-clear streams, and frothy creeks tumbling down cliffs and gullies.

LOCAL ADVENTURES
Day Trip
› Explore Kimberley Nature Park.

3 or 4 Days
› Bypass Gray Creek Pass by cycling south to Creston, then east and north through Cranbrook to Kimberley. (See page 288.) → 202 km
› Stay in Kimberley and spend several days hiking, cycling, horse riding, snowshoeing, or cross-country skiing in Kimberley Nature Park.

TCT ACCESS POINTS
Gray Creek (Km 0) Hamlet on Highway 3A, 12 kilometres south of the Kootenay Bay ferry terminal, 67 kilometres north of Creston. ▲ ↻ *general store*

Kimberley Nature Park (Km 79.2) On St. Mary Lake Road, 2.7 kilometres west from Highway 95A, just south of Kimberley. There is also TCT access at another park entrance at Burdett Street and Swan Avenue (Km 87.2) near downtown Kimberley.

Kimberley (Km 88.5) Small city on Highway 95A, 32 kilometres northwest of Cranbrook.

18

THE PURCELL MOUNTAINS

ONE RANGE WEST OF THE ROCKIES

Trans Canada Trail travellers who started their journeys in Victoria will have explored parts of no fewer than five major mountain ranges before reaching the Purcells. This heart-heaving climb—and hair-raising descent—over Gray Creek Pass is warm-up for the final mountain assault in BC: the Canadian Rockies.

Though not as famous, the Purcells are at least as toilsome as the Rockies for TCT cyclists. "Gruelling" is not an exaggeration of the pedal over Gray Creek Pass from Kootenay Lake to Kimberley. It seems the steepest patches are also the roughest, often potholed and washboarded from trucks struggling up the 14-percent grades. This is an extremely challenging route in the middle of wilderness; vehicle traffic is light and cell phone service is not available for most of this trip.

The first 17.6 kilometres from Gray Creek could mainly be a bike-push, taking as long as four hours. Besides cyclists, a few hard-core backpackers take this route, and it is becoming increasingly popular among equestrians. Oliver Lake campground, about 800 metres west of the summit, offers a reprieve for travellers in need of overnight rest. After this stop a healthy horse or cyclist could complete the ride to Kimberley Riverside Campground and through Kimberley Nature Park to Kimberley in a day.

Travellers do have the option of taking a detour, an albeit much longer route, on various highways to Kimberley. (See page 288.) There also have been discussions about using a more trail-like old power-line road as an alternate route around certain sections of the Gray Creek Pass forest service road. Check for updates at www.trailsbc.ca (look up "Rocky Mountains" under "BC Regions"), and watch for signs on the road.

THE TRANS CANADA TRAIL

Place names with asterisks are included in the **Communities, Parks, and Places to Stay** section (page 287).

Km 0   *Gray Creek** 🛖 560 metres. From the general store, head south on Highway 3A for 200 metres to Oliver Road.

Km 0.2   *Highway 3A + Oliver Road* Turn left (east) off Highway 3A up Oliver Road, a gravel road leading to Gray Creek Pass.

Km 0.5   *T junction* Turn right across a bridge over Gray Creek and continue uphill.

Km 1.4   *Gray Creek Pass forest service road* 📟 north 49.37.354, west 116.46.571 ▲ 670 metres. Continue uphill. A large sign (perhaps obscured by bush) indicates it's 84 kilometres to Marysville, just south of Kimberley.

Km 6.9 *Gate/possible alternate route* GPS north 49.37.181, west 116.42.727 ▲ 1,200 metres. The road makes a hairpin turn and passes though an open gate. (There may be a sign here indicating a 7.2-kilometre alternate route on an old power-line road. It runs over a different pass to reconnect with Gray Creek Pass forest service road on the east side of Gray Creek Pass.)

Km 16.8 *Oliver Lake recreation site** GPS north 49.35.101, west 116.41.096 ▲ 1,982 metres. Wooded campsites, basic but usable. (Outhouses.)

Km 17.6 *Gray Creek Pass summit* GPS north 49.34.866, west 116.40.542 ▲ 2,053 metres. A Ministry of Forests sign: "Steep grades to 14% over next 11 km, use lower gears, excessive use of brakes may result in brake failure."

Km 20.8 *Gate* GPS north 49.35.280, west 116.39.934 ▲ 1,855 metres. The road goes through an open gate.

Km 22.4 *Fork* GPS north 49.36.437, west 116.39.050 ▲ 1,749 metres. Stay on the main road, heading east, where another road forks back toward the west.

Km 24.2 *Fork/possible alternate route* GPS north 49.36.820, west 116.37.736 ▲ 1,634 metres. The TCT continues on the main road. (There may be a sign here indicating an alternate route on an old power-line road. It is ten kilometres shorter than the TCT/Gray Creek Pass forest service road, but has grades of up to 25 percent. It could be better suited for serious mountain bikers than touring cyclists.)

Km 25.8 *Rock slide* ▲ 1,601 metres. The first of several roadside rock slides, this one recognized by overhead utility lines.

Km 29.8 *Junction* GPS north 49.36.492, west 116.34.607 ▲ 1,363 metres. At a junction near a red-roofed building, one road goes up to the right while the TCT route veers to the left on the main road. A sign on the westbound side indicates Gray Creek Pass.

Km 46 *Mountain views* GPS north 49.39.468, west 116.24.742 ▲ 1,194 metres. Openings in the trees provide impressive mountain views to the southeast.

Km 52.7 *St. Mary River* GPS north 49.39.189, west 116.19.671 ▲ 1,002

Gray Creek Pass rockslide

metres. The road crosses St. Mary River, flowing down from the north. There is a primitive riverside campsite below the bridge. Just ahead is a junction: go right. Westbound travellers see a sign indicating Gray Creek Pass.

Km 65.1   *Cabins* Private cabins line the beach at the eastern end of St. Mary Lake.

Km 65.4   *Pavement where the gravel road ends* Near a junction with Lakeside Road, continue east on the main paved road.

Km 79.2   *Kimberley Nature Park** **GPS** north 49.38.100, west 115.59.864 ⛰ 976 metres. A parking lot and information kiosk on St. Mary Lake Road marks the start of the marked TCT route through Kimberley Nature Park to Kimberley. (Wooded campsites at Kimberley Riverside Campground near St. Mary River. A luxury accommodation option would be Canadian Mountain Lodging Company*, which is next to the campground.)

Km 79.3   *Intersection* The trail crosses a dirt road. Continue straight, following a sign to Jimmy Russell Road.

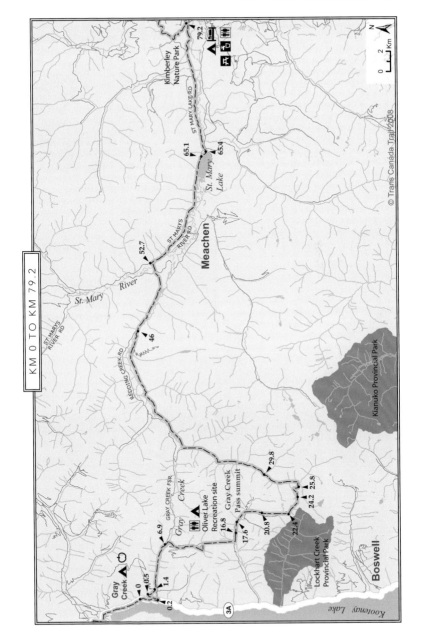

© Trans Canada Trail 2008

KM 79.2 TO KM 88.5

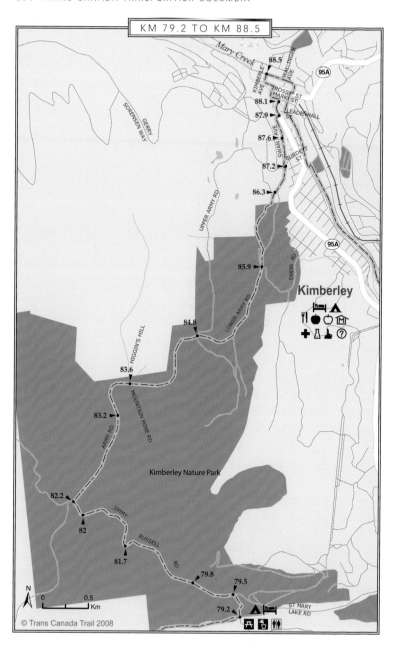

Kimberley

Kimberley Nature Park

© Trans Canada Trail 2008

Purcell Mountains, Gray Creek Pass

Km 79.5	*Jimmy Russell Road* Turn left onto Jimmy Russell Road.
Km 79.6	*Fork* Stay to the right, going uphill.
Km 79.8	*Fork* Continue on Jimmy Russell Road to the left. (Duck Pond Trail goes to the right.)
Km 81.6	*Fork* Again, continue on Jimmy Russell Road to the left.
Km 81.7	*Bridge* The TCT crosses a creek on a small bridge.
Km 82	*Jimmy Russell Road + Army Road* The TCT leaves Jimmy Russell Road and takes Army Road to the right.
Km 82.2	*Fork* Continue to the right on the main trail. (The Bear Trail takes a hairpin turn to the left, while a sign saying "Lunchroom" points back on the TCT.)
Km 83.2	TCT *+ Creek Trail* Continue on the main trail, past the Creek Trail.
Km 83.6	*Army Road + Mountain Mine Road + Higgin's Hill* Continue straight on Army Road.
Km 84.7	*Fork* The TCT continues up to the left.
Km 84.8	*Richardson's Sidehill + Upper Army Road + Lower Army Road* At a Kimberley Nature Park kiosk near the junction, go right on Lower Army Road.
Km 85.6	TCT *+ Pat Morrow Trail* At a junction with Pat Morrow Trail, continue on the main trail down a steep, rocky stretch.

Km 85.9   *Three Corners* Eimers Road goes down to the right while Lower Army Road and another trail go up to the left. Take the steep and rocky wider trail on the extreme left, passing a sign about 60 metres up the trail that indicates you are on Lower Army Road.

Km 86.3   *Lower Army Road + Ponderosa Trail* A Kimberley Nature Park kiosk with a map stands near the junction of the Ponderosa Trail, which goes to the right, and Lower Army Road, which loops around to the left. Stay on Lower Army Road.

Km 86.5   *Clearing* Where the trail opens to a large clearing, veer to the right on the main road.

Km 86.8   *Clearing* At another clearing, veer to the right again.

Km 86.9   *Fork* At a fork, veer uphill to the right.

Km 87   *Fork* The TCT continues straight. (The Ponderosa Trail goes to the right.)

Km 87.2   *Gate* A gate at the entrance to Kimberley Nature Park meets pavement at a subdivision near the intersection of Burdett Street and Swan Avenue. The TCT crosses Burdett and goes along Swan Avenue.

Km 87.6   *Swan Avenue + Diamond Street* Cross the street kitty corner to a chain-link fence around a basketball court and continue on a gravel trail alongside the chain-link fence.

Km 87.9   *Swan Avenue + Highway 95A/Wallinger Avenue* With gas stations on both sides, the end of Swan Avenue looks across Highway 95A (Wallinger Avenue) toward All Saints Anglican Church. Turn left and take the sidewalk for about 60 metres to Leadenhall Street, then go left behind some buildings on an alley that leads to a pedestrian bridge.

Km 88.1   *Bridge, Mark Street* Cross the bridge and immediately turn left on Mark Street. Continue straight across Deer Park Road, passing a "No Exit" sign on a paved road that leads to a steel pedestrian bridge across Mary Creek. Cross the bridge and turn left on Ross Street, which veers to the right on Kimberley Avenue to the Platzl West Entry.

Km 88.5   *Kimberley* Platzl* Kimberley's pedestrian-only downtown centre. (The TCT takes the brick road through the Platzl and heads out of town, south toward Marysville.)

KOOTENAY ROCKIES REGION

Tourism region that encompasses British Columbia's mountainous southeast corner, including the southern Monashees, Selkirks, Purcells, and Rockies. (For detailed information, see page 250 in Chapter 15.) Unofficially, the Kootenays consist of the "West Kootenay" and "East Kootenay," with a dividing line generally along the height of the Purcell Mountains. The TCT crosses this line in Gray Creek Pass, leaving Trails BC's West Kootenay region and entering the Rocky Mountain/East Kootenay region.

› TCT **Info** Look up "Rocky Mountains" under "BC Regions" on the Trails BC website at www.trailsbc.ca.

COMMUNITIES, PARKS, AND PLACES TO STAY

Information on each provincial park in BC can be found on the BC Parks website at www.env.gov.bc.ca/bcparks/.

♣ Gray Creek (Km 0)

See page 276 in the previous chapter.

▲ Oliver Lake Recreation Site (Km 16.8)

Primitive campsite with outhouses, 800 metres west of Gray Creek Pass summit. An overnight stop for people who don't want to travel the entire 79 kilometres to the Kimberley Riverside Campground in one day.

18

ROCKY MOUNTAIN ELK: BC'S SECOND-LARGEST DEER

As spring brings the first burst of greenery, herds of Rocky Mountain elk (*Cervus canadensis nelsoni*) forage the south-facing slopes of mountain ranges throughout the Kootenays. Weakened by winter, they feed voraciously, snipping new shoots and grasses as quickly as they grow. On some days between March and May, herds of a dozen or more might assemble on open meadows.

A mature Rocky Mountain bull elk may weigh nearly 500 kilos. (BC's biggest deer, the moose, might weigh 800 kilos.) An elk could carry massive six- or eight-point antlers that span 150 centimetres and weigh 13 kilos, requiring extra-strong neck muscles to hold upright. Antlers reach maximum size by midsummer; they are shed in late winter or early spring when a new rack begins to grow.

Elk can be spotted throughout southeastern BC; best times for sightings are the low-light hours of dawn and dusk.

DETOUR

BYPASSING GRAY CREEK PASS → 202 KM

Travellers who favour pavement and civilization over gravel roads and wilderness can opt out of the "Gray Creek Pass Challenge" and take an easier, albeit much longer 202-kilometre route from Gray Creek to Kimberley. It takes in some of the most scenic parts of the Kootenays, with expansive views of lakes and valleys, and orchards and farms, hemmed in by the humongous rock walls of the Selkirk, Purcell, and Rocky mountains.

A view of the Steeples in the Rockies

Place names with asterisks are included in the Communities, Parks, and Places to Stay section, starting on page 287 as well as page 290.

Km 0   *Oliver Road + Highway 3A, Gray Creek** Go south on Highway 3A.

Km 13.4   *Lockhart Beach Provincial Park** Continue south on Highway 3A.

Km 64.5   *Highway 3A + Highway 3, Creston** Go south on Highway 3 through Creston and continue east on Highway 3.

Km 108.6   *Community of Yahk* and Yahk Provincial Park* Head northeast on Highway 3.

Km 142.6   *Moyie** Continue north on Highway 3. General store.

Km 153.6   *Moyie Lake Provincial Park** Go north on Highway 3.

Km 168.5   *Jimsmith Lake Provincial Park** Continue north on Highway 3. (To reach the park turn left (west) off the highway and go four kilometres.)

Km 174.2   *Highway 3 + Highway 95A, Cranbrook** Where Highway 3 veers left, continue straight onto Highway 95A to Kimberley*.

Km 186.2   *Cranbrook Airport* Continue northwest on Highway 95A.

Km 193.9   *Marysville* Continue north on Highway 95A.

Km 201.6   *Highway 95A (Wallinger Avenue) + Ross Street, Kimberley** Turn left (east) on Ross Street at the traffic light and go to Kimberley Avenue and the Platzl West Entry.

Km 202   *Platzl West Entry* The TCT out of Kimberley is described in Chapter 19.

🌲 Kimberley Nature Park (Km 79.2)

One of Canada's largest municipal parks, twice the size of Vancouver's Stanley Park. Several kilometres of (non-motorized) multi-use trails linking ponds and viewpoints. ⑦ ▲

> **Size** 800 hectares
> **Visitor Info** *Kimberley Nature Park Society* Box 398, Kimberley, BC V1A 2Y9; www.rockies.net/kimberley/naturepark/. The website is an excellent source of information, including maps, photos, history, natural history, geology, contacts, and more. The *Kimberley Nature Park Trail Guide*, with detailed maps and descriptions, is available from the *Kimberley Visitor Centre* at 270 Kimberley Avenue, and from numerous local outlets, listed at www.rockies.net/kimberley/naturepark/maps.htm.
> **TCT access** Across from the Kimberley Riverside Campground, and in Kimberley near the intersection of Burdett Street and Swan Avenue (Km 87.2).
> **Attractions** An extensive network of old roads and paths for hikers, cyclists, equestrians, cross-country skiers, and snowshoers, providing a "soft-wilderness experience for residents and visitors alike." No motorized use of trails is allowed.
> **Camping** *Kimberley Riverside Campground* RV and tent sites, each with picnic table and fire pit. On the Trans Canada Trail across the road from Kimberley Nature Park; owned by the city of Kimberley. PO Box 465, Kimberley, BC V1A 3B9; 1-877-999-2929; www.kimberleycampground.com. ○ *small store* 🚻 🚮 | *shower, laundromat, swimming pool, tour bookings*

🛏 Canadian Mountain Lodging Company (Km 79.2)

Luxury log cabins; year-round vacation rentals. Next to Kimberley Riverside Campground. PO Box 26006 BVPO, Calgary, AB T2P 4L2; 1-877-771-4653; 250-423-5743 (Kimberley); www.ultimaterm.com/rentals/kimberley.html.

♣ Kimberley (Km 88.5, Detour Km 202)

On Highway 95A, 32 kilometres northwest of Cranbrook. Kimberley claims to be the highest city in BC, at an elevation of 1,113 metres. Its downtown core features a red-brick pedestrian-only street running through "the Platzl." Once a mining town, Kimberley now relies more on tourism. Attractions include the mining history and ski hill.

> **Population** 6,700
> **Visitor Info** *Kimberley Visitor Centre* 270 Kimberley Avenue, Kimberley, BC V1A 3N3; 250-427-3666; www.kimberleychamber.ca.
> **Attractions** The Platzl, Cominco Gardens, Bavarian City Mining Railway, Kimberley Heritage Museum, Kimberley Alpine Resort.

› **Cycling/Outfitting** *Bavarian Sports and Hardware* 235 Spokane Street; 250-427-2667. *Poser Sports* 270 Spokane Street, 250-427-4449; www .posersports.com. *Rocky's Ride and Glide Cycle and Ski* 250 Spokane Street, 250-427-4244; www.rockysrideandglide.com.
› **Greyhound Bus** (1-800-661-8747; www.greyhound.ca) Depot located at *Blarchmont Tire & Service* at 1625 Warren Avenue.

ALONG THE GRAY CREEK PASS DETOUR

♣ Lockhart Beach Provincial Park (Detour Km 13.4)
On Highway 3A, 53 kilometres north of downtown Creston. ⊞ ▲ ♦♦ *outhouses* 🚻
› **Size** 3 hectares
› **Camping** 18 forested sites across the highway from Kootenay Lake.

♣ Creston (Detour Km 64.5)
A forestry and agriculture centre with sawmills nearby and grain elevators at the edge of downtown. Creston is the commercial hub in one of BC's

Creston Valley Wildlife Centre

Sasquatch crossing near Creston

most picturesque scenes. With the Purcells at its back door and the Selkirks out front, the town gazes across a broad flood plain of the Kootenay River. It's a lush green meld of farms and wetlands flanked by forests and mountainous rock walls. ⑦ ● ◬ ✕ ⍩ ▲ | *most needs and services*

› **Population** 4,800
› **Visitor Info** *Creston Visitor Info Centre* 1171 Canyon Street, Box 268, Creston, BC V0B 1G0; 250-428-4342; www.crestonbc.com.
› **Attractions** Creston Valley Wildlife Centre, Creston Valley Museum, Columbia Brewery, Cresteramics, Kootenay Candle Factory, Wayside Gardens and Arboretum.
› **Cycling/Outfitting** *Summit Outdoor Sports* 1029A Canyon Street; 250-428-2630.
› **Greyhound Bus** (1-800-661-8747; www.greyhound.ca) Depot located at 125 15th Avenue North.
› **Camping** *Pair-A-Dice RV Park & Campground* is near downtown at 1322 Northwest Boulevard; 1-866-223-3423; www.crestonvalley .com/pairadice/.

🍁Yahk (Detour Km 108.6)
Riverside hamlet on Highway 3/95, 42 kilometres east of Creston. ⑦ ↻ general store ⍩ ▭ ▲ | *post office, telephone*
› **Population** 200

> **Visitor Info** www.yahkkingsgate.homestead.com
> **Attractions** Antiques and collectibles.
> **Greyhound Bus** (1-800-661-8747; www.greyhound.ca) Depot located at *Grouse Mountain Variety* at 8741 Highway 3/95.
> **Accommodation/Camping** *Cozy Quilt Motel* 8849 Highway 3/95; 250-424-5558; www.cozyquilt.ca. *Riverside Campground* 8741 Highway 3/95; 250-424-5454. *Yahk Provincial Park* Nine-hectare park, beside Moyie River in Yahk, with 26 campsites. 🏕 ⛺ 🚻 *outhouses* 🚰

♣ Moyie (Detour Km 142.6)
On Highway 3, 34 kilometres northeast of Yahk. � *general store* 🏕 🍴 *Kokanee Cove neighbourhood pub | post office, telephone, no restrooms*
> **Population** 170
> **Attractions** Moyie Lake

🌲 Moyie Lake Provincial Park (Detour Km 153.6)
Take a marked turnoff from Highway 3, about 11 kilometres north of Moyie. This is the only public access to Moyie Lake. 🏕 ⛺ 🚻 🚰 | *showers*
> **Size** 91 hectares
> **Attractions** Sandy beach, grassy picnic area, playground, hiking trails.
> **Camping** 111 sites. *Reservations* 1-800-689-9025 (or 604-689-9025 in Metro Vancouver). www.discovercamping.ca

🌲 Jimsmith Lake Provincial Park (off the Gray Creek Pass detour at Km 168.5)
26 kilometres north of Moyie on Highway 3. Turn left (southwest) off Highway 3 onto Jimsmith Lake Road, a four-kilometre paved route to the park. ⛺ 🚻 *outhouses* 🚰
> **Size** 14 hectares
> **Attractions** Hiking trails; small lake for swimming, paddling, and fishing.
> **Camping** 34 campsites in a lakeside forest of Douglas fir and larch.

♣ Cranbrook (Detour Km 174.2)
On Highway 3, 30 kilometres north of Moyie. Also on the Trans Canada Trail. See page 311 in Chapter 19.

19 KIMBERLEY TO BAYNES LAKE

> "This is the most exciting part, down across the trench and up into the Rockies. It'll blow you away.
> —*A cyclist heading from Cranbrook toward the Rocky Mountains after riding the TCT all the way from the Okanagan*

Lake Koocanusa and
Rocky Mountains near Wardner

TRAIL TRIVIA

Koocanusa is an artificial lake on the Kootenay River created by the Libby Dam, which is downstream in Montana. The name is made up from the words *Kootenay*, *Canada*, and U.S.A.

TOTAL DISTANCE

102.5 km

HIGHLIGHTS

› Views of the Rocky Mountains
› Isidore Canyon rail trail
› Lake Koocanusa

CONDITIONS

› **Kimberley (Km 0) to Cranbrook (Km 30.6)** About 800 metres of city streets, followed by a mix of streets and trail for 5.5 kilometres, then paved highway and roads for 24.3 kilometres. → 30.6 km
› **Cranbrook (Km 30.6) to Wardner (Km 67.3)** Paved bike/hike trail for about 4.4 kilometres, followed by 13.3 kilometres of gravel road and rail trail, then paved highway and road for 19 kilometres. → 36.7 km
› **Wardner (Km 67.3) to Baynes Lake (Km 102.5)** 1.4 kilometres of pavement, followed by 23.6 kilometres of gravel industrial roads, then 9.3 kilometres of paved roads, ending with 900 metres of gravel. → 35.2 km

CAUTIONS

› Bears.
› Logging trucks.

TOPOGRAPHIC MAPS

1:250,000	Fernie 82/G
1:50,000	St. Mary Lake 82F/9, Lake Koocanusa 82G/3, Moyie Lake 82G/5, Elko 82G/6, Cranbrook 82G/12

OVERVIEW

Unlike regions to the west, the eastern Purcells and Rocky Mountains have fewer abandoned railway corridors conveniently ripe for transformation into long, continuous rail trails. The TCT here is comprised largely of highways, back roads, and provincial forestry roads still used by loggers.

Between Kimberley and Baynes Lake, just over 59 kilometres of the TCT route are paved highway and road, while slightly more than 43 kilometres are gravel road or rail trail.

Thirteen kilometres of the Isidore Canyon rail trail, east of Cranbrook, make up the only rail trail section on this stretch of TCT, at the time of writing. However, an abandoned 26-kilometre Canadian Pacific Railway line was expected to become a new TCT link between Kimberley and Cranbrook (see page 309). There were also hopes that the TCT would eventually take unused railway corridors beyond Isidore Canyon southeast to Wardner, eliminating several kilometres of road travel.

Until these rail trails are developed, much of the TCT route here will be shared with vehicle traffic. The upside is that they are scenic roads, with striking views of the Rocky Mountains, Lake Koocanusa, and the Rocky Mountain Trench.

LOCAL ADVENTURES
Day Trip
› Explore the forests, grasslands, streams, swamps, and lakes on the trails through Cranbrook Community Forest (Km 35).
› Take the Isidore Canyon rail trail (Km 35.3 to Km 48.3). → 13 km
› Take the TCT and Fort Steele Connector back in time to the 19th century. (See page 308.) ⇆ ±38 km

TCT ACCESS POINTS
Kimberley (Km 0) Small city on Highway 95A, 32 kilometres northwest of Cranbrook.

Marysville (Km 6.9) A small community that has been absorbed into the municipality of Kimberley, on Highway 95A, approximately 25 kilometres northwest of Cranbrook.

Cranbrook (Km 30.6) On Highway 3/95, 109 kilometres northeast of Creston. **P** *Parking lots and street parking. Inquire about long-term parking at the visitor centre (2279 Cranbrook Street North).*

Isidore Canyon trailhead (Km 35.3) Take Highway 3/95 north from downtown Cranbrook; just south of the overpass at Highways 3/95 and 95A, turn (right) east onto Stahl Road to the trailhead.

Fort Steele Connector (to Km 42.7) A trail known as the Fort Steele Connector meets Highway 3/93 at a pullout with parking for a small number of vehicles. This pullout is on Highway 3/93, approximately 11 kilometres from downtown Cranbrook, and 2.9 kilometres southeast of Highway 3/93 and Highway 95 (a junction north of Cranbrook). Follow the marked connector trail through the woods for 2.5 kilometres to Km 42.7 on the TCT/Isidore Canyon rail trail.

Rampart Rest Area (to Isidore Canyon rail trail) On Highway 3/93, approximately 14 kilometres from downtown Cranbrook, and 4.5 kilometres southeast of Highway 3/93 and Highway 95 (a junction north of Cranbrook). From this rest area, the TCT/Isidore Canyon rail trail is reached by a marked trail through bush and meadow. Take the trail to the northwest for 800 kilometres to a point where it joins the Fort Steele Connector. Turn left onto the connector and stay on the trail for 700 metres to the TCT/Isidore Canyon rail trail.

Baynes Lake (Km 102.5) Take Jaffray–Baynes Lake Road south from Jaffray on Highway 3/93 for about 18 kilometres to the small community of Baynes Lake.

19

THE ROCKY MOUNTAIN TRENCH

CLIMBING TOWARD THE GREAT DIVIDE

The mountain views get bolder as Trans Canada Trail travellers move from the eastern edge of the Purcells at Kimberley, down through the Rocky Mountain Trench beyond Cranbrook, and up toward the western fringes of the Rockies. People rolling into Cranbrook are confronted by an imposing rock ridge known as the Steeples, the first major glimpse of the Rocky Mountains. More than 2,400 metres above sea level, the Steeples are 25 kilometres away on the far side of the trench yet seem like they're right on the edge of town. They continue to overwhelm the views as the TCT runs down into the trench and along the shore of Lake Koocanusa.

Cranbrook is the last large helping of humanity as the TCT pushes east. Fernie, population 4,600, is the biggest town between Cranbrook and Alberta. Beyond Cranbrook, the route to the Rockies is mainly farms, forests, and mountains—and a few surprises, too, for those who get up as early as elk or black bears.

Rocky Mountains near Wardner

Populations along this stretch of TCT are slim and traffic is often light. Wardner, with its general store, is the only pocket of civilization until the TCT reaches Baynes Lake. From Baynes Lake the TCT continues to climb out of the Trench, to the town of Elko and into the Lizard Range of the Rocky Mountains.

THE TRANS CANADA TRAIL

Place names with asterisks are included in the **Communities, Parks, and Places to Stay** section (page 311).

Km 0   *Kimberley** From Kimberley Avenue, the Trans Canada Trail heads southeast through the pedestrian Platzl.

Km 0.2   *Kimberley Platzl East Entry* Cross Wallinger Avenue and head down Spokane Street past City Hall onto St. Mary's Avenue, which veers to the right.

Km 0.4   *St. Mary's Avenue + Ross Street* Make a short jog to the right, crossing Ross Street. Continue down St. Mary's Avenue, passing Mark Street, then crossing a bridge over St. Mary Creek. St. Mary's Avenue dead-ends at Leadenhall Street. Turn left onto Leadenhall, which veers to the right and becomes Beale Avenue.

Km 0.8   *Beale Avenue + Bingay Street* The road comes to an end at the start of the Mark Creek Trail, which is the TCT route to Marysville.

Km 1.1   *Bridge* A bridge to the left crosses the creek, while the
TCT continues straight on the trail. Ignore a steep trail up
to the right.

Km 1.2   *Information panel* A panel explains how trout habitat has been
restored in Mark Creek.

Km 1.3   *Victoria Avenue + Mackenzie Street* At this junction a bridge
on the left crosses the creek: don't cross it. Continue straight
down Victoria Avenue, following the creek.

Km 1.6   *Victoria Avenue + Archibald Street* A bridge on the left crosses
the creek near an RCMP station on the opposite corner. Continue straight on Victoria Avenue.

Km 1.8   *Victoria Avenue + Lindsay Street* The trail leaves paved roads
and becomes trail again, following Mark Creek downstream.

Km 1.9   *Montgomery Avenue* Where the trail comes out to Montgomery, continue to the left along the road.

Km 2.3   *Montgomery Avenue + Marsden Street* Turn left (northeast)
onto Marsden Street, crossing a bridge over Mark Creek, then
immediately turn right past a riverside parking area.

Km 2.5   *Lions' Way* A gateway called Lions' Way is the start of the
TCT/Mark Creek trail route down the east side of the creek.

Km 3.5   *Crosswalk* The TCT crosses Rotary Drive on a crosswalk just
up from a junction with Highway 95A. Cross the road and
continue down to where the trail takes a bridge over Mark
Creek and goes behind a kiosk with information about the
Kimberley Trail Network. Continue downstream on the trail.

Km 5.3   *Creek crossing* The TCT crosses the creek again. About
70 metres beyond the bridge, the trail forks. Take the fork
to the right over a small hump.

Km 6.3   *Kiosk* At a kiosk with information about the Kimberley Trail
Network, the trail meets pavement and a residential area.
Go right downhill and stay on the main road, following trail
markers down to Highway 95A.

Km 6.9   *Highway 95A* When you approach Highway 95A, you will see
a highway bridge across Mark Creek and a parking and picnic
area decorated with fish sculptures. While the Mark Creek
trail continues across the highway to Marysville Falls, the TCT
heads left (southeast) toward Cranbrook on Highway 95A,

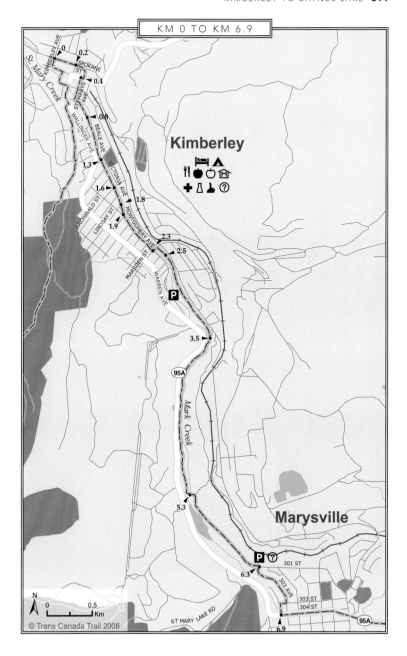

KM 0 TO KM 6.9

Kimberley

Marysville

19

Farmland southeast of Kimberley

which has paved bike lanes and scenic farmland on both sides, and views of the Rocky Mountains ahead.

Km 15.2   *Highway 95A + Wycliffe Park Road* Turn right off the highway onto Wycliffe Park Road, and continue downhill over railway tracks.

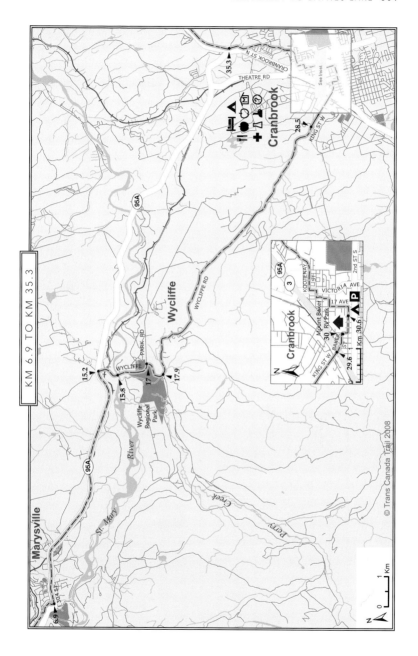

KM 6.9 TO KM 35.3

Marysville

30A SL

6.9

St. Mary

River

95A

15.2

15.8

WYCLIFFE

PARK RD

17

17.9

Wycliffe
Regional
Park

Perry Creek

Wycliffe

WYCLIFFE RD

95A

35.3

CRANBROOK ST N

THEATRE RD

Cranbrook

28.5

KING ST W

19

Inset:

N

Cranbrook

95A

3

KOOTENAY

1 ST

VICTORIA AVE

2nd ST S

17 AVE

Mount Baker

30 RV Park

1 ST

KING ST W

BAKER

29.6

Km 30.6

P

See Inset

N

0   1 Km

Km 15.8   *Bridge* The route crosses a long bridge over St. Mary River, where ospreys nest on utility poles. After the bridge continue straight uphill.

Km 17   *Wycliffe Park Road + Wycliffe Road* Turn right on Wycliffe Road.

Km 17.9   *Wycliffe Regional Park* Don't take the turnoff to Wycliffe Park; continue straight on Wycliffe Road.

Km 28.5   *Armour Road* Continue on Wycliffe Road, which becomes King Street West. King Street/the TCT passes Armour Road.

Km 29.6   *Cranbrook*, Railway tracks, Highway 3/95* Cross the tracks and highway. Continue about 100 metres to Baker Street, where you turn left.

Km 30   *12th Avenue South* Turn right on 12th Avenue South, go one block, then turn left on First Street up a hill. Continue about 400 metres, crossing 14th Avenue South.

Km 30.6   *Mount Baker RV Park* The RV park is a good overnight stop. (A TCT Pavilion is located here.) From here the TCT takes a paved bike path through Cranbrook*, then continues on a rail trail toward Lake Koocanusa, Baynes Lake*, and the Rocky Mountains. Go north on the Rotary Way cycle/walk path for nearly two kilometres to cross Victoria Avenue at Kootenay

Osprey nest near St. Mary River

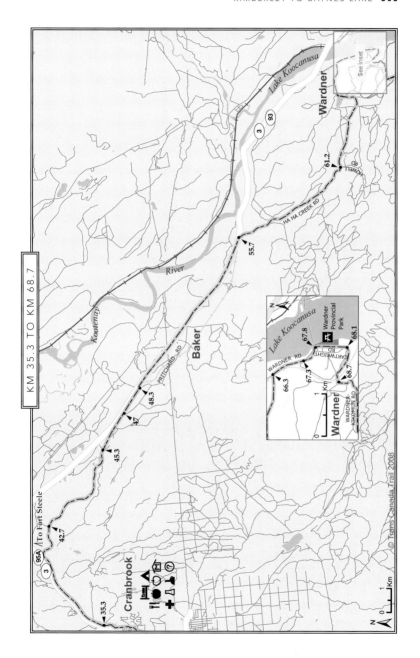

KM 35.3 TO KM 68.7

Wardner

Lake Koocanusa

93

3

61.2

HOWELL RD

HA HA CREEK RD

55.7

Kootenay River

Baker

PRITCHARD RD

48.3

47

45.3

42.7

35.3

95A

3

/To Fort Steele

Cranbrook

19

Inset:

N

Lake Koocanusa

67.8

Wardner Provincial Park

68.1

WARDNER RD

CARTWRIGHT RD

66.3

67.3

68.7

Wardner

WARDNER-KIKOMUN RD

Km 0   1

© Trans Canada Trail 2008

N   Km 0   1

Street. Stay on the bike path another 2.5 kilometres to the end of the pavement, then continue on a gravel trail marked "Cranbrook Community Forest North Entrance." Three hundred metres ahead is the Isidore Canyon rail trail.

Km 35.3   *Isidore Canyon trailhead* TCT markers show the way onto one of the few rail trails in this region, a nicely developed double track through the woods, with good birding in the wetlands beside the trail.

Km 42.7   TCT *marker/Fort Steele* Connector* The TCT continues straight on the rail trail toward Wardner and Baynes Lake. (The Fort Steele Connector is a trail to the left, off the rail trail through a small gate. This route and the historic town of Fort Steele make an interesting side trip into BC history—see page 308.)

Km 42.9   *Pond* A small trailside pond with a Rocky Mountain backdrop is a good stop for birders and photographers.

Km 45.3   *Road crossing* The TCT/rail trail crosses a gravel road. (Access Highway 3/93 by going left.) Continue straight on the rail trail.

Km 47   *Cattle guard* The rail trail crosses a cattle guard. (Again, you can access Highway 3/93 by going left.) Continue straight on the rail trail.

Km 48.3   *Pritchard Road* The rail trail crosses Pritchard Road onto private property. The TCT, however, turns left onto Pritchard and crosses a cattle guard to Highway 3/93. Go right (southeast) on the highway, which has paved shoulders.

Km 55.7   *Highway 3/93 + Ha Ha Creek Road* Turn right off the highway onto Ha Ha Creek Road.

Km 61.2   *Ha Ha Creek Road + Howell Road* Howell road goes to the right. Continue straight on Ha Ha Creek Road.

Km 66.3   *Ha Ha Creek Road + Wardner Road* At a T-junction where Highway 3/93 can be seen behind the trees about 100 metres to the left, turn right (south) toward the community of Wardner.

Km 67.3   *Wardner* The TCT continues through Wardner toward Lake Koocanusa. (A right turn on Cartwright Street leads to Wardner General Store.) Lake Koocanusa with the Steeples (in the Hughes range of the Rockies) as a backdrop makes a good photo op.

19

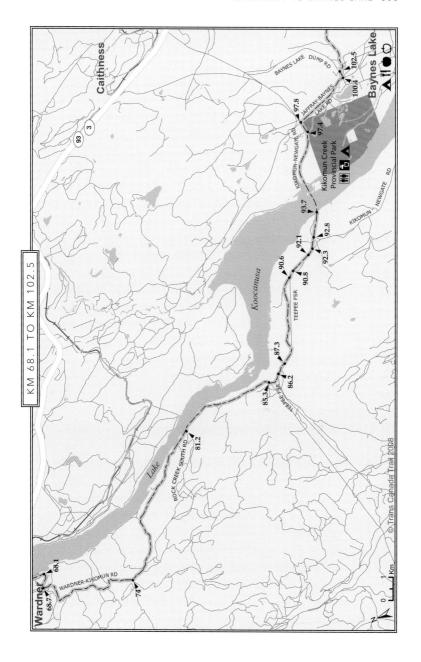

KM 68.1 TO KM 102.5

19

Km 67.8   *Wardner Provincial Park* A four-hectare lakeside park with hiking trails, used mainly by locals. Continue straight (south), along the lakeshore, on Laurier Road.

Km 68.1   *Wardner–Kikomun Road* The paved TCT route goes right (west) on Wardner–Kikomun Road.

Km 68.7   *Pavement ends* Where the pavement ends, the TCT continues on gravel road up around a hairpin turn.

Km 74   *Fork* Continue straight on the left fork, along a forest service road through a forest of larch trees.

Km 81.2   *Fork* Where Rock Creek South Road goes up behind to the right, continue straight ahead, following Lake Koocanusa, which is visible through the trees on the left (east).

Km 85.3   *Gas line* The TCT route passes a marked gas line.

Km 86.2   *Teepee forest service road* Continue straight on the left fork onto Teepee forest service road, an active logging road. A sign on a tree near this junction says Wardner is 20 kilometres from here.

Km 87.3   *Side road* You can choose to go on the left (east) side of the road where there is an abandoned side road that takes cyclists, hikers, and equestrians off the busy logging road for nearly five kilometres. It parallels the main road.

Km 90.6   *Side road/Teepee forest service road* Travellers on the side road must return to the main logging road for 200 metres.

Km 90.8   *Side road* The side road resumes on the right (west) side of the main road.

Km 92.1   *Side road ends* The side road ends and the route continues on the gravel road.

Km 92.3   *TCT + Caven Creek Road, pavement begins* Near an intersection where Caven Creek Road goes to the right, continue straight on the pavement.

Km 92.8   *Kikomun–Newgate Road* Kikomun–Newgate Road looks like two separate roads here. The TCT route continues straight (southeast) toward Lake Koocanusa. (The "other" Kikomun–Newgate Road runs to the right (south) down the west shore of the lake.)

Km 93.7   *Lake Koocanusa Bridge* (A campground with a small store is on the west side of the bridge.) Cross Lake Koocanusa on the bridge.

Km 97.4   *Kikomun Creek Provincial Park** A right (south) turn off the

Dutch Creek Hoodoos in the Rocky Mountain Trench

road and across a cattle guard leads into the park
and campground.

Km 97.8   *Kikomun–Newgate Road + Jaffray–Baynes Lake Road* Turn
right (south) on Jaffrey–Baynes Lake Road.

Km 100.4   *Jaffray–Baynes Lake Road + Baynes Lake Dump Road* (To
reach "downtown" Baynes Lake, stay on Jaffray–Baynes Lake
Road at this intersection.) The TCT goes left onto Baynes
Lake Dump Road, and at a fork about 300 metres up the
road, goes to the left, continuing on Baynes Lake Dump Road
as it crosses a cattle guard near Chief Daniel Road.

Km 101.6   *Pavement ends and gravel road begins*

Km 102.5   *TCT marker on Baynes Lake Dump Road, Baynes Lake** A TCT
marker indicates a rough industrial road on the right (east) off
of Baynes Lake Dump Road. This is the TCT route into the
heart of the southern Rockies.

THE ROCKY MOUNTAIN TRENCH: BC'S LONGEST VALLEY

A satellite image of British Columbia reveals a geographic oddity—a valley
that stretches the full length of the province from Montana in the south
almost to Yukon in the north. This is the longest valley in BC, the Rocky

LOCAL ADVENTURE

A RAIL TRAIL FROM KIMBERLEY TO CRANBROOK → 26 KM

An abandoned 26-kilometre Canadian Pacific Railway line was expected to replace the current Trans Canada Trail route between Kimberley and Cranbrook. Scenic and easy, this rail trail would provide off-road travel for hikers, cyclists, equestrians, and cross-country skiers. Check for updates at www.trailsbc.ca (look up "Rocky Mountains" under "BC Regions"). (These convoluted directions will likely become irrelevant when the route is finalized and signs are erected.)

Kimberley, Highway 95A/Ross Street Head southeast toward Jennings Avenue. At this junction, Highway 95A begins to curve to the left, but stay on Ross Street as it continues southeast.

Concrete barrier A concrete barrier on Ross blocks vehicle traffic but not hikers or cyclists—continue past the barrier for about 200 metres to Knighton Road, turn left on Knighton, and go another 200 metres to the start of the rail trail.

Rail trail to Cranbrook At the Cranbrook end, getting off the rail corridor and getting back on the TCT is more complicated, and still to be formalized.

Railway + Echo Field Road + Highway 95A At this intersection, the rail line parallels the highway as it approaches Cranbrook. Continue past the Echo Field Road junction for nearly one kilometre to where the highway veers left while the railway veers right. Get off the railway onto Highway 95A, and continue southeast for about 430 metres to Theatre Road.

Highway 95A + Theatre Road Turn right onto Theatre, and go 1.8 kilometres to McPhee Road.

Theatre Road + McPhee Road Turn left onto McPhee, continuing about 150 metres to where McPhee veers left, meeting an unnamed road to the right. Take the unnamed road past Wal-Mart's parking lot, then jog right to Ridgeview Drive. Turn right onto Ridgeview, go one block, then turn left onto Willowbrook Drive.

Willowbrook Drive + Highway 3/95 Continue on Willowbrook through traffic lights across Highway 3/95 until you reach Kootenay Street.

Kootenay Street + Rotary Way cycle/walk path The road joins the Rotary Way cycle/walk path. Turn right onto the paved pathway and stay on it to Mount Baker RV Park (TCT Km 30.6), site of a TCT Pavilion.

Mountain Trench. It runs along the western fringe of the Rockies for 1,400 kilometres, varying in elevation from 600 to 1,000 metres, widening to approximately 20 kilometres.

Each of BC's four largest rivers—the Columbia, Fraser, Peace, and Liard—travels through parts of the trench. Hydroelectric dams have drastically altered the landscapes here, creating huge artificial lakes. Williston Lake, on the Peace River, is the province's largest lake at 1,750 square kilometres; it took five years to fill after the W.A.C. Bennett Dam blocked the river in 1967.

Archaeological evidence of aboriginal inhabitants in the southern area of the trench dates back to the Ice Age. Explorer David Thompson crossed the trench in 1807, the Canadian Pacific Railway came in the 1880s, and the Trans Canada Trail arrived in the 1990s.

FORT STEELE'S FUTURE: A THING OF THE PAST

There's air conditioning in Wild Horse Theatre and a modern highway outside the stockade, but not much else at Fort Steele made it beyond the 19th century. A designated BC Heritage site, Fort Steele is a village on the east bank of the Kootenay River with 60 original or reconstructed buildings and a backdrop of Rocky Mountain peaks reaching over 2,800 metres.

LOCAL ADVENTURE

FORT STEELE → 23.8 KM FROM CRANBROOK
(→ 11.7 KM FROM THE ISIDORE CANYON RAIL TRAIL)

To make Fort Steele a side trip from the Trans Canada Trail, follow the TCT route from Cranbrook to Km 42.7, where the Fort Steele Connector heads east off the TCT/Isidore Canyon rail trail toward Highway 3/93.

Km 0 *TCT marker/Fort Steele Connector (TCT Km 42.7)* Go left (northeast) off the railway. The Fort Steele Connector takes a winding, single-track course across ranchlands and through open forests.

Km 1.2 *Rocky Mountain Trench viewpoint* A jumbo picnic table looks across the Rocky Mountain Trench to the Rockies.

Km 2.5 *Highway 3/93* The trail makes a kitty-corner crossing over the highway and a driveway and continues through cow fields and pine forests. Listen for the whistles of ground squirrels warning their neighbours of human intruders.

Km 5 *Eager Hill Road* Turn right (northeast).

Km 8 *Eager Hill Road/ Highway 93/95* Turn right onto the highway and breathe in the views of the Rockies as this route moves toward Fort Steele.

Km 11.7 *Fort Steele Heritage Town* Left off the highway into the 19th century.

19

Across southern British Columbia east of the Cascade Mountains, sagebrush (*Artemesia tridentata*) gives a desertlike look to much of the land at lower elevations. Its fragrance and pastel grey-green hue are particularly noticeable though the Okanagan and Boundary regions, and in the southern Rocky Mountain Trench along the Kootenay River.

Growing to two metres high, this aromatic evergreen shrub bears small yellow flowers in summer. Aboriginals made tea from the leaves and branches for relief from common colds. The bark was woven into mats and clothing.

Sagebrush readily takes root in arid areas where other plants have been displaced. Overgrazing by cattle has caused significant increases in the amount of sagebrush across southern BC.

19

Tourists see the town from carriages drawn by working Clydesdales, or from a two-kilometre ride aboard a steam locomotive. Children follow chickens around, visit goat pens, and see cows milked and butter churned at Lambi House. There's fresh bread at City Bakery, and candy just along the boardwalk at Mrs. Sprague's Confectionery. Actors in period costume perform indoors and out, and if there's "trouble" in the streets an officer of the North West Mounted Police—perhaps even Superintendent Sam Steele himself—can be summoned from the force's Kootenay Post.

Originally dubbed "Galbraith's Ferry," Fort Steele burst onto the Rocky Mountain landscape with the Kootenay gold rush of 1864. It was a commercial, social, and administrative hub until 1898 when the BC Southern Railway bypassed it in favour of Cranbrook.

Now, in the 21st century, Fort Steele is much like it was in the 19th.

KOOTENAY ROCKIES REGION

Tourism region that encompasses British Columbia's mountainous southeast corner, including the southern Monashees, Selkirks, Purcells, and Rockies. (For detailed information, see page 250 in Chapter 15.)

› TCT Info Look up "Rocky Mountains" under "BC Regions" on the Trails BC website at www.trailsbc.ca.

COMMUNITIES, PARKS, AND PLACES TO STAY

Information on each provincial park in BC can be found on the BC Parks website at www.env.gov.bc.ca/bcparks/.

🌲 Kimberley (Km 0)

See page 289 in the previous chapter.

🌲 Cranbrook (Km 29.6)

On Highway 3/95, 109 kilometres northeast of Creston. Cranbrook is southeastern BC's largest centre and the TCT's gateway to the Rocky Mountains. It sits on a broad plain with the Rockies to the east, the Purcells to the west, and at least 16 kilometres of Rocky Mountain Trench in between. This was a pasture and Ktunaxa camp before the railway came to Cranbrook in 1898. Canadian Pacific remains an important employer. Forestry, tourism, and service industries also help sustain the local economy. *all needs and services for a surrounding population of 60,000*

› **Population** 19,000

› **Visitor Info** *Cranbrook Visitor Centre* 2279 Cranbrook Street North, Box 84, Cranbrook, BC V1C 4H6; 1-800-222-6174; www.cranbrook chamber.com.

19

Pond beside Isidore Canyon rail trail

> **Attractions** Cranbrook Community Forest, South Star recreation trails, Rotary Way cycle/walk path, self-guided heritage walking tour, Canadian Museum of Rail Travel.
> **Cycling/Outfitting** *Gerick Sports* 320 Cranbrook Street North; 250-426-6171; www.gericksports.com.
> **Greyhound Bus** (1-800-661-8747; www.greyhound.ca) Depot located at *Sun City Couriers* at 1229 Cranbrook Street North.
> **Camping** *Mount Baker R V Park*, a municipal campground. 1501 First Street South; 1-877-502-2288; www.mountbakerrvpark.com.

🌲 Fort Steele (side trip off of Km 42.7)

A BC Heritage historic site on Highway 93/95. See page 308. The site is open specific hours; check websites below. ⊘ ⏱ *general store* 🍴 *1890s-style restaurant* 🛏 *available near heritage town area* 🚻 | *candy store, bakery, ice cream*

> **Visitor Info** *Fort Steele Heritage Town* 9851 Highway 93/95, Fort Steele, BC V0B 1N0; 250-417-6000; www.fortsteele.bc.ca. BC *Heritage* Look up "Fort Steele" at www.tsa.gov.bc.ca/heritage/.
> **Attractions** Living museum from the late 1800s.

🌿 Kikomun Creek Provincial Park (Km 97.4)

> From Highway 3/93 at Jaffray, go south on Jaffray–Baynes Lake Road for 16 kilometres to the park entrance. ▲ 🚻 *outhouse* 🚿 | *showers*
> **Size** 682 hectares
> **Attractions** Lake Koocanusa. Forests of Douglas fir and ponderosa pine with bunchgrass, six small lakes, hiking trails, adventure playground, fishing.
> **Camping** 105 campsites. *Reservations* 1-800-689-9025 (or 604-689-9025 in Metro Vancouver). www.discovercamping.ca

🌲 Baynes Lake (Km 102.5)

Small lakeside village at south end of Jaffray–Baynes Lake Road, 19 kilometres south of Jaffray (on Highway 3/93). ✂ *tack and camping supplies* ● 🍴 ▲ | *telephone*

> **Camping** P.R. *Campground & RV Park* 250-529-7696

20 BAYNES LAKE TO SPARWOOD

> "These mountains are sheets and wedges of striated rock from the bed of an inland sea. They have been sheared, twisted, folded, and heaped on edge like split cedar.
> —*Paul St. Pierre on the Rockies in*
> British Columbia: Our Land

Fernie ski hill as seen from the TCT near Cokato

TRAIL TRIVIA

The Canadian Rockies encompass 180,000 square kilometres, stretching 1,350 kilometres from the BC–Montana border to Liard River, and averaging 150 kilometres in width.

TOTAL DISTANCE

81.9 km

HIGHLIGHTS

> The Elk River Valley
> Trails in Fernie
> The Sparwood heritage walk

CONDITIONS

> Baynes Lake (Km 0) to Cokato (Km 41.5) Rough dirt road and single-track trail through cow fields, followed by active logging roads. → 41.5 km
> Cokato (Km 41.5) to just north of Fernie on Highway 3 (Km 52.9) 3.5 kilometres of paved road followed by 7.9 kilometres of single- and double-track hard-packed trail. → 11.4 km
> North of Fernie (Km 52.9) to Sparwood (Km 81.9) Paved road. → 29 km

CAUTIONS

> Confusing logging roads. Keep a close watch for TCT markers.
> Bears.

TOPOGRAPHIC MAPS

1:250,000	Fernie 82G
1:50,000	Lake Koocanusa 82G/3, Elko 82G/6, Flathead Ridge 82G/7, Fernie 82G/11, Crowsnest 82G/10

OVERVIEW

When people talk of being in the heart of the Rockies, this is it: a near-straight and narrow valley hemmed in by great hulks of raw rock chiselled against the sky. Some peaks are clad in patchy snow; most are naked from treeline to summit; and all confirm why they're called the Rockies.

For more than a century, coal miners have built their livelihoods on these mountains. Coal is still the economic backbone of the Elk Valley, employing hundreds of workers from Fernie, Sparwood, Elkford, and nearby towns in Alberta. TCT travellers share the corridor with trains transporting coal to tidewater at Vancouver, for export to Japan and other foreign markets. A colossal dump truck displayed at Sparwood symbolizes the region's mining heritage.

LOCAL ADVENTURES

Day Trip

› From Baynes Lake (Km 0), hike, bike, or ride a horse to Fusee Lake (Km 4.3). ⇆ 8.6 km

› On mountain bike or horse, make a return trip between Fernie (Km 52.9) and Sparwood (Km 81.9) on the Coal Discovery Trail. (See page 325.) ⇆ 68 km

› Or combine the Coal Discovery Trail and the TCT for a longer loop. (See page 325.) ↺ 63 km

› In Sparwood (Km 81.9), take a tour of heritage murals and sundry mining equipment by following painted footprints.

2 or 3 Days

› Stay at Fernie (Km 50) and explore dozens of trails outlined in the *Fernie Trail Guide* (which details 85 easy, moderate, or expert trails in the area. It can be purchased online at www.fernie.com/activities_intro/trail_map .html).

TCT ACCESS POINTS

Baynes Lake (Km 0) From Jaffray, on Highway 3/93, take Jaffray–Baynes Lake Road for about 18 kilometres to the small community of Baynes Lake. **P** *parking near the* TCT *marker on Baynes Lake Dump Road*

Elko, River Road (Km 14.8) The village of Elko is 65 kilometres east of Cranbrook on Highway 3. Just before the Elko store, turn right off the highway onto Bate Avenue, and follow the main road through Elko to the TCT at River Road. **P** *street parking*

Fernie, James White Park (formerly Mountview Park) (Km 47) From Highway 3 at downtown Fernie turn right (east) onto Fourth Street. Continue to Park Drive, turn right (south) and cross the bridge over Coal Creek, then turn right (west) on Mount Minton Street to the park.

Fernie Visitor Centre (Km 54) Located at 102 Commerce Road, near Highway 3 on the north side of Fernie.

Hosmer (Km 64.4) On Highway 3, 11.5 kilometres northeast of Fernie.

Sparwood (Km 81.9) On Highway 3, 29 kilometres northeast of Fernie. 🅿
parking at visitor centre

A ROCKY ROUTE TO THE ROCKY MOUNTAINS

CLIMBING OUT OF THE TRENCH

The Trans Canada Trail leaves the Rocky Mountain Trench from Baynes Lake on logging roads that head northeast into the Rockies. The mountains begin at Elko, where the TCT runs between the Lizard Range to the north and Mount Broadwood to the south. This is the start of a 175-kilometre trek up the Elk River Valley to Alberta. It is somewhat like a backwoods rendition of the famous Icefields Parkway in Jasper and Banff national parks, where the sculpted peaks of the southern Rockies appear within touching distance of the road. With summits on both sides reaching more than 3,000 metres, mountains overwhelm this route—Mount Fernie, Three Sisters, Mount Hosmer, and dozens more, each a landmark in its own right.

The TCT takes unused and active logging roads from Baynes Lake for most of the way to Fernie. Road conditions vary with use: the busier the road, the better the maintenance. People who want to avoid loaded logging trucks can take Highway 3. Beyond Fernie, Dicken Road (a delightful secondary route) and Highway 3 take the TCT traveller past a string of peaks and ridges to Sparwood.

THE TRANS CANADA TRAIL

Place names with asterisks are included in the **Communities, Parks, and Places to Stay** section (page 324).

Km 0   *Baynes Lake*, TCT marker on Baynes Lake Dump Road* Turn left (east) off Baynes Lake Dump Road at the TCT marker onto a rough industrial road; another TCT marker at a fork just ahead points right.

From "downtown" Baynes Lake, get to the intersection of Jaffray–Baynes Lake Road and Baynes Lake Dump Road, and turn right (east) onto Baynes Lake Dump Road. At a fork about 300 metres up the road, continue left on Baynes Lake Dump Road as it crosses a cattle guard near Chief Daniel

Road. You will see the TCT marker 2.1 kilometres from the intersection.)

Km 1.2   *Cattle gate* Go through the gate and continue straight, following TCT markers on a rutted mud track across a farmer's field. Where the track meets another track (near a gate on the left), follow the TCT markers to the right.

Km 4.3   *Fusee Lake* A placid pond in the forest; cattle sometimes graze near shore. (A primitive campsite to the left.) The TCT makes a sharp right turn up a short, steep hill.

Fusee Lake

Km 6.2   *TCT + Highway 93* The TCT crosses the highway and passes through a wooden cattle gate. It continues straight (east) across a field for a 100 metres to Sheep Mountain Road, a dirt forestry road that parallels the highway. Turn left (north) onto the dirt road. (Travellers who shy away from gravel roads can take Highways 93 and 3 to Elko (Km 13.2).)

Km 8.5   *Sheep Mountain Road + a haul road for Elko's sawmill* Sheep Mountain Road comes to a stop sign at a junction with the busy main haul road for Elko's sawmill. Turn right, and stay on the road as it veers away from Highway 93. At a junction, continue straight for about 200 metres.

Km 9.4   *TCT–marked trail* Go up a short hill to the left. This trail is an old road that leads to Elko.

Km 10.1   *Pipeline* The trail crosses a pipeline.

Km 10.7   *Fork* The TCT goes to the left continuing on the old road. (To the right is a single-track trail.)

Km 11.1   *Railway corridor* The TCT/old road continues on part of the Great Northern Railway corridor for about 200 metres, marked by yellow squares with figures of a bicycle or hiker.

20

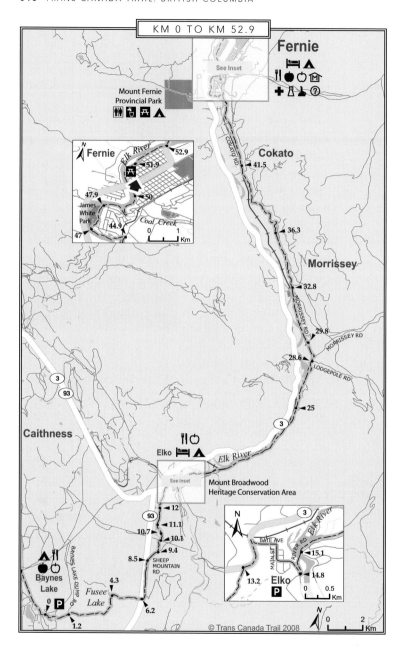

KM 0 TO KM 52.9

Fernie

Mount Fernie
Provincial Park

Fernie

Elk River

52.9
51.9

47.9
50

James
White
Park

44.9
Coal Creek

47

0   1
Km

Cokato

COKATO RD

41.5

36.3

Morrissey

32.8

MORRISSEY RD

29.8

MORRISSEY RD

28.6

LODGEPOLE RD

25

3

Caithness

Elko

Elk River

Mount Broadwood
Heritage Conservation Area

See Inset

12

93

11.1

10.7

10.1

9.4

8.5

SHEEP
MOUNTAIN
RD

BAYNES LAKE DUMP RD

Baynes
Lake

4.3

Fusee
Lake

0

1.2

6.2

N

3

Elk River

BATE AVE

RIVER RD

15.1

MAIN ST

13.2

Elko

14.8

P

0   0.5
Km

© Trans Canada Trail 2008

N   0   2
Km

3
93

20

Km 12   *Meadow* The TCT makes a transition out of the trees into a meadow. The trail is marked by signs with yellow decals.

Km 13.2   TCT + *Highway 3* The trail meets Highway 3 at a T-junction. Turn right (northeast) onto Highway 3, which continues over a railway bridge to the Elko store. To continue on the TCT, turn right off Highway 3 before the store onto Bate Avenue, and follow the main road through the village of Elko* to River Road.

Km 14.8   *River Road* The TCT takes River Road, a logging road, down over the Elk River and along the eastern bank through forests that frequently open to expansive mountain-and-river views.

Km 15.1   *Mount Broadwood Heritage Conservation Area* (Just beyond the bridge over the Elk River is a gated gravel road up to the right. This is a scenic alternate route that runs through a nature conservancy. It is approximately 28 kilometres from this gate back to the TCT route at Lodgepole and Morrissey roads (Km 28.6). See page 324 for more details.)

Km 25   *Elk River, View of the Highway 3 tunnel* Across the river the highway runs through an old Great Northern Railway tunnel.

Rocky Mountain meadow south of Cokato

Three Sisters, a backdrop to Cokato village

Km 28.6 *Lodgepole / Morrissey roads* **GPS** north 49.21.923, west 114.58.769. At a three-way junction, go left on Lodgepole/Morrissey.

Km 29.8 *Morrissey Road + River Road extension* **GPS** north 49.22.282, west 114.59.447. Go left on Morrissey Road.

Km 32.8 *Morrissey Road + Domin Road* **GPS** north 49.23.572, west 115.00.846. Just beyond this junction, a TCT marker points straight over a cattle guard; don't go left over the railway tracks.

Km 36.3 TCT *marker* **GPS** north 49.25.193, west 115.01.613. At a road that follows a hydro line, stay on the main road.

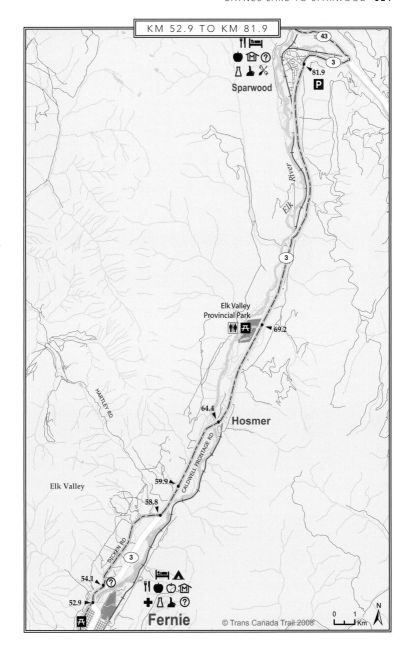

KM 52.9 TO KM 81.9

Sparwood

43

3

81.9

P

Elk River

3

Elk Valley
Provincial Park

69.2

Hosmer

64.4

HARTLEY RD

Elk Valley

CALDWELL FRONTAGE RD

59.9

58.8

DICKEN RD

3

54.1

52.9

Fernie

© Trans Canada Trail 2008

20

0 1 Km

N

Km 41.5 *Village of Cokato* Pavement begins at a village in a postcard setting of green meadows at the foot of Mount Fernie, with the prominent Three Sisters to the north.

Km 44.9 *Cokato Road + Mount McLean Street* Follow the TCT marker left onto Mount McLean Street, and after 100 metres turn left onto a trail marked by a TCT post. Wooden posts mark a forested trail that follows the Elk River through James White Park (formerly Mountview Park) and Fernie*.

Km 47   *TCT marker, fork* Stay right at the fork. About 100 metres ahead, continue across a road on the Fitness Trail. Where it crosses another road 400 metres farther along, turn right on the road.

Km 47.9 *TCT marker* The TCT leaves James White Park, runs beside the Elk River, then veers right up Coal Creek to a bridge on Park Drive. Turn left over the bridge, then left again at the TCT marker back toward the Elk River. The TCT takes a dyke that curves around Fernie for four kilometres.

Km 50   *TCT Pavilion, Fernie** In recognition of TCT donors. (To reach trails and campsites at Mount Fernie Provincial Park*, leave the trail here and take the Highway 3 bridge across the Elk River. Head southeast on the highway for approximately three kilometres. Turn right (west) off the highway on Mount Fernie Park Road and go nearly one kilometre to the park.)

Km 51.9 *Picnic site* A treed riverside spot in the shadow of the Three Sisters peaks.

Km 52.9 *Highway 3 (north)* The TCT goes under a bridge and loops on a paved trail up to Highway 3. (From Fernie, the TCT penetrates deeper into the mountains as it heads northeast up the Elk River Valley out of Fernie on Highway 3.)

Km 54.1 *Fernie Visitor Centre, Highway 3 + Dicken Road* Just beyond the visitor centre, go left off the highway at Dicken Road. The TCT veers right on Dicken, a pleasant paved back road. It wanders away from the highway and moves up the Elk Valley, flanked by Three Sisters and Mount Procter on the northwest and Fernie Ridge to the east.

Km 58.8 *Dicken Road (north) + Highway 3* Turn left (northeast) onto the highway.

Km 59.9 *Highway 3, Caldwell Frontage Road* (Caldwell Frontage Road can be used as a paved off-highway route for 1.3 kilometres,

20

but it requires two hazardous highway crossings.)

Km 64.4   *Hosmer* Former mining town with heritage sites.

Km 69.2   *Rest area and Elk Valley Provincial Park* On the left (west)
            side of the highway. (Outhouses, picnic tables.)

Km 81.9   *Sparwood** Ponder maps of Sparwood's heritage walking tours
            while ogling the world's largest dump truck (see below). From
            here the TCT continues north on Highway 43.

BIGGEST DUMP TRUCK A GUINNESS RECORD

There is no constructed landmark on the Trans Canada Trail that matches the grandiosity found at the gateway to Sparwood—the 350-tonne Terex Titan.

It's in the *Guinness Book of World Records* as the largest tandem-axle, rear-dumping hauler ever made. Built by General Motors of Canada, it came to Sparwood in 1978 on eight rail flatcars. It was assembled by the roadside and driven to the nearby Kaiser Resources coal mine. Three hundred and fifty tonnes is the load capacity, and although there are now newer trucks that carry more, they are not of such prodigious dimensions. The Titan weighs 260 tonnes. At 20 metres long, nearly eight metres wide, and seven metres high with the dumper down (17 with it up), the Titan could hold two humpback whales and a medium-sized school bus.

20

Terex Titan dump truck at Sparwood

LOCAL ADVENTURE

MOUNT BROADWOOD HERITAGE CONSERVATION AREA → 28 KM
A lightly travelled alternative to the logging roads of the TCT beyond Elko is a
route through an 8,900-hectare sanctuary. It is owned by the Nature Conservancy
of Canada and inhabited by grizzlies, bighorn sheep, elk, and other wildlife. The
land was donated by Shell Canada in 1992 to celebrate Canada's 125th birthday.
Cyclists, hikers, equestrians, and cross-country skiers can use the property, but at
their own risk. Vehicles are permitted at specified times during summer.

Access the Mount Broadwood Heritage Conservation Area from a gate near the
bridge over the Elk River outside Elko (TCT Km 15.1). The first ten kilometres up
the road run through Crown and private land (some owned by BC Hydro—at the
time of writing, BC Hydro allowed the public to travel across its land on the road).
Once you reach the conservation area, continue for seven kilometres to another

gate, which you pass through. Take
Ram Creek Road (a logging road)
for 3.1 kilometres to its junction
with Lodgepole Road (**GPS** north
49.18.572, west 114.55.886). From
here, Lodgepole Road continues
for 7.9 kilometres to the TCT route
at Lodgepole/Morrissey roads
(TCT Km 28.6).

Bighorn ewes with lambs

20

The Terex Titan retired in 1990 to become one of several outdoor artifacts that portray Sparwood's mining heritage. The area's history is also
depicted in murals, which can be viewed by following painted footprints
along the streets.

KOOTENAY ROCKIES REGION
Tourism region that encompasses British Columbia's mountainous south-
east corner, including the southern Monashees, Selkirks, Purcells, and
Rockies. (For detailed information, see page 250 in Chapter 15.)
› **TCT Info** Look up "Rocky Mountains" under "BC Regions" on the Trails BC
website at www.trailsbc.ca.

COMMUNITIES, PARKS, AND PLACES TO STAY
Information on each provincial park in BC can be found on the BC Parks
website at www.env.gov.bc.ca/bcparks/.

♣ Baynes Lake (Km 0)

See page 312 in the previous chapter.

♣ Elko (Km 13.8)

A sawmill town on Highway 3, 65 kilometres east of Cranbrook. ♻ general store 🍴 ▲ | *telephone, camping supplies*

› **Population** 160

› **Camping** *Mountain Tracks Wilderness Campground*, on Highway 3 two kilometres east of Elko; 250-529-6994. *West Crow Motel & R V Park*, at the junction of Highways 3 and 93; 250-529-7349.

♠ Mount Fernie Provincial Park

Cross the Elk River on the Highway 3 bridge near Km 50 and head southeast on the highway for approximately three kilometres. Turn right (west) off the highway on Mount Fernie Park Road and go nearly one kilometre to the park. ▦ *sheltered picnic tables* ▲ 🚻 *outhouses* 🚰

› **Size** 259 hectares

› **Attractions** Hiking trails.

› **Camping** 40 campsites. *Reservations* 1-800-689-9025 (or 604-689-9025 in Metro Vancouver). www.discovercamping.ca

---

LOCAL ADVENTURE

20

COAL DISCOVERY TRAIL → 34 KM / ↻ 63 KM

Opened in 2004, the Elk Valley Coal Discovery Trail is a 34-kilometre link between Fernie and Sparwood. The trail is on private land but is open to the public, and is widely used by hikers, equestrians, cross-country skiers, and mountain bikers. ATVers and motorbikes are not allowed, and it is not suitable for cyclists with panniers or trailers. (There has been discussion about combining stretches of the trail with back roads to create an off-road route for touring cyclists. Check for updates online at www.trailsbc.ca.) The trail is one of the first projects undertaken by the Canadian Coal Discovery Centre. There are plans to build an interpretive centre in Sparwood, focusing on the coal-mining industry.

From Fernie, take the Trans Canada Trail to where it loops up onto Highway 3 on the north side of town (Km 52.9). Rather than cross the bridge on the TCT route, continue nearly two kilometres along the southeast side of the river on the Great Northern Trail, crossing Canadian Pacific Railway tracks. Just beyond the tracks is a trailhead for the Coal Discovery Trail. It follows the east side of the Elk River to Mountain Shadows Campground, on Highway 3 near the southern entrance to Sparwood. Mountain bikers can ride a 63-kilometre loop, going one way on the Coal Discovery Trail, the other way on the TCT.

♣ Fernie (Km 50)

On Highway 3, 32 kilometres north of Elko. A coal-mining and tourist town bisected by the Elk River, and surrounded by mountain peaks exceeding 2,500 metres. Fernie is a four-season outdoor destination with snow sports in winter, and hiking, mountain biking, and kayaking in summer. The *Fernie Trail Guide*, which can be purchased online (www.fernie.com/activities_intro/trail_map.html), details 85 easy, moderate, or expert trails in the area. *all needs and services*

> **Population** 4,600
> **Visitor Info** *Fernie Visitor Centre* 102 Commerce Road, Fernie, BC V0B 1M5; 1-877-433-7643; www.ferniechamber.com. See also www.fernie.com.
> **Attractions** Historic oil derrick, Fernie and District Historical Museum, heritage walking tour, Ghost Rider. Outdoor adventure companies offer horseback, bicycle, and hiking trips on local trails; check the websites listed under "Visitor Info."
> **Cycling/Outfitting** *Ski Base* 432 Second Avenue; 250-423-6464; www.skibase.com. *Straight Line Bicycle & Skis* 461B Second Avenue; 250-423-3532; www.straightlinefernie.com. *The Guides Hut Outdoor Limited* 671 Second Avenue; 1-888-843-4885; 250-423-3650; www.thehut.ca.
> **Greyhound Bus** (1-800-661-8747; www.greyhound.ca) Depot located at *Park Place Lodge* at 742 Highway 3.

20

♣ Sparwood (Km 81.9)

On Highway 3, 29 kilometres northeast of Fernie. A resource community that proudly exhibits its coal-mining history with murals and artifacts, including the world's biggest dump truck. *all needs and services*

> **Population** 4,200
> **Visitor Info** *Sparwood Visitor Centre* 141 Aspen Drive, Box 1448, Sparwood, BC V0B 2G0; 1-877-485-8185; www.sparwoodchamber.bc.ca or www.sparwood.bc.ca.
> **Attractions** Heritage walking tour, mine tours, the Terex Titan dump truck.
> **Greyhound Bus** (1-800-661-8747; www.greyhound.ca) Depot located at D & M *Courier* at 127 Centennial Square.
> **Accommodation/Camping** *Valley Motel* Highway 3; 1-800-918-9305. *Black Nugget Motor Inn* 102A Red Cedar Drive; 1-800-663-2706. *Mountain Shadows Campground* Highway 3; 250-425-7815.

21 SPARWOOD TO ELK PASS

> **"** We did it!
> —*TCT's trail identification officer*
> *Mike LeBlanc after 23 days of cycling the*
> *Trans Canada Trail across southern BC*

Rocky Mountains near Elk Lakes Park

TRAIL TRIVIA

Early Canadian Pacific Railway brochures described the mountains of southeast BC and southwest Alberta as "Fifty Switzerlands in One."

TOTAL DISTANCE

107.7 km

HIGHLIGHTS

› Elkford's hiking and biking interpretive trails
› Completing the Trans Canada Trail in southern British Columbia

CONDITIONS

› **Sparwood (Km 0) to Elkford (Km 34.6)** A paved Highway 43. → 34.6 km
› **Elkford (Km 34.6) to Elk Pass (Km 107.7)** Rough and dusty gravel logging road for 68.9 kilometres, then a 4.2-kilometre grind (with an elevation gain of 200 metres) up Elk Pass Road. (The total elevation increase from Sparwood to Elk Pass is 800 metres.) → 73.1 km

CAUTIONS

› Wilderness for approximately 80 kilometres from Elkford. No supplies or groceries—the next store is eight kilometres beyond Elk Pass.
› The gravel road/TCT between Elkford and Elk Pass is well defined, but is known by a number of names. Elk Valley Road appears on a sign where the pavement ends 1.1 kilometres north of Elkford. Other signs may refer to the road as Elk Main, Elk River forest service road, or Elk Valley Highway.
› Logging trucks.
› Grizzly bears and black bears.

TOPOGRAPHIC MAPS

| 1:250,00 | Fernie 82G, Kananaskis Lakes 82J |
| 1:50,000 | Crowsnest 82G/10, Tornado Mountain 82G/15, Fording River 82J/2, Mount Head 82J/7, Mount Rae 82J/10, Kananaskis Lakes 82J/11 |

OVERVIEW

When it seems the Trans Canada Trail has passed every size and shape of mountain in the Cordillera, the serrated ridges of the Wisukitsak Range and the pyramidal summit of Mount Peck leap out of the landscape.

With mountains in all directions, the dilemma is fitting them all into a photograph.

Ascending the western slope of the Continental Divide is an arduous journey, especially for cyclists riding all the way from Elkford in a single day. Logging trucks, road dust, potholes, and long inclines make for slow headway. The last push up Elk Pass is a bog slog, with running water gouging ruts in the trail, and ambushes by bloodthirsty mosquitoes.

Survivors ignore the discomforts and let the euphoria take over. For those who began this cross-province trek in Victoria, the landmark at the top of the hill is both geographic and personal. They've come all this way expecting a grand finale, and there's not much grander than the Canadian Rockies.

LOCAL ADVENTURES

Day Trip

> Cycle or hike Elkford's 40 km interpretive trail system.

2 or 3 Days

> Camp at Upper or Lower Elk Lake and take day hikes in provincial parks on both sides of the BC–Alberta border.

TCT ACCESS POINTS

Sparwood (Km 0) On Highway 3, 29 kilometres northeast of Fernie. **P** *parking at visitor centre*

Elkford (Km 34.6) At the north end of Highway 43, 35 kilometres north of Sparwood. Elkford is the last community on the TCT in eastern BC, just over 73 kilometres from the BC–Alberta boundary, 81 kilometres from the next grocery stop (in Alberta).

Elk Lakes Provincial Park ranger's cabin (Km 103.5) At the end of the gravel road, 70 kilometres north of Elkford. Trailhead for Elk Lakes, and for Elk Pass Road, which is the TCT route to the Continental Divide.

Peter Lougheed Provincial Park/Elk Pass parking lot In Alberta, 5.6 kilometres below Elk Pass, on the BC–Alberta border (see page 337). Albertans commonly hike from here, over Elk Pass into BC's Elk Lakes Provincial Park. 🚻 | *no camping*

21

Rocky Mountains at Elkford

CONQUERING THE CONTINENTAL DIVIDE

AN UPHILL BATTLE

Highway 43 runs north from Sparwood and ends at Elkford, where Elk Valley Road, a logging road, begins. Elkford is a final dose of civilization before the last leg of the TCT in BC. Walled in between Mount Hadiken and Profile Mountain to the west, and Fording Mountain and the Greenhill and Wisukitsak ranges to the east, the little town marks the start of more than 70 kilometres of gravel road. The route from Elkford is more up—700 metres up—than down.

Those who venture onto this logging road enter the realm of grizzlies and black bears, elk and bighorn sheep, white-tailed deer, moose, beavers, and birds. The Elk Valley has long been a mecca for hunters and anglers, and recent years have seen growing numbers of birders, photographers, artists, and TCT travellers. Where there are logging roads there are loggers, and this final leg of the TCT in British Columbia showcases harvesting methods of the province's largest industry. At several points these mountain vistas make spectacular backdrops to acres of clearcuts.

The TCT runs north along the eastern border of Elk Lakes Provincial Park, a 172-square-kilometre wilderness laced with hiking trails. Near the end of the TCT in BC at Elk Pass, the park's northern boundary follows the Continental Divide, adjoining Peter Lougheed Provincial Park in Alberta's Kananaskis Country. TCT travellers here can peer down from the Continental Divide into the glacier-green waters of Kananaskis Lakes.

THE TRANS CANADA TRAIL

Place names with asterisks are included in the **Communities, Parks, and Places to Stay** section (page 342).

Coal operations south of Elkford

Km 0   *Sparwood** At Sparwood, Highway 3 runs east across the Rockies through Crowsnest Pass. The TCT, however, takes Highway 43 north to Elkford. From the visitor centre at 141 Aspen Drive, go east on Aspen through downtown Sparwood for 400 metres to the junction of Highways 3 and 43. Turn left (north) on Highway 43.

Km 4.3   *Highway 43 + Lower Elk Valley Road (south end)* While the TCT route stays on Highway 43 as it veers left here, Lower Elk Valley Road to the right is a 13-kilometre paved alternative to the busier highway.

Clearcut logging in Elk Valley

Km 14.9   *Highway 43 + Lower Elk Valley Road (north end)* The alternate route returns to Highway 43. The TCT continues north on Highway 43.

Km 22.8   *Elk Valley Regional Park* A 25-hectare day-use park, with a baseball diamond and swimming area. (Restrooms, drinking water, picnic shelters.)

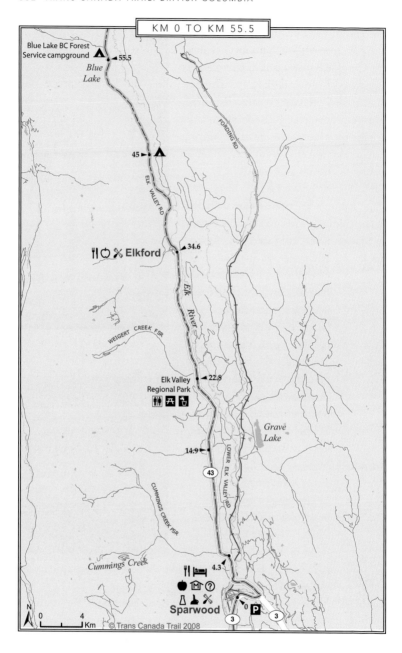

KM 0 TO KM 55.5

Blue Lake BC Forest
Service campground
▲ ◄ 55.5
*Blue
Lake*

FORDING RD

45 ► ▲

ELK VALLEY RD

¶ ☼ ✗ **Elkford**
◄ 34.6

*Elk
River*

WEIGERT CREEK FSR

Elk Valley
Regional Park
◄ 22.8

*Grave
Lake*

14.9 ►

43

LOWER ELK VALLEY RD

CUMMINGS CREEK FSR

Cummings Creek
¶ 🛏 ◄ 4.3
🍎 🗺 ❓
⚗ 🏔 ✂
Sparwood ◄ 0 🅿

3   3

N
0   4
Km
© Trans Canada Trail 2008

21

Km 34.6 *Highway 43 + Alpine Way, Elkford** Last chance to buy food and supplies for more than 80 kilometres. At the four-way stop, continue north on Highway 43 for just over one kilometre to its end. Keep going north along the west side of the Elk River on Elk Valley Road (a logging road).

Km 45 *Campsite* Basic campsite to the right (east) on the Elk River.

Km 55.5 *Blue Lake bc forest service campground* **GPS** north 50.11.207, west 114.58.993 📷 1,358 metres. On the left (west) side of the road.

Km 80.8 *Weary Creek bc forest service campground* One- or two-tent creekside/roadside campground. Beautiful stream. (Outhouse, picnic table.) From here the road narrows, crosses the Elk River, and begins to follow power lines up the river's east side. The surface generally improves, but there are still lots of potholes and long hills.

Km 81.7 *Fork* **GPS** north 50.23.992, west 114.55.100 📷 1,615 metres Veer left on the main road.

Km 86.6 *Cadorna–Abruzzi Wolverine Lakes trailhead, Elk Lakes Provincial Park** (A hiking trail into the provincial park is to the left.) The TCT stays on the main road.

Km 92 *Riverside bc forest service campground* **GPS** north 50.28.815, west 114.57.896 📷 1,668 metres. (A user-maintained site left (west) off the road. Outhouses, picnic tables.)

Km 98.3 *Tobermory bc forest service campground* **GPS** north 50.31.385, west 115.00.802 📷 1,707 metres. The epitome of mountain

21

Tobermory campsite

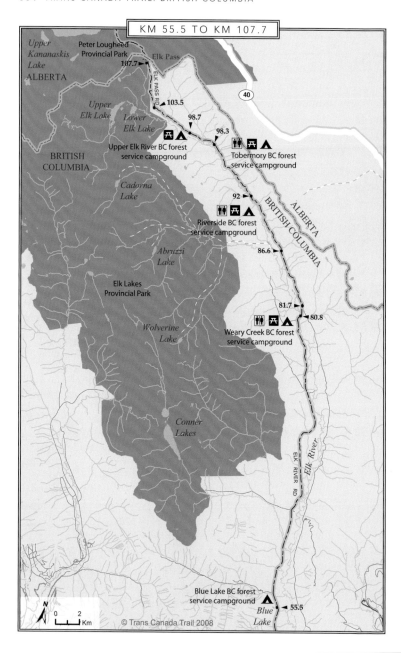

KM 55.5 TO KM 107.7

Upper Kananaskis Lake

Peter Lougheed Provincial Park

Elk Pass

107.7

ALBERTA

ELK PASS RD.

103.5

Upper Elk Lake

Lower Elk Lake

98.7

98.3

Upper Elk River BC forest service campground

Tobermory BC forest service campground

BRITISH COLUMBIA

Cadorna Lake

92

Riverside BC forest service campground

BRITISH COLUMBIA

ALBERTA

Abruzzi Lake

86.6

Elk Lakes Provincial Park

81.7

80.8

Wolverine Lake

Weary Creek BC forest service campground

Conner Lakes

ELK RIVER RD.

Elk River

Blue Lake BC forest service campground

Blue Lake

55.5

N

0   2
Km

© Trans Canada Trail 2008

21

TCT staffer Mike LeBlanc (left) and author at Elk Pass

scenery enveloping a one-room log cabin with bunks, table and chairs, and a wood stove for TCT–weary travellers. User-maintained, as is another campground across the road. (Outhouse, picnic table, creek water.)

Km 98.7   *Upper Elk River BC forest service campground* (Campground is left off the main road.) Veer right on the main road to stay on the TCT.

Km 103.5   *Elk Pass Road* **GPS** north 50.33.004, west 115.03.972 🔺 1,764 metres. (A ranger's cabin and Elk Lakes trailhead in Elk Lakes Provincial Park* are about 400 metres down the road to the left.) The TCT goes right (north) through a gate and up Elk Pass Road, which is closed to vehicles. Smear on liberal amounts of bug repellent before starting the climb.

Km 107.7   *Elk Pass—end of the TCT in southern BC* **GPS** north 50.34.999, west 115.04.066 🔺 1,960 metres. The final kilometre point in British Columbia for eastbound Trans Canada Trail travellers, on the border between BC's Elk Lakes Provincial Park and Alberta's Peter Lougheed Provincial Park in Kananaskis Country. Congratulations.

Alberta Rockies

TCT ROUTES TWICE CROSS THE ROCKY MOUNTAINS

Though not the highest of British Columbia's mountains (peaks in the Coast Mountains are higher), the Rockies are without question the most famous. They are the geographic backbone of North America, the location of a UNESCO World Heritage Site, and birthplace of national parks at Banff, Alberta.

The Rocky Mountains are the continent's largest range, running through 40 degrees of latitude from Mexico to Yukon. Tectonic forces created the Rockies, and glaciers sculpted raw rock into sawtooth ridges, hanging valleys, and pyramidal peaks. BC's Mount Robson, not far from Jasper, Alberta, is the highest in the Canadian Rockies at 3,954 metres; Colorado's Mount Elbert, at 4,402 metres, is the highest in the entire range.

The World Heritage Site here consists of Banff, Jasper, Yoho, and Kootenay national parks, and Mount Robson, Hamber, and Mount Assiniboine provincial parks in BC. They encompass the largest unbroken tract of mountain parkland on earth.

From Elko, the TCT slips between Mount Broadwood and the Lizard Range and continues through the Rocky Mountains for nearly 200 kilometres to Alberta. It crosses the Continental Divide at Elk Pass, just south of the World Heritage Site. Travellers on the TCT's northern BC route—the Alaska Highway—also cross the Rockies, near Summit Lake.

THE CONTINENTAL DIVIDE SPLITS THE NATION

Travellers who stand at Elk Pass with one foot in BC and the other in Alberta straddle the line that topographically separates the country west from east. At 1,960 metres, this is the second-highest point on the Trans Canada Trail in BC, after Gray Creek Pass in the Purcells.

This Great Continental Divide is the birthplace of Canadian rivers that flow to three oceans. Puddles that soak the shoes of TCT travellers on the Alberta side of Elk Pass are the headwaters of the Kananaskis Lakes and River, a tributary to the Bow River. These waters are part of the Saskatchewan River watershed, which eventually drains into the North Atlantic via Lake Winnipeg and Hudson Bay.

On the BC side, those wet feet are treading in the upper reaches of the Elk River, part of the Columbia River system, which flows through BC and the United States to the Pacific Ocean. The "Mother of Rivers" is the Columbia Icefield, on the Continental Divide north of Elk Pass, on the boundary between Jasper and Banff national parks in Alberta. Among the many rivers that originate here is the Athabasca, which flows northeast

---

BACK TO CIVILIZATION

OVER THE HILL TO ALBERTA → 90+ KM TO CANMORE, 130 KM TO CALGARY

Although the Trans Canada Trail in British Columbia ends at Elk Pass, the journey doesn't. Elk Pass is the proverbial "middle of nowhere," more than 130 kilometres from Calgary, Alberta, the closest big city, or about 90 kilometres from Canmore, Alberta. TCT travellers can either arrange to be picked up at the Elk Pass parking lot in Peter Lougheed Provincial Park, or continue on highways to Calgary or Canmore. The precise location of the TCT link here between BC and Alberta is not yet finalized.

The following route offers directions to Canmore, where there is a Greyhound bus depot, and to the eastern edge of Calgary, continuing on its roads and bike trails to the Calgary Greyhound depot (141 kilometres) and Calgary International Airport (161 kilometres). Campgrounds, accommodations, and other amenities can be found along the route.

Place names with asterisks are included in the Communities, Parks, and Places to Stay section.

Km 0   *Elk Pass, Peter Lougheed Provincial Park** On the Alberta side at the top of the pass go around the right side of a picnic table and head north on a steep, rough road that follows a power line down toward Kananaskis Lakes.

BACK TO CIVILIZATION (CONTINUED)

Km 3.1 *Power-line road ends* **GPS** north 50.36.326, west 115.05.834 🔺 1,924 metres. The route veers to the left on a service road, making an extremely steep descent.

Km 4 *Fork* After crossing a bridge, the route forks and makes a sharp climb to the left. It crosses under a power line and continues on a rough road to the paved parking lot.

Km 5.6 *Elk Pass parking lot, Peter Lougheed Provincial Park* From the parking lot, take Kananaskis Lakes Trail (paved road) north toward Kananaskis Trail (Highway 40). (Outhouses, no camping.)

Km 7.5 *Lower Lake campground* In Peter Lougheed Park on Lower Lake Drive. (104 campsites, restrooms, drinking water, telephone.)

Km 8 *Boulton Creek campground* In Peter Lougheed Park on Boulton Creek Trail. (118 campsites, restrooms, showers, drinking water, telephone.)

Km 11.7 *Elkwood campground* In Peter Lougheed Park. (130 campsites, restrooms, showers, drinking water, telephone.)

Km 13.9 *Canyon campground* In Peter Lougheed Park. (51 campsites, restrooms, drinking water, telephone.)

Km 14.4 *Peter Lougheed Provincial Park Visitor Information Centre** Information about Peter Lougheed Provincial Park and Kananaskis.

Km 15.7 *Smith-Dorrien/Spray Trail (road)* If you wish to go to Canmore*, it is 64 kilometres to the west by gravel road.

Km 26.7 *Fortress Junction Service Centre* Continue north on Highway 40. (Restrooms, drinking water, fuel, food, telephone.)

Km 32.4 *Opal* (Picnic site.)

Km 33.3 *Eau Claire campground* (403-591-7226; www.kananaskiscamping.com. 51 campsites, outhouses, drinking water.)

Km 38.7 *Wedge Pond* (Picnic site.)

Km 40.3 *Mount Kidd RV Park* (403-591-7700; www.mountkiddrv.com. 229 campsites, all amenities for campers.)

Km 45.6 *Lodge at Kananaskis Junction* (Go left (west) for one kilometre to reach Delta Lodge at Kananaskis. 1-866-432-4322; www.deltahotels.com.)

Km 47.7 *Sundance Lodges campground* (403-491-7122; www.sudancelodges .com.Teepee rentals, outhouses, showers, laundry, groceries.)

Km 50.5 *Mount Lorette Ponds* (Picnic site.)

Km 52 *Wasooch Creek* (Picnic site.)

Km 57.9 *Barrier Lake* (Picnic site.)

Km 60.3 *Barrier Dam* (Picnic site.)

Km 61.3 *Highway 40 + Highway 68* Continue north on Highway 40.

Km 62.4 *Barrier Lake Visitor Information Centre* (403-673-3985;

ELK PASS TO ALBERTA • KM 0 TO KM 120.9

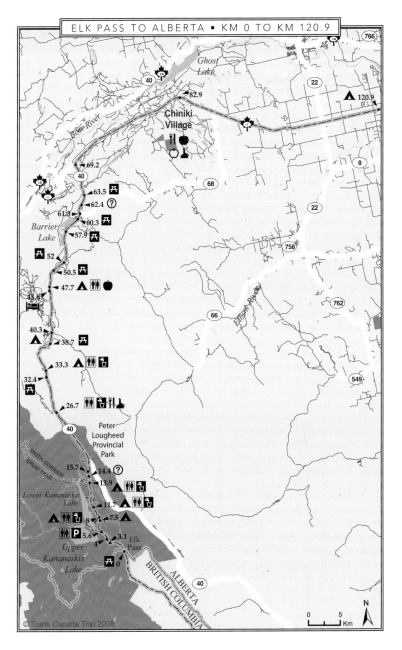

BACK TO CIVILIZATION (CONTINUED)

look up "Facilities Barrier" at http://tprc.alberta.ca/parks/.) Information on trails, backcountry camping, and facilities in Kananaskis Country. Sells maps, guidebooks, and posters.

Km 63.5 *Canoe Meadows* (Picnic site.)

Km 69.2 *Highway 40 + Highway 1* Left (west) to Canmore, 23 kilometres, right (east) to Calgary, 75 kilometres to city centre.

Km 82.9 *Chiniki First Nation village* Most amenities.

Km 120.9 *Calaway RV Park* (403-240-3822; www.calawaypark.com. 104 campsites, all amenities, amusement park.)

Km 129.6 *KOA campground* (1-800-562-0842; www.aroundcalgary.com/koa/. 365 campsites, all amenities.)

Km 135.1 *Highway 1 (16 Avenue) + Home Road Northwest* Turn right (south) on Home Road Northwest and continue to the end.

Km 135.6 *Montgomery Boulevard Northwest* Turn left and go to the end of the road then take the bike path to the east along the north bank of the Bow River.

Km 141.3 *14 Street + Bow River crossing to Greyhound bus depot* Travellers going to the Greyhound bus depot turn right on 14 Street, crossing the Bow River on Mewata Bridge. Turn right to the depot, which is clearly visible at 877 Greyhound Way Southwest. Travellers going to Calgary International Airport, where there is another Greyhound depot at 2000 Airport Road Northeast, should stay on the north side of the river and continue east on the path.

Km 143.6 *Trans Canada Trail* At the bridge across the Bow River to Prince's Island Park, the bikeways on both sides of the river become the Trans Canada Trail. Continue east along the north bank toward the airport.

Km 147.5 *Nose Creek* The TCT veers left (north) and follows Nose Creek up the west side of Deerfoot Trail Northeast (Highway 2).

Km 149.5 *Highway 1 underpass + Calgary Airport turnoff* The TCT crosses under the Trans-Canada Highway (Highway 1) and continues north, but the route to the airport takes a trail east then north along the east side of Fox Hollow Golf Course.

Km 151.5 *Deerfoot Trail Northeast (Highway 2) crossing* The trail crosses Highway 2 on a pedestrian bridge to a T-junction. Take the pathway to the right for 1.5 kilometres to another pathway intersection. Turn left (north) on 18 Street and continue north. Turn right (east) on 30 Avenue, left (north) on 19 Street, crossing 32 Avenue then McKnight Boulevard, where 19 Street becomes McCall Way and veers to the right. Hikers and cyclists can take a trail here that parallels the west side of McCall Way north to Barlow Trail at the entrance to the airport terminal.

Km 160.7 *Calgary International Airport* Served by more than two dozen airlines.

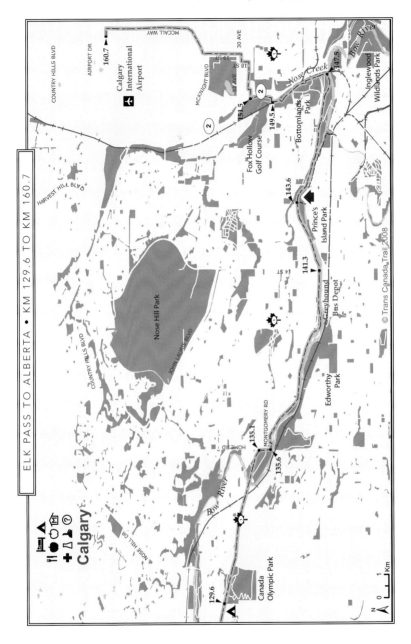

ELK PASS TO ALBERTA • KM 129.6 TO KM 160.7

© Trans Canada Trail 2008

21

Alberta's Kananaskis Country, beyond Elk Pass, the end of the TCT in southern BC

through Wood Buffalo National Park. It is part of the vast Mackenzie River system, which spills across the Arctic tundra to the Beaufort Sea.

KOOTENAY ROCKIES REGION

Tourism region that encompasses British Columbia's mountainous southeast corner, including the southern Monashees, Selkirks, Purcells, and Rockies. (For detailed information, see page 250 in Chapter 15.)

› **TCT Info** Look up "Rocky Mountains" under "BC Regions" on the Trails BC website at www.trailsbc.ca.

COMMUNITIES, PARKS, AND PLACES TO STAY

Half a dozen basic BC forest service campgrounds are spaced along the route between Elkford and Elk Pass: *Elk River* (Km 45), *Blue Lake* (Km 55.5), *Weary Creek* (Km 80.8), *Riverside* (Km 92), *Tobermory* (Km 98.3), and *Upper Elk River* (Km 98.7). Tobermory, which has a log cabin for public use, and Upper Elk River make good overnight stops for TCT travellers headed for Elk Pass and beyond.

Information on each provincial park in BC can be found on the BC Parks website at www.env.gov.bc.ca/bcparks/.

🌲 Sparwood (Km 0)

See page 326 in the previous chapter.

♣ Elkford (Km 34.6)

A coal-mining town that bills itself as the "Wilderness Capital of BC," a claim TCT travellers could substantiate. ⑦ ☿ *general store and camping supplies* ✕ ‖ | *post office*

> **Population** 2,600
> **Visitor Info** *Elkford Visitor Centre* 4A Front Street, Box 220, Elkford, BC V0B 1H0; 250-865-4614; www.tourismelkford.ca.
> **Attractions** More than 40 kilometres of maintained interpretive trails for cyclists, hikers, cross-country skiers, and snowmobilers in and around the town.

♠ Elk Lakes Provincial Park (Km 86.6, Km 103.5)

North of Elkford, and west off the Elk River. Biking on hiking trails is not allowed. ▲ | *no amenities near the* TCT

> **Size** 17,245 hectares
> **Attractions** At least a dozen designated trails as well as crude bush paths to scenic spots make this the stomping grounds for hikers from both BC and Alberta. Hikers can reach Lower and Upper Elk lakes in less than an hour from the trailhead near Elk Pass Road (Km 103.5). See the BC Parks website for trail details.
> **Camping** Four backcountry camping areas are reached by hiking trails. Three have pit toilets; two have food caches.

♠ Peter Lougheed Provincial Park, AB

On the Alberta side of Elk Pass in Kananaskis Country. Highway 40 runs through the southeast edge of the park to join Highway 1, the route to Canmore or Calgary.

> **Size** 50,142 hectares
> **Visitor Info** 1-800-366-2267 or 403-591-7726; www.albertaparks.ca; http://tprc.alberta.ca/parks/ (search for "Peter Lougheed").
> **Attractions** Hiking, camping, cycling, skiing, boating.
> **Camping** Four campsites within the park are located along the described route between Elk Pass and Canmore or Calgary.

♣ Canmore, AB

An attractive mountain town used year-round as a base for outdoors lovers exploring surrounding Kananaskis Country.

> **Population** 16,000

21

> **Visitor Info** *Tourism Canmore* 907 Seventh Avenue, PO Box 8608, Canmore, AB TIW 2V3; 1-866-226-6673 (press "1"); www.tourismcanmore .com.

> **Attractions** Opportunities to explore Kananaskis Country. Hiking, mountain biking, white-water kayaking and rafting, snowshoeing, downhill and cross-country skiing.

> **Cycling/Outfitting** *Bicycle Café* 102–630 Main Street; 403-678-3021; www.bicyclecafe.com. *Couloir Ski and Bike* 105–712 Bow Valley Trail; 403-678-0088; www.couloirskiandbike.com. *Rebound Cycle* 902 Main Street; 1-866-312-1866; www.reboundcycle.com. See also the Canmore business directory at www.canmorebusiness.com.

> **Greyhound Bus** (1-800-661-8747; www.greyhound.ca) Depot located at 701 Bow Valley Trail.

> **Accommodation** A wide selection of lodges, guest ranches, resorts, motels, hotels, hostels, B&BS, and campgrounds. Check www.tourismcanmore .com.

♣ Calgary, AB

One of Canada's fastest-growing cities; home of the annual Calgary Stampede and Exhibition.

> **Population** 952,000

> **Visitor Info** *Tourism Calgary* Suite 200, 238–11th Avenue Southeast, Calgary, AB T2G 0X8; 1-800-661-1678; www.tourismcalgary.com.

> **Attractions** Calgary Science Centre, Calgary Zoo, Calgary Tower, Canada Olympic Park, Devonian Gardens, Inglewood Bird Sanctuary, Heritage Park Historical Village, Fort Calgary, Eau Claire Festival Market.

> **Transportation**

Land The *Greyhound Canada* bus depot is at 877 Greyhound Way Southwest; 403-260-0877. Another Greyhound depot is located at *Calgary International Airport* at 2000 Airport Road Northeast (1-800-661-8747; www.greyhound.ca).

Air More than two dozen airlines fly to *Calgary International Airport* (www .calgaryairport.com). Among the major Canadian carriers are *Air Canada* (1-888-247-2262; www.aircanada.com) and *WestJet Airlines* (1-888-937-8538; www.westjet.com).

Bike Paths Map Look up "cycling maps" at www.calgary.ca to download a variety of maps.

> **Accommodation** See accommodation listings at www.tourismcalgary.com or www.explorealberta.com.

PART TWO: NORTHERN BC

YUKON *to the* BC–ALBERTA

BORDER

> "There are strange things done in the midnight sun.
> —*From the classic poem "The Cremation of Sam McGee" by Robert Service, a.k.a. the Bard of the Klondike*

The Alaska Highway forms most of the Trans Canada Trail across northern BC

TRAIL TRIVIA

Northern BC is a land of midnight sun, with daylight lasting as long as 19 hours a day around the time of the summer solstice.

The Trans Canada Trail route across northern British Columbia takes the Alaska Highway (BC Highway 97) to Dawson Creek, BC, where it continues on secondary roads to the BC–Alberta boundary.

This route is categorized by the TCT as a "temporary road link," although there is currently no plan to build a trail alongside the highway corridor. The Alaska Highway can be cycled safely, or hiked by ambitious walkers.

Summit Lake, Stone Mountain Park

Liard River Hot Springs Park

A total of 1,051 kilometres, the TCT in northern BC is part of a 5,700-kilometre loop through northwestern Canada. Beyond BC the trail continues east across northern Alberta where it becomes a water-based route, running down the Slave and Mackenzie rivers across the Northwest Territories out to Tuktoyaktuk, on the Beaufort Sea. The coastline to the east across the Arctic toward Hudson Bay is being considered as a TCT route for Nunavut. Meanwhile, trail builders in Yukon have completed much of a TCT route that incorporates historic gold-mining and fur-trading trails with roads and highways.

The TCT in northern BC actually begins in Watson Lake, Yukon, 13 kilometres from the BC border because it's the only town of any size near the western end of the trail. All but 73 of the total 1,051 kilometres are on the Alaska Highway. The Alaska Highway in BC is remote, wild, and somewhat daunting to people accustomed to the security of travelling the populated south. Communities in the northern half of the province are literally few and far between, separated by vast tracts of wilderness where moose and bears may outnumber people. Many of the towns named on Alaska Highway maps are listed by the *Gazetteer of Canada* simply as "locality"—"a named area with or without a scattered population." Some are truck stops, some *were* truck stops, and a few are villages in the middle of nowhere. The only full-service communities are Watson Lake (Km 0), Fort Nelson (Km 522), Fort St. John (Km 903), and Dawson Creek (Km 978).

It is undoubtedly the boundlessness of the northern BC landscape that entices travellers. And the chance to encounter Canada's biggest and

ADVICE FOR CYCLISTS

Horrific tales of transport trucks bearing down on cyclists at 130 kilometres an hour are exaggerated. While the Alaska Highway may be busy at certain times and places, it is, for the most part, a long, often lonely road through the hinterland. When traffic is light, cyclists may ride for hours and see vehicles only once every three or four kilometres. Of all the drivers on the Alaska Highway, commercial truckers set the example for courtesy; they rarely crowd cyclists and usually give a wide berth when passing. Cyclists can reciprocate by pulling off-road in particularly tight places.

The Alaska Highway between Watson Lake and Dawson Creek has paved shoulders for all but 200 kilometres. Gravel shoulders too rough or soft for continuous riding may be safe for emergency pull-offs.

Updated road reports. In Yukon: www.gov.yk.ca/roadreport/; 867-456-7623. In BC: www.drivebc.ca; 1-800-550-4997. In the section in BC between Wonowon and Yukon border: 250-774-7447.

wildest land animals—caribou, moose, elk, mountain goats, thinhorn sheep, black bears, grizzlies, and wood bison (the biggest of all).

From Watson Lake, just north of 60°N, to the BC–Alberta border the highway cuts through boreal forests, climbs over the northern Rocky Mountains, and rolls onto the Canadian prairie. While each of these landscapes holds its own intrigue, the Rockies are the most staggering: blue-green rivers and turquoise lakes, broad valleys laid out below peaks over 2,000 metres, and a travel route that sometimes gropes along the edge of sheer rock walls.

The eastern end of this leg of the TCT is a geography lesson for those who maintain that BC is a Pacific province, west of the Rockies. About one-tenth of BC is on the Alberta Plateau, east of the Rockies. This is the only place where the Canadian prairie spills into BC, and travellers who wheel into Dawson Creek on the Alaska Highway see all the prairie-like hallmarks—big skies and thunderheads, mosaics of cultivated fields, grain elevators, and rivers that cut deep ravines in hairpin turns across the plains.

PLANNING YOUR TRIP

Vehicle is the main mode of travel on the Alaska Highway, but a bicycle is more in keeping with the non-motorized theme of the Trans Canada Trail. This is a route for seasoned cyclists, a 10- to 14-day ride of more than one thousand kilometres. Most of the route is a paved, two-lane corridor with challenging gradients, changing weather, worrisome bears, and a few inconsiderate drivers.

It can be a long journey, especially at the pace of a touring cyclist. A trip by bike should be carefully planned around available overnight stops. Though reservations for accommodation or campsites may not be needed, it is wise to call ahead. When the next stop could be 80 kilometres up the road, a "no vacancy" sign is disconcerting after a daylong trek. Cyclists should also schedule in extra hours of daylight in case of unexpected setbacks, and be prepared to pitch tents by the roadside.

The main places for serious grocery shopping are Watson Lake at the start, Fort Nelson just beyond the middle, and Fort St. John and Dawson Creek near the eastern end. Meals are available at restaurants along the highway, but touring cyclists should ensure they have ample food for the long distances and for emergencies. Expect to pay about one-third more than in the south for food and restaurant meals, and for drinking water, which can be bought by the bottle from truck stops.

Bike parts and repair services are available in Fort Nelson and Fort St. John, but cyclists should be mechanically self-sufficient, and reasonably adept at roadside repair.

FINDING THE TRANS CANADA TRAIL

Watson Lake and other TCT communities are served by Greyhound Canada buses, and a few are served by airlines. Fort St. John (Km 903) is the largest city in the Peace River region; Dawson Creek (Km 978), Mile 0 on the Alaska Highway, can also be reached from Alberta via Highway 2 and Highway 49.

Those from southern BC planning to hike or cycle the TCT/Alaska Highway may want to avoid a long drive and use planes and buses instead. It's fairly uncomplicated and inexpensive to buy a bike box from Greyhound Canada ($10 at last check) and ship a bicycle to Watson Lake. Travellers can then fly Air Canada to Fort St. John, take a 14-hour bus ride (or even charter a plane) to Watson Lake, and then assemble bikes and ride back down the Alaska Highway to any destination where Greyhound buses stop, such as Fort Nelson, Fort St. John, or Dawson Creek. Some Greyhound drivers are good tour guides, pointing out landmarks and often stopping so people can take pictures of landscapes and wildlife.

MORE INFORMATION

Northern BC Tourism Association For general travel information: 1274 Fifth Avenue, PO Box 2373, Prince George, BC V2N 2S6; 1-800-663-8843; www.northern bctravel.com.

Northern Rockies Alaska Highway Tourism Association For more details on the Alaska Highway and northern environs: Suite 300, 9523–100th Street, Box 6850, Fort St. John, BC V1J 4J3; 1-888-785-2544; www.hellonorth.com.

Land

Greyhound Canada bus stops include Watson Lake, Contact Creek, Fireside, Coal River, Liard River Hot Springs, Muncho Lake, Toad River, Fort Nelson, Prophet River, Buckinghorse River, Pink Mountain, Wonowon, Fort St. John, Taylor, and Dawson Creek (1-800-661-8747; www.greyhound.ca).

Air

A number of airlines serve the largest communities on the Alaska Highway. For scheduled flights to Fort Nelson, Fort St. John, and Dawson Creek check *Air Canada* (1-888-247-2262; www.aircanada.com), *Central Mountain Air* (1-888-865-8585; www.cmair.bc.ca), and *Peace Air* (1-800-563-3060; www.peaceair.com).

NAVIGATING THE TCT IN NORTHERN BC

Unlike in southern British Columbia, the TCT in northern BC is not expected to change significantly. The kilometre points in the nothern route descriptions, therefore, run continuously from chapter to chapter—that is, the 1,051-kilometre route begins at "Km 0" at Watson Lake, Yukon, and ends at "Km 1,051" on the BC–Alberta border. (Each chapter in Part One, describing the TCT's southern route in BC, begins at Km 0.) The format used here in Part Two is the same as in official Trans Canada Trail guidebooks covering other regions.

AMENITIES, LODGING, AND CAMPING

Watson Lake (Km 0), Fort Nelson (Km 522), Fort St. John (Km 903), and Dawson Creek (Km 978) are the main population centres and TCT access points. Each offers a range of amenities and services, including Internet access for travellers at cafés and places of accommodation.

"Campers" in yacht-sized motorhomes, invariably with compact "dinghies" in tow, make up much of the summer traffic on the Alaska Highway. Campgrounds that cater to RVs usually have tent sites as well. RV camps may also have motel rooms or cottages. Reservations may not be needed but it's wise to call ahead.

Communities, truck stops, restaurants, and specific accommodations along the Alaska Highway are listed in the **Communities, Parks, and Places to Stay** section in each chapter. Other resources include www .hellonorth.com and Karo Enterprises' RV Park and Campground Directory at www.karo-ent.com.

CAUTIONS

Cautions for the TCT in southern BC apply as well to the north. (See page 15 in the introduction.) In the north, however, populations are smaller and distances between communities are larger. Be prepared for emergencies or mechanical breakdowns. Though often sparse, traffic on the Alaska Highway is steady—help is usually available from other travellers.

Only the larger communities along the Alaska Highway have 911 emergency-calling service. Smaller centres may have individual telephone numbers for police, fire, and ambulance; check **Communities, Parks, and Places to Stay** in each chapter.

Stone sheep at roadside salt lick

66 You should be more concerned about bears. Best thing you can do is smear sardines on your buddy's bike.

—*Park ranger when asked about the hazards of cycling with truck traffic on the Alaska Highway*

Watson Lake
Sign Post Forest

TRAIL TRIVIA

BC's most northerly point is anywhere along 60°N parallel, BC's border with Yukon and the Northwest Territories.

TOTAL DISTANCE

212 km

KM POINTS

Km 0 to Km 212

HIGHLIGHTS

› Watson Lake Sign Post Forest
› Northern Rocky Mountains
› Liard River Hot Springs Provincial Park

CONDITIONS

No paved shoulder for the first seven kilometres, then for 195 kilometres the paved shoulder is often too narrow for cycling. The adjacent gravel shoulder is usually hard-packed and safe as a pull-off lane. There's no paved shoulder for the final ten kilometres to Liard River Hot Springs.

CAUTIONS

› Few groceries available for 522 kilometres between Watson Lake and Fort Nelson.
› Bears along the highway and at campgrounds.
› Bison blocking the highway, especially between Km 136 and Km 212.
› Horses on the highway.
› Motorhomes cutting close to cyclists.

TOPOGRAPHIC MAPS

| 1:250,000 | Rabbit River 94M, McDame 104P, Watson Lake 105A |
| 1:50,000 | Vents River 94M/8, Teeter Creek 94M/9, Grant Lake 94M/10, Fireside 94M/11, Egnell Lakes 94M/13, Egnell Hillgren Lakes 94M/14, Irons Creek 95D/4, Lower Post 104P/16, Watson Lake 105A/2 |

OVERVIEW

From Watson Lake in Yukon to Liard River Hot Springs, the Alaska Highway descends about 230 metres over 212 kilometres. This is easy cycling

22

as the route crosses the Liard Plain and follows the Liard River through British Columbia's most northerly reaches.

The Liard River is the main stem of BC's second-largest watershed (after the Fraser) and skirts the northern extremity of the Rocky Mountain Trench, a valley that runs the full length of the province (see page 307 in Chapter 19). There are views of the Liard River from roadside pullouts. Near Liard River Hot Springs, the river continues east, then north to join the Mackenzie River at Fort Simpson (in the Northwest Territories). The Alaska Highway and TCT leave the river and climb into the Rockies to the south.

LOCAL ADVENTURES
Day Trip
› Spend a day or more at Watson Lake (Km 0) walking nearly 100 km of local trails, perusing the famous Sign Post Forest (see page 359), and viewing the multimedia displays at the Northern Lights Centre.

2 or 3 Days
› Set up camp at Liard River Hot Springs Provincial Park, site of Canada's second-largest hot springs. Loll in the springs and hike the boardwalk. (See page 361.)

TCT ACCESS POINTS
Watson Lake, YK (Km 0) On the Alaska Highway (Highway 97) near the BC border.

Liard River Hot Springs Provincial Park (Km 212) On the Alaska Highway, 212 kilometres from Watson Lake, 310 kilometres from Fort Nelson, 691 kilometres from Fort St. John, and 766 kilometres from Dawson Creek.

22

FROM YUKON TO BRITISH COLUMBIA

THE ALASKA HIGHWAY:
GATEWAY TO THE NORTHERN ROCKIES
Yukon's Watson Lake, just outside British Columbia's northern boundary (60°N latitude), is the only sizable community on this stretch of the Alaska Highway. It is the southern end of the TCT's Yukon route, which begins 1,600 kilometres to the northwest at the Yukon–Northwest Territories

Swampland at Liard River Hot Springs Park

border on the Beaufort Sea. (Watson Lake is the only place for major grocery shopping until Fort Nelson, more than 500 kilometres along the Alaska Highway. A few items, including bottled water, can be purchased at truck stops, where restaurant meals may also be available.)

The forests on the outskirts of Watson Lake give way to mountains as the road starts to follow the Liard River toward the northern Rockies. The first hints of mountain terrain appear near Liard River Hot Springs as the highway moves toward the Muskwa Ranges.

THE TRANS CANADA TRAIL

Place names with asterisks are included in the **Communities, Parks, and Places to Stay** section (page 361).

Km 0   *Watson Lake*, ʏᴋ* Begin at the Sign Post Forest in Watson Lake. The route heads southeast on the Alaska Highway, criss-crossing the Yukon–ʙᴄ border seven times between Watson Lake and Contact Creek, Yukon.

Km 7.1   *Paved shoulder* Often dangerously narrow.

Km 9.3   *Liard Canyon recreation site/Lucky Lake* Sandy beach with outhouses, picnic tables, barbecue pits, and the "only

KM 0 TO KM 212

Watson Lake

Lower Post

Contact Creek

YUKON

BRITISH COLUMBIA

Coal River

Liard River

Alaska Highway

Fireside

Coal River

Smith River

Liard River

Liard River

Kechika River

Liard River Hot Springs Provincial Park

0

7.1

9.3

66.1

97.3

135.4

136.2

144.3

153.1

180.5

202.2

212

© Trans Canada Trail 2008

N

0   10

Km

22

waterslide north of 60°." Short hike to Liard River rapids.

Km 66.1 *Contact Creek, Yukon* (Amenities available at Contact Creek Lodge*.)

Km 97.3 *Liard River viewpoint* High view over the river and across to Goat Mountain. (Outhouse.)

Km 135.4 *Cranberry Rapids* A long stretch of whitewater whipping around several islands.

Km 136.2 *Fireside car/truck stop**

Km 144.3 *Whirlpool Canyon rest area* A small riverside campsite with a dumpster; no other facilities. Overlooks Mountain Portage Rapids. From here the Alaska Highway follows the Liard River downstream to the east.

Km 153.1 *Coal River* (Camping and lodging at Coal River Lodge and RV*.)

Km 180.5 *Smith River Falls* (Take a two-kilometre gravel road to a short hiking trail to get to the base of the falls.)

Km 202.2 *Paved shoulder ends*

Km 212 *Liard River Hot Springs Provincial Park** One of northern BC's most popular campgrounds. There is a commercial lodge (the Liard Hotsprings Lodge*) and restaurant across the highway from the park entrance. (The TCT continues on the Alaska Highway, south through Muncho Lake Provincial Park.)

WATSON LAKE'S SIGN POST FOREST

Watson Lake is the only town in Yukon, perhaps in all of Canada, where travellers can stroll through a forest and *read* the trees—in several languages. Licence plates, street signs, names of towns and their populations, directional signs, even decorated moose antlers are nailed to rows of upright poles in the Sign Post Forest.

"Reading the signs and messages can take you on a textual tour of the world for as long as you care to keep reading and walking," writes Yukon historian Murray Lundberg on his website, ExploreNorth.

Like a natural forest, the Sign Post Forest is growing. It was "seeded" in 1942 by an American soldier who nailed to a post a sign pointing to his home in Danville, Illinois. When he returned 50 years later there were well over 10,000 signs. Last count was at more than 55,000, and the forest was growing by as many as 4,000 signs a year.

22

Liard River

NORTHERN BC'S TROPICAL PARADISE

The swamps and thermal pools at Liard River Hot Springs Provincial Park form part of Canada's second-largest hot springs system. Closer to the Arctic Circle than to southern BC, this ecological oddity has been referred to as a "Tropical Valley." Air temperatures near the springs are 2°C higher than the surrounding area, creating a microclimate in which plants grow bigger and flowers bloom earlier.

Liard River Hot Springs

Wild sarsaparilla and fleabane are among more than 80 plants not normally found at such northerly latitudes. At least 14 species grow here only because of the springs.

It's easy to imagine dinosaurs here. A lambeosaurus, perhaps, or an amblydactylus, placidly nibbling the fiddleheads of giant ostrich ferns in the steamy jungle of northern British Columbia. The lush vegetation is cloaked in hoarfrost and snow until spring. The annual thaw brings back the prehistoric look—succulent new greenery dappled with the colour of blooming orchids. Sundew, butterwort, and other carnivorous plants lie in wait for mosquitoes and blackflies, and hairy cow parsnip grows taller than a one-horned monoclonius.

Tourists must be content with non-prehistoric wildlife, however. Bull moose or cows with calves are commonly seen knee-deep in the swamps, slurping up aquatic vegetation. Porcupines waddle about the forest, and Bohemian waxwings perch in black spruce trees above the water. Warm-water lake chub, thought to be remnants from the last Ice Age, loiter in the shadows of a boardwalk.

Today's boardwalk is an improvement over one laid out in 1942, when Alaska Highway construction crews had a camp here. It leads to views of hot water cascading through a hanging garden, and to bathing pools heated by springs that ooze from the earth at about 50°C.

COMMUNITIES, PARKS, AND PLACES TO STAY

Information on each provincial park in BC can be found on the BC Parks website at www.env.gov.bc.ca/bcparks/. Also note that the Greyhound Bus stops at many of the places listed below. Contact Greyhound at 1-800-661-8747 or go to www.greyhound.ca.

♣ Watson Lake, YK (Km 0)
"Yukon's Gateway" for travellers heading northwest on the Alaska Highway from BC. Originally a service centre for American army engineers building the Alaska Highway in the 1940s, Watson Lake now bases its economy on forestry, oil and gas, and tourism. ⑦ ⟳ △ ✗ ▲ ⌹ | *laundromat, most needs and services*

› **Population** 1,600
› **Visitor Info** *Town of Watson Lake* PO Box 590, Watson Lake, YK Y0A 1C0; 867-536-8000; www.watsonlake.ca. The *Watson Lake Visitor Reception Centre* (867-536-7469) is behind the Sign Post Forest. Call *Environment Canada* at 867-668-6061 for weather information.
› **Attractions** Northern Lights Space and Science Centre, Alaska Highway Interpretive Centre, Sign Post Forest, Heritage House Wildlife and Historic Museum, Watson Lake Walking Tour. Watson Lake's website lists 18 multi-use trails totalling 96 kilometres (www.yukoninfo.com/watson/watsonlakerecreation/).

GIVE A WIDE BERTH TO WILD BISON

It's heart-stopping to round a bend in the road and come face-to-face with a one-tonne bison. One belligerent bull on the Alaska Highway had a habit of stepping into the paths of oncoming vehicles, forcing drivers to slow down and cautiously creep past the rest of the herd grazing on the roadside.

The wood bison (*Bison bison athabascae*) is North America's biggest land mammal. Once plentiful, they declined in the face of over-hunting and human encroachment. BC's last bison was shot in 1906. Since the 1980s, introductions of brood stock from Elk Island National Park in Alberta have brought BC's population back to about 120 so far.

Two herds totalling about 80 animals migrate through the Liard River Valley. Travellers may see wood bison on or alongside the road between Fireside (Km 136.2) and Liard River (Km 212).

While fascinating to observe and photograph from a distance, a protective bull standing two metres at the shoulder can be intimidating at close range, particularly to cyclists. It may be safe to pass if all the herd is on one side of the highway, but if the animals are split by the road it might be wise to back off. They rarely graze in one place for more than an hour or two.

› **Greyhound Bus** (1-800-661-8747; www.greyhound.ca) Depot located at *Watson Lake Recreational Complex* at 912 Lakeview Drive.
› **Accommodation/Camping** *Downtown RV Park* (867-536-2646) in town centre. For other campgrounds as well as hotels, motels, B&BS, check www .watsonlake.ca.
› **Emergency** *Police* 867-536-5555 *Fire* 867-536-2222 *Ambulance* 867-536-4444

Contact Creek Lodge (Km 66.1)
Lodging only, no camping. 867-536-2262 🅻 ⅋ *coffee shop | telephone*

▲ Fireside Car/Truck Stop (Km 136.2)
Motel, RV camping. 250-776-7303 ⅋

▲ Coal River Lodge and RV (Km 153.1)
Lodge and campsite. 250-785-8775 ⅋ 🅻 | *showers, laundromat, telephone*

⚘ Liard River Hot Springs Provincial Park (Km 212)
On the Alaska Highway, 212 kilometres southeast of Watson Lake, YK, 766 kilometres northwest of Dawson Creek, BC. This park, established in 1957, lies at the western edge of Liard River Corridor Park—more than 83,000 hectares set aside in 1997 to protect natural features such as fossils and archaeological sites, bears, and bison. **Note:** Be bear wary; two people were killed by a malnourished black bear here in 1997. Park operators may provide small, spotlessly clean, stainless steel food caches for campers without vehicles. ⊞ ▲ ⚹ *outhouses* ⛿ | *telephone, playground*
› **Size** 1,082 hectares
› **Attractions** Unique microclimate created by hot springs; two hot bathing pools, a boardwalk and trails (some wheelchair accessible) through bogs and boreal spruce forests. (See page 361.)
› **Camping** 53 drive-in campsites that fill early in the day. Reservations 1-800-689-9025 (or 604-689-9025 in Metro Vancouver). www.discover camping.ca

22

▲ Liard Hotsprings Lodge (Km 212)
Directly across the highway from Liard River Hot Springs Provincial Park. 250-776-7349; www.liardhotspringslodge.com. ⅋ *café with home baking | campground has showers*

23 LIARD RIVER HOT SPRINGS TO FORT NELSON

> " Just keep moving, even if you're pedalling uphill. If you stop, the bear figures you're invading its space.
> —*Park ranger on how cyclists should deal with roadside bear encounters*

Alaska Highway through Stone Mountain Park

TRAIL TRIVIA
With 1,138 vertebrate species—142 mammals, 488 birds, 22 amphibians, 18 reptiles, and 468 fish species—BC supports more wildlife than any Canadian province.

TOTAL DISTANCE
310 km

KM POINTS
Km 212 to Km 522

HIGHLIGHTS
> Northern Rocky Mountains
> Muncho Lake Provincial Park
> Toad River and Reflection Lake
> Stone Mountain Provincial Park
> Alaska Highway summit

CONDITIONS
The two-lane highway is paved, but shoulders are paved sporadically. Even the paved shoulders are often rough and unrideable, but traffic is generally light. Terrain varies from gentle roll to gruelling climb. Steamboat Mountain's ten-percent grade is the steepest on the Alaska Highway.

CAUTIONS
> Bears on the highway and in campgrounds.
> Stone sheep on the highway.
> Strong headwinds near Muncho Lake.
> Motorhomes that cut close to cyclists.

TOPOGRAPHIC MAPS
1:250,000	Fort Nelson 94J, Tuchodi Lakes 94K, Toad River 94N
1:50,000	Chischa River 94J/12, Kledo Creek 94J/13, Raspberry Creek 94J/14, Fort Nelson 94J/15, North Tetsa River 94K/9, Mount St. George 94K/10, Yedhe Mountain 94K/11, Muncho Lake 94K/13, Toad Hot Springs 94K/14, Vents River 94M/8, Trout River 94N/4, Mount Prudence 94N/5

23

OVERVIEW

For anyone who's travelled the Rocky Mountains through the national parks of southern BC and Alberta, this journey through the northern Rockies is déjà vu with a touch more wildness. As in the south, mountains engulf the route: they are the foreground, the background, and most of the space between.

As the Alaska Highway winds through the valleys, each bend in the road brings new sights, invariably as stunning as the last, of mountains and more: Mount St. Paul reflecting on the emerald surface of Summit Lake; a highway squeezed between Toad River and a barren rock wall; curious Stone sheep, unsure whether to move off the road for equally unsure cyclists.

The mountain pass near Summit Lake (Km 381.9) is one of two points where the Trans Canada Trail crosses the Rocky Mountains; the other is at Elk Pass, on the TCT's southern BC route. Although parts of the route make an arduous ride for cyclists, much of it is surprisingly painless for such mountainous terrain.

LOCAL ADVENTURES

Day Trip
› Spend a day at Toad River (Km 331.1), viewing moose, beaver, waterfowl, and other wildlife at Reflection Lake.

2 or 3 Days
› Set up camp at Summit Lake (Km 381.9) and hike trails into the mountains on both sides of the lake.
› Stay at Tetsa River Guest Ranch & Campground and ride horses into the wilderness of the northern Rockies.
› From Fort Nelson, take a bicycle and camping gear on a Greyhound bus to Liard River Hot Springs, then cycle back over the Rocky Mountains.

TCT ACCESS POINTS

Liard River Hot Springs Provincial Park (Km 212) On the Alaska Highway, 212 kilometres from Watson Lake, 766 kilometres from Dawson Creek.

Fort Nelson (Km 522.1) On the Alaska Highway, 522 kilometres southeast of Watson Lake, 381 kilometres north of Fort St. John, 456 kilometres northwest of Dawson Creek. Served by airlines and Greyhound Canada buses; a good starting or end point for cyclists taking a ride through the northern Rockies between here and Liard River Hot Springs.

THE NORTHERN ROCKIES

A WILDER RENDITION OF ICEFIELDS PARKWAY

With five million tourists a year, the Icefields Parkway through the Banff and Jasper national parks in the southern Rocky Mountains attracts about 15 times as many travellers as the Alaska Highway. And though the southern scenery is more accessible, that of the northern Rockies is just as spectacular. Folded mountains and pyramidal peaks, ice-clear rivers, alpine wildflower meadows, and wild animals licking salt from the roadsides—all that's missing in the north are heavy highway traffic and overcrowded towns.

The mountains close in around the Alaska Highway as the route follows the Trout, Toad, and Tetsa rivers. It crosses the Rockies and moves down the eastern slopes onto the Alberta Plateau. Paved shoulders appear and disappear while the road gains about 800 metres in elevation between Liard River Hot Springs and Summit Lake, near the highest point on the Alaska Highway, then drops nearly 900 metres to Fort Nelson. Gradients can be long, steep, and challenging uphill, or hair raising downhill.

THE TRANS CANADA TRAIL

Place names with asterisks are included in the **Communities, Parks, and Places to Stay** section (page 372).

Km 212   *Liard River Hot Springs Provincial Park** The TCT/Alaska Highway heads south from Liard River Hot Springs through Muncho Lake Provincial Park*, then east toward the highway's highest point.

Km 212.2   *Muskwa-Kechika Management Area, western boundary* The Alaska Highway enters an area encompassing 64,000 square kilometres of northern Rocky Mountain habitat, where wildlife and environmental concerns must be incorporated in work plans of local industries—see page 371. A number of provincial parks are located in the Muskwa-Kechika.

Km 239.4   *Muncho Lake Provincial Park*, northern boundary* Within Muskwa-Kechika, the glacial-green waters of Muncho Lake fill a narrow valley for more than 12 kilometres. (There are

23

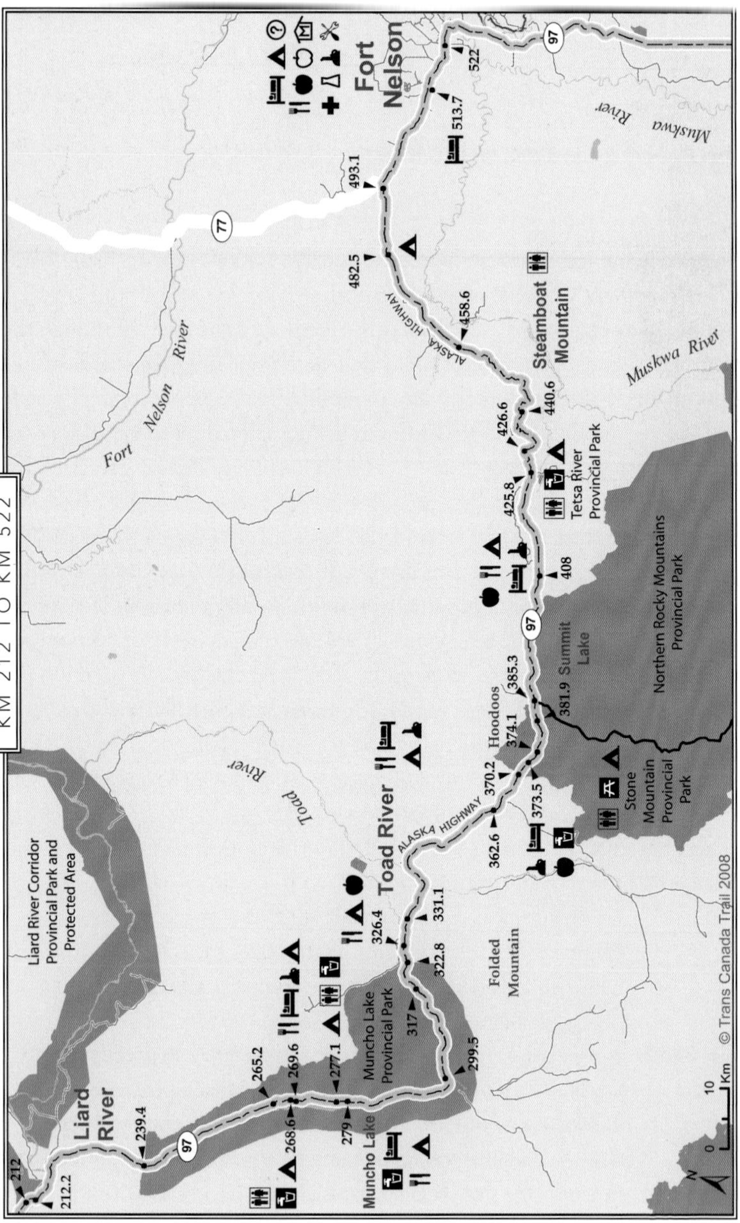

KM 212 TO KM 522

© Trans Canada Trail 2008

Muncho Lake

roadside campsites within the park at Km 268.6 and
Km 277.1.)

Km 265.2 *Muncho Lake viewpoint* A well-known Alaska Highway
stop overlooking the lake flanked by mountains over
1,500 metres high.

Km 268.6 *MacDonald campground* Campsites beside Muncho Lake,
with outhouses and drinking water.

Km 269.6 *Northern Rockies Lodge** RV camping also available.

Km 277.1 *Strawberry Flats campground* Campsites at the south end of
the lake, with outhouses and drinking water.

Km 279   *Muncho Lake** A blink of a community within the provincial
park just beyond the south end of the lake.

Km 299.5 *Muskwa-Kechika Designated Route* (A rough trail for hikers,
cyclists, motorbikes, all-terrain vehicles, and snowmobiles that
follows the West Toad River for about 25 kilometres.)

Km 317   *Folded Mountain* A massive peak, one of many, formed by
tectonic faulting and folding.

Km 322.8 *Muncho Lake Provincial Park*, eastern boundary* From Liard
River Hot Springs to here, the road has climbed from 470

metres to 750 metres.

Km 326.4 *The Poplars Campground & Café** (Cabins available as well.)

Km 331.1 *Toad River**, *Reflection Lake* Look for moose and beaver in the lake behind Toad River Lodge.

Toad River

Km 362.6 *Rest area* No facilities but could be an emergency campsite.

Km 370.2 *Stone Mountain Provincial Park**, *western boundary* A wilderness park within Muskwa-Kechika that adjoins Northern Rocky Mountains Provincial Park. Watch for Stone sheep.

Km 373.5 *Rocky Mountain Lodge** The start of a steady eight-kilometre climb. (Lodging as well as camping.)

Km 374.1 *Hoodoos* Gargantuan pinnacles.

Km 381.9 *Stone Mountain Provincial Park**, *Summit Lake campground* The Alaska Highway near Summit Lake reaches its highest point—1,295 metres. From here, only minor inclines interrupt a downhill run of more than 20 kilometres to Tetsa River—there's hardly a need to crank a pedal for the first seven kilometres from Summit Lake.

Km 385.3 *Stone Mountain Provincial Park**, *eastern boundary* The TCT/Alaska Highway leaves Stone Mountain Park and follows the north edge of Northern Rocky Mountains Provincial Park.

Km 408 *Tetsa River Guest Ranch & Campground**

Km 425.8 *Tetsa River Provincial Park** (To get to a riverside campground, turn right (south) off the Alaska Highway and follow the signs for 2.5 kilometres.)

Km 426.6 *Muskwa-Kechika Management Area*, *eastern boundary* As the Alaska Highway heads east away from Muskwa-Kechika, there is still one more elevation obstacle—Steamboat Mountain. This is another 375 metres up and 14 kilometres farther into the Rockies.

Km 440.6 *Steamboat Mountain summit* A much-needed rest stop with an outhouse and pay phone, reached via long hills

Northern Rockies Bison Ranch

with minimal reprieve. Great views of the Muskwa Valley and northern Rockies.

Km 458.6 *Indian Head Mountain* A mountain that resembles the profile of an aboriginal.

Km 482.5 *Raspberry Creek campsite* Roadside campsite with minimal facilities.

Km 493.1 *Alaska Highway (Hwy 97) + Liard Highway (Hwy 77)* (Turn left (north) to get to Fort Liard and Fort Simpson in the Northwest Territories.)

Km 513.7 *Northern Rockies Bison Ranch* Herds of bison graze in fenced pastures alongside the Alaska Highway on the outskirts of Fort Nelson.

Km 522 *Fort Nelson** A busy mix of neighbourhoods and industry on the western edge of the Alberta Plateau, where the Canadian Prairies spread into northeastern British Columbia. (The TCT then heads south on the Alaska Highway toward Fort St. John.)

MUSKWA-KECHIKA: THE SERENGETI OF NORTH AMERICA

After leaving northern BC's "Tropical Valley" at Liard River Hot Springs, the Alaska Highway crosses into an area sometimes called the "Serengeti

23

of North America," referring to the famous national park in Africa. At 6.4 million hectares, Muskwa-Kechika is four times the size of the Serengeti, and although there are no wildebeests, cape buffalo, or jackals here, there are grizzlies, caribou, and timber wolves.

The Muskwa-Kechika Management Area, designated in 1998, encompasses 1.6 million hectares of provincial parkland surrounded by nearly five million hectares where logging, mining, and oil and gas development is allowed only with a view to conserving important wildlife habitat. The largest protected area in Muskwa-Kechika is Northern Rocky Mountains Provincial Park, 665,709 hectares set aside in 1999. It covers large tracts of the Muskwa and Kechika ranges. U-shaped valleys, mountain cirques, and big rivers form the habitat for animals such as moose, Stone sheep, mountain goats, caribou, red foxes, and black bears, which may be seen here by TCT travellers.

For more on Muskwa-Kechika, go to www.muskwa-kechika.com or http://ilmbwww.gov.bc.ca/lup/lrmp/ (scroll down).

COMMUNITIES, PARKS, AND PLACES TO STAY

Information on each provincial park in BC can be found on the BC Parks website at www.env.gov.bc.ca/bcparks/.

Red fox in Muskwa-Kechika

SALT-LICKING STONE SHEEP: A TRAFFIC HAZARD

When Stone sheep (*Ovis dalli stonei*) come down to the Alaska Highway to lick salt, they cause "sheep jams." Traffic slows to a crawl as drivers nudge past bands of unwary sheep preoccupied with getting their daily dose of minerals. From June to mid-August, travellers through northeastern BC may see herds of 10 to 50 sheep, mainly ewes with lambs, though stocky rams occasionally appear.

Like Dall's sheep (*Ovis dalli dalli*), Stone sheep inhabit the wildest parts of northern BC. *Ovis dalli* are thinhorn sheep; their large curled horns are slenderer and spread farther apart than those of southern BC's bighorn sheep (*Ovis canadensis*).

♠ Liard River Hot Springs Provincial Park (Km 212)
See page 363 in the previous chapter for details.

♠ Muncho Lake Provincial Park (Km 239.4 to Km 322.8)
The Alaska Highway travels through the park for more than 80 kilometres, including a stretch where the road runs within metres of the lake. The jade-coloured waters of Muncho Lake are a contrast to the dark, forested mountains above. 🛏 *commercial lodges within the park boundaries* ▲ | *amenities available in the small community of Muncho Lake*
› **Size** 86,079 hectares
› **Attractions** Hiking to viewpoints, wildlife viewing.
› **Camping** Muncho Lake Park has two provincial campgrounds, each with 15 drive-in sites, outhouses, and drinking water. MacDonald campground (Km 268.6) is about halfway along the eastern lakeshore. Strawberry Flats campground (Km 277.1) is near the south end.

🛏 **Northern Rockies Lodge (Km 269.6)**
Elegant log lodge with chalets, motel rooms, lakeside RV park. 1-800-663-5269; www.northernrockieslodge.com. ⚓ 🍴 *fine dining | telephone*

♣ Muncho Lake (Km 279)

Near the south end of Muncho Lake, one of the few BC communities within a provincial park. ○ *convenience store* ❙❙ *café* ⛟ *motel* ▲ 🗑 | *post office, take-off point for guided lake cruises*

› **Population** 24
› **Accommodation** *Double "G" Service*, near the south end of Muncho Lake. Amenities listed above. 250-776-3411
› **Greyhound Bus** (1-800-661-8747; www.greyhound.ca) Depot located at *Double "G"* at the south end of Muncho Lake.
› **Emergency** *Police* 250-774-2777 *Ambulance* 250-774-2344

⛟ ▲ The Poplars Campground & Café (Km 326.4)

Cabins and campground, between Muncho Lake Park and the community of Toad River. 250-232-5465 ○ ❙❙ | *showers*

WORLD'S LARGEST DEER IS AN AQUATIC UNGULATE

Taller than a saddle horse, the moose (*Alces alces*) is British Columbia's lordly loner of the woods. This largest member of the deer family is mostly a solitary animal, although it is known to gather in groups to forage at swamps and rivers. Alaska Highway travellers look for moose at Toad River's Reflection Lake.

A full-sized bull moose may stand two metres at the shoulder and carry palmate antlers that stretch nearly as wide. Weighing a massive 800 kilograms, it consumes up to 23 kilograms of food a day. With strong teeth, a powerful neck, and flexible lips, a moose can strip willow or birch twigs three centimetres thick. In summer it wades ponds, streams, and lakes in search of sedges or horsetails. A moose may dive as deep as five metres and stay submerged for 30 seconds when looking for pond weeds or water lilies.

Moose are strong swimmers. Maintaining a steady pace for a couple of hours at a time, they may swim 20 kilometres when seeking new territories. They commonly swim across coastal inlets, occasionally falling prey to killer whales. On land a moose is equally adept, using its long legs to travel through tangles of fallen trees and deep snow. Its cloven hooves support its heavy body when wading in mushy muskeg.

Travellers who encounter moose should not be deceived by their docile appearance. Both bull and cow moose are known to charge at wolves, horses, people, vehicles, and locomotives.

♣ Toad River (Km 331.1)

A tiny town with a school and airstrip. ⚲ ⑂ ⌸ *motel* ▲ *cabins and camp-sites | showers, laundromat, post office, telephone*

› **Population** 60

› **Attractions** *Toad River Lodge* (250-232-5401; www.toadriverlodge.com) is the place to "hang your hat where it's at"—more than 7,000 hats adorn the ceilings. Behind the lodge, Reflection Lake is a marshy feeding ground for moose: as many as 13 at one time have been seen eating aquatic vegetation. Beavers maintain a large lodge in the lake, and waterfowl are abundant. Best viewing times are dawn and dusk.

› **Greyhound Bus** 1-800-661-8747; www.greyhound.ca.

› **Emergency** *Police* 250-774-2777 *Ambulance* 250-744-2344

♠ Stone Mountain Provincial Park (Km 370.2 to 385.3)

One in a complex of provincial wilderness parks within the Muskwa-Kechika Management Area of the northern Rocky Mountains. (See page 371 for more on the Muskwa-Kechika.) ▣ ▲ ⑂ *outhouses*

› **Size** 25,691 hectares

› **Attractions** Wildlife viewing, hiking.

› **Camping** *Summit Lake Campground* (Km 381.9) has 28 drive-in sites beside the lake. Though open and sometimes breezy, the scenery is extraordinary, a quintessential Rocky Mountain lake with a view to the southwest of Mount St. George (at an elevation of 2,261 metres). The campground is a good base for day hikes to viewpoints, alpine meadows, lakes, and hoodoos.

⌸ ▲ Rocky Mountain Lodge (Km 373.5)

Motel and campground. 250-774-2052 ↻ *convenience store* ⚲ 🗉 *"best water on the highway"*

⌸ ▲ Tetsa River Guest Ranch & Campground (Km 408)

Cabins and campground. Otherwise known as the "Cinnamon bun centre of the galactic cluster." Besides great baking, a frontier-style general store is stocked with coon-skin hats and wolf pelts, and the walls are hung with

Tetsa River Guest Ranch

antlered ungulates and mounted fish. Daily and weekly packhorse trips into the northern Rocky Mountain parks. 250-774-1005; www.canadianrocky mountainadventures.ca. ○ ⚓ ⅋| *telephone*

♠ Tetsa River Provincial Park (Km 425.8)

A family favourite in the Rocky Mountain foothills, within 100 kilometres of Fort Nelson. Be wary of bears. ▲ ⅋⅋ *outhouses* ⛟

› **Size** 115 hectares
› **Attractions** Riverside location, fishing for Arctic grayling.
› **Camping** 25 drive-in campsites.

♣ Fort Nelson (Km 522)

On the Alaska Highway, 522 kilometres southeast of Watson Lake, YK, 381 kilometres northwest of Fort St. John, 456 kilometres northwest of Dawson Creek. The only sizable pocket of civilization between opposite ends of the Alaska Highway in northern BC. Once a fur-trading post, "resource-full" Fort Nelson now has an economy rooted in forestry, oil and natural gas, and agriculture. The Westcoast Energy gas-processing plant here is the largest in the world. *most amenities and services for a regional population of about 6,400*

› **Population** 4,200
› **Visitor Info** *Fort Nelson Visitor Centre* 5500 50 Avenue North, Box 196, Fort Nelson, BC V0C 1R0; 250-774-6400; www.fortnelsonchamber.com; www.northernrockies.org.
› **Attractions** Fort Nelson Heritage Museum.
› **Cycling** CMP *Sports* 5407 Alaska Highway; 250-774-2944.
› **Transportation**
  Land Greyhound Canada (1-800-661-8747; www.greyhound.ca) Depot located at 5031 51st Avenue West.
  Air Air Canada (1-888-247-2262; www.aircanada.com); *Central Mountain Air* (1-888-865-8585; www.cmair.bc.ca); *Peace Air* (1-800-563-3060; www.peaceair.com).
› **Accommodation/Camping** A range of accommodation in and around Fort Nelson—go to www.northernrockies.org (click on "Visitor Information").
› **Emergency** *Police* 250-774-2777 *Fire* 250-774-2222 *Ambulance* 250-774-2344

> 66 You mean you can't even carry a weapon
> to protect yourself?
> —A woman from the U.S. when told
> that Canadian cyclists don't pack
> guns in bear country

Stone sheep seem
unfazed by Alaska Highway traffic

TRAIL TRIVIA

BC's northeast corner, in Peace River Country, is the same distance from the Pacific Ocean as from the Arctic Ocean—1,055 kilometres.

TOTAL DISTANCE

529 km

KM POINTS

Km 522 to Km 1,051

HIGHLIGHTS

› Charlie Lake Provincial Park
› Beatton Provincial Park
› The Peace River
› Dawson Creek/Alaska Highway's Mile 0

CONDITIONS

Paved, rideable shoulders for most of the route; gravel road for the last 14 kilometres. Mainly rolling terrain with a few serious hills.

CAUTIONS

› No major grocery stores between Fort Nelson and Fort St. John, or beyond Dawson Creek toward Alberta.
› Accessible creeks may be too silty to filter for drinking water; carry extra bottled water.
› Bears.
› Motorhomes cutting close to cyclists.

TOPOGRAPHIC MAPS

1:250,000	Dawson Creek 93P, Charlie Lake 94A, Halfway River 94B, Trutch 94G, Fort Nelson 94J
1:50,000	Dawson Creek 93P/16, Shearer Dale 94A/1, Fort St. John 94A/2, Bear Flat 94A/6, North Pine 94A/7, Alces River 94A/8, Murdale 94A/11, Deadhorse Creek 94A/12, Aitken Creek 94A/13, Blair Creek 94B/16, Julienne Creek 94G/1, Pink Mountain 94G/2, Caribou Creek 94G/7, Trutch 94G/10, Bougie Creek 94G/15, Prophet River 94J/2, Big Beaver Creek 94J/7, Jackfish Creek 94J/10, Fort Nelson 94J/15

24

OVERVIEW

Beyond the eastern foothills of the northern Rockies, the TCT/Alaska Highway skirts the western edge of the Alberta Plateau as it moves south from Fort Nelson. This is, perhaps, more a route for thinkers than gawkers: the mountain scenery has given way to boreal forest, a more subdued landscape with fewer distinguishing features. At times the road is hemmed in by walls of stubby spruce trees. Then it may crest a hill to reveal a rolling expanse of forest and swamp, or a patchwork of farm fields, many that turn lemon-yellow when the canola blooms in mid-summer.

Drivers, at 100 kilometres an hour, may marvel at the vastness of northeast BC's open terrain. For cyclists, this can be a long five- or-six-day ride.

LOCAL ADVENTURES

2 or 3 Days

› Camp at a provincial park on Charlie Lake and hike the trails, swim, and fish for walleye and northern pike; good winter snowshoeing and cross-country skiing.

TCT ACCESS POINTS

The following towns are served by airlines and Greyhound Canada buses.

Fort Nelson (Km 522) On the Alaska Highway, 381 kilometres north of Fort St. John, 456 kilometres north of Dawson Creek.

Fort St. John (Km 903) On the Alaska Highway, 75 kilometres northwest of Dawson Creek. Northern BC's largest city.

Dawson Creek (Km 978) Near the BC–Alberta border at the junction of BC Highway 97 and Alberta Highways 2 and 49. Mile 0 on the Alaska Highway.

THE ALBERTA PLATEAU

BC'S CANADIAN PRAIRIE

The scene becomes more prairielike as the Alaska Highway rolls onto the Alberta Plateau. Only here does the Canadian prairie come to BC. Dawson Creek, only 15 kilometres from the BC–Alberta boundary, is enveloped by farm fields where grain elevators and oil derricks stand almost side by side against the horizon.

Although the Rocky Mountains may be a diminishing sight in a rear-view mirror, this final leg of the Alaska Highway is not without notable terrain. From an elevation of 422 metres at Fort Nelson, the road climbs to 1,097 metres at Pink Mountain, then drops to 666 metres at Dawson Creek.

THE TRANS CANADA TRAIL

Place names with asterisks are included in the **Communities, Parks, and Places to Stay** section (page 385).

Km 522   *Fort Nelson** The TCT/Alaska Highway heads south.

Km 526.1 *Muskwa River Bridge* At 305 metres, this is the lowest point on the Alaska Highway.

Km 530.3 *Trapper's Den* Frontier products in a log cabin owned by trappers. Includes fur hats, antler carvings, native crafts, moccasins, and more.

Km 530.9 *Fort Nelson Truck Stop**

Km 542.1 *Duke Energy gas processing plant* Processes natural gas from gathering fields near Fort Nelson and in the Northwest Territories and Yukon.

Km 547.1 *Andy Bailey Provincial Park** (Turning left (east) off the highway onto a 16-kilometre gravel road will lead you to a park with campsites.)

Km 612.1 *Prophet River**

Km 627.6 *Prophet River Wayside Provincial Park** (Turning right (west) onto a 500-metre gravel road will lead you to a campground.)

Km 698.8 *Buckinghorse River Lodge**

Km 699.1 *Buckinghorse River Wayside Provincial Park**

Km 720.9 *Sikanni Chief River Bridge* River crossing (about 300 metres from Sikanni River RV Park*). Challenging hills ahead.

Km 739.1 *Time Zone* Set clocks to Mountain Time (one hour ahead).

Km 744.2 *Beatton River Bridge* Beatton River is a major tributary to the Peace River.

Km 745   *Sasquatch Crossing Lodge**

Km 751.1 *Pink Mountain** Community with various amenities. From Fort Nelson the route has climbed nearly 700 metres. Dawson Creek, at 666 metres above sea level, is 431 metres lower than Pink Mountain.

KM 522 TO KM 889.6

Muskwa River

522
530.3
526.1
530.9

Fort Nelson

542.1

547.1

Prophet

Andy Bailey
Provincial Park

97

River

612.1

**Prophet
River**

Prophet River Wayside
Provincial Park

627.6

Sikanni

Chief

River

ALASKA HIGHWAY

**Buckinghorse
River**

698.8

699.1

Buckinghorse
River Wayside
Provincial Park

Sikanni Chief

720.9

739.1

744.2

745

751.1

**Pink
Mountain**

Wonowon

814.6

Beatton

River

Graham-Laurier
Provincial Park

850.1

861.1

Charlie Lake
Provincial Park

N

0   10
└──┴──┘ Km   © Trans Canada Trail 2008

29

889.6

24

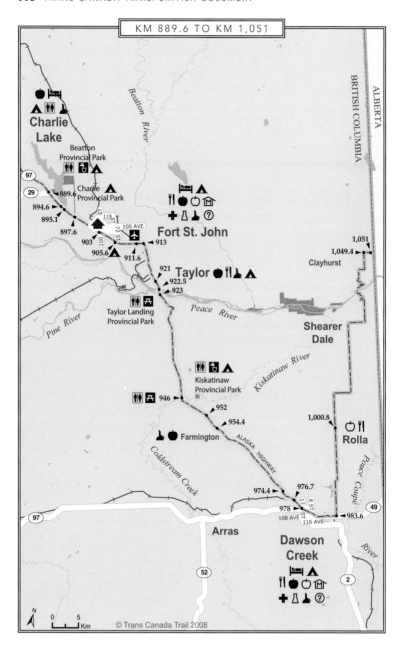

KM 889.6 TO KM 1,051

Charlie
Lake

Beatton
Provincial Park

97

29

889.6

Charlie
Provincial Park

894.6

895.1

897.6

903

905.6

911.6

913

Fort St. John

100 AVE

921

Taylor

922.5

923

Taylor Landing
Provincial Park

Beatton River

Pine River

Peace River

Kiskatinaw River

1,051

1,049.4

Clayhurst

Shearer
Dale

Kiskatinaw
Provincial Park

946

952

954.4

1,000.8

Rolla

Farmington

ALASKA HIGHWAY

Coldstream Creek

974.4

976.7

978

108 AVE

116 AVE

983.6

49

97

Arras

52

Dawson
Creek

2

BRITISH COLUMBIA

ALBERTA

Peace Coupe River

N

0   5

Km

© Trans Canada Trail 2008

24

Farmland near Fort St. John

Km 814.6   *Wonowon** At historic Mile 101 on the Alaska Highway.

Km 850.1   *Rest area* (Restrooms, picnic tables.)

Km 861.1   *The Shepherd's Inn**

Km 889.6   *Charlie Lake Provincial Park** Stop at Charlie Lake Provincial
            Park for camping. (Highway 29, near the turnoff to Charlie
            Lake, goes to Hudson's Hope, w.a.c. Bennett Dam, Moberly
            Lake, Chetwynd, and Tumbler Ridge.)

Km 894.6   *Rotary r v Park* Camping on Charlie Lake.

Km 895.1   *Hamlet of Charlie Lake**

Km 897.6   *Beatton Provincial Park** (The park is on the east shore, oppo-
            site Charlie Lake Park. Turn left (north) and follow the road
            for 13 kilometres.)

Km 903   *Fort St. John** Largest community in northeastern bc.

Km 911.6   *The Honey Place* World's largest glass beehive. Honey, pollen,
            leathercraft.

Km 913   *Fort St. John Airport* Scheduled flights to major centres.

Km 921   *Taylor*, Peace Island Park* Small town on a bench overlooking
            the Peace River. Site of an attractive park with campsites.

Km 922.5   *Taylor, Peace River Bridge* The bridge across the Peace River
            south of Taylor was originally the biggest on the Alaska

Highway. It collapsed in 1957 and was replaced three years later.

Km 923   *Taylor Landing Provincial Park** A 2.4-hectare riverside day-use park; river access for boaters, anglers, swimmers.

Km 946   *Kiskatinaw River Bridge* (Picnic tables, outhouses.)

Km 952   *Kiskatinaw Provincial Park** (To get to the park, go left (east) off the highway onto Road 64; it is five kilometres to reach the park.)

Km 954.4   *Farmington Store* Groceries, fuel, and telephone available. (A wink of a village is just over one kilometre farther down the highway.)

Km 974.4   *The Trading Post* Native crafts and carvings, and handmade *mukluks* (northern aboriginal traditional boots).

Km 976.7   *Walter Wright Pioneer Village* Step back in time to Dawson Creek before the arrival of the Alaska Highway.

Km 978   *Dawson Creek** Mile 0 on the historic Alaska Highway. From Dawson Creek Visitor Centre, continue east on Highway 49.

The following TCT link between BC and Alberta was not confirmed as this book went to press:

Km 983.6   *Highway 49 + Rolla Road (Road 3)* Turn left (north) up Rolla Road.

Km 1,000.8   *Rolla* (Pub, restaurant, store.) After Rolla, the paved road continues about 37 kilometres to cross the Peace River and continues on gravel road (Road 110).

Km 1,049.4   *Clayhurst* Agricultural hamlet with no services. Turn right (east) to Alberta.

Km 1,051   BC–*Alberta border* The tentative TCT route crosses into northern Alberta by going east then north on Road 717, for about 25 kilometres through Cherry Point and Bear Canyon to join Alberta's Highway 64.

Peace River at Taylor

PEACE RIVER: THE LIFEBLOOD OF NORTHEAST BC

The Peace River is unique. It is the only river in BC that flows from west to east across the Rocky Mountains. The province's third-largest watershed, the Peace drains nearly 130,000 square kilometres in BC. More than 1,900 kilometres long, it runs from BC across northern Alberta, through Wood Buffalo National Park, and into Lake Athabasca, an Arctic drainage.

As the Peace River runs down the eastern slopes of the Rockies it spins the turbines at two generating stations, producing one-third of BC's hydro-electricity. The larger operation is at W.A.C. Bennett Dam: 183 metres high and nearly two kilometres wide, this is one of the world's biggest earth-filled dams. (Behind the dam is Williston Lake Reservoir, at 1,750 square kilometres, the largest lake in BC.)

The northeast corner of BC is known as Peace River Country, yet not until Fort St. John (Km 903) do travellers on the TCT come close to the mighty waterway for which this region is named. The highway crosses the Peace downstream at Taylor, but the TCT's "temporary road link" and the river don't meet again for 115 kilometres, near Clayhurst.

With rivers that cut deep trenches across the prairie, and wheat fields curling over the horizon, northeast BC is more akin to Alberta than BC. Farmland dominates the landscape, and the Peace and its tributaries make a climatic contribution to the region's agriculture. Heat radiated from riverbanks here creates a moderating affect on the cold northern climate, allowing for the growth of crops as delicate as melons. But this area is better known as BC's bread basket. Nearly 90 percent of the province's grain is grown here. It is also the main producer of canola, which blankets the fields in bright blooming yellow through mid-summer.

COMMUNITIES, PARKS, AND PLACES TO STAY

Information on each provincial park in BC can be found on the BC Parks website at www.env.gov.bc.ca/bcparks/.

🏠 Fort Nelson (Km 522)

See page 376 in the previous chapter.

🌲 Fort Nelson Truck Stop (Km 530.9)

250-774-7270 ⭘ 🏕 🍽 ⛺

24

Ravens are common along the TCT in northern BC

🌲 Andy Bailey Provincial Park (Km 547.1)

Turn left (east) off the highway, and take a 16-kilometre gravel road to the park in the Fort Nelson Lowlands between the Fort Nelson and Prophet rivers. ▲ 🚻 *outhouses* 🚰

› **Size** 196 hectares
› **Attractions** Typical northeastern BC forests of white and black spruce; sandy beach on Andy Bailey Lake; moose, beaver, foxes, migratory waterfowl.
› **Camping** 5 drive-in campsites.

🌳 Prophet River (Km 612.1)

A native village with a school and church. ⛵🍴 *Lum N' Abners Restaurant* (250-773-6366) 🛏 ▲ | *post office*

› **Population** 100
› **Greyhound Bus** 1-800-661-8747; www.greyhound.ca.
› **Emergency** *Police* 250-774-2777 *Ambulance* 250-774-2344

🌲 Prophet River Wayside Provincial Park (Km 627.6)

Turn right (west) off the highway onto a gravel road; 400 metres to the park on a bank above the Prophet River; originally a U.S. Army camp, now a stopover for Alaska Highway travellers. ▲ ⚇ *outhouses* 🝙 *water from natural springs | concession stand*

› **Size** 113 hectares
› **Attractions** Good birding in forests of white and black spruce; occasional sightings of moose, elk, deer, and grizzly bears.
› **Camping** 45 drive-in campsites.

🛏 ▲ Buckinghorse River Lodge (Km 698.8)

Lodge and campground. Buildings adorned by sun-bleached antlers. 250-772-4999; www.buckinghorseriverlodge.com. ⛽ 🍴 *café | telephone*

🦌 Buckinghorse River Wayside Provincial Park (Km 699.1)

East of the Rocky Mountain foothills, a stopover for Alaska Highway travellers. ▲ ⚇ *outhouses* 🝙 *drinking water from a hand pump*

› **Size** 36 hectares
› **Attractions** Moose, fishing for Arctic grayling.
› **Camping** 33 drive-in campsites.

🛏 ▲ Sikanni River RV Park (Km 720.7)

Cabins, riverside camping. 250-772-5400 🍎 ⛽ ⚇ | *telephone, showers, laundromat*

🛏 ▲ Sasquatch Crossing Lodge (Km 745)

Lodge, camping. 250-772-3220 ⛽ 🍴

ALASKA HIGHWAY—THE MIRACLE ROAD

"Miracle Road" is a fitting byname for the Alaska Highway. It is also known as the Alaska-Canadian Highway, or the "Alcan." This was a wartime supply route, a crude track bulldozed across the mud, muskeg, and mountains of northern BC, Yukon, and Alaska. Over eight months in 1942, 10,000 American troops built nearly 2,400 kilometres of road from Dawson Creek, in BC's northeastern Interior, to Fairbanks, Alaska, just shy of the Arctic Circle.

The Alaska Highway was opened to the public in 1948, and over subsequent years was improved to meet modern four-season standards. Today it is a paved, two-lane corridor used mainly by truckers and RVers. As many as 300,000 people a year may travel the Alaska Highway. No one knows how many cycle it, but the general consensus is "not very many." The most intrepid Alaska Highway travellers are hikers, who are occasionally seen walking the road shoulders, sometimes pulling carts.

24

♣ Pink Mountain (Km 751.1)

Village near the highest point (1,097 metres) between Fort Nelson and Fort St. John. ● ⊨ ▲ | *amenities available at places of accommodation; see below*

› **Population** 99

› **Accommodation/Camping** *Pink Mountain Campsite and* rv *Park also has lodging.* 250-772-5133. ⟳ ♨ ♚ | *showers, laundromat, post office, telephone. Pink Mountain Motor Inn* 250-772-3234. ♨ ♚ | *laundromat*

› **Greyhound Bus** 1-800-661-8747; www.greyhound.ca.

› **Emergency** *Police* 250-787-8100 *Ambulance* 250-785-2079

♣ Wonowon (Km 814.6)

Historic Alaska Highway Mile 101. Largest population centre between Fort Nelson and Fort St. John. ⟳ ● ♨ ♚ *restaurants and pub* ⊨ *motels* ▲ | *post office, telephone*

› **Population** 150

› **Accommodation** *Blueberry Esso & Motel* 250-772-3363; *Hall's Motel* 250-772-3301.

› **Greyhound Bus** (1-800-661-8747; www.greyhound.ca) *Depot located at Hall's Food & Gas.*

› **Emergency** *Police* 250-787-8100 *Ambulance* 250-785-2079

⊨ ▲ The Shepherd's Inn (Km 861.1)

Motel and campground. 250-827-3676 ♨ ♚ *restaurant with home baking* | *showers, telephone*

♣ Charlie Lake Provincial Park (Km 889.6)

On the southwest shore of a 13-kilometre-long lake, part of the Peace River watershed. A favourite holiday spot for people from Fort St. John. ▲ ♛ *outhouses* ▣

› **Size** 85 hectares

› **Attractions** Walking trails, fishing for northern pike and walleye.

› **Camping** 58 drive-in campsites. *Reservations* 1-800-689-9025 (or 604-689-9025 in Metro Vancouver). www.discovercamping.ca

♣ Charlie Lake (Km 895.1)

Unincorporated hamlet at the south end of Charlie Lake. ⟳ ♨ ♚ *pub* ⊨ ▲ | *post office, other amenities available at accommodation listed below*

› **Attractions** Natural trails, "best walleye fishing in BC."

› **Accommodation** *Rotary* RV *Park* (and campground) borders a nature reserve between Charlie Lake Provincial Park and the community of Charlie Lake. 250-785-1700. 🚻 🍴 | *showers. Charlie Lake* RV *& Leisure* (and campground) 250-767-1569. 🔀 🚻 🚽 | *showers*

🛶 Beatton Provincial Park (Km 897.6)

On the east shore across from Charlie Lake Provincial Park. Turn left (north) off the Alaska Highway near Km 897.6 and follow the road for 13 kilometres. ▲ 🚻 *outhouses* 🚽

› **Size** 310 hectares
› **Attractions** Fishing, hiking, 12 kilometres of snowshoeing and cross-country skiing trails.
› **Camping** 37 drive-in campsites. *Reservations* 1-800-689-9025 (or 604-689-9025 in Metro Vancouver). www.discovercamping.ca

🏕 Fort St. John (Km 903)

The "capital" of northern BC, a supply centre for industries on both sides of the BC–Alberta border. With its economy firmly rooted in gas and oil, Fort St. John bills itself as the "Energetic City," the hub of an industry that employs more than 5,000 people in northeastern BC, where more than 10,000 wells have been drilled. *all amenities required by a regional population of 60,000*

› **Population** 17,000
› **Visitor Info** *Fort St. John Visitor Centre* 9523 100th Street, Fort St. John, BC V1J 4N4; 1-877-785-6037; www.cityfsj.com.
› **Attractions** Fort St. John–North Peace Museum, North Peace Cultural Centre, Peace River Lookout.
› **Cycling/Outfitting** *Lugi's Source for Sports* 9628 100th Street; 250-785-7771.
› **Transportation**
  Land Greyhound Canada (1-800-661-8747; www.greyhound.ca) Depot located at *Metobe Enterprises* at 10355 101 Avenue.
  Air Air Canada 1-888-247-2262; www.aircanada.com. *Central Mountain Air* 1-888-865-8585; www.cmair.bc.ca. *Peace Air* 1-800-563-3060; www.peaceair.com.
› **Accommodation/Camping** There is a variety of motels, B&Bs, and campgrounds in and near Fort St. John. Go to www.cityfsj.com/accommodations.html.
› **Emergency** Call 911.

24

♣ Taylor (Km 921)

A forestry and gas-processing centre above the Peace River. ⦿ ● ⚓ ⁌

› **Population** 1,200
› **Visitor Info** *Taylor Visitor Centre* 10316 100 Street, Box 300, Taylor, BC V0C 2K0; 250-789-9015; www.districtoftaylor.com.
› **Emergency Call** 911.

♣♣ Taylor Landing Provincial Park (Km 923)

Day-use park on the south side of the Peace River, east side of the Alaska Highway. ⚹ *outhouses* ⊞ | *boat ramp, river access for boaters, anglers, swimmers, no drinking water or camping facilities*

› **Size** 2.4 hectares
› **Attractions** Beaver, raptorial birds, moose, white-tailed deer, black bears. Boat access to the Peace, Pine, Beatton, and Halfway rivers. Water levels, controlled by BC Hydro, can fluctuate.

♣♣ Kiskatinaw Provincial Park (off Km 952)

On Kiskatinaw River, five kilometres via Road 64, east of the Alaska Highway. ▲ ⚹ *outhouses* ⚰ *water from hand pump*

› **Size** 54 hectares
› **Attractions** Old bridge on original Alaska Highway.
› **Camping** 28 drive-in campsites.

♣ Dawson Creek (Km 978)

Best known as Mile 0 on the Alaska Highway. Dawson Creek's grain elevators, emblazoned by "Alberta Pool Elevators," are conspicuous evidence of the town's agricultural ties to its neighbouring province. *all services and amenities for a surrounding population of more than 17,000*

› **Population** 11,000
› **Visitor Info** *Tourism Dawson Creek, Dawson Creek Visitor Centre* 900 Alaska Avenue, Dawson Creek, BC V1G 4T6; 1-866-645-3022; www.tourismdawsoncreek.com.
› **Attractions** Historic Mile 0, NAR Station Museum, Dawson Creek Art Gallery, Walter Wright Pioneer Village; hiking and ski trails.
› **Transportation**
   Land Greyhound Canada (1-800-661-8747; www.greyhound.ca) Depot located at GCM *Enterprises* at 1201 Alaska Avenue.
   Air Central Mountain Air 1-888-865-8585; www.cmair.bc.ca.
› **Emergency Call** 911.

24

INDEX